PREHISTORIC STONE TOOLS OF EASTERN AFRICA

Stone tools are the least familiar objects that archaeologists recover from their excavations and, predictably, they struggle to understand them. Eastern Africa alone boasts a 3.4 million-year-long archaeological record, but its stone tool evidence remains disorganized, unsynthesized, and all-but-impenetrable to non-experts, and especially so to students from Eastern African countries. In this book, John J. Shea offers a simple, straightforward, and richly illustrated introduction in how to read stone tools. An experienced stone tool analyst and an expert stone-worker, he synthesizes the Eastern African stone tool evidence for the first time. Shea presents the EAST Typology, a new framework for describing stone tools specifically designed to allow archaeologists to do what they currently cannot: compare stone tool evidence across the full sweep of Eastern African prehistory. He also includes a series of short, fictional, and humorous vignettes set on an Eastern African archaeological excavation that illustrate the major issues and controversies in research about stone tools.

John J. Shea is Professor of Anthropology at Stony Brook University, New York. He is the author of *Stone Tools in Human Evolution* (Cambridge University Press, 2016) and *Stone Tools in the Paleolithic and Neolithic Near East: A Guide* (Cambridge University Press, 2012).

PREHISTORIC STONE TOOLS OF EASTERN AFRICA

A Guide

JOHN J. SHEA

Stony Brook University

CAMBRIDGE
UNIVERSITY PRESS

CAMBRIDGE
UNIVERSITY PRESS

University Printing House, Cambridge CB2 8BS, United Kingdom

One Liberty Plaza, 20th Floor, New York, NY 10006, USA

477 Williamstown Road, Port Melbourne, VIC 3207, Australia

314–321, 3rd Floor, Plot 3, Splendor Forum, Jasola District Centre, New Delhi – 110025, India

79 Anson Road, #06–04/06, Singapore 079906

Cambridge University Press is part of the University of Cambridge.

It furthers the University's mission by disseminating knowledge in the pursuit of
education, learning, and research at the highest international levels of excellence.

www.cambridge.org
Information on this title: www.cambridge.org/9781108424431
DOI: 10.1017/9781108334969

First published 2020

Printed in the United Kingdom by TJ International Ltd. Padstow Cornwall

A catalogue record for this publication is available from the British Library

Library of Congress Cataloging-in-Publication Data
NAMES: Shea, John J. (John Joseph), author.
TITLE: Prehistoric stone tools of Eastern Africa : a guide / John J. Shea.
DESCRIPTION: New York : Cambridge University Press, 2020. | Includes
    bibliographical references and index.
IDENTIFIERS: LCCN 2019046107 (print) | LCCN 2019046108 (ebook) | ISBN 9781108424431
    (hardback) | ISBN 9781108440165 (paperback) | ISBN 9781108334969 (epub)
SUBJECTS: LCSH: Tools, Prehistoric–Africa, Eastern. | Stone implements–Africa, Eastern.
CLASSIFICATION: LCC GN861 .S55 2020 (print) | LCC GN861 (ebook) | DDC 930.1/209676–dc23
LC record available at https://lccn.loc.gov/2019046107
LC ebook record available at https://lccn.loc.gov/2019046108

ISBN 978-1-108-42443-1 Hardback

Additional resources for this publication at www.cambridge.org/PSToEA

For all students of African archaeology.

CONTENTS

FIGURES

TABLES

BOXES

PREFACE

I wrote this book in order to improve Eastern African archaeological stone tool analysis. *Prehistoric Stone Tools of Eastern Africa: A Guide* describes how to measure and identify stone artifacts. This book introduces the East African Stone Tool (EAST) Typology, a framework for describing individual lithic artifacts from any period of Eastern African prehistory. In this respect, the EAST Typology differs from nearly all the other stone tool typologies currently in use in Eastern Africa. I envision the EAST Typology as a means for establishing concordances among typologies now in use. That is, Professor Jones' artifact type X and Professor Smith's artifact type Y are both equivalent to EAST Type IX.A.1.g (a convergent sidescraper). This work builds on Mehlman's (1989) efforts to establish concordances among typologies then in use for Middle and Later Stone Ages. I do not intend it to replace existing stone artifact typologies that archaeologists find adequate for their own research purposes. This being said, I have tried to make the EAST Typology as user-friendly as possible and adaptable to variable circumstances. One can use it in whole or in part and equally well to describe stone tools from Early Pleistocene sites as those from Iron Age contexts. In this respect the EAST Typology also differs from all lithic artifact typologies currently used anywhere else in the world.

Developing an artifact typology is an odd errand for me. A previous book (Shea 2013b) documented how colleagues working in the East Mediterranean Levant classified stone tools. Having shifted my research interest to Eastern Africa, I wanted to write a book that would make it easier for students to learn about the Levant's lithic record than my own experience. It was the most difficult thing I have ever written. As a stoneworker and archaeologist, I have never felt myself drawn to debates about artifact classification. As a stoneworker, questions about how earlier humans made and used stone tools interest me much more (Shea 2015). As an archaeologist, I care more about how we can use stone tools to answer questions about human evolution than about what we call them (Shea 2017b). As an anthropology professor, I exhort my own students to "measure first, only classify if you must." Still, one needs words for things. There may well come a day when archaeologists develop "wholly parametric" (exclusively measurement-based) ways of characterizing the stone tool evidence, but that day is not yet here nor even in sight on the horizon. Even if it was archaeologists would still need "a bridge to the twentieth century," terms for the evidence we have unearthed in Eastern Africa so far. If we have to classify stone tools in order to describe them to one another, we might as well "intelligently design" these classifications. I hope *Prehistoric Stone Tools of Eastern Africa: A Guide* will help Eastern Africanist archaeologists (indigenous scholars and those who work in that region) understand stone tools and assist them in answering important research questions about African prehistory.

Stone tools suffer an undeserved reputation for being uninteresting. Indeed, some of this book's more technical sections, namely Chapters 6–9, may be as tough a slog to read as they were to write. To convey some of the intellectual adventure of trying to make sense out of stone tools, this work punctuates its chapters with "Uwazi Valley Tales." These short fictional episodes illustrate, from a student's-eye perspective, some of the major issues in stone tool analysis in Eastern African archaeology. Kent Flannery (1976) adopted a similar strategy in his *The Early Mesoamerican Village*, a book I read as an undergraduate archaeology student. Flannery's vignettes and archetypal characters (the Real Mesoamerican Archaeologist, the Skeptical Graduate Student, the Great Synthesizer) helped me better understand archaeology. I hope my Uwazi Valley characters will do the same for others. These episodes are works of fiction. Any resemblances to actual events or persons living or dead are entirely coincidental.

I do not expect that all of my colleagues in Eastern African archaeology will agree with all of my choices of terms or the distinctions I make (or fail to make) among artifact-types. So be it. All those things I have done, I have done in good faith and above all in hopes that they will improve Eastern African archaeology.

ACKNOWLEDGMENTS

For advice on how to improve the EAST Typology, I thank Justin Pargeter, Hilary Duke, and the numerous colleagues who commented on the earlier version of the typology that I posted online. I thank Steve Brandt and Stan Ambrose for helping fill gaps in my knowledge about more recent phases of Eastern African prehistory. For suggesting the fictional vignettes that comprise the Uwazi Valley Tales, I thank Katheryn Twiss. I thank Erik Otarolla-Castillo, Sonia Harmand, Jason Lewis, and particularly Christian Tryon, for reading and commenting on drafts of the manuscript-in-progress. Finally, I thank the Stony Brook University Inter-Library Loan Service, especially Jay Levenson and Donna Sammis, for their help in procuring references I needed to write this book. I thank, my wife, Patricia Crawford, for her patience and advice (even such of it as I ignored in writing the Uwazi Valley Tales). Opinions expressed herein and any errors or omissions are entirely my responsibility.

Because in-text citations would interrupt the narrative flow of Uwazi Valley Tales, I here acknowledge the following sources for ideas expressed in them:

Tim White (2000) for paleoanthropology's "inverted ecosystem."

Jonathan Kingdon (1993) for elephants' possible roles as Pleistocene trailblazers.

Corbey and colleagues (2016) for their theory that earlier hominins' long core-tools might arise from some sort of genetic programming and the bird song/nest analogy.

Louis Liebenberg (1990) for proposing that the scientific method originated from animal tracking.

Mentioned by name but not cited in the vignettes are Eric Boëda's (1995) work defining the Levallois methods, Shannon McPherron's (2006) comparative study of handaxes, and Richard Leakey's anti-poaching strategy (Leakey and Morell 2001).

For the "Eskimo seal hunting" story, I thank the late Irven DeVore but with a qualification. I am confident he told it in Harvard's Science B-29 Sex and

Human Behavior as an example of human strategic variability, but I cannot remember if he explicitly invoked it as a metaphor for scientific authorship. It was a long time ago, and memory fails me. If you like it, credit Irv. If it offends, blame me.

That "the shortest line between two people is laughter, for humor is truth," is a quote from the Danish composer, pianist, and comedian, Victor Borge (1909–2000).

CHAPTER 1

INTRODUCTION

This chapter introduces the book's key concepts, including systematics, Eastern Africa, prehistory, stone tools, and guidebooks. It also outlines the book's structure and its goals:

1 To provide students of Eastern African archaeology with a state-of-the-art introduction to stone tools.
2 To make it easier for archaeologists to compare stone tools, in detail, over the full sweep of African prehistory.
3 To nudge archaeologists closer to being able to investigate evolutionarily and historically important questions using evidence from Eastern Africa.

What we call things matters. Names can clarify, confuse, or do both simultaneously. Finding names for prehistoric stone tools poses special difficulties. When archaeologists unearth ceramics or metal tools, we do so from sediments no more than a few thousand years old – relatively recently on a geological timescale. As a result, we have familiar household words for ceramics (e.g., bowl, plate, jar) and metal implements (e.g., axe, knife, nail). Stone tools, in contrast, range in age from the ethnographic present to more than three million years ago. Few people make and use stone tools any longer, and for this reason we lack subject-specific common words for them. Instead, we borrow words for Industrial Era metal tools (e.g., scraper, pick, awl). In developing terms for stone tools, the nineteenth- and early twentieth-century archaeologists who developed the artifact typologies we still use today relied on their intuition, but those archaeologists' intuitions about stone tools and their functions reflected their experience excavating artifacts, not making or using them or observing others who did. Yet archaeologists have been reluctant to reform these stone tool systematics. We cannot blame their reluctance on sloth. Archaeologists are among the world's hardest-working scientists; nobody looking for a life of leisure becomes an archaeologist. Nor can we blame ignorance, for critiques about theory and method in stone artifact analysis have a long history and have grown increasingly trenchant (e.g., Shea 2011b, Holdaway and Douglas 2012, Dibble et al. 2017). If the explanation for archaeologists' reluctance to reform stone tool systematics remains an enigma, the need for such reform has become ever more pressing, and no more so than in Eastern Africa. Eastern Africa provides unique fossil evidence about long-term patterns in human evolution. Even so, Eastern Africa's lithic record makes only a fraction of its potential contribution to African prehistory and to human origins research. Why is this so?

For me, studying and interpreting stone tools has always felt a bit like following animal tracks, an activity I learned at a young age, and one I still enjoy today. One can learn a lot about animal behavior from following a short segment of one animal trackway, but to know what is going on across the landscape, one has to follow tracks for longer periods and mentally correlate and integrate one's observations about different sets of tracks. A galloping deer track makes more sense after noting the accelerating pace of nearby coyote tracks. As matters stand today, archaeologists investigating Eastern African prehistory easily see only short segments of individuals' tracks; they use different terms for tracks left by the same animal, and similar terms for tracks left by different animals. Had our hunter-gatherer ancestors done this with actual animal tracks, they would have starved, and we would not be here.

Around the year 2000, I decided to compare the stone tools my colleagues and I found together with early *Homo sapiens* fossils in the Lower Omo Valley Kibish Formation, Ethiopia, to lithic artifacts from other sites of roughly the same age (104,000–195,000 years ago) as well as to some from older and younger periods of Eastern African prehistory. Surveying the archaeological literature, I found few archaeologists described stone tools the same way. Basic cardinal measurements, such as length, width, and thickness, went undefined. Stone tool systematics not only varied between time periods (as it does throughout much of the world) but also within time periods and between and within individual countries. Some archaeologists had imported artifact typologies intact from other regions. Others had devised their own idiosyncratic typologies. Still others combined these approaches. Few archaeologists illustrated their artifact typologies in any great detail but instead used terms such as "point" and "microlith" that enjoy different definitions among various research traditions. The more sites I tried to include in my comparisons, the less and less confidence I had in my findings. Often, when I thought I had found differences between stone tools from different sites, I could not reject the hypothesis that those differences arose not from variation in prehistoric human behavior but from variation in how archaeologists described the stone tool evidence. This "lithics systematics anarchy" contrasted starkly with what I had previously experienced in other regions, such as the Near East, Europe, and North America, where archaeologists use standardized systematics (although different ones in each region).

Calling this situation "anarchy" references the term's original political meaning, a landscape of small, self-governing communities, not its modern use as a synonym for lawless social chaos. Some Eastern African research traditions and research projects use internally consistent lithics systematics, but they differ among one another. One could also call the situation "lithics systematics diversity," but in modern usage, diversity has generally positive connotations, whereas lithics systematics anarchy does not. There is also the matter of the unfortunate acronym, LSD.

When I raised these concerns with colleagues, their responses varied widely. Some pointed out that prominent Eastern African archaeologists' calls for top-to-bottom reform in stone tool systematics made decades ago (Clark et al. 1966, Bishop and Clark 1967: 896–7, Kleindienst 1967) had little or no effect on archaeological practice. Others argued for reforming existing systematics by refining definitions of specific problematical artifact categories. I had enough experience with such "reform" efforts in Southwest Asian lithic analysis (Shea 2013b) and in Eastern Africa to know that such efforts had no chance of success whatsoever. (Getting academics to cooperate in this way is like herding cats with a compressed-air horn.) Others had full confidence in their own ways of describing stone tools but expressed suspicion about the methods their colleagues used. Such views may arise because so few Eastern Africanist archaeologists work in more than one country or with colleagues trained in different research traditions. Most indigenous Eastern African archaeologists *only* work in their home countries. A third group thought the problem too complex to solve, but, as a young Alexander of Macedon (later "the Great") showed when he undid the Gordian Knot by slicing it in half with his sword, complex does not mean unsolvable.

For answering questions about long-term change and variability in human evolution, no other region of the world has greater potential than Eastern Africa. Right now, because archaeological stone tool systematics are so variable, Eastern African archaeologists find themselves limited to single-site-focused narratives about the past – essentially short segments of longer animal trails. More integrative questions require inter-site comparisons, but differences in how archaeologists describe the stone tool evidence make such comparisons difficult. Those attempting them quickly discover that they have to collapse artifact-type categories in rough proportion to the number of samples included. Such comparisons further assume, based on no evidence whatsoever, that archaeologists all measure stone tools the same way. Changing the ways we measure and describe stone tools seems a trivially small price to pay for progress in answering "big" evolutionarily significant questions using the stone tool evidence. This first chapter explains the book's purpose by defining each component part of its title: Eastern Africa, prehistory, stone tools, and guidebooks.

WHAT IS EASTERN AFRICA?

Eastern Africa lies between roughly 30–52° East Longitude and approximately +18.00° North and -12.00° South Latitude. It encompasses both the Horn of Africa (Eritrea, Ethiopia, Djibouti, and Somalia) and East Africa (Kenya, Tanzania, Uganda, Rwanda, and Burundi), as well as parts of adjacent countries, such as South Sudan, the Democratic Republic of the Congo, Zambia, Malawi, and Mozambique (Figure 1.1). Eastern Africa encloses the southern end of the Red Sea and the western equatorial Indian Ocean coastline, the whole of the Ethiopian plateau, and the East African Rift Valley. The Equator divides the region more or less in half.

Both unique and a transition zone, Eastern Africa enjoys overall higher elevations and more varied topographic relief than adjacent regions. Relatively young volcanic deposits comprise a much greater proportion of the Eastern African landscape than elsewhere on the continent. Ancestral Eastern Africans' use of volcanic rocks, such as basalt and obsidian, created a distinctive lithic archaeological record. Eastern Africa has also enjoyed sustained and intense archaeological research since the mid-twentieth century. It joins South Africa, the East Mediterranean Levant, and southern France/northern Spain ("Franco-Cantabria") in contributing disproportionately to global prehistory. It differs from these other regions by preserving a much older archaeological record, one currently dating from around 3.5 million years ago, or ca. 3.5 Ma (see Box 1).

Eastern Africa sits at the conjunction of three "worlds," an arid zone stretching across North Africa to Southwest Asia, a humid and densely forested Sub-Saharan Africa, and the Indian Ocean's seasonally arid and humid western periphery. This conjunction makes Eastern Africa a conduit, a route by which plants, animals, humans and, in earlier times, human ancestors circulated. Few, if any, major human cultural institutions spread from any one of these three worlds to the others without leaving a footprint in Eastern Africa.

WHAT IS PREHISTORY?

Prehistory describes both the time before written historical records and scientific accounts of events during that time. A maximally inclusive prehistory could stretch backward from roughly 5,000 years ago, when precursors to Egyptian hieroglyphs and Mesopotamian cuneiform writing appear, to the Earth's geological origins some 4.5 billion years ago. Archaeologists use a more restricted definition, one starting the period after the oldest-known archaeological sites, or, since 3.5 Ma.

Deciding when prehistory "ends" in any given region can be far from simple and straightforward. Many early written records are economic records (Mesopotamia), political-religious tracts (the Nile Valley), elite records (Mesoamerica),

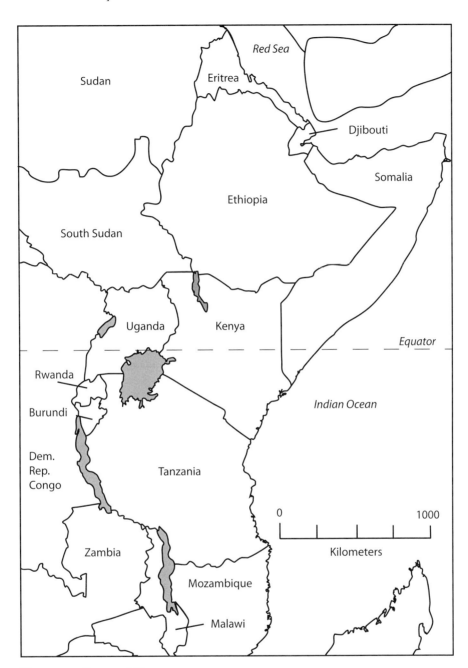

Figure 1.1 Eastern Africa.

or documents concerning supernatural phenomena (China). Scholars in Western societies with long traditions of written history produced the first nonsupernatural scientific accounts of prehistoric events during the eighteenth and nineteenth centuries (Daniel and Renfrew 1988). Predictably, prehistory's definition privileges written records over oral histories. Historical records for the Horn of

Box 1 *Time*

Prehistoric Stone Tools of Eastern Africa: A Guide uses the following abbreviations for dates, Ma = millions of years ago, Ka = thousands of years ago. Where dates are calibrated radiocarbon ages, they are designated Ka cal. BP. "BP" means "before present," i.e., the International Radiocarbon Year, AD 1950. Dates referenced as Ka derive from dating techniques other than radiocarbon, such as Uranium-series (U-S), thermoluminescence (TL), electron spin resonance (ESR), optically stimulated luminance (OSL) dating, or various radiopotassium-based techniques, such as potassium-argon (K-Ar) and single-crystal argon dating (^{40}Ar/^{39}Ar). These dating techniques can disagree with one another to varying degrees without necessarily invalidating one or the other set of results. Table 1.1 lists the dates for major cultural periods and geological epochs.

TABLE 1.1 *Cultural and geological periods. Youngest periods are listed in the upper row of each column. Note: Cultural and geological periods on the same row are not equivalent.*

Cultural Periods/Age-Stages	Geological Periods/Epochs
Iron Age – iron metallurgy, extensive trade with external regions, since around 0.5–2.5 Ka cal. BP.	Anthropocene – ongoing, begins 2 Ka cal. BP.
Neolithic – domesticated plants and animals, pottery, 2–6 Ka cal. BP.	Holocene – ongoing, begins 11.7 Ka cal. BP at boundary of MIS[*] 1 and 2.
Later Stone Age – geometric microlith production, 6–50 Ka cal. BP.	Later Pleistocene – begins 128 Ka, at the start of MIS 5.
Middle Stone Age –"Levallois" prepared cores, 50–300 Ka.	Middle Pleistocene – begins at boundary of Brünhes Normal Paleomagnetic Chron, 728 Ka.
Early Stone Age – stone tools modified by controlled fracture, 0.3–3.5 Ma.	Early Pleistocene – begins at 2.6 Ma.[**]
	Pliocene 2.6–5.3 Ma.

[*] MIS = marine oxygen isotope stage
[**] In 2009 the International Union of Geological Sciences reset the start date for the Pleistocene. Formerly it was 1.8 Ma.

Cultural periods (aka "ages" or "age-stages") divide time based on variation in the contents of archaeological deposits. Since the nineteenth century, European and Asian archaeologists have divided prehistoric time into Stone, Bronze, and Iron Ages and split the Stone Age into Lower, Middle, and Upper Paleolithic periods, followed by Mesolithic (aka Epipaleolithic) and Neolithic periods. For the most part, Eastern Africa's earlier cultural periods use the Earlier, Middle, and Later Stone Age.

Box 1 (*Cont.*)

framework originally developed in Southern Africa (Goodwin and van Riet Lowe 1929) and the Neolithic and Iron Ages from Eurasian prehistory. (The term, "Bronze Age" rarely appears in the Eastern African archaeological literature.) Some researchers combine terms from Eurasian and Southern African frameworks, such as "Earlier Paleolithic" or "Later Paleolithic."

Geologists define geological periods, or "epochs," in terms of changes in rocks and fossils and dated geochronometrically, usually by radiopotassium, Uranium-series, or radiocarbon dating. Most of Eastern Africa's Stone Age prehistory falls within the Pleistocene Epoch, 2,600,000 years ago (2.6 Ma) to 11,700 years ago (12 Ka). This was a period of increased aridity and ever wider climatic variability. The Pliocene Epoch (2.6–5.3 Ma) precedes the Pleistocene, and the Holocene Epoch (<12 Ka) follows it. During the Pliocene Epoch, Eastern Africa was generally warm and humid with minor climatic oscillations. Hominins evolved and differentiated themselves from other anthropoids (apes) during the Pliocene. Geologists divide the Pleistocene into Early, Middle, and Later periods that they define in terms of changes in paleomagnetism and variation in marine oxygen-isotope stages. The Holocene Epoch was generally warmer and more humid than the Later Pleistocene. It is, thus far at least, also more stable than any period of Middle-Late Pleistocene prehistory of equivalent duration.

Many archaeologists and other paleoanthropologists use the informal term "Plio-Pleistocene" for the later Pliocene and early Pleistocene, roughly 1.6–3.5 Ma. The "Anthropocene," a recently proposed term for a geological epoch marked by global-scale human impacts on the environment, has neither been formally defined nor recognized as yet, but the term appears in some recent popular and scientific works.

In 2009, the International Union of Geological Sciences redefined the boundary between the Plio-Pleistocene from 1.8 Ma to 2.6 Ma.

Africa stretch back thousands of years, while in Eastern Africa's interior, "prehistory" ended after nineteenth-century European colonial incursions.

Why is prehistory important? It provides answer to anthropology's existential questions: namely, why humans differ from other primates and why humans differ from one another. All of the major behavioral differences between humans and non-human primates evolved during prehistoric times. Tool making, bipedalism, controlled use of fire, art and symbolic artifacts – of these things' origins, history offers mere hints. Prehistory offers evidence. Root causes for the major differences among living humans: language, geographic dispersal, farming and herding, trade, religion, even early cities, all developed in prehistoric times, and during periods when humans made, used, and discarded stone tools. The differences between Israelis and Palestinians, between Irish and British, between Chinese and Vietnamese pale to insignificance compared to the differences between any living human and earlier hominins.

WHAT ARE STONE TOOLS?

Stone tools, also known as lithics or lithic artifacts, are portable objects made from rocks and nonmetallic minerals that deliberate fracturing and abrasion have altered from their natural state. This definition excludes immovable features such as modifications to bedrock as well as large stones used for architectural purposes. Most archaeologists do not consider figurative stone sculptures, stone vessels, beads, pendants, and other personal adornments lithics. Archaeological reports usually tally such artifacts separately from more utilitarian flaked and groundstone artifacts. This work includes beads and vessels among stone tools because archaeologists who describe fractured and abraded stone tools often have to describe these other artifacts as well. If only for convenience, it makes sense to include guidance about how to describe and measure these artifacts in this guidebook.

Why devote an entire book to stone tools? Stone tools are a common denominator for nearly all of prehistory and a logical starting point for research into behavioral differences among "technological primates" (i.e., humans and other primates who use tools). Every stone tool ever made has either been collected, destroyed by geological processes, or still awaits discovery. Since at least 1.7 Ma, hominins appear to have been at least habitual stone tool users (Shea 2017a). That is, at least some artifacts made and discarded since that point in time exhibit such "patterned imposition of non-intrinsic shape" that they almost certainly reflect intergenerational transmission of technological knowledge rather than just latent (spontaneously generated) solutions to needs for cutting edges and percussive surfaces. In Eastern Africa, as in much of the world (Australia, the Americas), archaeological traces of human activity appear without stone tools only during the last thousand years, after iron and steel implements largely displaced stone tools from their longstanding roles. People still make and use stone tools in various remote parts of Eastern Africa.

WHY A GUIDEBOOK FOR EASTERN AFRICAN STONE TOOLS?

A guidebook aids its readers in identifying meaningful differences among its subjects. Guidebooks for birds, for example (e.g., Van Perlo 2009), include colloquial and scientific names, illustrations showing male versus female and adult versus juvenile birds of a given species, definitions of key identifying features (different kinds of beaks or wing feathers) as well as descriptions of common ways to describe and measure those features. As with its author's previous guidebook for the Southwest Asian lithic record (Shea 2013b), this book provides similar information about stone tools from Eastern Africa. It differs from previous works by devoting chapters to major artifact categories rather than to different time periods. Unlike in Southwest Asia, where different age-stages have strikingly different lithic evidence (although less so than generally thought), the same stone artifact types and ways of making stone tools cross-cut traditional Eastern African prehistoric age-stages.

Differences in Eastern African stone artifact systematics make it difficult to compare evidence archaeologists have gathered, not just within and between countries but also within and between prehistoric time periods. This problem is especially acute in recent prehistoric periods for which lithic evidence is abundant and in which more archaeologists conduct research; but no time period is immune, and our understanding of Eastern African prehistory suffers. Even though the number of archaeologists working in Eastern Africa has grown since the 1960s and millions of dollars have been spent on research, more than sixty-five years have passed since Sonia Cole published the last major synthesis of the region's Stone Age record, *The Prehistory of Eastern Africa* (1954).

Eastern Africa's "lithics systematics anarchy" reflects it colonial history, but postcolonial factors perpetuate it. Unlike North and South Africa, where single colonial powers controlled vast regions, Eastern Africa had diverse British, Italian, German, and French colonizers. European prehistoric archaeologists work largely within their own countries and those countries' past and former colonies. As a result, their methods for describing stone tools diverge from one another. When European archaeologists began working in Eastern Africa, they described stone tools using conventions developed in their national research traditions. Researchers from the United States, Canada, Japan, and other countries with no prior colonial presence in Eastern Africa further increased variation in how archaeologists describe stone tools. Today, Eastern Africans seeking professional archaeological training abroad absorb further different ways of dealing with the stone tool evidence. Others develop their own stone tool systematics. Because most indigenous Eastern African archaeologists only work in their home countries, and because relatively few foreign researchers work in more than one East African country concurrently, stone tool systematics vary widely within and between countries – more so than anywhere else in Africa, and possibly more so than anywhere else in the world.

Eastern Africa's systematics anarchy is not just a problem for archaeologists working in that region. When prehistoric research began and fieldwork took place mainly in Europe and the Mediterranean Basin, archaeologists projected their inferences about human biological and cultural evolution in these regions to global scales. As evidence accumulated from Asia, Africa, Australia, and the Americas over the course of the twentieth century, archaeologists recognized that the European evidence possessed its own uniquely derived features, ones not shared globally (Clark 1977). Today, prehistoric archaeologists aspire to a global prehistory – to developing and testing hypotheses about variation and variability in the evidence for human behavior evolution (e.g., Gamble 2013, Shea 2017b). To do this, we need to compare evidence over long time periods and between major regions. Humans and our evolutionary precursors made and used stone tools in Eastern Africa longer than anywhere else on Earth. Eastern Africa is the logical place to search for patterns of long-term change and variability in the stone tool evidence. That the ways archaeologists have organized Eastern Africa's stone tool record obstructs this search ranks among paleoanthropology's greatest ironies.

HOW IS THIS BOOK ORGANIZED?

Prehistoric Stone Tools of Eastern Africa: A Guide has three major parts. The first, Chapters 2–3, provides a basic introduction to stone tools and lithic technology. *Prehistoric Stone Tools of Eastern Africa*'s target audiences include college students and professional archaeologists not already deeply familiar with stone tools. For this reason, these chapters assume little or no prior knowledge of that subject. They introduce essential terms and concepts, including the vocabulary archaeologists use to describe the lithic evidence and advice on how to "read" (visually examine and interpret) stone tools.

The second part, Chapters 4–5, describe Eastern Africa and its archaeological stone tool evidence. Chapter 4 introduces Eastern Africa's geology and other geographic properties that influence its paleoanthropological record. It also discusses the history of prehistoric research in the region and contemporary frameworks for Eastern African prehistory. Chapter 5 focuses more narrowly on the Eastern African lithic record, describing the artifact-types and industries that characterize major prehistoric periods. To gauge the extent to which Eastern Africa's lithic record fits with this stadial (stage-wise) framework, Chapter 5 compares more than two hundred and fifty archaeological stone tool collections from the full range of Eastern Africa's prehistoric record using Stoneworking Modes A-I, a framework specifically designed for such comparisons. By any conceivable measure, the lithic evidence and archaeologists' stadial framework correlate poorly with one another. Difficulties comparing lithic evidence across the full sweep of the region's prehistory justify the book's centerpiece, the Eastern African Stone Tool (EAST) Typology.

The third part, Chapters 6–9, presents the EAST Typology. This typology describes stone tools in terms of nine major technological categories (Groups I–IX), each of which it further subdivides into more specific artifact types. This hierarchical typology has three goals. First, it enables Eastern African archaeologists to develop concordances among the many different stone tool typologies they currently use. Second, it allows archaeologists to more effectively compare archaeological lithic evidence from different prehistoric periods.

Finally, it makes it easier to compare the Eastern African lithic record to evidence from other regions. These chapters also discuss measurement conventions. Recognizing that different research questions require different measurements, these discussions focus on the most commonly made "conventional" measurements, the ones most researchers make no matter what their specific research questions.

Concluding this work, Chapter 10 considers larger questions about the Eastern African stone tool evidence as well as ways to make the region's lithic record more relevant to prehistoric research.

UWAZI VALLEY TALES, EPISODE 1: WAZUNGU

Our Landrover bounced and rattled along the red dirt road dividing green thorn forest. Herds of sheep, goats, cattle, and throngs of children lined the road. Tall men in scarlet cloaks strode slowly alongside the animals. Crisply dressed women in floral print dresses walked briskly around them carrying bundles and baskets on their heads. I liked the Uwazi Valley already.

"*Wazungu!*" three boys shouted together as the car approached.
"What's *wazungu?*" I asked my traveling companions.
Our driver remained silent, his eyes never leaving the road ahead of us.

The Old Africa Hand spoke from the front passenger seat. "In the old days, it meant someone who wanders around without a purpose, but now it refers to Europeans or white people, more generally."

The Old Africa Hand was dressed for safari in khaki trousers and bush jacket. A broad-brimmed canvas hat with a zebra-skin band perched on his head. Short-cropped white hair peeked out beneath it. I had heard that his parents were European missionaries in rural Africa, where he grew up. Educated at Cambridge and Oxford, the Old Africa Hand had taught for decades at Big American University, where his adventure-filled tales of African fieldwork filled lecture halls. Although his days of supervising graduate students were behind him, they clamored to be his teaching assistants. African masks, statues, baskets, and spears decorated the Old Africa Hand's office. Rumor held that he kept an antique elephant gun squirreled away in there somewhere.

"The people who wander without a purpose. Sounds like a perfect term for academics in general and archaeologists in particular." The Polymath smirked, put down his camera, and made some jottings in an orange geological notebook. A weathered copy of *Collins Birds of Eastern Africa* sat on the seat between us. Hirsute, and tanned the color of an old penny, the Polymath was in his late fifties. He wore faded blue jeans, a short-sleeved shirt, and a sleeveless synthetic fleece vest. The Polymath was Professor of Anthropology at Big American University, co-director of the Uwazi Valley Prehistory Project, and my doctoral thesis advisor. On campus, one only saw him fleetingly. The Polymath's wide-ranging research interests and university committee service kept him continuously scurrying from office to lab, to lectures, to library, to administration buildings pretty much all week long. Stacks of "to be read" papers, ostensibly organized by subject, rose like skyscrapers from every horizontal surface in his office. This six-hour ride from the Capitol was the longest I had ever been in the same place with him continuously.

"You see, Robin," the Polymath continued, emphasizing my first name – possibly thinking to remind the Old Africa Hand of it, "unlike other parts of Africa, Eastern Africa had many different colonial occupiers. Different countries have different names for foreigners. *Wazungu* here and in other Swahili-speaking countries, *Fereng* in Ethiopia – probably derived from French or "frankish," and *Talian* in Eritrea, a former Italian colony.

"Will there be a quiz on this, Professor?" the Old Africa Hand harrumphed as the Landrover swerved around a cow. The Polymath had once been an undergraduate student in the Old Africa Hand's class.

"MMBA," the Old Africa Hand had called it hours ago, "miles and miles of bloody Africa."
"Are we there yet?" I asked. (Sometimes one just cannot resist)

Several hours later, after dark, we arrived at the Uwazi Valley Prehistory Project's base camp. I could not see much. A distant generator powered a few bare electric lights around two long cinder-block buildings with corrugated steel roofs. About a dozen people sat around a long table made of plywood and saw horses. A woman wearing a loose-fitting red tracksuit approached us as we stepped from our car. A young archaeologist, Aya was co-director with the Polymath of the Uwazi Valley Prehistory Project. Tall and thin, with her straight black hair tied in a ponytail, Aya was in her third year as a tenure-track professor. During my first year in graduate school, I saw even less of her than of the Polymath. She traveled back and forth to Africa often. Inviting the Old Africa Hand and me to join the project had been the Polymath's idea. The Old Africa Hand's role as a senior "advisory" member on several international research projects increased those projects' funding. That I had my own in-house university grant for my research weighed in my favor, too.

Aya greeted us, announcing that dinner had already been served to the staff, but plates had been set out for us. Cloth napkins kept insects out of them. We ate quickly and quietly. Aya had had a grueling day and was clearly tired, but she warmed to conversation after we finished our meals. Staff morale was good. The excavations continued to turn up rich deposits of stone tools, although other than in the most recent layers, there were few animal bones – Aya's specialty. An email last week announced that the previous year's site report had been accepted for publication.

The staff had pitched three tents for the Old Africa Hand, the Polymath, and me. After we ate, we three and Aya relocated to a cleared area behind our tents overlooking the moonlit Uwazi Valley. This, the "Gentlemen's Smoking Lounge," featured four canvas chairs arranged in an arc around a small wooden table on which sat a whiskey bottle and four small glasses. Only the Old Africa Hand smoked, a battered wooden pipe he kept in a jacket pocket.

I tried to stay awake and listen to the Old Africa Hand, the Polymath, and Aya's conversation. But their stories involved persons unknown to me, and after half an hour I faded, slinking off to my tent. As I dozed, I heard the distinctive "thunk" of a whiskey bottle uncorking again, the gurgling splash of glasses refilling. I caught the faintest whiff of the Old Africa Hand's pipe smoke.

CHAPTER 2

STONE TOOLS

Essential Terms and Concepts

This chapter introduces essential terms for the archaeological lithic evidence. Next, it considers the principal sources of information about stone tools and lithic technology. Finally, the chapter reviews some common mistakes archaeologists make in interpreting the stone tool evidence.

TERMS FOR STONEWORKING AND FOR STONE TOOLS

Stoneworking versus Flintknapping

Archaeologists commonly describe stone tool production as *flintknapping* and those who make stone tools as *flintknappers* (Johnson 1978, Whittaker 1994, Patten 2009). The original flintknappers were industrial craftsmen who shaped gunflints from the eighteenth century onward (Skertchly 1879, Clarke 1935). Archaeologists also use the terms flintknapper/flintknapping and knapper/knapping for modern-day craftspeople and hobbyists who make reproductions of archaeological stone tools. To avoid implying false equivalency between these modern-day craft specialist activities and prehistoric stone tool production, this work uses the terms *stoneworking/stoneworker* and *craft/hobby stoneworker*. Also, relatively few Eastern African stone tools are made of flint.

Stoneworking Mechanics and Techniques

Stoneworkers shape the overwhelming majority of stone tools using controlled fracture. A *fracture* is a cleavage plane that forms when applying force to an object (*loading*) causes that object to deform (*fail*). Stoneworkers initiate fractures by striking a brittle rock, or *core*, with a nonbrittle stone, metal, wood, or bone/antler *percussor* or *hammerstone* (see Figure 2.1). The surface on which the percussor lands, initiating the fracture is the *fracture initiation surface*. The opposite side of the edge under which the fracture spreads (*propagates*) until it emerges to the rock surface (*terminates*) is the *fracture propagation surface*.

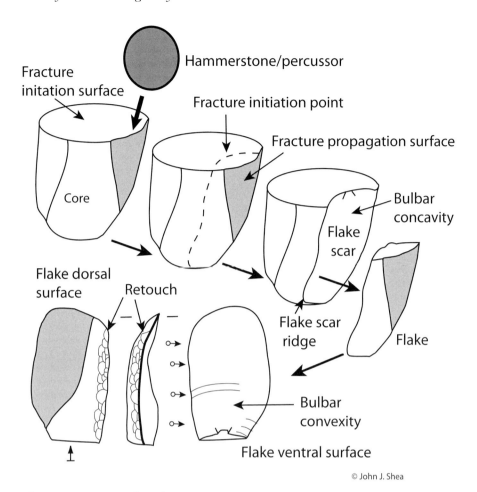

© John J. Shea

Figure 2.1 Stoneworking basics

The piece of rock that fracture detaches from the core is called a *flake* or a *flake fragment*, and the concavity its detachment leaves on the fracture propagation surface is a *flake scar* (or, less commonly, a *fracture detachment scar*). Archaeologists call the ridge at the flake scar's margin either a *flake scar ridge*, or an *arris* – an architectural term for the conjunction of two flat or curved surfaces. A fresh flake scar usually features a concave area near its fracture initiation point. This area is called the *bulbar concavity*, a remnant of the bulbar convexity on flake ventral surfaces. *Retouch* describes patterned distributions of small fractures on flake or core edges that archaeologists think were detached intentionally. (It also references the act of creating retouch.) Archaeologists describe incidental and unpatterned fractures as *edge damage*. Because retouch is also technically edge damage, a qualifying term, such as *incidental/unpatterned edge-damage* is advisable.

Many of the brittle rocks stoneworkers use possess conchoidal fracture properties. By varying the amount of force applied, the speed at which they

apply it, and the fracture initiation point, stoneworkers influence how conchoidal fractures start, spread, and end, thereby controlling the resulting
artifacts' shapes and dimensions (Cotterell et al. 1985, Lin et al. 2013). Stoneworking requires a degree of manual dexterity, hand to eye coordination, and
patience, but it is really not that difficult. In the author's experience, most
American college students grasp the basics after 30–60 minutes' practice,
and children as young as 10 years can proficiently detach flakes from cores
(Shea 2015).

Fracture-based stoneworking works best when one strikes near the edge of a
stone whose surfaces intersect at 90 degrees or less. Many factors influence
fracture trajectories (for review, see Lin et al. 2013). Mechanical experiments
confirm the influence of *striking platform depth* (the distance from the edge of a
rock at which fracture initiates) and *edge angle,* (the angle at which fracture
initiation and fracture propagation surfaces intersect). All other things being
equal, greater edge-angle values correlate with longer fracture propagation.
Insufficient or incorrectly directed loading can cause a fracture to propagate
incompletely, to break during propagation (*step-terminated fracture*), or to curve
sharply as it terminates, creating *hinge-terminated* fractures that curve sharply up
from the fracture propagation surface or *plunging* fractures that turn sharply in
the opposite direction.

Modern-day stoneworkers fracture stones using a variety of techniques
(Crabtree 1972, Inizan et al. 1999, Patten 2009) (Figure 2.2). *Percussion* involves
striking a rock swiftly and forcefully with some other hard object. Many
modern-day stoneworkers do this while holding the core in their hand, resting
it on their thigh (with a leather pad underneath) or on the ground (a much
safer arrangement for large-scale fracturing). *Hard-hammer* percussion uses
percussors made of stone or metal (Figure 2.2a), while *soft-hammer* percussion
uses bone, antler, wood percussors (Figure 2.2b). In *pressure flaking*
(Figure 2.2c), one places an object against a stone tool edge and then increases
pressure until a fracture occurs. Other ways of initiating fracture include anvil
percussion, throwing, bipolar percussion, and indirect percussion. In *anvil
percussion*, one strikes the rock to be fractured against a larger stationary rock,
bedrock, or some other hard substrate (Figure 2.2d). A variant of anvil
percussion, *throwing*, involves forcefully casting a stone against bedrock or
other large rock until it fractures. Perhaps because throwing offers little control
over the resulting fracture products, recent craft/hobby stoneworkers do not
do it very much, although ethnographic stoneworkers often do so. In *bipolar*
percussion (Figure 2.2e), one places a rock on top of a hard surface (another
rock or bedrock) and initiates fracture by striking the uppermost rock from
above. With *indirect* percussion (Figure 2.2f), one places one end of a hard
bone, antler, or metal cylinder on a rock's edge and then strikes the cylinder's
opposite end, initiating a fracture. Both pressure flaking and indirect percussion
provide greater control over fracture initiation and propagation, but they

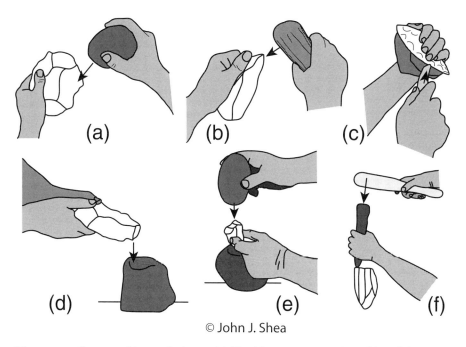

© John J. Shea

Figure 2.2 Stoneworking techniques. (a) Hard hammer percussion. (b) Soft hammer percussion. (c) Pressure flaking. (d) Anvil technique. (e) Bipolar percussion. (f) Indirect percussion.

require considerable skill and more time to remove equivalent mass than other percussion techniques.

Retouch is both noun and a verb. The noun describes small (>2–10 mm long) flake scars on a flaked-stone tool's edge. The verb references the act of detaching those small flakes. One can create retouch using either pressure or percussion and pretty much any hard object, including wood. Archaeologists have no single objective standard for distinguishing purposeful retouch from edge damage due to use, trampling, or geological forces. The consensus holds that such damage should be sufficiently large and continuous along an edge to rule out causes other than human agency, although criteria for recognizing such human agency vary.

Stone Tools

Stone tools/lithic artifacts owe their shape to human activity. *Ecofacts*, in contrast, are unmodified stones or other objects found together with other archaeological evidence. For larger unmodified stones found in archaeological excavations, many Eastern African archaeologists use the term *manuport*, ("hand-carried" from the Latin *manus* [hand] and *portare* [to carry]). This usage occurs more often in Early and Middle Pleistocene archaeology than in later prehistory and usually refers to *exogenous* stones, stones that differ from the local geological substrate.

Archaeologists' terms for stone artifacts commonly distinguish hammer-stones, groundstone, and flaked-stone tools. *Hammerstones* are rocks damaged from repeated percussion. *Groundstone* artifacts owe much of their shape to abrasive processes, such as cutting with an edged or pointed tool (sawing or engraving, respectively), rotary cutting/piercing (drilling), or by sliding one stone tool surface against another (shearing/abrasion).

Flaked-stone tools owe much of their final shape to fracture. Flaked-stone tools comprise the majority of all known stone tools, and archaeologists divide them into cores, flakes, retouched pieces, and core-tools. *Cores* feature at least one edge featuring flake scars longer than 10 mm. *Flakes* are relatively long, wide, and thin pieces of stone detached from cores. *Retouched pieces* are flakes whose edges preserve retouch. Many archaeologists use the terms, "tool" or "retouched tool" as synonyms for retouched pieces. A *core-tool* is a core whose edges preserve retouch. Some archaeologists use the terms *objective piece* or *flaked piece* for cores and *detached pieces* for flakes.

Archaeologists have opportunities to observe craft/hobby stoneworkers, but few of these modern-day craftspeople (or archaeologists, for that matter) also habitually *use* stone tools. Possibly as a result, archaeologists' terms for stone tools and stone-tool functions borrow words for historic metal tools (e.g., knife scraper, pick, awl) and commonplace Industrial Era activities (e.g., butchery, carpentry/woodworking, hide-working). Archaeologists frequently assume strong form-function correlations existed among prehistoric stone tools in much the same way as one sees them among Industrial-Era metal tools, but little evidence supports this assumption. Instead, functional variability seems to be the rule. Stone tools of similar size and shape often preserve wear traces on analogous portions of their edges and surfaces, but the specific motions and worked material combinations archaeologists reconstruct and infer from those wear traces vary widely. As the late George H. Odell (1942–2011) puts it (1981), stone tools do not provide archaeologists with a "Morphological Express to Function Junction."

Many extensively retouched prehistoric stone tools may have been multi-functional tools similar to multipurpose components in recent residentially mobile humans' portable toolkits. Much like a Swiss Army knife™ or multi-tools, these artifacts may not work optimally in any one task, but they perform adequately well in enough tasks to be worth carrying around as "insurance" against not having a tool at hand for some important but unanticipated task. Recent prehistoric contexts preserving evidence for prolonged residential sedentism and agriculture often feature more functionally specialized artifact designs, such as bits for rotary drills, seed-pulverizing stones, and carved stone vessels (Kelly 1992, Shea 2017b).

Perhaps because most small and/or unretouched stone tools from archaeological sites preserve little or no obvious evidence of use, archaeologists' terms for these artifacts imply they were unused. Such terms include *blank* (an unretouched flake), *débitage* (French for small pieces detached from a larger worked object), and *debris* (small flakes and flake fragments). And yet, ethnographic humans routinely used unretouched flakes and flake fragments, including ones less than 20–30 mm long. Gripping stone tools less than 20–30 mm long while cutting can be difficult (Key and Lycett 2014), but it is not impossible. Moreover, one can increase such small tools' potential gripping surface by embedding them in mastic (glue) and/or by attaching them to a handle (hafting). Experimental studies suggest many archaeological stone tools preserve little or no visible evidence of use because prehistoric stone tool users abandoned them before fracturing, and abrasion perceptibly degraded cutting edge effectiveness (Key et al. 2018).

Archaeologists' longstanding assumption that prehistoric stoneworkers did not use small and unretouched stone tools has serious negative consequences. Historically, archaeologists have seen small and unretouched artifacts as less informative than retouched pieces and cores. Prior to the 1960s–1970s, many archaeologists routinely discarded small and/or unretouched flakes and flake fragments in the field, at or near excavation sites. Archaeologists no longer discard such artifacts, thankfully, but they do much less, analytically, with unretouched flakes of any size than they do with retouched pieces and cores.

Stone Tool Groups

Stone tools occur at archaeological sites – locations where survey and excavations have identified artifacts and other traces of human activity. Site complexes feature more than one artifact-bearing deposit, the latter of which are called *levels*, *strata*, or *units*. Caves and rock-shelters nearly always contain multiple discrete archaeological levels. Most archaeologists name levels at multilevel sites in the order in which they encounter them during excavation (from the surface downward) using either ascending series of numbers or letters. The term *assemblage* describes artifacts and other remains from the same site or same level of a multilevel site. A *subassemblage* comprises a subset of artifacts within a larger assemblage that share some observed quality, such as being made of the same kind of rock, preserving similar patterns of modification, or being found in proximity with one another.

Naming conventions for archaeological sites vary widely in Eastern Africa. Generally speaking, names reflect either local place-names, serial numbers assigned in the course of survey, or registration numbers in national archives. The combinations of letters and numbers in Kenyan and Tanzanian site names in (e.g., FxJj 50, GnJh 42, GvJm 22, etc.) come from the Standard African Site Enumeration System (SASES), a hierarchical grid framework for all of Africa that researchers devised during the 1970s (Nelson 1993). By offering precise longitude, latitude, and altitude coordinates, Global Positioning Systems (GPS) make this framework obsolete. Nevertheless, Kenyan and Tanzanian authorities and researchers working in those countries retain it.

An example shows how these concepts articulate with one another. Olduvai Gorge, Tanzania, incorporates a local Maasai place-name ("place of the wild sisal"). The Gorge is a site complex within which HWK East is one among many individual named sites (Leakey 1971). HWK stands for Henrietta Wilfrida Korongo. *Korongo* is Swahili for "gully." HWK East Level 3 is one level among several at HWK East whose assemblage contains stone artifacts made of lava, quartz, quartzite, and chert. The quartz artifacts comprise a subassemblage of HWK East Level 3.

A typology lists recognized artifact-types. Nearly all typologies subdivide cores, flakes, retouched pieces, groundstone artifacts, and other implements into more specific types and subtypes.

Somewhat confusingly, many archaeologists use the term "typology" in two different ways. A noun, "capital-T" Typology is an artifact list. An adjective, "lower-case-t" typology references artifact morphological variation. To minimize confusion, this work uses "morphology/morphological" in its place.

An *artifact-type* groups together artifacts with shared technological, morphological, and/or metric properties. Technological variables include rock physical qualities as well as morphological and metric properties that archaeologists think respond to differences in manufacturing methods and techniques, artifact use, and discard behavior. Morphological variables mainly concern artifact shape and modification patterns (usually variation in retouch and surface fracture scar patterning). Archaeologists assume that technological variability reflects patterns of human economy and ecological adaptation (activities), while morphological variability reflects culturally conditioned choices of functionally equivalent artifact design. This identity/activity dichotomy creates many difficulties, if only because it is a false dichotomy. Social identities influence technological choices, and vice versa (Carr 1995, Schiffer and Skibo 1997). (The entire advertising industry depends on this principle for its very existence.)

The archaeological literature often refers to stone tool morphological variation as *style*, thereby implying a rough equivalence between lithic artifact variation and symbolic variation in modern-day clothing, folk art, and other overtly symbolic media (Sackett 1982). Some artifact morphological variation may have had overt social/cultural significance, but such equivalence is an assumption, not a fact so well established that one should accept it unquestioningly and under all circumstances. Because lithic technology is reductive (i.e., continued use results in a loss of mass), some variation may reflect morphological convergence. That is, two artifacts may look similar because both have been used to the same extent, in similar ways, or both. Other lithic variation may be "neutral," varying in ways similar to genetic drift. That our

capacity for using artifacts as symbols ("exosomatic symbols") in social interactions so differs from other primates' behavior suggests that it evolved
recently, and unlike stone tool use, perhaps uniquely among our immediate
ancestors. How recently, under what circumstances, and among which hominins? Nobody knows. One has to remain alert to the possibility that hominins
made, used, and discarded stone tools before that symbolic capacity evolved
(Shea 2017b).

   Naming conventions for the artifact-types listed in typologies vary, as do
conventions for measuring and illustrating them (see Box 2). Some names may
express artifact morphology (e.g., point or notch), others an inferred function
(e.g., scraper or awl). Others, such as Kombewa (a Kenyan village) flake or
Acheulian (the French town, St. Acheul) handaxe, may refer to a particular site

---

Box 2 *Lithic artifact illustration*

Archaeologists' conventions for positioning artifacts in drawings and photographs differ among various research traditions. This work uses "American"
conventions (Aprahamian 2001). These minimize movement when showing multiple views of the same artifact. For example, a profile view of an
artifact's right side appears to the right of the figure showing that artifact in
plan view. Longer lines between drawings indicate artifact pairs of plan and
profile views. Short lines at the edge of plan-view drawings indicate the
endpoints of cross-section drawings. Section drawings are darkly shaded.

   Archaeologists employ various techniques for conveying the impression
of three dimensions on two-dimensional representations of lithic artifacts.
In photographs, projecting a focused beam of light at a low ("raking") angle
to the core surface shows contour. In drawings, which better convey artifact
appearance, one achieves a similar effect by drawing concentric radial lines
on flake scars (Addington 1986). These lines' convex sides indicate inferred
flake scar propagation direction. Their length and spacing indicate contour
and shadow. Unfortunately, these conventions create drawings that do not
resemble actual stone tools, and they are difficult to replicate with
computer-assisted drawing. Instead, and as in the author's previous works
(Shea 2013b, 2017b), *Prehistoric Stone Tools of Eastern Africa* uses multiple
views of the same object to indicate three-dimensional shape. On cores and
some retouched tools, arrows positioned on flake scars show flake scar
directionality. If the flake scars are too small for arrows to be drawn on
them, they appear next to the edge of the core. Arrows with rings at their
base indicate flake scars with visible fracture initiation points. Simple arrows
show flake scars where fracture initiation points are missing. Cortical
surfaces appear lightly shaded.

at which the artifact-type was first identified or a stone tool industry (see below) of which it is thought to be characteristic.

Archaeologists have long debated their goals in identifying artifact-types. It is possible that some of archaeologists' artifact-types correspond with prehistoric stoneworkers' ideas about different stone tool designs, but hypotheses claiming such correspondences remain difficult to test directly. (After all, doing so to the exclusion of alternative hypotheses would require one to interview extinct stoneworkers.) Today, most archaeologists see stone artifact-types as heuristics – as concepts devised for particular analytical goals. Many work well in the purposes for which archaeologists originally defined them, such as documenting variation in artifact morphology. Historically, however, archaeologists have proven reluctant to abandon artifact-types when analytical goals change. Very few artifact-types are ever *sunk* (permanently abandoned), and few rules seem to govern such sinkings or whether archaeologists adopt newly proposed artifact-types and other terms. Archaeologists first identified many of the artifact-types we now use in Eastern Africa and elsewhere throughout much of the Old World more than 50 years ago. Few other sciences boast (or suffer?) such enduring conventions for recording their observations.

Archaeologists aggregate stone tool assemblages together into named stone tool industries, cultures, age-stages, and technological complexes. An *industry* combines assemblages from the same region and time period that preserve similar inventories of lithic artifact-types. When archaeologists define an assemblage-group in terms of both lithic and nonlithic evidence (e.g., ceramics, bone or metal tools, architecture), they may refer to that grouping as an archaeological *culture*, but this practice varies. Today, named archaeological cultures appear most often in references about recent (i.e., Holocene) prehistory. Many archaeologists think differences among stone tool industries correspond with cultural, even biological/behavioral, differences among prehistoric stoneworkers, but little direct evidence supports this assumption.

Technological complexes group together industries sharing similar distinctive ways of making tools or technologies. Common synonyms for technological complexes include *industrial complex* and *technocomplex*. Technological complexes differ from industries in their geographic extent. While industries occur at local or subcontinental scales, a technological complex encompasses assemblage groups at continental or intercontinental scales. Archaeologists differ over where to draw the line between a widespread industry and a technological complex.

Archaeologists define *age-stages* in terms of the presence/absence of specific artifacts, industries, and technological complexes. Prehistoric Eastern African age-stages include three periods imported from Southern African prehistory: the Earlier Stone Age (ESA), Middle Stone Age (MSA), and Later Stone Age (LSA) (Goodwin and van Riet Lowe 1929), and two periods imported from Eurasian prehistory, the Neolithic and Iron Ages (see Table 1.1).

TABLE 2.1 *Clark Modes 1–6*

Mode	Defining features	Eurasian prehistoric period
1	Pebble-tools	Lower Paleolithic
2	Handaxes	Lower Paleolithic
3	Levallois prepared cores	Middle Paleolithic
4	Prismatic blades	Upper Paleolithic
5	Geometric microliths	Mesolithic/Epipaleolithic
6	Groundstone artifacts	Neolithic

References: Clark (1969a, 1970)

Since the 1970s, increasing numbers of archaeologists working in Africa and elsewhere use *Clark Modes 1–5* to describe technological-complex-level variation among flaked-stone tools (e.g., Phillipson 2005, Barham and Mitchell 2008) (Table 2.1). Some use the terms to reference specific ways of making stone tools; others use them to classify groups of assemblages based on the highest-numbered mode in evidence. British archaeologist J.G.D. ("Grahame") Clark, introduced Modes 1–5 in his popular textbook, *World Prehistory: A New Outline* (1969a). Clark did not emphasize stone tools much in this book (or in his other writings), and one suspects he devised Modes 1–5 to minimize the number of named stone tool industries he had to cover in a work intended for undergraduate students. A later work, Clark (1970), added a sixth mode for groundstone artifacts, although few other archaeologists use it. Although some archaeologists use Modes 1–5 as a framework for global-scale stone tool variability (Foley and Lahr 2003, Gamble 2013), closer examination reveals the characteristics that define Modes 1–5 are just the defining characteristics of major periods of European and Western Asian Stone Age prehistory. Put simply, Clark Modes 1–5 are little more than traditional European age-stages expressed as whole numbers. They confer the illusion of quantification without the increased precision of an actual change in measurement scale.

Archaeologists disagree over how well or poorly Modes 1–5 work for any given purpose, but it is beyond dispute that because Modes 1–5 use a single term for multivariate phenomena. They overlook complex patterns of stone tool variability. Noting occurrences of Mode 5 technology among a group of lithic assemblages affirms microliths' presence but nothing about those artifacts' commonness or scarcity in those assemblages. Similarly, calling a group of assemblages, "Mode 5 industries," tells colleagues little about variation in Modes 1–4 among those assemblages. Some studies note occurrences of multiple modes within lithic assemblages, but these are exceptions to general archaeological practice.

Artifact-types, cultures, industries, technological complexes, age-stages, and Clark Modes 1–5 articulate with one another in complex ways. Continuing with the Olduvai HWK East Level 3 example, some of the stone artifacts from that site are called *choppers*. Archaeologists who work in earlier phases of African prehistory often call these artifacts "Oldowan choppers," indicating their affinity with the Oldowan assemblage group. In her earlier writings, Mary Leakey (1966) identified the Oldowan as a culture. This was appropriate, because at that point in time only Olduvai Gorge itself preserved Oldowan assemblages. Today, most archaeologists call the Oldowan an industry. They do so for two reasons. First, lithic assemblages as old as those from Olduvai have come to light in many other parts of Eastern Africa, and over a much longer time span than that of any human culture. Second, archaeologists define the Oldowan Industry exclusively in terms of its lithic characteristics. The Oldowan Industry is one among several assemblage groups dating to the Earlier Stone Age. Some archaeologists invoke the term *Oldowan Technological Complex* or *Clark Mode 1* for Oldowan-like lithic assemblages found throughout Africa and Eurasia. Recent years have seen former industries "promoted" to technological/industrial complex in the archaeological literature, but to what purpose or benefit remains unclear.

Technological Organization

Circumstances can cause stoneworkers to choose from among a range of possible solutions to a given problem in patterned ways. Raw material scarcity, for example, can cause them to adopt less wasteful production methods and more labor-intensive strategies for preserving artifact functionality. If, on the other hand, stoneworkers only need stone tools for simple, brief, "expedient" tasks, weak incentives to conserve materials may not influence their behavior. Archaeologists use the terms *technological organization* or "organization of technology" for variation in the stone tool evidence arising from strategic responses to such contextual variables. Crucial concepts in technological organization include curation, discard thresholds, operational chain, and flaking/shaping.

 Curation describes efforts to recover more potential utility, or use, from an artifact (Binford 1979, Shott 1996). The most common strategies for curating an artifact include retouch – resharpening a use-damaged edge – and transport – carrying an artifact from one place to another. These strategies are neither mutually exclusive nor inevitably correlated. Ethnographic stoneworkers can retouch/resharpen a tool and transport it, transport a tool without retouching it, or retouch a tool without transporting it. Hafting stone tools encourages transport, retouch, and prolonged use in many tasks (Keeley 1982). Greater or lesser amounts of curation can influence what kinds of artifacts appear in archaeological assemblages as well as their abundance or scarcity. For example, artifacts that are intensively curated and transported may appear rarely, represented only by small retouch-related flakes detached from them.

Prolonged curation by retouch may cause artifacts made by different cultures to resemble one another, or "converge" morphologically.

Discard threshold is the point at which the costs for curating an artifact exceed the benefits for doing so (Schiffer and Skibo 1997). Archaeologists differ in how they describe discard thresholds. Its use here follows previous works (Shea 2017b) in that a high discard threshold describes prolonged curation through reuse and recycling, while a low discard threshold implies expedient, or shorter-term, tool use. (*Reuse* describes tool use resuming after a period of disuse, while *recycling* describes reuse following substantial modification.) Discard thresholds can vary along with the geological substrate. Recent human stoneworkers living near rock sources typically discard tools after much less use than their counterparts in lithic raw-material impoverished areas. As with curation, variation in discard thresholds can cause artifacts and assemblages to differ from one another or to converge independently of other variables, such as tool use or stoneworkers' cultural affinities.

Operational chain (from the French, *chaîne opératoire*) describes the entire sequence of transformations to stone from raw material procurement, through tool production and use, to discard and recycling (Lemmonier 1992, Sellet 1993). In principle, archaeologists' reconstructions of operational chains encompass all these activities, but in practice those reconstructions concentrate on raw material procurement and tool production, activities for which American and other Anglophone archaeologists often use the term *reduction sequence* (Shott 2003). Archaeologists' reconstructions of operational chains can depict simple linear staged sequences or branching flowcharts. Operational chains are not necessarily things that existed in prehistoric stoneworkers' minds, but rather archaeological models (groups of linked hypotheses) about prehistoric stoneworker behavior. (It is extremely unlikely that prehistoric stoneworkers thought about their activities in terms of flowcharts or other modern-day systems-theory concepts that archaeologists use to represent operational chains in the professional literature.) Operational chains can be a useful way to connect prehistoric lithic assemblages with one another (Boëda 2013). If the particular series of toolmaking operations defining them are highly idiosyncratic, then one can make a stronger claim for cultural connections among prehistoric toolmakers than one based solely on appearances of artifact-types among which similarities and differences may reflect convergences and divergences arising from curation and discard threshold variation. Comparing operational chains is like comparing recipes rather than what remains on plates after finished meals.

Archaeologists often characterize operational chains holistically, as flaking or shaping (Anglophone works commonly use the French terms *débitage* and *façonnage*, respectively, Inizan et al. 1999). In flaking/*débitage* stoneworkers detach flakes in bulk from cores in order to provision themselves with flakes intended either for immediate use as cutting tools or for further shaping-related modification. In shaping/*façonnage* stoneworkers detach flakes from cores or flakes in order to modify the core/flake into a desired shape. Neither strategy is mutually exclusive of the other. Flakes detached during shaping can be used as cutting tools, and in-bulk flake production necessarily entails some shaping. Perhaps the best way to think about flaking/shaping is as archaeological "shorthand" – broad and hypothetical generalizations about operational chains rather than robust analytical categories for them.

SOURCES OF INFORMATION ABOUT STONE TOOLS

Most of what archaeologists think we know about prehistoric stone tool technology comes from either actualistic or contextual observations.

Actualistic Observations

Actualistic observations involve witnessing stone tool production, use, and discard; that is, from actually seeing tools made, used, and discarded. The three main sources for such observations include ethnography, experimental archaeology, and nonhuman primate ethology.

Ethnography Today, few people habitually make and use stone tools, but as recently as 6,000 years ago, nearly every living human was either a stone-tool maker/user or depended on stone tools others made for them. In a striking contrast with the thousands of years it took for early metal tools to replace stone tools in the Near East (Rosen 1996), ethnographic nineteenth- and twentieth-century stone-tool-users everywhere abandoned lithic technology for industrial mass-produced metal implements almost instantaneously. Even so, early ethnographers and anthropologists managed to amass an impressive body of observations about stone tool production and use in the Americas, Australia and New Guinea, Africa, and Asia (see Holdaway and Douglas 2012, McCall 2012). These observations can inform archaeological interpretation, but one needs to be aware of their limitations. Few ethnographers had formal training in archaeology or stone-tool analysis. Their descriptions of tools and toolmaking activities can be imprecise. Even the best such accounts emphasize normative or "typical" activities at the expense of information about behavioral variation and variability. "Ethnoarchaeological" research specifically focused on lithic technology did not become commonplace until the 1970s. Even so, because there are so few such high-quality ethnographic accounts, over-generalizing from them can risk equating local idiosyncrasies with widespread or evolutionarily primitive behaviors. The stone tools modern-day Ethiopian hide-workers employ have been well documented (Gallagher 1977, Clark and Kurashina 1981, Brandt and Weedman 1997, Sahle et al. 2012, Weedman Arthur 2018), but their distinctively modified stone tools resemble only a small number of prehistoric artifacts, mostly scrapers and bipolar cores.

The published evidence about ethnographic stoneworking suggests the following hypotheses about prehistoric human behavior:

- People gathered stone tool materials during excursions with that goal in mind (as in mining or *direct procurement*) as well as during daily foraging activities or other work (*embedded procurement*).
- Stoneworkers selected lithic materials not only based on mechanical properties, rock morphology, and size but also guided by aesthetic qualities and supernatural beliefs about rocks and rock sources.
- People carried tools and tool materials with them beyond daily foraging areas.
- Much stoneworking focused on obtaining sharp cutting edges in quantities vastly exceeding immediate needs.
- Tool uses included both pre-oral food processing and making tools out of other materials.
- Tool designs included shapes not intrinsic to the rocks themselves.
- When people transported stone tools, they often used them for multiple purposes.
- Prestige goods and trade items included elaborate and "overdesigned" tools.
- Multicomponent implements often integrated lithic and nonlithic materials (e.g., tips and barbs of projectile weapons, stone axes attached to wooden handles).
- Artifact designs varied geographically, chronologically, and functionally in patterned ways.
- People procured, manufactured, used, and discarded stone tools at many points on the landscape, including former habitation sites and along pathways between sites.

Not all examples of ethnographic stone tool use exhibit all of these features, but their widespread occurrence suggests they result from evolutionarily primitive (i.e., ancestral) capacities that we may share with at least more-recent extinct hominins. These features also distinguish human from nonhuman primate stone tool use (Shea 2017b).

Experimental Archaeology Archaeologists have gained many insights into prehistoric lithic technology through experimental archaeology, making and using stone tool themselves. Archaeologists' experiments with stone tools began early on, and they now encompass a vast and diverse literature (for an overview, see Eren et al. 2016). The earliest such experiments focused on stone tool manufacturing techniques and methods (Johnson 1978). Experiments testing how stone tools performed in different tasks, the wear traces resulting from use, and investigations into how natural forces can modify tools and tool materials soon followed. Recent controlled experiments furnish insights into the mechanical forces involved in stone tool production (for a review, see Dibble and Rezek

2009, Lin et al. 2013). Other experiments overturn longstanding archaeological assumptions about the efficiency of various toolmaking methods (Eren et al. 2008, Pargeter and Eren 2017) and the functional significance of morphological variation among tool types (Sisk and Shea 2009, Key and Lycett 2017). Informative as they can be, experiment and experience are not the same things. Archaeologists' experiments almost certainly do not replicate the conditions under which prehistoric hominins made and used stone tools. They demonstrate the possible rather than the probable.

Ethology *Ethology* describes research on nonhuman animal behavior. Living nonhuman primate stone tool use can suggest what aspects of hominin stone tool use are either evolutionarily primitive or likely to have evolved convergently. Nineteenth-century scientists knew that nonhuman primates use tools. Indeed, Darwin mentioned this in his *Descent of Man* (1871: 50–51), but primatologists only began systematically studying nonhuman primate stone tool among wild-living primates during the 1960–1970s (Panger et al. 2003, Haslam et al. 2009). Many primates use tools, but our nearest relatives, chimpanzees (*Pan troglodytes*) and bonobos (*Pan paniscus*), appear to be the most versatile tool users (McGrew 1992). Chimpanzees transport unmodified stone tools and use them as percussors to split open nuts. This practice is not universal, however, and primatologists report age- and sex-based differences among stone-tool-using groups (Boesch and Boesch 1984). Chimpanzees do not modify stones before using them as tools – something they do routinely with other kinds of tools made of wood. Human tutors have taught captive bonobos how to make and use simple flaked-stone cutting tools (Toth et al. 1993), but this speaks as much to the apes' capacity to learn (and their tutors' persistence) as to the probability that bonobos and humans' last common ancestors used stone tools. Whether or not those last common ancestors made stone tools, differences between human and nonhuman primate stoneworking and tool use can be fertile sources of hypotheses about the evolutionary basis for changes in hominin lithic technology (Shea 2017b).

Just what to call research on nonhuman primate tool use remains somewhat controversial. Haslam and colleagues (2009) propose *primate archaeology*, but this term is problematic for several reasons. First, it expands the original definition of archaeology beyond the field's original and exclusive focus on past *human* behavior. Second, although a few self-identified "primate archaeologists" actually excavate, most study living animals. Therefore, the most accurate term for such research on living nonhuman primates using methods developed in archaeology would be *archaeological primatology*.

Contextual Observations

Contextual observations arise from interpretations of archaeological evidence following generally accepted principles from other scientific fields. For the lithic evidence, stratigraphic associations are the most-commonly-cited such observations. Other fruitful sources of contextual observations include artifact-refitting, stone tool-marks on other materials, lithic microwear, and residues adhering to artifacts.

Stratigraphic Associations The geological "Principle of Association" holds that artifacts enclosed in the same sediment were last buried at the same time. Finding stone tools and other objects enclosed together in the same sediments can inspire hypotheses about how they came to be associated, but one has to remember that "at the same time" can encompass weeks, years, decades, even centuries, depending on variability in local rates of sediment accumulation.

Refitting Artifacts On well-preserved stone tool surfaces, one can sometimes match (*refit*) surfaces that are the opposite sides of the same fracture. Archaeologists call groups of artifacts that link up to one another in this way *refitting constellations* or simply *constellations*. Different kinds of refitting constellations tell one different things (Cziesla 1990, Laughlin and Kelly 2010) (see Figure 2.3). Constellations comprising flake dorsal surfaces, flake ventral surfaces, and core surfaces (refits *sensu stricto*) tell one about core reduction strategies. Constellations between flakes and retouched pieces (*modifications*) inform one about artifact shaping and curation strategies. Constellations consisting of flake fragments (*breaks*) potentially tell one about geological disturbance, trampling, or other mechanical forces that affect stone tools on the surface or while buried.

Any kind of refitting constellation can shed light on how artifacts might have moved around prior to burial, or afterward. Refitting has great potential, but one has to interpret such evidence with care. Many interpretations of refitting constellations assume sets of refitting artifacts were detached near to one another in time. This is not necessarily true. Constellations can result from stoneworking events far separate from one another in time. Many (indeed, nearly all) ethnographic stoneworkers collect and recycle artifacts eroding from former habitation sites and archaeological deposits, frequently modifying them on the spot.

Systematic artifact-refitting studies are relatively uncommon. Seeking refits takes a lot of time and table space, as well as a certain imprecisely definable "eye" for the activity. An assemblage may lack refitting constellations due to inadequate scrutiny rather than from a failed search for them.

Perhaps because refitting studies are so uncommon, how archaeologists document and report refitting artifacts varies widely. They will usually report such refits as they find, but they often do not report details about the circumstances under which they found them. Did they sample systematically or judgmentally? How many people searched, and who were they? How much time did they spent searching? All of these things can affect refitting search outcomes. As with any experience-based skill involving visually assessed information, individuals' abilities differ. Such details are important if one wants to compare statistical variation in artifact-refitting between lithic assemblages.

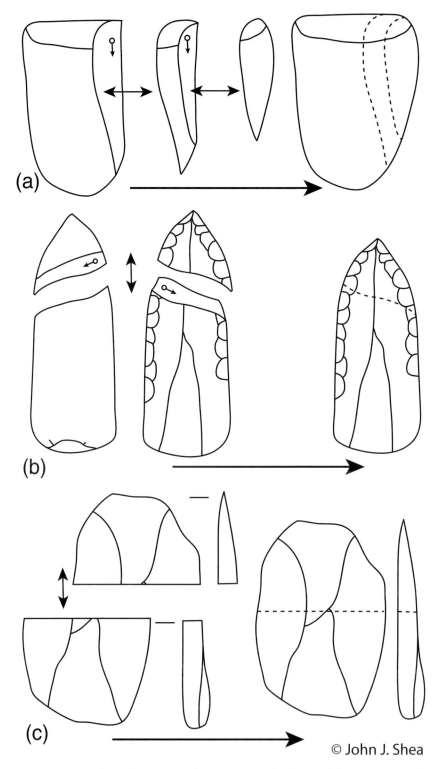

Figure 2.3 Artifact refitting constellations: (a) Refit, (b) Modification, (c) Break.

Surprisingly few experimental studies document what factors influence success in artifact refitting. In the author's experience (Sisk and Shea 2008) and based on published illustrations, larger artifacts, artifacts with cortex, and artifacts comprised of uncommon lithic raw materials are more likely to be refit to others. Experience and anecdotes from colleagues suggest success at refitting usually occurs early on: that first find encouraging an intense search for more of them. Success declines after 20–30 minutes or so. If one seeks refits, 30 minutes need not be a permanent "point of diminished return" but rather a point of cognitive overload at which one should take a break and return to the task later with a fresh perspective. These generalizations parallel closely "success profiles" for doing jigsaw puzzles. Someone good at assembling jigsaw puzzles will probably be good at refitting. Doing jigsaw puzzles can be good practice for artifact-refitting.

Tool-Marks Favorable circumstances can preserve bone or wood with stone tool cut-marks on them. Such preservation is exceptional, but one has to remain alert to false negative findings. Wooden objects lacking tool-marks might have been used as tools. Friction between tool users' hands and wooden tool surfaces can abrade away stone tool cut-marks. Stone tool cut marks on animal bones can indicate tool-assisted butchery, but the absence of stone tool cut-marks does not necessarily rule out butchery.

Microwear Fractures, striations, and polishes form when stone edges and surfaces make forceful contact with one another and with other media. Archaeologists describe such damage collectively as *microwear*, even though in some cases one can see the phenomena without artificial magnification. Microwear on stone tool edges and surfaces furnishes clues about the parts of the tools that were used – including attachments to handles, the motions employed, and the nature of the worked materials. Archaeologists have explored microwear's potential value for a very long time (Semenov 1964). Controlled experiments routinely inform this research, and these reveal likely interpretive biases (Keeley 1980, Rots 2003). Activities involving heavy force, prolonged use, and work on relatively hard or abrasive materials leave more distinctive wear traces than tasks involving light force, brief use, and cutting softer and/or lubricated materials. It follows that one should not take relative frequency variation in occurrences of different wear traces as straightforward reflections of prehistoric tool use. Post-depositional mechanical wear, such as flowing water, soil move-ment, trampling, and other factors can significantly alter microwear traces (Shea and Klenck 1993, Levi-Sala 1996). Some archaeologists use the term *use-wear* for microwear. It is wise to avoid this practice, for doing so implicitly accepts that the wear in question arises from human activity and not from geological or other sources.

Novice lithic analysts often try their hand at microwear analysis, but those who do should be aware that the field is a research specialization within archaeology. Microwear analysts employ expensive high-magnification microscopes that require considerable care and maintenance. Though micro-wear analysts have made impressive progress in moving away from the field's early reliance on visually assessed morphological analogies and towards para-metric (measurement-based) interpretations, microwear analysis retains a strong subjective and interpretive component. Novice lithic analysts should not be surprised that microwear specialists question their interpretations.

Residues All manner of substances can adhere to stone. Archaeologists have found DNA, blood, hair, starch particles, plant fibers, and inorganic substances, such as red ochre (iron oxide) on stone tool edges and surfaces (Monnier et al. 2012, Rots et al. 2015, Nowell et al. 2016). One encounters residues less frequently in older assemblages, but techniques for recovering organic residues continue to advance. Interpreting residues requires differentiating residues bonded to the tool surface as the result of cutting, residues from handles, fibers and mastic use to attach tools to handles, and residues from sediments enclosing the tools. Archaeologists have made great progress in visual identifications of residues. Still, many such residues are ambiguous, and interpreting them in detail requires physical or chemical analyses.

HOW TO MISINTERPRET STONE TOOLS

Time and again, the history of archaeology shows archaeologists realizing that they have misinterpreted stone tools (Dibble et al. 2017, Shea 2017b). Such misinterpretations make a certain amount of sense; after all, stone tools are the least familiar artifacts archaeologists recover from excavations, and, therefore, our theories about such unfamiliar artifacts are intrinsically likely to be wrong. (One invites younger readers to test this hypothesis by visiting an antiques market, older readers by visiting any consumer electronics store.) This section reviews the following common assumptions that lead archaeologists to misin-terpret stone tools:

- Preservation equals significance.
- Artifact forms reflect stoneworkers' intended artifact designs.
- "Type-sites" preserve evidence for larger regional patterns of stone tool variation.
- Artifact relative frequencies in an assemblage indicate relative frequencies of particular activities undertaken while that assemblage accumulated.
- Lithic assemblages are spatially homogeneous.
- Specific stone tool assemblages can be linked to specific human groups.
- Similarities among stone tools matter more than differences.
- Stone tool variation primarily reflects adult economic activities and ecological adaptations.
- Making and using stone tools confers expertise in archaeological lithic artifact interpretation.

- Excavating stone tools confers expertise in archaeological lithic artifact interpretation.
- Past archaeological practices in stone tool analysis remain valid and analytically powerful.

Preservation equals significance. Stone tools resist weathering better than any other kinds of artifacts and fossils, but this does not make them relevant to every question we want to ask about the prehistoric past. Just because people made stone tools when something happened does not mean that event influenced the stone tool evidence. It would be nice if stone tool variation told us something about cattle domestication or about changing gender roles in prehistory, for example, but it is far from clear that they do (Gero 1991). Archaeologists formulate many such "relevance claims" after the fact of artifact discovery, rather than by deducing predictions about them from prior anthropological theory. Inasmuch as one can fit facts to any theory, and vice versa, one should reserve skepticism about theories that fail to predict new findings and place more confidence in those that do.

Artifact forms reflect stoneworkers' intended artifact designs. Davidson and Noble (1993) coined the term "Finished Artifact Fallacy" for archaeologists' all too common assumption that the forms in which stone tools appear in the archaeological record reflect intentional designs, or "finished artifacts." While some stone tools may reflect such designs, as do craft/hobby stoneworkers' artifacts, ethnographic studies also suggest prolonged use and resharpening/recycling affect artifact forms as well. Numerous artifact-refitting studies show cores and retouched pieces undergoing changes during use that would result in their being classified differently at correspondingly different intervals prior to discard. American archaeologists often use the expression *Frison Effect* for use-related changes in artifact morphology. (The term references George C. Frison [1924–present] who documented this phenomenon among North American prehistoric sites (Frison 1969)).

"Type-sites" preserve evidence for larger regional patterns of stone tool variation. This idea developed during the prehistoric archaeology's early phases. When few sites had been excavated, it made sense to extrapolate widely from those with deep stratigraphic sequences and stone tool assemblages, but in every region where early archaeologists applied this "type site" approach, subsequent research revealed lithic assemblages that did not "fit" comfortably into the type-site's cultural sequence. In hindsight, archaeologists should not have expected them to do so. Humans do different things in different parts of the landscape. While a group might have known perfectly well how to construct free-standing shelters, one would hardly expect them do to so in a cave. (The whole point of living in a cave is to avoid building a shelter.) Similarly, one would not expect a people capable of killing an elephant to do so near habitation sites and thereby draw carnivores to the vicinity of their children and other predation-vulnerable group

members. (Nearly everyone who has taken up stoneworking as a hobby has at one time or another been admonished to relocate their work area elsewhere.)

Artifact relative frequencies in an assemblage indicate relative frequencies of particular activities undertaken while that assemblage accumulated. This might be true, but contemporary human material culture offers sufficient counterexamples to suggest caution in assuming so. For example, many people who smoke tobacco do so using cheap paper cigarettes, and, as a result, cigarette butts litter many contemporary landscapes in rough proportion to their usage. That is, they are common where people smoke a lot, uncommon elsewhere. Others use expensive pipes or electronic cigarettes whose users transport and maintain them. Predictably, one rarely finds usable pipes or functioning electronic cigarettes lying about on the ground. Like paper cigarettes, stone tools engaged in activities with high rates of edge-attrition and low discard thresholds likely occur pretty much everywhere humans used them and in rough proportion to their usage. Relative frequencies of more curated artifacts, stone tool equivalents of pipes or electronic cigarettes, likely reflect other factors, such as the ease or difficulty of repairing or replacing them.

Lithic assemblages are spatially homogeneous. Some measure of what stone tools one recovers from excavation may reflect where one chose to put the excavation trenches. Nearly every archaeological site for which archaeologists have published maps shows differences in artifacts' horizontal distribution. This means that if one sampled the same area using a different excavation strategy, one would recover a stone tool assemblage with different characteristics. Trench locations reflect modern-day topography and ease of access (e.g., game trails, cultivated fields, large trees with thorny branches), factors utterly irrelevant to how prehistoric humans arranged their activities at those places thousands, if not millions, of years previously.

One can link specific stone tool assemblages to specific human groups. Many archaeological sites are either caves/rock-shelters or open-air sites near perennial water sources that preserve deeply stratified sequences of human occupations. Unless prehistoric human settlement patterns followed completely different principles than recent human ones, such sites were almost certainly "settlement magnets." Any humans in the vicinity for any length of time likely resided there. Absent compelling evidence to the contrary, one should assume assemblages from such locations combine and commingle traces of multiple occupations – ones by different people for different reasons. When archaeologists recognize and distinguish different lithic assemblages at these sites, they nearly always do so in terms of geological stratigraphy. No prior theory whatsoever predicts that interruptions in sediment deposition at such sites should coincide with changes in the identities of the humans or earlier hominins active there. The longer the interruptions, the more likely such changes occurred, but the durations of such interruptions in sediment deposition are less often known than unknown. Deep skepticism ought to greet archaeologists' all-too-common practices of (1) assigning all the artifacts from a single sedimentary deposit to one, and only one, prehistoric culture or stone tool industry and (2) assuming such cultures or industries correspond to only one group of stoneworkers. Stone tools aren't people.

Similarities among stone tools matter more than differences. Archaeologists routinely assume that when artifacts resemble one another, they do so due to similarities in stoneworkers' activities, identities, or some combination of both. They might; but this is not necessarily true. Stone tools can resemble one another due to continued use and resharpening, as well as to constraints on how one can hold a stone tool or attach it to a handle. Retouched artifact-types, such as so-called thumbnail scrapers and Acheulian handaxes, that enjoy global or near-global distributions lasting hundreds of thousands of years or more, may result from such convergences. Alternatively, they may reflect the retention of ancestral ways of making stone tools, or simply archaeologists' perceived morphological analogies. Differences are more important than similarities for, in evolution, only differences matter. (Darwin titled his seminal work, *Origin of Species* [1859], not *Why So Many Animals and Plants Look Alike*.)

Stone tool variation primarily reflects adult economic activities and ecological adaptations. Humans are primates, and primates are neophilic ("novelty-loving" or "novelty-seeking"). Adults seek out unfamiliar objects and engage with them, and children do so, too. Indeed, "child's play" emulating adult activities is one of the principal ways humans and our nearest nonhuman primate relatives learn how to make and use tools (Riede et al. 2018). It is also potentially a source of variability in the archaeological record (Hammond and Hammond 1981, Shea 2006). It seems vanishingly unlikely that archaeologists will develop a single set of criteria that discriminates stone tools that children and juvenile hominins used from those that adults used. Nevertheless, some of the ways children interact with modern-day artifacts sound cautionary notes about prehistoric *teleoliths* – stone artifacts modified in the course of learning.

Anecdotal evidence from modern-day stoneworkers suggest that most children younger than about ten years old lack the physical strength and hand to eye coordination to undertake competent core reduction and fracture-based artifact shaping for prolonged periods (Shea 2015). When children try to imitate adult stoneworking, the resulting artifacts feature extensive percussion-related damage, including *comminution* (incompletely propagated flake scars) and other crushing damage on all edges, ridges, and surfaces. Instances of such seemingly "obsessive stoneworking" grace all periods of Stone Age prehistory. Some such instances may reflect children imitating adult toolmaking gestures without being able to initiate controlled fractures.

Children's hands are smaller than adults' hands. Children's toys that imitate adult implements are often smaller and less functionally efficient than their adult counterparts, although this quality can vary with a child's age. Many parents might allow their twelve-year-old to carry a sharp *panga* (machete) or a loaded rifle, but few would allow their five-year-old to do so. Stone tools with blunted tips and dull edges may be tools discarded due to their mechanical inutility, but some of them may be artifacts specifically designed for children's safe use.

Children often collect adult implements and aggregate them in play areas within adult living spaces or at the margins of those spaces. The author well remembers thoroughly canvassing his parents' home one Thanksgiving Day in search of a television remote control that his nephews were using as a pretend 'space ship' in a game they were playing in the bedrooms upstairs.

Such child's play involving stone tools is neither necessarily less symbolic nor less informative than adult stone tool use. While conducting a field survey in West Turkana, Kenya, the author several times came upon rectangular arrangements of small pebbles (including stone tools) arranged in even rows and columns. A single larger rock or two often lay off to the side. Our local Turkana staff informed us these were the handiwork of children "playing school." The smaller rocks arranged in rows were children, the larger ones, teachers. One older staff member wistfully remembered that he played a similar game as a child, but that his small stones were cattle and arranged in circles rather than rectangles.

This experience reminds one that our capacity to imbue artifacts with symbolic meanings can influence our interactions with them, and with one another. Among adults, such interactions follow culturally prescribed and proscribed patterns, whereas few rules prevail among children still learning these prescriptions/proscriptions. For example, among adults the "Queen" chess piece is an artifact one can use on a chessboard in a limited set of ways. For a child, it could just as well be a space ship.

Making and using stone tools confers expertise in archaeological lithic artifact interpretation. It does not. David Hurst Thomas (1986) memorably named this assumption, the "flintknappers' fundamental conceit," although one thinks "Flintknapper's Fantasy" more appropriate. Most craft/hobby flintknappers are humble artists. Some craft/hobby flintknappers may imagine they are recreating prehistoric stonework, but few claim their experience gives them special insights into prehistory. That sort of syllogism exists mainly in archaeologists' imaginations. (Anybody bragging about having "replicated" prehistoric stone tools is far more likely to be an archaeologist!) Some archaeologists who study lithic artifacts (including the author) have considerable experience, even expertise, making and using stone tools (Shea 2015). Such experiences can inspire hypotheses, but those hypotheses still have to be tested using archaeological evidence (Eren et al. 2016). Who proposed the hypothesis, what experience led them to propose it, and similar such appeals to authority are irrelevant. Modern-day stoneworkers' claims to have "replicated" prehistoric human activities, as opposed to merely having crafted artifact reproductions, have to be independently tested and verified. Experimental archaeologists should not describe modern-day experimental artifacts using terms originally developed for prehistoric stone tools, such as "Oldowan" chopper or "Acheulian handaxe" without noting that these artifacts are reproductions.

Excavating stone tools confers expertise in archaeological lithic artifact interpretation. It does not. This "Digger's Delusion," the conceit that excavating stone tools qualifies one to interpret those artifacts, is even less convincing than claims based on self-reported stoneworking experience. While stoneworking is at least plausibly analogous to prehistoric stone tool production, archaeological excavation skills are utterly irrelevant. Nothing about the experience of digging rectangular holes in Africa or wandering around deserts picking up artifacts confers expertise stone artifact analysis.

This syllogism arose and persists because during prehistoric research's earlier phases, excavators reported their lithic artifacts and ceramic findings themselves. Formal training in archaeology involved in-depth studies about how to identify, describe, and measure stone tools and ceramics. Excavators usually engaged specialist researchers to analyze animal bones, plant fossils, and other residues. Today, those directing archaeological excavation may be geoarchaeologists, zooarchaeologists, or generalist researchers without specialized training in stone tool analysis. In such cases, describing stone tools may be a task assigned to a specialist or to an inexperienced graduate student. In evaluating hypotheses about prehistoric stone tools, the only things that matter are how well those hypotheses explain the known evidence, how well they predict new findings, and how well they withstand challenges from competing hypotheses. All else is irrelevant.

Past archaeological practices in stone tool analysis remain valid and analytically powerful. Archaeologists devised many of the ways we measure, classify, and organize the prehistoric stone tool evidence in the late nineteenth and early twentieth centuries. They meant well, but these researchers, literally, knew less about stone tools than any other humans before or after them. Stone tool use had largely vanished from Europe by this point, and such ethnographic descriptions of stone tool use as archaeologists had at the time lacked detail. Given these odds against them, early archaeologists made impressive contributions to prehistory. Nevertheless, since the late nineteenth and early twentieth centuries archaeologists have accumulated many observations about prehistoric and ethnoarchaeological stone tool variability. Many of their observations contradict early archaeologists' assumptions. Seeking support in some modern-day debate by invoking early archaeologists' published views amounts to little more than appeal to authority. That someone did something a long time ago does not mean that they did it well. Arguments backed up with claims of long experience analyzing stone tools carry little weight either. Such are little more than self-directed appeals to authority. Just because archaeologists, collectively or individually, have been measuring, describing, and classifying stone tools in one way or another for a very long time doesn't mean they have been doing it well, or that these are the best ways of doing so. It could simply indicate the absence of strong selective pressure to the contrary. The history of science abounds with examples of entire communities of scholars doing the same thing for long periods (e.g., trying to convert base metals into gold) until strong selective pressure from evidence-based hypotheses finally forced them to do things differently (Kuhn 1962).

UWAZI VALLEY TALES, EPISODE 2: THE VALLEY OF CLARITY

A brilliant copper disk, the rising sun, chased the evening's mist downslope into the Uwazi Valley.

"Some colonial cartographer must have been making a joke." The Polymath approached holding a steaming tin coffee cup. "Densest fog in Eastern Africa."

"Valley of Clarity, indeed," said the Old Africa Hand as he strode briskly past us towards the breakfast table. A short, gray-haired African man wearing a waterproof jacket, shorts, and hiking boots followed. Joseph, the Polymath's assistant, smiled.

"*Jambo*. Welcome to Africa," Joseph said passing us.

"*Asante sana, Mzee*," (Thank you very much, Elder), I replied.

Joseph, I would learn, was born among hunter-gatherers who still lived in nearby hills. A few of them still hunted and gathered, but most, like Joseph, had transitioned to wage-work in town. The Polymath hired Joseph as his assistant during the Uwazi Valley Project's first year and then retained him as at the project's "guide," thereafter.

What was I doing here, so far from home? The Polymath and Aya had invited me to join the Uwazi Valley Prehistory Project to measure, describe, and analyze stone tools. If anyone had told me ten months ago that this would be the doctoral research project to which I devoted most of my twenties, I would have laughed in their face.

I grew up in the mountains and deserts of the American Southwest. From an early age I became interested in stone tools and other aspects of Ancestral Native American material culture. This interest tracked in various directions until, as a senior undergraduate, I read a paper by Big American University's Professor Scott. The paper argued that humans had lived in the Americas 40,000 years ago. This was nearly three times the generally accepted date for humans' first appearance there. Scott was an authority on stone tools from the Southwest but a bit of a maverick. A fistfight with colleagues had gotten him banned from the Faculty Club. On the other hand, he published yearly progress reports on all of his excavations, and he and his wife richly endowed a scholarship fund for Native American students.

"Boys and girls," he said in his classes, "if you don't publish it, it didn't happen."

Much of Scott's argument about his early tools hinged on being able to tell stone tools from naturally damaged rocks. I sought him out in his office, hoping to join Scott's expedition in search of Late Pleistocene cave sites in southern New Mexico. My reputation as an amateur stoneworker preceded me, and he asked to see some of my stone tools. I had read Scott's classic work, *The Stone Age in the American Southwest*, and crafted some reproductions of Clovis and Folsom points and others of the more complex-looking artifacts illustrated in his book. We hit it off thereafter, but he insisted that if I wanted to work with him, I had to go to graduate school. Scott encouraged me to apply to study with him the next year. Big American University accepted me into their anthropology doctoral program on scholarship. Scott perished in an automobile accident just before the start of my first semester.

The Polymath was then in his last year as Department Chair. I met with him to tell him that I was dropping out of the doctoral program.

"Don't be foolish, Robin," the Polymath said. "You haven't even got started, yet. Your skills with stone tools could transfer to any other part of the world. Look, Aya and I have started a project in Eastern Africa focusing on later prehistory – basically everything since 200,000 years ago. At Pango Wa Kwale, we hit a gold mine, but Aya lacks the expertise to analyze the stone tools, and I haven't got the time to do it. So, let's put our heads together, get you a grant, and turn you into an Africanist archaeologist."

"But I've never taken a course in African archaeology."

"So, register for the Old Africa Hand's course on African prehistory. Come to weekly meetings with me, and we will discuss Eastern African stone tools. Next summer, we'll head off to the field and get you started on your thesis research."

I enjoyed the Old African's course, and I learned a lot, but the Polymath's weekly meetings quickly wandered from stone tool analysis to whatever topic happened to have caught his interest. One week we discussed chimpanzee meat-eating, the next Aboriginal Australian ethnography, a third the results of paleoclimate reconstructions from Indian Ocean sediment cores. The only thing one could predict about these sessions was that stone tools played ever-diminishingly central roles in them.

Aya had risen just before dawn and had already set out for the site. I had not seen much of her during my first year on campus. Aya had come to Big American University from Old Private University three years earlier, winning a fierce competition among job candidates. A whirlwind since arriving, Aya won a National Science Foundation grant for early-career scientists. Aya's lab went from office furniture storage to a richly provisioned archaeozoology lab overnight. Her popular courses were fully enrolled. She had organized two symposia at the Society for American Archaeology Annual Meetings. One of these she compiled into a special issue of a scientific journal, the other was in review as an edited book. Several of her papers and ones she wrote with graduate students had appeared in prestigious scientific journals. Aya's pretenure review praised her solid publication record, but it also noted her modest success in obtaining grants for her research. The small annual grants she and the Polymath had secured for the Uwazi Valley Prehistory Project had been adequate, the review wrote, but for permanent appointment, she needed a larger grant with multiyear funding.

A decade before, the Polymath had been Aya's undergraduate academic advisor at Old Private University. Students and faculty noted their closeness, and a few hinted at a possible romantic relationship between them. The photographs in the Polymath's office told a different, sad story. Older photos showed the Polymath and his wife with their son and daughter at steadily older ages. Aya first appears in the photos when the children were college-age. She and the Polymath's daughter, Susan, were together, smiling, in graduation robes. "Sisters by different mothers," read a handwritten caption. Susan did not appear in later photos. Aya stood alone with the Polymath's family.

I looked forward to working with Aya, but I was also a bit intimidated. I tried to meet with her during my first year, but I was run ragged with courses, and our schedules conflicted. She taught her classes, held office hours, and spent time in her lab with undergraduate students. Aya had no graduate students of her own yet. Other than this, she worked in her office with the door closed and a "do not disturb" sign on it.

Speaking about Aya at the wine and cheese reception for first-year graduate students, one tipsy senior professor quipped, "You can smell the ambition wafting down the hallway."

"Nothing wrong with ambition," said the Polymath, sidling up to us. "Without it, we'd still be living in trees yelling and throwing poop at each other. Instead, we get to do so in this nice faculty lounge."

"You'd better be careful, Professor, people talk."

"Yes, speech is one of our species' most over-rated behaviors," he replied, smiling broadly. The older professor turned away towards the fast-dwinding stacks of cheese and crackers on the refreshment table.

CHAPTER 3

HOW TO READ STONE TOOLS

Much like "reading" animal tracks and signs, reading a stone tool involves examining it and interpreting it in behavioral terms. What kind of rock is it? Is it an artifact and, if so, what kind of artifact? This chapter introduces the methods by which archaeologists answer these questions.

WHAT KIND OF ROCK IS IT?

Rocks are aggregates of minerals. Many of the rocks prehistoric humans shaped into cutting tools are *silicates* – rocks predominantly comprised of silica or quartz. Quartz is a relatively hard mineral (7 out of 10 on geology's Moh's hardness scale). Fractured silicate rocks preserve sharp, durable cutting edges and hard surfaces. Silicate rocks dominate archaeological lithic assemblages from most regions and time periods. Rocks used as percussors to create fractures and as groundstone artifacts vary more widely and include nonsilicate rocks as well.

Lithic Raw Materials

Archaeologists discuss lithic raw materials, or the rocks out of which stone-workers make implements, in terms of four major geological categories: minerals, igneous rocks, sedimentary rocks, and metamorphic rocks.

Quartz occurs as large crystals suitable for stoneworking when heat and pressure cause smaller quartz crystals to recrystallize inside other rocks. Quartz is usually either translucent or white and opaque. Its fracture properties vary. Sometimes it fractures along crystal boundaries, other times across them. These variable fracture properties encourage some archaeologists to rate quartz as a low-quality material, and yet, perhaps because of its sharpness, prehistoric humans used quartz as tool material wherever it occurred.

Igneous (volcanic) *rocks* form during exposure to heat. Igneous rocks commonly utilized as tool materials include obsidian (volcanic glass), rhyolite, ignimbrite, and basalt. Eastern African obsidians are usually black and opaque with a vitreous luster, but some are gray or dark green and partly translucent. Rhyolite is a silica-rich (felsic) volcanic rock whose appearance varies widely, from glassy and fine grained to coarser with large crystals (phenocrysts). Ignimbrite is volcanic tuff (silica-rich ash) reheated and fused together. Ignimbrites may exhibit flow-bands. Comprised mainly of plagioclase with pyroxene and olivine, basalt is black or gray with a dull luster, and it weathers to brown, green, and other earth tones. Basalts vary widely in their fracture qualities. In contrast with rhyolites, basalts have relatively low silica content. Some basalts are dense and tough (mafic basalt), others brittle and glassy. Vesicular basalts contain numerous small air pockets (vesicles) that impede fracture propagation. Nevertheless, prehistoric stoneworkers sometimes selected vesicular basalt to make groundstone vessels, abrading stones, pulverizing equipment, and other tools.

Sedimentary rocks consist of sedimentary particles and organic matter (fossils) accumulated near the Earth's surface and deposited under water. In some sedimentary rocks, such as cherts and shale, pressure causes rock particles to cement themselves to one another. In others, such as jasper, chalcedony, and flint, the rocks precipitate out in solution. Chert is the most common sedimentary rock used by Eastern Africans to make stone-cutting tools. Because chert includes quartz particles derived from older rocks, its color, texture, and composition can vary widely within the same deposit, even within the same stone. Cherts usually form in horizontal sedimentary deposits in lakes and oceans, but "fissure cherts" can also form as chemical precipitates in cracks and fissures of other, denser rocks. Precipitated siliceous rocks, such as jasper and chalcedony, occur in some Eastern African assemblages, though usually in small quantities. Reflecting its iron content, jasper is usually red, yellow or brown. Chalcedony is either white or semitranslucent with a waxy texture. Limestone and shale have relatively low silica content and preferred cleavage/breakage planes that impede and constrain fracture propagation. In some parts of Eastern Africa, prehistoric humans also shaped tools out of petrified (fossil) wood.

Metamorphic rocks, such as quartzite, form due to combined heat and pressure. Recrystallized sandstone, quartzite, varies widely in color and preserves a rough, "sugary" texture.

Lithic Raw Material Use in Prehistoric Eastern Africa

Eastern Africa is a geologically diverse region. The same stone tool assemblage may preserve multiple kinds of sedimentary, igneous, and volcanic rocks together with quartz. While the best way to learn how to identify such rocks is in a formal college-level lab course in geology, reference works can assist in making field identifications. Over the course of his career, the author has found *Simon and Schuster's Guide to Rocks and Minerals* (Prinz et al. 1978) very useful, its large color figures especially helpful. Other well-reviewed reference works include the *National Audubon Society Field Guide to Rocks and Minerals: North America (1979)* and Cairncross's (2005) *Field Guide to Rocks & Minerals of Southern Africa.*

The most common lithic materials in Eastern African archaeological stone tool assemblages include quartz, various coarse-grained volcanics (chiefly basalt), and obsidian (Leakey 1931). Basalt and quartz occur throughout Eastern African prehistory, but obsidian is more common in younger contexts. Few obsidian artifacts appear in deposits more than a million years old. While this might reflect an evolutionary shift in hominins' raw-material selection strategies, it could also result from preservation bias or eruption age. Most obsidians appear near the end of volcanic eruption cycles. Obsidian weathers relatively quickly on a geological timescale. If hominins made obsidian stone tools more than a million years ago, those artifacts may have so disintegrated that archaeologists can neither recognize nor recover them.

Identifying Rocks' Sources

When geologists identify rock types, they use samples extracted from bedrock deposits that provide contextual clues about rock formation. Making specific rock identifications without such information can be difficult. Other than tools found at quarry sites, archaeological stone tools rarely provide such unambiguous evidence about their geological origin. Humans and earlier hominins routinely moved stone tools many kilometers from their geological sources.

Obsidian is so distinct that one rarely misidentifies it as such, although there is always the possibility that one is actually holding industrial glass. Louis Leakey's father dismissed many of the obsidian stone tools young Louis collected as a youth as simply shards of broken bottles (Leakey 1937). Quartz and quartzite can grade into one another. In general, if the rock has a rough, "sugary" texture (like sugar crystals fused together), it is probably quartzite. If the rock is translucent with a glassy texture, it is probably quartz. Distinguishing among various kinds of volcanic and sedimentary rocks can be more difficult. As a temporary measure one can group them together as "volcanics" and later consult with geologists to develop more precise volcanic rock identifications.

Mechanically inconsequential variation in iron, manganese, or other minerals can cause quartz to vary from translucent to opaque, from white to red to yellow to black. Such variation can occur within the same rock, as well as within larger deposits. These color change properties can complicate identifications of cryptocrystalline silicate rocks, such as chert, chalcedony, and jasper. Luedtke (1979, 1992) provides valuable guidance about this problem.

Identifying rock sources by visual inspection alone risks error. In general, lithic material classifications in the Eastern African archaeological literature are more complex for older assemblages and less complex for younger ones.

Rock surfaces exposed to chemical weathering and mechanical damage develop cortex and patina that conceal a rock's inner structure and make rock-type identifications difficult. *Cortex* is a soft surface condition that develops when a rock is exposed to chemical or mechanical weathering. *Patina* (or patination) describes chemical staining, i.e., a rock absorbing minerals from its surroundings while buried. Archaeologists often use these terms interchangeably or refer to them collectively as *cortex*.

Desert varnish is a kind of abrasive wear: a brilliantly reflective polish that forms on tool surfaces from collisions with wind-driven sand particles. Desert varnish on an artifact suggests that the tool suffered prolonged subaerial exposure on eroding surfaces. One has to be cautious about accepting such a hypothesis because chemical weathering and collisions with sand and silt particles in flowing water can create abrasion similar to desert varnish on stone tool surfaces.

When different surfaces of the same artifact exhibit different degrees of weathering, archaeologists call this phenomenon *double patination*. Double patination can be evidence that prehistoric toolmakers reused and recycled stone artifacts from older deposits.

Archaeologists searching for the lithic material sources for a particular assemblage usually survey the area within at least two days' walk around the excavation site. That survey includes bedrock sources, sedimentary deposits, as well as archaeological sites of greater or equal antiquity from which stone-workers might have procured tool materials. Yet, the present-day "lithic landscape" differs from past ones. Recent high sea- or lake-level stands, sediment deposits, dense vegetation, farms and pastures, and housing construction may cover formerly accessible rock sources. Conversely, low lake and river levels, land clearance, and mining may expose rock sources that were inaccessible to prehistoric stoneworkers. Papers in Church (1994) provide some useful guidance about lithic resource studies.

Geologists and archaeologists who specialize in rock source identifications typically compare petrographic thin sections viewed under polarized light and/ or ratios of trace elements (rare stable isotopes), but these can vary within a geological source. Odell (2004) provides a review of various such methods. Eastern African archaeologists increasingly investigate obsidian sources using X-ray florescence to detect variation in these trace elements (Ndiema et al. 2010, Shackley 2011, Dillian 2016).

IS IT AN ARTIFACT?

Other scientists and nonscientists often express surprise that archaeologists lack a simple, objective, and universally applicable diagnostic test that reliably discriminates lithic artifacts from naturally fractured stones. One needs to keep this in perspective. Stone tools are durable residues of human behavior, and human behavior varies more than that of any other tool-using organism. That archaeologists have not devised an "artifact/nonartifact" test after more than a century of research may simply show that it is impossible to do so. Therefore, rather than seeking a simple "yes or no" answer to the question, "Is this an artifact?" a better approach considers whether the object in question differs significantly from naturally modified stones. For comparative purposes, students of archaeological lithic analysis should also collect and examine naturally damaged stones.

Deciding whether or not a lithic object is an artifact requires an understanding of the mechanics of how humans and natural forces modify stone. Those mechanisms include abrasion, fracture, and thermal alteration.

Abrasion

Abrasion results from sliding (shear) contact between two surfaces and creates two phenomena: striations and polish. When rocks abrade, shearing forces detach individual rock particles, or grit. Grit particles dragged across rocks surfaces leave linear depressions (*striations*) in their wake that align parallel with the direction of tool movement during wear formation. Striation is a familiar abrasive process. Nearly everyone who has worn eyeglasses has had scratches/ striations accumulate on their lenses. *Polish* describes the cumulative flattening of rock surfaces and the resulting increase in how well those surfaces reflect light.

Large-scale abrasion and polishing can make cutting edges work more efficiently than fractured/retouched ones. Abraded edges lose less energy to drag/friction, and transfer more energy into cutting (Hayden 1989). Abrasion can resharpen use-worn and damaged edges with less loss of tool mass than retouch, but it takes more time to accomplish. However, small-scale abrasion can dull a stone cutting edge, increasing the amount of energy necessary to accomplish a cutting task.

Ethnographic stoneworkers often shape rocks with poor fracture qualities by alternating cycles of percussion and abrasion, or "pecking and grinding" (Holmes 1919, Hayden and Nelson 1981, Dickson 1982, Adams 2014, Shoemaker et al. 2017). To weaken stone surfaces, they first strike the rock repeatedly with a hard percussor. Such percussion creates patches of incompletely propagated fractures, or *comminution*. Next, they detach these comminuted rock particles by abrading them with a coarse-surfaced rock. Stoneworkers repeat these cycles of percussion and abrasion until they achieve the desired shaping effect on the rock. At various points, they may introduce grit to accelerate striation formation and/or water and other substances to increase surface polishing.

Recent stoneworkers also use abrasion to perforate stones and to cut them into smaller pieces. *Perforation* usually involves a mechanical device to accelerate abrasion, such as a bow drill or a pump drill, (Holmes 1919). In either case, one moves a cord wrapped around a wooden spindle back and forth, thereby rotating the spindle on its long axis. A stone tool or sand embedded in mastic at one end of the spindle excavates a concavity in the rock surface. One can also do this by rotating the spindle back and forth between one's hands in much the same way as a fire drill (a primitive device for kindling fire).

Sawing through rock takes more time and energy than fracture, but one can control and apply it with greater precision than fracture. As abrasive incisions in stone grow deeper, they "seat" the stone-cutting tool, restricting its range of movements. Consequently, artificial incisions and perforations in stone are usually somewhat wider near the rock surface and grow narrower with depth. These smooth margins on incisions and perforations made using stone tools contrast starkly with the sharply delimited tool-marks that metal saws and drills leave on worked stone.

Few constraints govern morphological variation among abrasion-shaped artifacts. Abrasion due to nonhuman forces modifies angular stones into rounded forms that resist further abrasion. Collisions between wind-driven rock particles and stones partly exposed in sediments can create discrete patches of relatively flat abrasive wear, but mobile stones subjected to forceful abrasion with sediments, rocks, and flowing water are usually rounded to roughly the same degree all over their surfaces. Concavities manually excavated into stone artifacts require considerable work. Their surfaces usually feature extensive tool-markings and polishing. Concavities in naturally abraded stones mostly reflect differential weathering on convexities and concavities rather than abrasive wear focused on a small part of the rock surface.

Fracture

The majority of the rocks that most lend themselves to shaping by large-scale fracture are isotropic, brittle, and cryptocrystalline. That is, force passes through them equally in any direction *(isotropy)*. When they fail under loading, a discrete cleavage plane (fracture) forms. Their individual crystals are too small to see without artificial magnification *(cryptocrystalline* = "hidden crystals"). These three properties result in rocks having conchoidal (shell-shaped) fracture. When one strikes near a stone tool edge with a percussor and sufficient force, a fractures begins ("initiates") on the side of the struck edge. This is the fracture initiation surface, and fractures spread away from that surface (propagate) under the opposite side of the edge, the fracture propagation surface (Figure 3.1 a). Shaping stone using controlled conchoidal fracture can involve Hertzian cone fractures, bending fractures, and shear fractures.

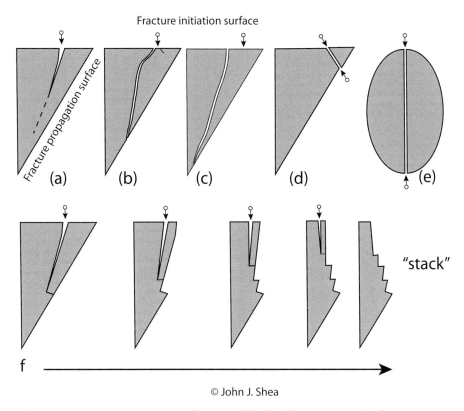

© John J. Shea

Figure 3.1 Cross–section view of stone tool edges illustrating major fracture types. (a) Fracture initiation and fracture propagation surfaces, (b) Hertzian cone fracture, (c) Bending fracture, (d) Shear fracture on edge, (e) Shear fracture on pebble, (f) Formation of a step–fracture "stack."

Hertzian *cone fractures* (or "cone fractures") form when compressive stress on a rock surface creates a ring-shaped crack that spreads into the rock as an expanding cone (Figure 3.1b). (The cone-shaped concavities that form when projectiles strike plate glass are cone fractures.) In stone tool production, toolmakers usually initiate cone fractures near the edge of a rock whose surfaces converge at angles of 90 degrees or less. Cone fractures initiated near such edges propagate deepest into the rock on the side of the cone most distant from the rock surface parallel the plane of fracture propagation.

Bending fractures start when compressive force loaded onto one part of a rock creates tensile stress (forces moving in diverging, opposite directions) sufficient to initiate a fracture some distance from the point where the load is applied (Figure 3.1c). (Shortening a stick or spaghetti strands by holding them at opposite ends an bending them until they break at their midpoint are familiar applications of bending fracture.) The rock surfaces bending fractures expose lack Hertzian cones at their fracture initiation point.

Shear fractures result when force aligns convergently and in parallel directions simultaneously. Splitting a nut or an ice cube by placing it on a hard surface and then striking it from above involve shear fractures. In rocks, shear fractures follow relatively flat trajectories. Prehistoric stoneworkers used shear fractures to blunt stone tool edges and to split open pebbles and cobbles (Figure 3.1d–e).

Radial lines and convex ripples (also called *undulations*) radiating away from the fracture initiation point on fracture scars provide clues about fracture propagation trajectories (see Figure 3.4). They also help to evaluate fracture scars on which subsequent flake detachments have removed traces of earlier ones. Fracture scars' overlapping patterns on artifact surfaces preserve a record of sequential flake removals in much the same way that animal tracks overlying one another record various creatures' serial passage over the same spot. Noting radial lines' and ripples' orientations on flake scars can reveal changes and continuities in stoneworking strategies between successive flake detachments.

Conchoidal fracture products vary widely, but they share characteristics that can help one distinguish them from naturally fractured rocks. Recent stone-workers often find it easier to initiate fractures and to predict their outcomes by striking a freshly fractured surface rather than a weathered surface. As a result, stoneworkers often strike core surfaces alternatingly, with each new fracture surface serving as the initiation point for the next fracture. Doing this creates an edge on which fracture initiation damage appears alternatingly on both sides. Natural fracture sources exhibit no such patterned preferences.

Experienced stoneworkers recognize deep, step- or hinge-terminated fractures on fracture propagation surfaces as obstacles to further fracture propagation. Once such a fracture termination is in place, subsequent fractures approaching them from the same direction experience a sharp increase in the distance between the fracture propagation front and the surface. This increase can stop the fracture from propagating and/or create a bending fracture between the step/hinge termination and the fracture initiation point. Such terminations create further obstacles to fractures propagating from the core's nearest edge (see Figure 3.1f). Some modern-day stoneworkers describe accumulations of successive step/hinge terminations as "stacks" (as in stack of books or plates), although one could make an equally compelling argument for calling them "stairs," for their step-wise progression.

Stoneworkers either detach such "stacks" or individual hinge/step fractures by undercutting them with fractures initiated from a different direction, or by detaching flakes from other core surfaces (see "core-repair flakes" in Chapter 7). A sufficiently large or inconveniently positioned stack can lead a stoneworker to discard a core. Natural fracture sources, in contrast, continue to detach fractures regardless of how previous fractures terminated. If the over-whelming majority of lithic objects in a large assemblage feature such repetitive step fracturing, one may be dealing with natural damage. One has to be careful, however, for children and novice stoneworkers can create such damage, too, simply because they either do not understand fracture mechanics or because they lack sufficient strength to initiate larger fractures.

Prolonged stoneworking results in fracture-damaged objects that are either extremely thin in one dimension or objects that approximate a disc, a cube, or an angular polyhedron. The fractures that natural forces initiate are less goal directed. Natural fracturing damage concentrates on weak points, such as projections and narrow edges, thereby creating more rounded, subangular, and spherical objects.

Aesthetic as well as mechanical considerations guide stoneworkers' choices of rocks. Natural fracturing indiscriminately affects local rocks in proportion to their susceptibility to fracture and regardless of their color or reflectivity. Fracturing damage concentrated on rocks sharing certain visual qualities, such as color or texture, but disproportionately scarce among rocks with different appearances but similar mechanical properties can be evidence of aesthetically guided stoneworking.

Special mention needs to be made about quartz. Simply put, when it comes to fracture, quartz does not always "play by the rules." Sometimes it fractures conchoidally, other times fractures follow crystallization planes. Its translucency makes visual examination of fracture surfaces difficult. Many modern craft/hobby stoneworkers disdain quartz, not a few archaeologists consider it a difficult material to analyze. Nevertheless, prehistoric humans used controlled fracture to shape quartz and employed the resulting artifacts as cutting tools pretty much wherever quartz was available. In practical terms, aspiring stone tool analysts should recognize that they may encounter difficulties recognizing and measuring the same surface features on quartz artifacts that they do on artifacts made from other rocks.

Thermal Alteration

Thermal alteration or "heat treatment" exposes quartz-rich sedimentary rocks to extreme heat (>500 degrees Fahrenheit) and cools them slowly. Doing this weakens the quartz crystals and makes the rock fracture more easily (i.e., at lower loading thresholds) (Crabtree and Butler 1964, Beauchamp and Purdy 1986). Recent stoneworkers heat treat tough rocks to improve their fracture qualities. However, because heat treatment also changes rock color and freshly fractured surfaces' reflectivity, one cannot entirely rule out aesthetic motivations for the practice. Natural fires and anthropogenic fires built on top of sediments containing stone tools can also alter lithic artifacts' appearance and fracture qualities. How sedimentary rocks respond to heating depends much on how fast they cool. Many natural fires burn hot and fast, cooling rapidly. Rapid cooling results in sharp temperature differentials in rock, differentials that cause fractures to form inside the rock or just below its surface. Distinctive products of such uncontrolled rapid cooling include shallowly concave hemispherical "pot-lid" fractures and flakes. Deliberate thermal alteration delays cooling by altering fuel sources and/or by insulating the heat-treated rocks in sandy sediments. The oldest-known evidence for deliberate and systematic thermal alteration of stone from the Pinnacle Point site complex in South Africa ca. 71 Ka shows precisely such sediment insulation (Brown et al. 2009).

Much like natural sources of abrasion and fracture, fire affects rocks indiscriminately. If stone tools were on the surface or shallowly buried when a fire swept across that part of the landscape, thermal damage ought to be widespread and appear on a plurality of artifacts. Evidence of artificial heat-treatment ought to be concentrated on sedimentary silicate rocks rather than igneous and metamorphic rocks that formed at far higher temperatures than pre-industrial fires can achieve. Many of the rocks Eastern African stoneworkers used are igneous rocks (obsidian, basalt) and quartz that are not amenable to thermal alteration. Obsidian exposed to heat often either melts or "devitrifies" – turning into white glass powder.

How does one tell whether a stone tool has been heat-treated? Visual inspection can provide some clues. Fracture surfaces are smoother than in nonheat-treated rocks and they have a more reflective luster. If the rock has significant amounts of iron in it, it is more red than unaltered rocks. These subjective guidelines are sufficient as sources of hypotheses, but conclusively identifying thermal alteration requires geophysical tests (Brown et al. 2009). One is more likely to find candidate artifacts for heat-treatment among sedimentary rocks, such as chert, jasper, and chalcedony.

Deciding: Artifact, or geofact, or both?

Most of the artifacts that Chapters 6–9 describe differ so much from naturally modified rocks as to leave no doubt about their artifactual status. Nevertheless, natural sources of abrasion and fracture can create *geofacts* – objects strikingly similar to some simpler artifact-types. For this reason, most archaeologists try to avoid making artifact/geofact determinations for single lithic objects. Instead, they prefer to assess samples of "candidate artifacts" recovered from the same deposit.

Affirmative artifact identifications gain strength if one can answer, "yes," to the following questions:

Did an experienced archaeologist identify the artifacts as artifacts? If so, this can count in their favor, but it remains an appeal to authority. Experienced archaeologists are no less immune to "confirmation bias" than younger ones. (Confirmation bias is the tendency to seek out, prefer, and recall information in ways that support one's preexisting hypotheses or other views.) Artifact versus. geofact identifications based on replicable measurements are superior to those based on appeals to authority.

Is one seeing all the stone objects from a given context, or is one looking at a selected sample? Natural forces can imitate the simpler sorts of lithic artifacts. Such pseudo-artifacts catch the eye and, all too often, enthusiastic people will gather them preferentially and present them as if they were representative samples. In the author's experience this is rarely deliberate deception but rather confirmation bias at work. The person has decided that they have found artifacts, and consciously or unconsciously, they seek out objects supporting that interpretation.

Do the objects come from low-energy sedimentary deposits, such as sand, silt, and clay, rather than gravel or rock scree (angular pieces of exfoliating rock)? While natural fractures occur commonly among gravel and rock scree, sand, silt, and clay usually accumulate with insufficient force to initiate large-scale fractures or to cause severe abrasion.

Do the objects vary in space and time at the same site? Geological processes routinely modify stone in similar ways across wide areas and over prolonged periods. Human stoneworking, in contrast, usually has a spatial focus and varies over time at particular localities.

Do at least some of the fractured objects found near one another also refit to one another? Geological forces sufficient to initiate large-scale fractures and extensive abrasion usually disperse pieces of the same fractured rocks widely across level surfaces. Human stoneworking, in contrast, can create immense piles of flakes and cores that resist dispersal by all but high-energy flowing water and erosion.

Do small flakes, flake fragments, and other debris accompany the candidate artifacts and refit to them? Small fracture products numerically dominate ethnographic and experimental stoneworking sites. Flowing water and other hydrodynamic geological forces powerful enough to fracture large stones move small fracture products away from one another and from the larger and heavier rocks from which they were detached.

Are the lithic objects stratigraphically associated with others that differ from naturally fractured and abraded stone? Natural sources of abrasion, fracture, and/or thermal alteration can create objects that superficially look like stone tools. Falling rocks, deteriorating and exfoliating boulders and bedrock exposures, wave action, and flowing water create geofacts that occur together in large numbers. Surfaces actively experiencing flash flooding and similar forceful geological processes do not attract prolonged human habitation. Large numbers of actual stone tools rarely appear among dense concentrations of geofacts, but excavated archaeological lithic assemblages may feature a few such objects. If abrasion, fractures, and/or thermal damage are not limited to a few "candidate artifacts" but are widespread among objects from the same sedimentary deposit, one may be examining selectively collected geofacts. *Pareidolia*, our distinctly human ability to identify patterns among randomly variable phenomena (e.g., animal figures in clouds) ensures anyone can find at least one lithic object that resembles an artifact among any sufficiently large group of naturally damaged rocks. Such candidate artifacts are often elongated, symmetrical, comprised of brightly colored and/or reflective rocks. Most of them are also usually large, but not so large as to be difficult to carry in one hand. These qualities contrast starkly with actual stone tools, most of which are short, asymmetrical, earth-tone-colored, and so small that one can carry dozens of them in one's hand.

Does other non-lithic evidence of human activity occur in the same deposit? Such evidence includes spatially discrete combustion features/hearths, architectural remains, percussion-damaged and cut-marked bone, ceramics, metal tools, or human fossils. Such finds establish human presence around the time of artifact deposition, strengthening hypotheses about an object's artifactual status.

Do the artifacts preserve use-related microwear traces? Archaeologists sometimes invoke lithic microwear evidence to bolster claims about morphologically ambiguous candidate artifacts. If the microwear evidence involves parametric measurements of wear traces that can be objectively compared with and contrasted to nonanthropogenic wear patterns, it can have probative value. Wear patterns assessed subjectively have less value (arguably, none whatsoever).

Can researchers other than those affiliated with the research team that found them examine the artifacts themselves? No one works long in Eastern African archaeology before encountering difficulties gaining permission to examine artifacts held in museum collections. Some of these difficulties are legitimate safeguards that ensure researchers who found the artifacts enjoy priority of access before publication. Others persist after publication, and stand in the way of independent verification, a crucial scientific principle. Some museums require those seeking access to accessioned collections\obtain the original excavators' written permission. In the author's experience, most excavators grant this permission. If there is a compelling reason to deny permission, an ethical archaeologist should state it explicitly in correspondence with all concerned. One should view with considerable skepticism any claim based on observations of artifacts unavailable for colleagues' firsthand scrutiny for any reason.

Are the artifacts presented as drawings or as photographs on which lines have been drawn to indicate fracture scars or other features? Drawings and lines superimposed on digitally modified images can help show otherwise unclear fracture propagation directions, but they can also conflate observations and inferences. In presenting lithic evidence to colleagues, one should strive to make one's observations in such a way that others can evaluate them separately from one's interpretations of them. (I name this Jelinek's Transparency Principle, after American archaeologist Arthur Jelinek [1928–present], whose work so exemplified it.) The simple solution to this problem is to publish, side-by-side, artifact images with and without such lines.

Do a plurality of the candidate artifacts appear clearly and convincingly artifactual? That is, do they look like the artifacts illustrated in Chapter 6–9? Admittedly, holistic visual assessments have inherent ambiguities. Nearly every archaeologist has been confronted with stone objects whose artifactual status they cannot establish beyond a reasonable doubt. One should describe such objects as "indeterminate." Large percentages of such indeterminate artifacts (>50%) in a given sample may be a sign one is dealing with rocks that geological forces have modified and/or stones gathered by collectors who lack formal training in recognizing lithic artifacts . Alternatively, one may be dealing with rocks that fracture irregularly or in ways that make reading them difficult.

Furthermore, it is well to remember that prehistoric stoneworkers did not make stone tools for modern-day archaeologists' benefit. If they behaved as many ethnographic stoneworkers do, the most important thing for them was obtaining a cutting edge. If they needed that cutting edge urgently, they may have selected rocks near-at-hand that they otherwise would not use. One imagines prehistoric humans knew their landscape well enough that mismatches between needs for cutting tools and rocks appropriate for the task would have been rare. Still, one should not dismiss candidate artifacts based solely on lithic raw material properties. One may have to develop, through experimentation, raw-material-specific criteria for recognizing human agency.

Chronological Outliers Special difficulties accompany efforts to evaluate lithic objects' artifactual status when they are candidates for the oldest stone tool evidence in a given region. Nearly every country in Eastern Africa and the wider world has one or more such putatively archaeological "chronological outlier." Extremely ancient stone tools attract vastly more scientific and popular interest than well-dated gravel. Consequently, scholarly disputes about such collections have high stakes (such as they are in academia). Proponents of these collections' antiquity and anthropogenic status may unconsciously relax artifact-recognition criteria. Or, they may "shop around" among lithic analysts for affirmative diagnoses. Critics and skeptics may unconsciously tighten artifact-recognition criteria, making them far more rigorous than they would apply to less controversial stone tool collections. Each may accuse the other of doing precisely these things. Both may insist on an "artifact/geofact" determination for an entire collection when that collection contains artifacts together with ecofacts and geofacts, as do nearly all lithic collections from all archaeological sites from all time periods. Disputes over chronological outlier collections count among the most vicious in archaeology, and they can run for decades. Students new to lithic analysis should avoid being drawn into such disputes at all costs. If one has to deal with chronological outlier collections, one should rate them probabilistically, as follows:

- Anthropological origin probable, natural origin improbable;
- Equivocal, impossible to decide human versus natural origin;
- Natural origin not refutable.

Doing this takes the absolutism out of artifactual/natural determinations. Journalists will not quote you if you do this, but neither will your colleagues cite you, decades later, when an overly hasty identification proves wrong. Table 3.1 reproduces some of the detailed criteria archaeologists use for making such determinations (Barnes 1939, Patterson 1983, Gillespie et al. 2004, Brown et al. 2009, Shea 2010). Most of these criteria require familiarity with terms introduced later in this book. One encourages readers to review

TABLE 3.1 *Criteria for recognizing the anthropogenic status of lithic artifact collections (adapted from Shea (2010).*

Category	Cores/retouched pieces	Flakes/detached pieces	Other considerations
Anthropological origin probable, natural origin improbable.	Large sample size (n > 30). Extensive and symmetrical scarring showing imposition of symmetry and asymmetry on different cardinal axes. Noncortical cores and retouched pieces predominate. A majority of cores feature more than one flake scar.	Large sample size (n > 100). Ventral radial lines common. Bulbar concavities visible on flake scars on >50% or more flakes. Surfaces mostly unweathered. Noncortical flakes predominate. More than one dorsal flake scar longer than 10 mm on most flakes. Majority of flakes have dorsal flake scars aligned parallel to one another.	Found together with vertebrate fossils preserving stone tool cut-marks identified by a professional archaeozoologist using microscopy. Flaked stone artifacts featuring thermal damage. Refitting sets of artifacts in close spatial proximity to one another in the same stratigraphic level. Low energy depositional context (clay, silt, or fine sand, rather than gravel). Majority of artifacts recovered from controlled archaeological excavation using hand tools.
Equivocal, impossible to decide human versus natural origin.	Small sample size (n = <5-10). Noncortical cores account for less than half of the sample. A minority of cores feature more than one flake scar.	Moderate sample size >10, <100. Even proportions of flakes with/without bulbar convexities. Heavily weathered artifacts about equal in number or more numerous than unweathered ones. Roughly equal proportions of cortical and noncortical flakes. Fewer than half feature more than one dorsal	Claimed stone tool cut-marks on vertebrate fossils. Majority of sample collected from surface or by other excavation methods (e.g., from backdirt left behind from mechanical excavation).

(continued)

TABLE 3.1 (*continued*)

Category	Cores/retouched pieces	Flakes/detached pieces	Other considerations
		flake scar longer than 10 mm. Fewer than 30% have dorsal flake scars aligned parallel to one another. Bulbar concavities present on 30–50% of dorsal flake scars.	
Natural origin not refutable.	A few candidate artifacts (n = 5 or fewer). Cortical core/ retouched pieces predominate. Relatively small flake scars on hypothetical cores/retouched pieces.	Small sample size (n = 10 or fewer artifacts). Ventral radial lines rare or absent. Bulbar convexities rare. Surfaces heavily weathered. Predominantly cortical flakes/flake fragments. More than one dorsal flake scar longer than 10 mm on fewer than 20% of the sample. Bulbar concavities visible on dorsal surfaces of fewer than 10% of the sample.	Candidate artifacts unavailable for direct examination (for *any* reason). Majority of sample collected from the surface. Stratigraphic provenience unclear or unverifiable (i.e., site has been destroyed).

Table 3.1 in detail after having finished this book and to consult it again, if and when the need arises.

WHAT KIND OF ARTIFACT IS IT?

Having decided that a stone artifact is to hand, one next needs to assign it to one of six major technologically defined lithic artifact categories – percussors, groundstone artifacts, cores, core-tools, flakes/flake fragments, and retouched pieces. Figure 3.2 shows this artifact-identification process as a flow chart. As the dashed lines at the end of the flowchart imply, actual stone tools may match criteria for more than one artifact category simultaneously.

Percussors and Groundstone Artifacts

If the artifact lacks fracture scars and fracture initiation points but preserves abrasive wear and/or percussion damage, then one is likely holding a percussor or a groundstone artifact.

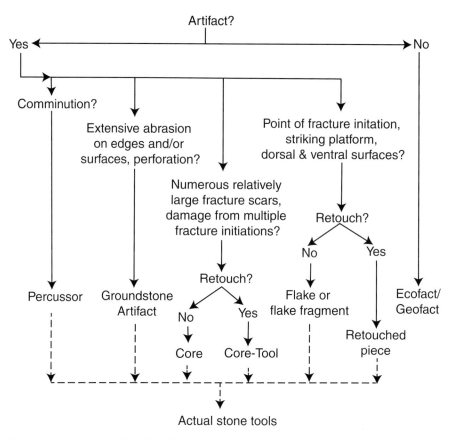

Figure 3.2 Lithic artifact identification flowchart.

Percussors feature comminution and other wear traces from repetitive force-ful percussion. This damage usually occurs in small patches and rarely covers a tool's entire surface. Most percussors are spherical, subspherical or tabular stones comprised of tough, nonbrittle rocks, but any lithic artifact can serve as a percussor. Archaeologists often call spherical and tabular percussors "ham-merstones." *Ad hoc percussors* are percussion-damaged cores, flakes, or other flaked-stone artifacts. Calling a tool an ad hoc percussor implies the implement was not a specialized tool but selected opportunistically, used briefly, then discarded. (Remember, this is an assumption, not a hypothesis easily tested.)

Groundstone artifacts suffer few constraints on their shape, and therefore one recognizes them from their abraded and polished surfaces. Macroscopic stri-ations, linear incisions and perforations may appear as well. Groundstone artifacts can include tools with abraded cutting edges, stone vessels, grinding stones and other pulverizing equipment, as well as grooved and/or perforated stones. Groundstone artifacts often preserve percussion damage, too. Some such damage may remain from manufacturing by "pecking and grinding"; other damage may result from reuse as a percussor. Many groundstone artifact fragments from Eastern African sites (as well as sites in many other parts of the world) appear to have been recycled in this way. Adams, (2014) book, *Ground Stone Analysis: An Anthropological Approach*, offers an excellent introduction to research on these artifacts. (Some archaeologists spell groundstone as two words, ground stone, others, as here, as one).

Cores and Core-Tools

If the artifact preserves numerous relatively large fracture scars and damage from multiple fracture initiations along one or more discrete edges, this is a *core* or a *core-tool*.

Cores feature at least one flake removal scar longer than 10 mm. Some of these fracture scars preserve the impressions of fracture initiations. When multiple such fracture initiations like this occur along one or both sides of an edge, archaeologists call that edge a *worked edge* (Figure 3.3). (Some sources use the term "working edge" for worked edge.) Core surfaces can intersect at variable angles along the same worked edge, but most do so at 90 degrees or less. Edges whose surfaces intersect at more than 90 degrees strongly resist fracture initiation. Cores can have more than one worked edge.

Conard and colleagues (2004) identify three main worked edge configurations, *inclined* – in which stoneworkers detach flakes alternatingly and more or less the same way from both sides of a worked edge (Figure 3.3a), *parallel* – in which stoneworkers consistently detach shorter flakes from one side of a worked edge than the other (Figure 3.3b), and *platform* – in which stoneworkers detach flakes from only one side of a worked edge (Figure 3.3c).

Fracture scars on core surfaces provide a cumulative record of detachments, but detachments that occurred just before toolmakers discarded the core are

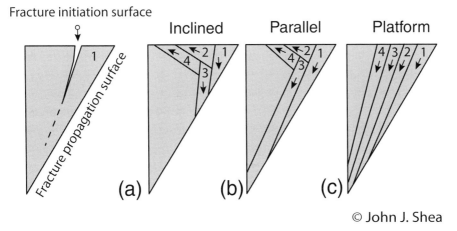

© John J. Shea

Figure 3.3 Worked edge terminology. (a) Inclined worked edge, (b) Parallel worked edge, (c) Platform worked edge.

more completely preserved than those detached earlier. Although it can be tempting to see core fracture scar patterning as representing that core's entire reduction sequence or operational chain (and many archaeologists do so), this is an assumption, not a hard and fast rule of stone tool use. Just as most sensible people conserve resources when they become scarce, prehistoric stoneworkers may have treated cores differently as they became smaller.

Cortex and patination also provide evidence about a core's geological origins. Cores preserving rounded and polished surfaces may have originated as *clasts* (pebbles, cobbles, and boulders rounded physical weathering) rather than tabular bedrock or nodules excavated from bedrock sources. Rocks procured from bedrock often retain features that impede fracture propagation, including hidden fractures and crystallization planes that abrasive processes and hydrodynamic forces have removed from clasts.

Most cores shown in archaeological illustrations are longer than 20–30 mm. Yet, excavations recover many cores shorter than this. Cores' upper size ranges remain imprecisely defined. One rarely sees cores much longer than 300 mm illustrated in archaeological reports. Nevertheless, some ethnographic tool-makers detached flakes from much larger pieces of stone, including bedrock (e.g., Gould et al. 1971, Toth et al. 1992).

If a core has a focused concentration of retouch along one or more edges (on one or both sides of the edge), archaeologists call it a *core-tool*. Most cores feature some incidental damage on their worked edges. Whether or not such damage is sufficiently patterned for archaeologists to recognize it as retouch is a subjective judgment. In general, archaeologists identify core-tools as such when the retouch is sufficiently invasive and extensive that it appears to have altered overall artifact shape, making the artifact elongated and/or symmetrical and/or making the edge straight when viewed edge on.

Flakes, Flake Fragments, and Retouched Pieces

If the artifact preserves a fracture initiation point, a striking platform, and recognizable dorsal and ventral surfaces, then one is holding a flake, flake fragment, or retouched piece.

Flakes and *flake fragments* are relatively flat pieces of stone that are more-or-less plano-convex or biconvex in cross-section (see Figure 3.4). Flakes preserve the entirety of the fracture that detached them from a core or retouched piece. Flake fragments preserve only a portion of this detaching fracture as well as relatively large scarring from subsequent shear and bending fractures. It can be difficult to distinguish between a step-terminated flake and a flake fragment that preserves the fracture initiation point. Most archaeologists do not make this distinction and treat both such artifacts as *proximal flake fragments*. Archaeologists describe complete flakes in terms of three named surfaces: the ventral surface, the dorsal surface, and the striking platform.

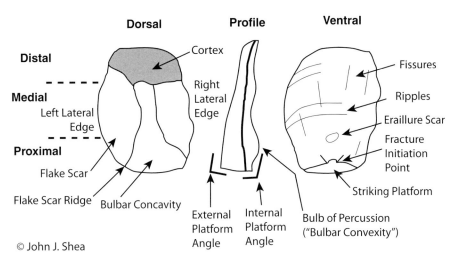

Figure 3.4 Flake features and orientation.

The *flake ventral surface* is the one that formed on one side of the fracture that detached the flake from another rock. Relatively smooth and lacking arrises or cortex, the ventral surface usually features a convexity, the "bulb of percussion," near the flake's fracture initiation point that becomes flatter or moderately curved further away from the fracture initiation point. The small concavity that appears on the bulb near its most prominent point is called an *eraillure scar*. Concentric half-circles (*ripples*) and linear fissures (*rays* and *fissures*) radiate away from the fracture initiation point.

The *flake dorsal surface* is a portion of a core's former exterior surface. Dorsal surfaces preserve variable combinations of fracture scars, arrises, and cortex. Part of the dorsal surface, the flake striking platform, is a detached part of a core's fracture initiation surface. The striking platform surface usually intersects the ventral surface at an angle greater than 90 degrees and intersects the rest of the dorsal surface at 90 degrees or less.

For consistency in orientation and measurement, archaeologists treat the striking platform as the *proximal* end of the flake. They call the edge opposite, where the detaching fracture terminated, the *distal* end.

Archaeologists differ in how they position distal versus proximal ends of flakes in artifact illustrations. This work puts the proximal end lowermost, in the "six o'clock" position. Others put the proximal end at the uppermost, in the "twelve o'clock" position. Debate about this issue seems to divide along age. Older researchers use the "six o'clock" position," younger ones "twelve o'clock" position.' As with so many intractable academic debates, this one will likely settle itself along Planckian lines. (After German physicist, Max Planck [1858–1947] who noted that many scientific debates only end after proponents of one or another argument die.)

How does one tell a whole flake from an unretouched flake fragment? Flake fragments vary widely, and Chapter 7 discusses them in detail. If dorsal and ventral surfaces are separated by a fracture scar aligned more or less perpendicularly to both of them, one is probably holding a flake fragment. Such fragments can be step-terminated fractures, lateral fragments of a flake split by simultaneous conchoidal and shear fractures, or pieces of a flake snapped by bending fractures. In any case, fracture scars in question are large. On distal/proximal flake fragments they are roughly equal to flake morphological width, and equal to flake length on lateral flake fragments.

Flakes and flake fragments range between microscopic pieces only a few millimeters long to specimens longer than 300 mm. Archaeological analyses of flakes/flake fragments focus mainly on artifacts longer than 20–30 mm. This arbitrary size cutoff enjoys support from studies showing that tools much smaller than this can only be grasped with great difficulty during cutting tasks (Key and Lycett 2014). On the other hand, the ethnographic and archaeological records abound with cutting tools this small or smaller. Using these size cutoffs for analysis may lead archaeologists to overlook episodes of systematic small stone tool production, or "lithic miniaturization" (Pargeter 2016, Pargeter and Shea 2019).

Retouched pieces are flake fragments whose edges feature retouch. How much retouch an artifact must exhibit in order for it to be recognized as a retouched piece varies among typologies and between individual archaeologists. All archaeologists interpret as retouch continuous fracture scars that are longer than 2–4 mm and continuously distributed along a tool edge for more than 10 mm. They interpret shorter and less extensive fracture scars less consistently. Archaeologists also differ in the extent to which they use artificial magnification, such as hand lenses and microscopes, to aid retouch identifications.

Major retouch categories include orthogonal retouch and burination (Figure 3.5). *Orthogonal retouch* initiates fracture scars that propagate across tool surfaces more or less perpendicular to an edge. *Burin retouch* (also called "burination") propagates a fracture parallel to an edge, undercutting it. Both retouch and burination can either restore functionality to a use-damaged edge, or impose a desired shape on an edge, or both.

Lithic typologies make many distinctions among orthogonal retouch. Most distinguish backing/truncation retouch versus scraper retouch. *Backing/truncation retouch* is usually minimally invasive (<5 mm), and it creates steep edge, one at or near 90 degrees in cross-section. *Scraper retouch* is usually no more invasive than 10 mm from an edge and it creates a relatively sharp edge, one less than 90 degrees in cross section. *Invasive retouch* is deeply invasive, often extending more than halfway across a tool surface. Its effects on edge shape vary. That is, it can create an edge that is either convex or concave in cross-section.

Archaeologists also usually distinguish whether the retouch occurs on only one side of an edge (*unifacial retouch*) or on both sides of an edge (*bifacial retouch*). Some artifacts feature points or other projections on which three or even four

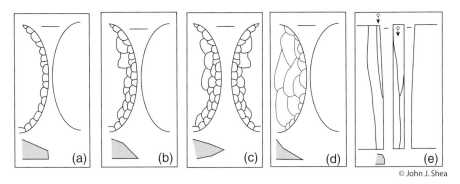

Figure 3.5 Retouch variation. Dorsal (left), ventral (right), and section (below, shaded) views of edges modified by (a) Backing/truncation, (b) Scraper retouch, (c) Bifacial retouch, (d) Invasive retouch, (e) Burin retouch (edge-on profile view also shown).

retouched edges intersect with one another. The terms trifacial retouch and quadrifacial retouch, respectively, are used for these phenomena.

Most orthogonal retouch appears on flake dorsal surfaces. This may be because detaching flakes from a flake's dorsal surface (i.e., by initiating fractures on its ventral surface) creates edges that are relatively straight and thus mechanically efficient in cutting tasks. Many typologies note when retouch appears on a flake ventral surface (ventral or inverse retouch), although this practice varies. Some typologies note whether backing/truncation retouch is unidirectional, bidirectional-opposed (fractures propagating towards one another from different directions), or divergent (fractures propagating away from one another); though again, this practice varies.

Archaeologists consider burin scars whose flake scars align more or less perpendicularly to the tool's ventral surface "normal" burins, for these are usually the most common. Burin flake scars aligned at low angles to the ventral surface and/or ones that propagate deeply onto either flake dorsal or ventral surfaces archaeologists describe using a variety of (mostly French) terms, including *burin à face plan, chanfrein, tranchet* flake. Some Anglophone works use the term, "chamfered piece," for these artifacts. Most typologies also distinguish among single- versus multiple-burin removals.

Retouched piece typologies also subdivide retouch modalities and retouched artifacts in terms of retouched edge shape (in plan view) and the artifact's overall shape. How many such retouch categories a typology recognizes and in what combinations reflects a mixture of personal preferences and differences among research traditions. In general, archaeologists trained in Continental European research traditions recognize more and more complex retouched piece typologies, while Anglo-American researchers recognize fewer. Novice lithic analysts often identify as retouch damage their senior colleagues view as either natural or ambiguous (Bisson 2001). One suspects this reflects their anxiety about overlooking actual retouched tools, but no direct evidence supports this hypothesis.

When stoneworkers resharpen use-damaged and/or retouched edges by undercutting them with a burin removal, they create flakes with retouch and/or use-damage on the flake's dorsal ridges. Some of the stone tools Louis Leakey (1931) identified as "fabricators" appear to be such artifacts. Archaeologists no longer consider such artifacts retouched pieces.

Older typologies identify stone tools featuring small-scale and discontinuous microfracturing damage on their edges as "utilized pieces" (or using other terms implying use, including, oddly, "nibbled pieces"). While stone tool use can cause such damage, trampling and geological forces can do so, too. Whatever one calls such artifacts, the current archaeological consensus does not treat them as retouched pieces.

Archaeological Reality

Few lithic artifact typologies survive intact their first collision with archaeological reality. Actual stone tools always crosscut archaeologists' neat and tidy artifact typologies. (I here name this Dibble's Rule, after the late Harold L. Dibble [1951–2018], who documented it so convincingly.) Many retouched pieces retain striking platforms and ventral surfaces indicating their origins as flakes or flake fragments. Stoneworkers sometimes used groundstone artifact fragments for percussors; percussors and flakes as cores, core-tools, and flakes and retouched pieces as cores and/or percussors. No typology can cover all these possible sequential transformations as well as the theoretically infinite range of morphological variation among their products. Any typology one would actually want to use for describing archaeological lithic artifacts has to balance completeness with ease of use. For ease of use, such typologies need to be holistic. That is, they need terms for whole artifacts. For completeness, they need to augment holistic identifications with measurements of specific variables that either actualistic or contextual observations justify. Such justifications are more convincing when proposed together with the typology rather than after the archaeologists have been using the typology for a long time. "Sunk costs" can make archaeologists retain familiar, if flawed, typologies rather than undertake the effort to devise new ones, even if those new typologies have stronger theoretical justifications (Bisson 2000).

UWAZI VALLEY TALES, EPISODE 3: OLD HABITS DIE HARD

Joseph had already eaten, so we three *wazungu* ate briskly, gathered our daypacks, and set off downhill into the Uwazi Valley on the narrow footpath to Pango Wa Kwale. Joseph carried the Old Africa Hand's pack as well as his own and a wooden bow and quiver of arrows.

The forest enclosed us instantly. The trees mixed flat-topped acacias and cactus-like euphorbia trees. Birds called out, scattering as we passed them. A black and white colobus monkey foraged in the treetops. As we walked, the

Box 3 *Comparing stone tool assemblages*

When archaeologists compare lithic assemblages, they usually do so in terms of artifact-type presence/absence or relative frequencies. They may compare artifact metric variation as well as occurrences of different attribute-states (values for discrete variables). The conventions for these comparisons vary between time periods and among different research traditions. Some researchers use cumulative percentage graphs whose x-axis lists artifact types in a prescribed sequence. Others list relative frequencies of major artifact-type groupings, such as scrapers, backed/truncated pieces, points, core-tools, etc.

Researchers who use cumulative percentage graphs, as well as those who do not, often report technological and typological (i.e., morphology-based) ratios or "indexes." For technological indexes, these are usually the percentage of artifacts with a given production-related property, such as dorsal cortex or various kinds of striking platform configurations. Their denominator usually includes all complete flakes, but they may include proximal flake fragments if the ratio in question relates to the striking platform. Typological indexes' numerators count the numbers of artifacts assigned to one or another major morphologically defined artifact category (e.g., scrapers, microliths, handaxes) Their denominators vary among researchers and research traditions. Separate indexes for cores, core-tools, and retouched pieces usually count all such artifacts. Few indexes combine artifacts from these different categories.

Researchers sometimes compare cardinal dimensions (length, width, thickness, or ratios of cardinal dimensions) for specific artifact-types whose variation they think particularly sensitive. Which artifact types they compare can differ between age-stages and among research traditions. To minimize difficulties later on, novice lithic analysts undertaking their own analysis of a stone tool assemblage should review those variables other researchers working in a given region and time period use to compare assemblages and then incorporate those variables into their own analytical protocols.

That we do not know to what degree archaeologists' morphological, metric, and technological observations are replicable remains a potentially significant, yet frequently ignored, problem with inter-assemblage comparisons using artifact typologies (Will et al. 2019). To what degree do individual archaeologists classify artifacts consistently throughout their careers? Is there significant age- and experience-related variation? One can marshal principled arguments in support of contradictory answers to both these questions. One assumes that we and our colleagues make these observations consistently, but little hard evidence supports this conclusion.

Box 3 (*Cont.*)

Nearly all artifact-type identifications involve subjective, visually–assessed morphological analogy. ("This artifact looks like one in that book, or like others I have seen before.") Just because two or more archaeologists use the same term for a stone tool does not mean that they use identical criteria for identifying such artifacts or that they do so consistently. Archaeologists rarely re-examine assemblages that they or their colleagues have published, or, having done so, find it possible to publish findings of "no difference."

Do expectations about an assemblage's age, the processes by which it accumulated, or its cultural affinities influence typological assessments? Absolutely! Archaeologists enjoy no special immunity to confirmation bias. Colleagues in archaeology's sister discipline, forensic science, share similar concerns about how memory and observer biases affect the reliability of visually assessed evidence (Loftus 1996, Kukucka et al. 2017). It would be difficult for archaeologists to adopt double-blind analysis – protocols in which analysts have minimal knowledge about sample provenience and no stake in the outcomes of their analysis – an approach increasing numbers of forensic scientists advocate. Unless archaeologists are willing to adopt wholly parametric (measurement-based) analytical methods, one has to retain inter-analyst variation as a possible explanation for differences among lithic assemblages.

Nor are measurement-based comparisons among stone tools entirely problem free. Many comparisons of artifacts and lithic assemblages focus on cardinal measurements, such as length, width, and thickness, or the angles of retouched edges. But there are different ways to measure each of these variables (Dibble and Bernard 1980, Andrefsky 2005). All too often, descriptions of lithic assemblages do not explicitly define which variant of these cardinal measurements they use. Ironically, Eastern African archaeologists (along with their colleagues elsewhere) make relatively little use of mass, the one variable with the least potential for inter-observer error. Always measure mass!

Polymath offered the Old Africa Hand a short history of the Uwazi Valley Preserve. A European settler family had bought this part of the valley and had fenced off portions of it as a cattle ranch and private game preserve. To help maintain the estate, the owners had invited several local families to live in a small village to which they brought a missionary, a teacher, and a dispensary. The buildings back at camp were remains of this village. By all accounts decent people, the owners had drilled a well near the village so that women and children did not have to fetch water from the distant spring. About a decade ago the settlers' grandchildren, who lived abroad, sold the property to the

National Government, which made it a nature preserve, albeit one in which they permitted scientific research. The terms of the sale provided funds for indigenous staff to move into a nearby town, one with a hospital, public schools, paved roads, and more employment opportunities.

A few minutes into our walk, Joseph exclaimed, "Leopard!" I looked back and forth into the bushes. The Polymath searched the tree branches overhead. The Old Africa Hand stood silently.

"No," Joseph said, pointing to the trail in front of us, "there." Big cat paw prints overlay the footprints Aya and the other excavators had left earlier that morning.

"Dragging something, maybe food for babies."

"Let's go," the Polymath said to Joseph. "Maybe we can get a nice photo of them." Off they went into the brush.

"That didn't take long," I sighed, looking to the Old Africa Hand.

"No worries, Robin, the trail is a green highway. They will be back with us as soon as my colleague loses patience following the leopard."

"The Polymath's a great teacher, and he knows a lot, but he doesn't seem much interested in archaeology."

The Old Africa Hand resumed walking. "I never had a student with such aptitude about stone tools or one who learned so quickly. His dissertation and his reports on the excavations up north are landmarks of clarity. You should read them. (I had.) Losing his daughter, Susan, to that car accident disarranged him. I think he's gotten bored with archaeology. He wants to hunt bigger game now."

"Such as?"

"Big questions. Anthropology really only has two big questions. How are we different from the other animals, and why do we differ from each other? That's it. If you can't connect what you are doing to one or both of those questions, you're off-trail, so to speak."

"Professor Scott complained about "Trivial Pursuits Anthropology."

"Scott could be harsh, sometimes. When there were few anthropologists, we could be generalists. As a younger man, I read and wrote about all kinds of things: ethnography, experimental archaeology, geology, stone tools, ceramics, and whatnot. Nowadays, though, there are so many anthropologists that everyone has to specialize.

"Do you think it will ever turn around, back to anthropologists being generalists.?"

"It has to. If the trend persists, each of us will be writing for an audience of one – ourselves."

"Might as well blog."

"That's different. Bloggers write for an audience, and some of them are quite good. They can tell how many people read what they have written and read their comments. The problem comes back to ecology. Academia's an ecosystem, but it's becoming an ecosystem of specialists, and ecosystems top-heavy with specialists are vulnerable to catastrophic failure."

"How so?"

"Our studies could become so esoteric and hyper-specialized that the public at large, the people whose taxes and charitable donations fund our research, could decide they were no longer interested in funding us. The whole enterprise of higher education could become just a bunch of trade schools and for-profit research and development centers. It will be hard for anybody to 'speak truth to power' if nobody knows what truth or power are, or how to make convincing arguments about them."

"To stabilize the academic ecosystem," the Old Africa Hand continued," we need some generalists, people who can connect the dots between digging holes in Africa and answering anthropology's big questions.

"Do you think that's what's up with the Polymath? That he's trying to become a generalist?"

"It's a wise move. Academics compete with one another, and in the long run generalists always beat specialists. The trouble is, he's off hunting elephants without an elephant gun."

"Joseph has a bow and arrows."

"Indeed, old habits die hard. So, Robin, you're Scott's "orphan," the grad student we admitted before he died. Scott was a good man, but those 'were-lithics' from his cave in New Mexico were something else."

"Were-lithics?"

"Some naturally fractured stones he claimed were 40,000-year-old artifacts. We called them 'were-lithics' because they only looked like artifacts when viewed by the light of the full moon and after the consumption of much tequila."

Scott had planned for me to write my dissertation on those "were-lithics."

Changing the subject, I asked, "What's the book you are reading after dinner?"

"That's my 'field book'. It's a longish novel by one of my former students. He says I inspired one of the characters, but I can't figure out which one, at least not yet."

"Field book?"

"Back in the old days, one had to choose a "field book" or two that one brought along to read in measured amounts over the course of a field season. Making your field books last the full season was a good lesson in self-discipline. One had to choose carefully."

"You're welcome to borrow my e-reader. It has more than one hundred books on it."

"Thank you, Robin. Enjoy your books. Just remember, not everything in books is true and not all truth is to be found in books."

CHAPTER 4

EASTERN AFRICA

This chapter describes Eastern Africa's geology and geography. It reviews the history of prehistoric archaeological research, and its chronostratigraphy – the major age-stages archaeologists recognize and what they think happened during each of them.

GEOLOGY AND GEOGRAPHY

Figure 4.1 shows Eastern Africa's major rifts, rivers, and lakes. The central part of the region is much higher than adjacent parts of Africa and drained to the north by the Nile River, to the west by the headwaters of the Congo River, and to the south by the Zambezi River. The Eastern African Rift Valley preserves numerous freshwater lakes, the largest and deepest of which include Lake Turkana, Lake Victoria, Lake Tanganyika, and Lake Malawi.

Eastern Africa lies at the conjunction of the Arabian, Nubian, and Somalian tectonic plates (Schlüter 1997). The fault lines between these plates radiate away from an upwelling of magma below the Afar triangle in Ethiopia. This "hot spot" drives a longer-running process of volcanic uplift that formed the Ethiopian highlands and the Kenya plateau around 20 Ma. Tectonic movements among these plates created Eastern Africa's two most distinctive geological features: its volcanic landscapes and its rift valleys.

Eastern Africa's landscape preserves evidence for recent volcanism more than any other African region of equivalent size. These relatively young volcanic rocks cover older quartz-rich Precambrian "basement rock" deposits. The Eastern African Rift Valley dominates the region in ways that influence habitats past and present and the course of human evolution and prehistory. Today the Rift Valley runs 4,500 km from southwest Asia to southeastern Africa. At the Equator, in Kenya and Uganda, the Rift Valley splits Eastern Africa longitudinally into two mountain ranges bracketing the Lake Victoria Basin. From Kenya, the Rift Valley runs north along the eastern side of Ethiopian highlands until it reaches eastern Ethiopia. There, it diverges sharply

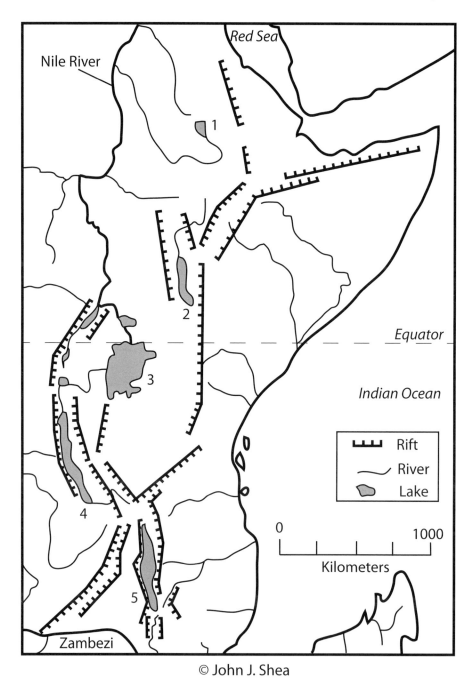

© John J. Shea

Figure 4.1 Eastern African physical geography. Lakes: (1) Lake Tana, (2) Lake Turkana (Lake Rudolf in older literature), (3) Lake Victoria, (4) Lake Tanganyika, (5) Lake Malawi.

northwest into the Red Sea Basin before emerging onto land in the Middle East's Jordan Valley. Southward from the Equator, Eastern and Western Rift valleys converge, continuing south into Mozambique.

Since more than 20 Ma, Eastern Africa's volcanism and rift valleys have created unique and evolutionarily significant topographic and hydrological conditions (Trauth et al. 2007, Maslin 2017). Volcanism has raised the Ethiopian Plateau and Rift Valley margins high above those parts of western and central Africa on the same latitude. When cyclonic storms track eastward across equatorial Africa, they shed much of their moisture on the Ethiopian Plateau and onto the Rift Valley's westward-facing slopes. Monsoons moving northward along the Indian Ocean coastline irrigate the eastward-facing hills flanking the Rift Valley. Due to rain shadow effects (decreased rainfall downwind of mountain ranges), the Rift Valley itself remains relatively dry, although dotted with lakes and crisscrossed by rivers. High topographic relief brings forest, woodland, and grassland communities closer together than they would occur on less topographically complex landscapes. Consequently, Eastern Africa preserves many *ecotones* – places where several distinct biotic communities conjoin to one another. Living in or near ecotones allows humans and other generalist feeders to exploit more than one distinct food source simultaneously.

Eastern Africa's topographic and hydrological features have important evolutionary implications. The region's major lakes' cyclical expansions and contractions have connected, divided, and reconnected animal populations, leading to high rates of speciation and to numerous instances where populations of "parent" and "daughter" species live in the same places (Trauth et al. 2010).

Elsewhere in northern and equatorial Africa, orbitally forced changes in temperature and rainfall patterns caused wide north–south latitudinal movements of vegetation zones and the fauna on which they depended for subsistence. High topographic relief in Eastern Africa insulated plant and animal life from abrupt climate change; not completely, of course, for droughts still afflict the region today but to a greater degree than in Africa's antipodes (Cowling et al. 2008). Eastern African vegetation zones shifted altitudinally, up- and downslope, allowing humans and animals to cope by moving along local elevation gradients (Ambrose and Sikes 1991). Eastern Africa's topography and hydrology likely sheltered hominins living there from the prolonged and severe megadroughts that afflicted hominins elsewhere. Rather than following shifting shorelines of west African Lake Mega-chad, or Lake Sudd, or chasing dying Saharan rivers when arid conditions struck, ancestral Eastern Africans could have shifted their settlement patterns among a chain of smaller Rift Valley lakes and the rivers draining the Ethiopia and Kenya–Uganda highlands (Ambrose 2001).

Eastern Africa's complex topographic variability and ecological heterogeneity support a wide range of human adaptations. No other part of the world preserves hunter-gatherers, fishers, nomadic pastoralists, seminomadic agropastoralists, sedentary farmers, coastal fishing villagers, and city dwellers, all of whom today live within a day or two's drive of one another.

Eastern Africa's high topographic relief and seasonal rainfall regimes create almost ideal conditions for fossilization. Seasonal rains charge lake margins with mineral-rich water, accelerating fossilization. Wide Rift Valley lakes preserve low-energy depositional environments in which fossils can become enclosed in clays and silts, improving their odds of fossilizing. Mineral extraction and large-scale earthmoving activities have accelerated in recent years, but nowhere near the scale they have near so many European and Asian fossiliferous deposits.

Eastern Africa is also uniquely "networked." By virtue of its north–south running coastline, Rift Valley lakes, and rivers that drain the region to all cardinal directions, Eastern Africa has been a corridor for movements of plants, animals, people, and culture between Saharan Africa, the Arabian Peninsula, and Sub-Saharan Africa. Proximity to the headwaters of the Congo and Nile rivers further enhances connections with western and central Africa. Eastern Africa's connectedness enhances its value for paleoanthropology and prehistory. Few major mammalian dispersals within Africa or between Africa and Eurasia failed to leave a trace in the region's fossil record (Werdelin and Sanders 2010). To the extent we can tell from the archaeological record (Barham and Mitchell 2008), no major prehistoric technological innovation bypassed Eastern Africa as it spread between Sub-Saharan Africa and Eurasia, and vice versa. All of southwestern Asia's three Abrahamic faiths, Judaism, Christianity, and Islam, found early converts among Eastern Africans (McKenna 2011). And as if this were not enough, Eastern Africa remains a leading contender for the origin of Earth's most broadly distributed primate, *Homo sapiens*.

PREHISTORIC RESEARCH: A BRIEF HISTORY

This section briefly reviews the history of Eastern Africa prehistoric research, focusing specifically on archaeologists who have dealt with the stone tool evidence. Gowlett (1990), Robertshaw (1990a), and Brandt and Fattovich (1990) offer more comprehensive histories of Eastern African archaeology. One can organize the history of Eastern African prehistoric research into three phases: an Exploratory Period (prior to the 1940s), a Culture-Historical Period (1940s–1970s), and a Processualizing Period (1970s onward).

The Exploratory Period

The Exploratory Period encompasses the late nineteenth and early twentieth century up to the end of World War II (1939–1945). While exploring the Rift Valley in the 1890s, J. W. Gregory (1921) observed lithic artifacts eroding from stratified deposits and collected samples. Between 1919 and 1939, E. J. Wayland (1924), chief geologist of Uganda Protectorate, also noted and reported stone artifacts. During the 1920s–1930s, excavations recovered stone tools in stratified deposits throughout Eastern Africa. Four major synthetic works dominate the literature of the Exploratory Period: Louis Leakey's (1931) *The Stone Age Cultures of Kenya Colony*, T. P. O'Brien's (1939) *The Prehistory of the Uganda Protectorate*, Paolo Graziosi's (1940) *L'Eta della Pietra in Somalia* [The Stone Age in Somalia], and J. Desmond Clark's (1954), *The Prehistoric Cultures of the Horn of Africa* (based on fieldwork carried out in 1942–3). Each of these books gathered together observations from their authors' excavations and surface collections, and they each proposed regional sequences of archaeological cultures and industries. The first continental synthesis of African prehistory, Louis Leakey's (1936) *Stone Age Africa*, appeared during this period.

The Exploratory Period witnessed many different approaches to the archaeological record. Individuals trained in geology and paleontology carried out much of the initial archaeological research. Field methods emphasized trenching and stratigraphic correlations. Early archaeologists used lithic artifact-types as markers of particular periods and industries in much the same way as paleontologists "index fossils," fossils diagnostic of one or another geological epoch.

Much early writing about East African prehistory and geochronology during the 1930s–1950s invoked Wayland's (1929) pluvial framework. Wayland argued that glacial periods in northern latitudes coincided with "pluvials," or periods of increased rainfall and higher lake levels in equatorial Africa. Due in significant measure to Louis Leakey's (1931) energetic promotion of his own interpretation of it, this pluvial framework dominated much prehistoric research, until radiometric dating and more sophisticated methods of paleoclimatic reconstruction overturned it during the late 1950s–1960s (Kingston and Hill 2005).

Exploratory Period archaeologists interpreted the stone tool evidence using models and metaphors from organic evolution. That is, they interpreted lithic artifact-types and stone tool industries as if they were organic life forms whose qualities reflected past interactions and evolutionary relationships among the hominins who made them. Archaeologists often attributed named stone tool industries to one or another specific ancient human population, or, using the terms of the day, "race." Most frameworks for prehistory assumed artifact-types and industrial sequences changed in parallel across wide regions. O'Brien (1939), however, sounded an early cautionary note about this, citing contrasts in habitats and lithic materials as possible causes for differences between Uganda's and Kenya's archaeological records.

Few archaeologists working in the Exploratory Period considered Eastern African evidence central to human evolution. Louis Leakey came to be a notable early exception in this respect, of course, but most early twentieth-century paleoanthropologists sought evidence for human origins in Europe or

Asia (Bowler 1986). Archaeologists generally did not link Eastern Africa's recent prehistoric cultures to living groups of Eastern Africans (Robertshaw 1990a). Instead, many attributed change and variability in the stone tool evidence to prehistoric migrations from other regions, such as the Nile Valley or Southwest Asia. Many archaeologists thought Eastern Africans' ancestors recent immigrants to the region whose arrival preceded European colonists by a matter of centuries (Sutton 2006).

The Culture-Historical Period

The First Pan-African Congress of Prehistory and Quaternary Studies in Nairobi in 1947 marks the start of the Culture-Historical Period. This meeting brought together researchers from across the continent (Leakey and Cole 1952). The 1947 event and subsequent Pan-African congresses encouraged efforts to correlate both geological and cultural stratigraphy across wider regions. This period witnessed publications of regional syntheses of the evidence for north Africa (McBurney 1960), South Africa (Clark 1959, Mason 1962), and Eastern Africa (Cole 1954). Examples of major published works in the Culture-Historical Period include Mary Leakey's monographs on Olduvai Gorge in Tanzania (Leakey 1971, Leakey and Roe 1994) and Hyrax Hill in Kenya (Leakey et al. 1943), and the first of J. Desmond Clark's (1969b, 1974) reports on Kalambo Falls, Zambia.

Postwar prehistoric research in Eastern Africa devoted more effort to identifying regional variation within age-stages and to reconstructing prehistoric activities. This culture-historical approach to archaeology found expression in growing numbers of stone tool industries whose names often hinted at connections to other regions, such as Europe or southern Africa. An increasingly rich ethnographic record inspired more detailed behavior reconstructions. These in turn spurred more horizontally extensive excavation strategies aimed at discovering intrasite spatial patterning. Archaeologists began interpreting their sites in explicitly ethnographic terms as campsites, kill/butchery sites, and quarries/workshops. They also began treating faunal remains accompanying stone tools as evidence for subsistence practices, rather than merely as aids to chronology and climate reconstruction.

Reflecting increased numbers of archaeologists with formal training in anthropology, Culture-Historical Period archaeologists interpreted the stone tool evidence using models and metaphors from history and ethnography. Lithic "index fossils" were still important, but paralleling developments in Europe and elsewhere (Bordes 1961), archaeologists also began defining and comparing artifact types in terms of measurements and comparing industries in terms of artifact-type relative frequencies. Individual archaeologists developed formal artifact typologies and published inventories of their finds from excavations and surveys. Artifact illustrations and measurements became more formalized, using consistent terms and artifact illustration conventions. Mary Leakey's (1971) stone tool typologies for Olduvai Gorge, Tanzania; Maxine Kleindienst's (1962) Eastern Africa Acheulian artifact typology; and J. Desmond Clark's (1974, 2001) typology for Kalambo Falls, Zambia are especially noteworthy in this respect, because they provided detailed descriptions and illustrations of individual lithic artifact-types.

Just as the 1947 Pan-African Conference benchmarks the Cultural-Historical Period's start, the 1965 Wenner-Gren Foundation Conference, "Systematic Investigation of the African Later Tertiary and Quaternary" at Burg Wartenstein, Austria (Bishop and Clark 1967) marks its end. Improvement in radiometric dating during the 1950s–1960s had nearly doubled the length of the Pleistocene Epoch from 1 Ma to 1.8 Ma. New fossil discoveries, especially those at Olduvai Gorge (Tanzania) nudged Eastern Africa's early Pleistocene evidence to the forefront of major debates about human origins and evolution. Radiocarbon dating also started to relieve archaeologists of previous concerns about relative chronologies for recent periods.

To their credit, the Burg Wartenstein Conference participants tried to bring some order to the lithics systematics anarchy that had developed over the previous two decades (Kleindienst 1967). Archaeologists generally accepted proposals to "sink" some stone tool industries (particularly those named after European industries), but they largely ignored proposals to cease using universal age-stages (e.g., Earlier, Middle, and Later Stone Ages), to standardize artifact typologies, and to follow consistent procedures for naming new industries (Clark et al. 1966, Kleindienst 1967). Even though the number of archaeologists and archaeological research projects in Eastern Africa grew steadily after the 1960s, it became ever more difficult to compare different researchers' published accounts of lithic evidence. Sonia Cole (1954) wrote the last major monographic synthesis of its prehistory, *The Prehistory of Eastern Africa*, before the Burg Wartenstein Conference.

During the 1960s, research on human origins increasingly attracted international attention from Americans, Canadians, and others from countries with no prior colonial possessions in Eastern Africa. Indigenous African scholarly participation increased as well. The British Institute in Eastern Africa, established in 1960, energized research on later phases of Eastern African prehistory.

The Processualizing Period

Processual archaeology, which began in the United States and the United Kingdom during the 1960s, adopted more explicitly scientific methods in research focused on testing hypotheses about human behavioral variability (Trigger 2006). Processual archaeology differed from culture-historical archaeology in viewing culture as a dynamic, changing adaptive system rather than as a fixed set of attributes that defined people living at specific times and in specific places. Processual archaeology began to influence archaeological research in Eastern Africa somewhat later, after the 1970s. Processual archaeology had deep roots in those American and UK institutions, such as the University of California at Berkeley, the University of Oxford, and the University of Cambridge, that conferred many doctoral degrees on Eastern Africanist archaeologists during the 1960s. Eastern African researchers already practiced the ethnographically informed behavior reconstruction and closer integration with mainstream anthropology and natural sciences (geology, zoology) that were among processual archaeology's goals.

Possibly because so many Anglo-American archaeologists work in Kenya, that country offers many examples of research in the processual tradition. Glynn Isaac's (1977) investigations at the Early Pleistocene site of Olorgesailie exposed large areas that allowed him to use geological measurements to test the longstanding hypothesis that these sites preserved "living floors" unaltered by hydrodynamic forces. Subsequently, Isaac brought similar techniques to bear on research in East Turkana, assembling an interdisciplinary team whose work integrated geological, lithic, and zooarchaeological evidence to reconstruct early Pleistocene hominin activities (Isaac and Isaac 1997). Elsewhere in Kenya, other notable field projects employing processual perspectives included Robbins' excavations at the early Holocene Lothagam site (1974), McBrearty and colleagues' (2005) investigations of Middle Pleistocene lithic assemblages from West Baringo, and Barut Kusimba's (2001) work at Lukenya Hill. Processual archaeology so thoroughly infused Eastern African prehistoric research from the 1970s onward that one struggles to find publications dating from that decade or more recently that did not adopt this approach to archaeology, often in addition to more explicitly culture-historical objectives.

Processual archaeologists interpreted lithic and other evidence using models and metaphors from systems theory and behavioral ecology. They continued to cite migration and diffusion as sources of archaeological variability but less so than formerly, and they also invoked environmental and demographic pressures as sources of change and variability. Many were skeptical about culture-historical archaeology's equating differences among stone tool industries with differences in prehistoric social cultural identities (especially in earlier Pleistocene time ranges). Instead, they attributed such differences to variation in adaptive strategies. Arguing that no single site likely captures the totality of human adaptation at any given moment, processual archaeologists emphasized reconstructing settlement patterns from surveys. During the 1970s, many survey projects were undertaken in Eastern Africa. These surveys usually described stone tools in internally consistent ways, but stone tool systematics often differed widely among research projects (Mehlman 1989).

Processual archaeology's emergence coincided with advances in geochronology that supplanted stone tools as the main basis for chronostratigraphy. Many Processual archaeologists, especially those who entered the profession after radiometric dating became routine, regarded questions about culture history and stone tool systematics as of secondary interest. Processual archaeologists did not neglect lithic artifacts entirely. Obsidian source tracing enabled those working in recent time periods to reconstruct exchange networks (Merrick and Brown 1984, Dillian 2016). Geoarchaeological perspectives on site formation processes became more common (Schick 1986). Perspectives on making and using stone tools derived from experiments and ethnoarchaeology became more systematic (Schick and Toth 1993, Brandt and Weedman 1997). Lithic microwear, residue analysis, and artifact-refitting studies appeared with increasing regularity (Keeley and Toth 1981). Analyses of lithic assemblages increasingly incorporated the operational chain perspectives used in European, Western Asian, and South African archaeology (e.g., Pleurdeau 2005, de la Torre and Mora 2005, Tryon et al. 2005, Harmand 2007).

Prehistoric research during the Processualizing Period diversified widely, but four research topics rose to prominence. These included the nature of early hominin subsistence – the "hunting versus scavenging debate" (Binford 1981, Bunn 1981, Isaac 1983, Shipman 1983, Blumenschine 1986, Domínguez-Rodrigo 2002), the evolution of "modern" human behavior (McBrearty and Brooks 2000, Shea 2011a, Marean 2015), the transitions to agriculture and pastoralism (Marshall and Hildebrand 2002, Fuller and Hildebrand 2013, Lane 2013), and connections between population movements and the spread of iron technology (De Maret 2013). Few processual archaeologists regarded the stone tool evidence as central to these issues. Stone tools' "dethroning," combined with their diminished role in chronostratigraphy, removed prior incentives to reform archaeological lithics systematics that had arisen during the Culture-Historical Period. Trends towards increasingly divergent and idiosyncratic artifact typologies and haphazardly defined lithic industries that so concerned participants in the Burg Wartenstein Conference continued unchecked.

The 1960s and subsequent decades also witnessed an enormous increase in the numbers of archaeological excavations in Eastern Africa. This development paralleled growing numbers of scholars joining academia and seeking careers as professional archaeologists. Many archaeologists sought to start their own research projects rather than joining established ones. This allowed them to secure funding under their own names and to publish findings promptly, requirements for permanent appointment at most academic institutions. Increased numbers of archaeological excavations during the Processualizing Period led to increasingly site-specific research questions, questions one could plausibly claim to answer by excavations at one site or at a group of sites close to one another in time and space. In an archaeological landscape dotted with many small inward-focused field projects led by individuals from diverse research traditions, lithics systematics diverged and diversified.

A steady shift away from book-length monographic publications toward publishing interim and final excavation reports in peer-reviewed journals (as paralleled throughout academia) further promoted differences in stone tool systematics. While the editorial board of a major university press might insist that an author use consistent artifact descriptions throughout a proposed book, journal editors reviewing papers about a single lithic assemblage might not even be aware of such differences within a single author's work, nor be in a position to reconcile differences between different authors.

This review's lithic-centric perspective might inadvertently convey the impression that the Processualizing Period was a bad time for prehistoric stone tool analysis. It was not. The Processualizing Period saw vast increases in the numbers of excavated and well-documented lithic assemblages overall and especially assemblages from prehistory's more recent phases. It also saw increased ethnoarchaeological research on stone tools, most notably among stone tool using hide-workers in Ethiopia (Gallagher 1977, Clark and Kurashina 1981, Brandt and Weedman 1997, Weedman Arthur 2018). Finally, archaeologists began closing the gap Exploratory Period archaeologists interposed between prehistory's latest phases and Eastern Africa's indigenous ethnographic and historic populations (Kusimba 2003, see papers in Kusimba and Barut Kusimba 2003). Still, some of the changes that took place in Eastern African archaeology over the last 50 or more years affect prehistoric research today. One of the most unfortunate of these changes for stone artifact analysis was that formal artifact typologies were increasingly relegated to doctoral dissertations (e.g., Nelson 1973, Merrick, 1975, Mehlman 1989) that were difficult for other scholars to obtain and expensive for them to photocopy. Because digital copies of most dissertations are now available on the internet through one source or another, this is not as much a problem today, but, at the time it was a factor in the lithics systematics anarchy discussed in Chapter 1.

Implications for Research Today

Differences in archaeological research between the Exploratory, Culture-Historical, and Processualizing Periods have profoundly affected archaeological research in Eastern Africa today.

At a very basic level, historical differences in research practices influenced how archaeologists recovered stone tools and how they conserved them (see Table 4.1). Surface collections and narrow sounding trenches characterize all phases of prehistoric research, but large-scale horizontal excavations and three-coordinate artifact plotting only became common during the Culture Historical Period. Earlier researchers often discarded unretouched artifacts and flake fragments, retaining only cores and retouched pieces, and sometimes only representative samples of the latter. As Eastern African museums developed the facilities to store and curate excavated remains, the formerly common practice of exporting whole lithic assemblages, or representative samples of them, to foreign museums and educational institutions largely ceased.

TABLE 4.1 *Historical contrasts in lithic artifact recovery and conservation practices.*

	Exploratory Period	Culture-Historical Period	Processualizing Period
Surface collections	+	+	+
Sounding trenches	+	+	+
Large horizontal area excavation	–	wide variation	+
3-coordinate plotting	–	wide variation	+
Sediment screening	wide variation	wide variation	+
Diagnostic cores, retouched pieces kept	+	+	+
All cores, retouched pieces, flakes kept	–	+	+
Flake fragments, objects less than 25 mm long kept	–	wide variation	+
Artifacts shipped abroad permanently	+	+	–

Key: + = yes, – = no.

Historical differences among excavation and artifact conservation practices affect how we can compare lithic evidence today. For example, a collection made in the 1930s will almost certainly over-represent culturally or chronologically diagnostic artifacts and under-represent small artifacts and unretouched pieces. More importantly, if students want to study stone tool assemblages excavated using modern techniques and up-to-date recovery procedures, they have to travel to Eastern Africa.

The regional archaeological synthesis was one casualty of the Processualizing Period in Eastern Africa. To understand these consequences, one needs to appreciate what regional syntheses do. First and foremost, regional syntheses present "the big picture." That is, they compare evidence from multiple sites and identify major trends in the evidence, as well as gaps in that evidence. Second, they go beyond site-specific research questions, posing hypotheses about major interpretive issues. Finally, and most importantly, used as college textbooks, they introduce students commencing their studies to the "state of the art" in prehistoric research in a given region. Archaeology students in Southern Africa can do this (Mitchell 2002), archaeology students in Eastern Africa cannot.

Elsewhere, as processual archaeology augmented culture-historical archaeology book-length regional syntheses continued to appear in print. Although the book-length regional syntheses by processual archaeologists differed from those that culture-historical archaeologists had written, they continued to write them. Events in Eastern Africa took a different course. Continental-scale syntheses included evidence from Eastern Africa (Phillipson 2005, Barham and Mitchell 2008), but the last major book-length synthesis of Eastern Africa's prehistoric archaeological record appeared in 1954 (Cole 1954).

As a result, higher-order research questions in Eastern African prehistory and efforts to reform stone tool systematics focus on either one time period or one region within a given time period (e.g., Will et al. 2019). The sorts of larger, integrative research questions that attract interest from archaeologists working in other regions and from scholars working in such allied fields as history, linguistics, and paleoanthropology, all too often go unasked. In order to understand how current frameworks for Eastern African prehistory constrain archaeologists' options, the next section reviews those frameworks.

CHRONOLOGICAL FRAMEWORKS FOR EASTERN AFRICAN PREHISTORY

This section briefly reviews the major age-stages of Eastern African prehistory and what archaeologists think happened during each of them. For detailed overviews, see Oliver (1975), Phillipson (1977b, 2005), Robertshaw (1995), Barham and Mitchell (2008), and individual papers in Clark (1984), Clark and Brandt (1984), Kusimba and Barut Kusimba (2003), Stahl (2005), and Mitchell and Lane (2013).

Archaeologists divide Eastern Africa's prehistory into five major age-stages: the Earlier, Middle, and Later Stone Age, the Neolithic Period, and the Iron Age (see Table 4.2). The three stone ages were originally defined in South Africa (Goodwin and van Riet Lowe 1929). Archaeologists began using them in Eastern Africa from about the mid-twentieth century onward. They imported the Neolithic and Iron Age concepts from European and Western Asian prehistory.

The Earlier Stone Age

The Earlier Stone Age (ESA) runs from the earliest occurrences of archaeological evidence, ca. 3.5 Ma (as of this writing) to around 0.2–0.3 Ma. This period witnessed dry grasslands replacing extensive forests and woodlands. A major turnover around 2.5 Ma among bovids signals a shift from browsers to grazers (Vrba 1988). A second shift around 1.6–1.8 Ma, the *Equus* Event, brought Eurasian fauna to the region (Werdelin and Sanders 2010). In evolutionary terms, the ESA's most significant events included the origin of the Genus *Homo*, its morphological differentiation and intercontinental dispersal, and the rise of our species, *Homo sapiens*. Unlike other hominin genera, such as *Paranthropus* and *Australopithecus*, who became extinct during this period, most species of the Genus *Homo* have relatively large brains as well as long feet and

TABLE 4.2 *Major anthropological events during East African age-stages.*

Age-stage and dates	Major anthropological events
Earlier Stone Age (3.4–0.3 Ma)	First appearance of *Homo* (*H. habilis*, *H. ergaster/erectus*, and *H. heidelbergensis*). Last appearance dates of australopithecines and paranthropines. First flaked stone tools. First stone tool cut-marks on large vertebrate remains. First evidence for controlled use of fire. Influx of Eurasian fauna ca. 1.6–1.8 Ma.
Middle Stone Age (300–50 Ka)	First appearance of *Homo sapiens*. Last appearance dates of *H. heidelbergensis*. First evidence for hafted stone tools, mineral pigments (red ochre), carved bone tools. Increased regional variation in stone tool designs.
Later Stone Age (50 to 4–6 Ka)	First appearance of geometric microliths, widespread occurrences of ostrich eggshell beads, ceramics, watercraft, rock art. Inland settlements focused on forest-savanna ecotones. Intensified use of aquatic resources along rivers and lakes.
Neolithic (5–3 to 1–2 Ka)	First appearances of domesticated cattle, sheep, goat, millet, sorghum, and other crops, as well as shaped groundstone artifacts (i.e., celts, stone vessels). Increased regional variation in ceramic styles. Small-scale monumental architecture.
Iron Age (<2.5–0.8–0.5 Ka)	First evidence for indigenous iron production. Widespread appearance of ceramics. Dispersal/migration of Bantu language-speaking populations. Urbanism and large-scale monumental architecture in Ethiopian highlands, and on Red Sea and Indian Ocean coasts. Increased and sustained trade contacts with Arabian Peninsula and European states.

legs, short arms, and an external nose – features that enhance long-distance walking/running and carrying things. They are also more consistently associated with stone tools than earlier hominins.

Eastern Africa's most famous ESA site complexes are Olduvai Gorge in Tanzania (Leakey 1971, Leakey and Roe 1994, Blumenschine et al. 2003, Domínguez-Rodrigo et al. 2007) and Lomekwi 3 in Kenya (Harmand et al. 2015). Other sites with well-documented ESA stone tool assemblages include those from East Lake Turkana's Koobi Fora and Burgi Formations (Isaac and Isaac 1997), the Nachukui Formation in West Turkana (Roche et al. 2003) and Olorgesailie (Isaac 1977, Potts et al. 1999), all of which are in Kenya, and Peninj, Tanzania (Domínguez-Rodrigo et al. 2009). Ethiopian ESA site complexes include Gona (Semaw et al. 2009), Hadar (Kimbel et al. 1996,

Goldman-Neuman and Hovers 2012), Melka Kunture (Chavaillon and Piperno 2004), and sites in Ethiopia's Middle Awash Valley (Schick and Toth 2017).

Stone tool assemblages identified as "transitional" ESA/MSA ones appear at Kalambo Falls (Clark 2001) and Twin Rivers (Barham et al. 2000), both in Zambia, as well as at sites from the western foothills of Lake Baringo, Kenya (McBrearty 2005), and Olorgesailie (Deino et al. 2018). Kalambo Falls very nearly preserves a complete sequence of all but the very earliest phases of Eastern African prehistory.

Nearly all Eastern African ESA sites are open-air sites, rather than caves. Some ESA sites preserve evidence for fire, but claims of systematic fire usage during the ESA remain controversial. Stone tool cut-marks on bone appear early on during the ESA and become more common after 1.8 Ma. These cut-marks and greater numbers of sites juxtaposing cut-marked and percussion-damaged bones suggest hominin diets increasingly incorporated protein and fat from large vertebrate carcasses (Domínguez-Rodrigo and Pickering 2003).

The Middle Stone Age

The Middle Stone Age (MSA) spans the period from 30–45 Ka cal. BP to 200–300 Ka, encompassing Marine Isotope Stages (MIS) 3–8 (see papers in Jones and Stewart 2016, Deino et al. 2018, Tryon 2019). Climate fluctuated widely during the MSA with at least two megadroughts, in ca. 75 and 135 Ka (Scholz et al. 2007, Potts et al. 2018). Fossil evidence suggests that *Homo sapiens* evolved out of regional *Homo heidelbergensis* populations during the early MSA (Fleagle and Grine 2014, Scerri et al. 2018). The MSA's end coincides with extensive desertification across northern Africa in the context of a generally colder but widely variable global climate (Barham and Mitchell 2008, papers in Jones and Stewart 2016).

Well-documented Ethiopian MSA stone tool assemblages include those from

Gademotta and Kulkuletti (Wendorf and Schild 1974, Sahle et al. 2014, Douze and Delagnes 2016) the Middle Awash Valley Aduma and Herto Beds (Clark et al. 2003, Yellen et al. 2005), the Lower Omo Valley Kibish Formation (Shea 2008), and Porc Epic Cave (Clark et al. 1984, Pleurdeau 2005).

Kenyan and Tanzania sites with MSA levels include a group of open-air sites near Ileret in East Turkana (Kelly 1996), lower levels of Enkapune Ya Muto (Ambrose 1998), Lukenya Hill (Merrick 1975, Gramly 1976, Tryon et al. 2015), Nyamita (Blegen et al. 2017), Prospect Farm (Anthony 1978), Carwright's Site (Waweru 2002), Panga Ya Saidi (Shipton 2018), sites in the West Lake Baringo Kapthurin Formation (Leakey et al. 1969, Cornelissen 1992, Tryon et al. 2005), Kisese Rockshelter II (Tryon et al. 2018), Mumba Cave (Mehlman 1989, Marks and Conard 2008, Gliganic et al. 2012) and Nasera Rockshelter (Mehlman 1989, Tryon and Faith 2016).

MSA occupations occur at the Zambian sites of Kalambo Falls (Clark 2001), Kalemba Cave (Phillipson 1976), and Mumbwa Cave (Clark 1942, Barham 2000).

In Ethiopia, MSA/LSA "transitional" assemblages appear at Goda Buticha (Leplongeon et al. 2017) and Mochena Borago, (Brandt et al. 2017). They follow MSA occupations at Enkapune Ya Muto, Panga Ya Saidi, Nasera Rockshelter, Kalambo Falls, Kalemba Cave, and Mumbwa Cave.

In contrast with the ESA, many MSA sites are caves/rock-shelters. These caves and some open-air sites preserve more cut-marked bones and somewhat more consistent evidence for fire. MSA contexts in Eastern Africa furnish some of the oldest-known evidence for the use of mineral pigments and for the production of barbed bone harpoons (Yellen 1998, Barham 2002, Brooks et al. 2018).

The Later Stone Age

The Later Stone Age (LSA) lasts from at least 40–50 Ka to around 4–6 Ka cal. BP. The LSA spans MIS 1–3, essentially the last major Pleistocene glacial cycle and the onset of the present Holocene Epoch. Multiple lines of geological evidence suggest generally cooler conditions in Eastern Africa during this period, accompanied by wide climatic variation (Gasse et al. 2008). As global temperatures increased after ca. 11 Ka, sea levels rose, and inland lake levels fluctuated widely. Consequently, sites from high lake stands and near-modern sea levels dominate the LSA record. The hominin fossil record for this period preserves only *Homo sapiens* remains.

Limited effectiveness of radiocarbon dating and variable criteria for identifying lithic assemblages as LSA versus MSA make this the LSA's beginning a bit "fuzzy" compared to the relatively swift, horizon-level "transition" between analogous Middle and Upper Paleolithic Periods in Europe and western Asia ca. 45 Ka. The date for the LSA's end varies with geography. As originally defined in South Africa, the LSA is the archaeological record of recent hunter-gatherers. Thus, for most archaeologists, first appearances of domesticated cattle, sheep, goats, and plants herald a "Neolithic" mode of food production and the "end" of the LSA. But, food production spread slowly in Eastern Africa, and Eastern Africans adopted it piecemeal (Crowther et al. 2017). Hunter-gatherers-fishers persisted alongside pastoralists, agro-pastoralists, and farmers for prolonged periods; indeed, some continue to do so today. As a result, dates for the youngest LSA assemblages vary widely within Eastern Africa and they overlap with first dates for the Neolithic Period and even the Iron Age.

Eastern African sites containing LSA lithic assemblages are considerably more numerous than those lithic-preserving MSA and ESA ones. Many are multilevel cave/rock-shelter sites.

Ethiopian sites with significant LSA deposits include Gobedra Rockshelter (Phillipson 1977a), Goda Buticha (Leplongeon et al. 2017), Brandt's (1982) Lake Besaka sites, and Mochena Borago, (Brandt et al. 2017).

In Somalia/Somaliland, Gutherz and colleagues' (2014) recent investigations at Las Geel Shelter 7 augment data from the surface collections and test excavations J.D. Clark (1954) conducted during his military service there during the 1940s.

In the Democratic Republic of the Congo, Ishango II (de Heinzelin 1962, Brooks and Smith 1987, Mercader and Brooks 2001) and Matupi Cave (Van Noten 1977) provide evidence for LSA adaptations at the easternmost edge of the Congo Basin.

Partly as the result of extensive survey projects and relative political stability, Kenya and Tanzania boast far more well-documented LSA sites than neighboring countries. Better-known Kenyan LSA sites include Barthelme's (1985) East Turkana sites GaJi 1 and 11, Enkapune Ya Muto (Ambrose 1998), Gamble's Cave 2 (Leakey 1931, Ambrose 1984, Frahm and Tryon 2018), Lopoy (Robbins 1980), Lothagam Lokam (Robbins 1974, Goldstein et al. 2017), Lowasera, (Phillipson 1977c), Lukenya Hill (GvJm 22 and 62) (Merrick 1975, Kusimba 2001), Maasai Gorge Rockshelter (Ambrose 1985), the Mtongwe Lower Group (Omi 1988), Muringa Rock Shelter (Sutton 1973), Nderit Drift (GsJi 2/T) (Merrick 1975), Panga Ya Saidi (Shipton 2018), and Tunnel Rockshelter (Sutton 1973).

In Tanzania, some of the best-documented LSA sites include Baura 1, Lusangi 1, and Markasi Lusangi 2 (Kessy 2013), Kirumi Isumbirira (Masao 1979), Kisese II Rockshelter (Tryon et al. 2018), Kuumbi Cave on Zanzibar (Sinclair et al. 2006, Shipton et al. 2016), Kwa Mwango-Isanzu (Masao 1979), Magubike Rockshelter (Werner and Willoughby 2017), Mlambalasi Rockshelter (Biittner et al. 2017), Mumba Cave (Mehlman 1989, Marks and Conard 2008, Gliganic et al. 2012), Nasera Rockshelter (Mehlman 1989, Tryon and Faith 2016), and the Naisusu Beds at Olduvai Gorge (Leakey et al. 1972).

Zambian sites with LSA occupations include Gwisho Sites A, B, and C (Gabel 1965, Fagan and van Noten 1971), Kalambo Falls (Clark 1974), Kalemba Cave (Miller 1969, Phillipson 1976), Makwe Cave (Phillipson 1976), Mumbwa Cave (Clark 1942, Barham 2000), and Mwela Rockshelter (Miller 1969).

Archaeologists view the LSA as a period during which Eastern African populations grew, recovering from hyperarid conditions during MIS 3–4. LSA humans' adaptations are thought to have been broadly similar to ethnographic Africa forager societies. That is, they settled near savanna-forest ecotones and along rivers and lakes, hunting a broad spectrum of terrestrial and aquatic prey using spears, bows and arrows, and nets and traps. Eastern African LSA sites preserve a wide variety of carved bone implements, including conical points and barbed bone "harpoons," of which smaller specimens may be arrow tips used for fishing. The plant component of LSA diets remains poorly documented, but the region boasts many species that could have been cultivated without domesticating them (Fuller and Hildebrand 2013). Pottery appears at some LSA sites, but it is uncommon. Ostrich eggshell beads, on the other hand, are nearly ubiquitous. Just when Eastern Africans obtained domesticated dogs (derived from the Eurasian wolf) remains unclear, but depictions in early Egyptian artwork suggest their presence in the lower Nile Valley by ca. 5–10 Ka.

The Neolithic Period

Many Eastern African archaeologists, especially those working in Kenya and Tanzania, identify a "Pastoral" Neolithic Period (Bower 1991, Marshall and Hildebrand 2002), but other than this, the idea of a "Neolithic Period," fits poorly with the Eastern African evidence. In Europe and Western Asia, where the term originated, and in current usage, "Neolithic" references the archaeological record of sedentary farmers and herders. The Eastern African Neolithic Period, in contrast, features hunter-gatherers-fishers, pastoralists, and agro-pastoralists all living near one another at the same time, doubtlessly interacting in complex ways. Aptly, Crowther and colleagues (2017) describe this as a "subsistence mosaic." Such hallmarks of the Eurasian Neolithic – groundstone artifacts, abraded-edge celts, and ceramics – occur in Eastern Africa, but they crosscut other paleoeconomic evidence, frustrating archaeologists' efforts to define an Eastern African Neolithic Period with clearly demarcated chronological boundaries. In Europe and western Eurasia, for example, ceramics generally occur among agro-pastoralists. Eastern Africa has a "ceramic LSA" in which hunter-gatherers used ceramics.

Consequently, beginning and end dates for Eastern Africa's Neolithic Period vary widely. If one dates the beginning of the Neolithic to first-appearance dates for livestock (cattle, for the most part) and the end of the period to first appearances of ironworking (or the ceramics associated with Early Iron Age societies), then the dates 3–5 to 1–2 Ka Cal BP bracket most Eastern African Neolithic occurrences.

Djibouti preserves two Neolithic sites featuring well-documented stone tool assemblages, Asa Koma and Wakrita (Gutherz et al. 2015). Near Aksum in Ethiopia, Anqer Baahti (Finneran et al. 2000b) contains Neolithic occupations. In Tanzania, Luxmanda (Grillo et al. 2018), Nasera Rockshelter (Mehlman 1989, Tryon and Faith 2016), and the Ngorongoro Burial Mounds (Leakey 1967, Sassoon) feature Neolithic stone tool assemblages.

Other than these, the overwhelming majority of Eastern African Neolithic sites with well-documented lithic assemblages come from Kenya. The northernmost of these are Dongodien (GaJj 4) and the Ileret Stone Bowl Site (FwJj 5), both in East Turkana (Barthelme 1985). Wright (2005) identifies a series of

Neolithic sites in Tsavo National Park. Most Kenyan Neolithic sites occur in the southern part of the country and in the Rift Valley. Excavated early on in the history of prehistoric research, the best known of these include Gamble's Cave 2 (Leakey 1931, Ambrose 1984, Frahm and Tryon 2018), Hyrax Hill Site I (Leakey et al. 1943, Sutton 1998), and Njoro River Cave (Leakey and Leakey 1950). A second wave of research into the Neolithic began in the 1960s to 1980s, resulting in excavations at Ilkek (Gilgil) (Brown 1966), Prolonged Drift (Nelson 1973, Bower et al. 1977, Larson 1986), Narosura (Odner 1972), Nderit Drift, (Ambrose 1984), Salasun (Bower et al. 1977), and Laikipia (Siiriäinen 1984). During the 1980s Robertshaw and colleagues (1990b) documented numerous Neolithic sites in southwest Kenya at Lemek, Ngamuriak, Old-orotua, Olopilukunya, Sambo Ngige. Odney-Obul (1996) published two Neolithic assemblages from Marula and Ndabibi. Ambrose's (1998) excavations at Enkapune Ya Muto have furnished valuable chronological information about the LSA, Neolithic, and Iron Ages in this region. As of this writing, increasing numbers of researchers are focusing on the origins and spread of agriculture and pastoralism in Eastern Africa. One expects the list of Neolithic sites from this region will grow much larger in the near future. Sugenya (southwestern Kenya) (Goldstein 2018) is one recently published example of this renaissance in Neolithic archaeology.

The oldest Eastern African evidence for food production using domesticated plants and animals appears around mid-Holocene times, ca. 5–6 Ka. Throughout the region, cattle pastoralism appears earliest and becomes widespread long before evidence for stable agrarian adaptations (Marshall and Hildebrand 2002). Cattle remains in Ethiopia and Eritrea date to ca. 5 Ka, with crops much later, ca. 3 Ka (Harrower et al. 2010). Further south along the Rift Valley, a similar offset occurs, with cattle pastoralism appearing around 4 Ka, spreading southward, and becoming widespread after 1 Ka. Other than in those parts of the region connected to international trade routes along the Nile Valley, the Red Sea, and Indian Ocean coasts, Eastern African agriculture did not give rise to large towns and villages occupied continuously for centuries or millennia. As in Europe, Neolithic lifeways' onset inspired monumental architecture, such as the stone pillar sites (*namoratunga*) of northern Kenya (Hildebrand et al. 2018).

Neolithic livestock included southwest Asian species: sheep (*Ovis*), goats (*Capra*), and cattle (*Bos*), the latter possibly combining stocks domesticated separately in Northern Africa and Southwest Asia. The plant economy offers some early and surprising evidence for plants brought into the region from Southeast Asia, such as banana (*Musa* spp.), taro (*Colocasia esculenta*), and Asian yam (*Dioscorea alata*). Indigenous hunter-gatherer-fishers probably obtained these crops from Austronesian explorers and dispersed them inland. Neolithic agricultural mainstays included pearl millet (*Pennisetum glaucum*), sorghum (*Sorghum bicolor*), finger millet (*Eleusine corcana),* and legume cowpea (*Vigna unguiculata*). With the exception of finger millet, which likely derives from the

Ethiopian highlands, these crops originated in the Sahel, the southern fringes of the Sahara Desert.

As in Europe and the Near East, Eastern African archaeologists identify Neolithic assemblage-groups in terms of ceramic wares (or "traditions"). Some examples of these include the Akira, Ileret, Kanysore, Maringishu, Narosura, and Nderit wares/traditions.

The Iron Age

The Iron Age begins with first-appearance dates for iron smelting. In Eastern Africa, the oldest such evidence occurs on Lake Victoria's western shores and hinterlands around 500 BC (ca. 2.5 Ka cal. BP). Additional such sites appear on the eastern edge of the Lake Victoria Basin around 100 AD (ca. 1.8 Ka). By around 200 AD, evidence for ironworking appears in eastern Kenya and northern Tanzania. Archaeological accounts of Eastern African prehistory generally cease using the term "Iron Age" for evidence dating to less than 1200–1500 AD (ca. 0.8–0.5 Ka cal. BP).

Most Iron Age sites with well-documented *in-situ* lithic artifacts are from Ethiopia. These include Aksum (Phillipson et al. 2000, Fattovich et al. 2012), Gobedra Rockshelter (Phillipson 1977a), Goda Buticha (Leplongeon et al. 2017), Mai Agam (Phillipson and Sulas 2005), and the Medogwe Workshop Locality (Capra 2017). Kokan Rockshelter (Brandt et al. 2008) and Sembel (near Asmara) (Teka and Okubatsion 2008) comprise two Eritrean Iron Age sites with lithic artifacts. Kenyan Iron Age sites with documented lithic assemblages include Hyrax Hill Site II (Leakey et al. 1943, Sutton 1998), Kulchurdo Rockshelter (Phillipson and Gifford 1981), and Maasai Gorge Rockshelter (Ambrose 1985). Tanzanian Iron Age lithic assemblages come from Jangwani I (Mehlman 1989), Kuumbi Cave (Sinclair et al. 2006, Shipton et al. 2016), and Malambasi Rockshelter (Biittner et al. 2017). Iron Age occupations with lithic artifacts cap the long prehistoric sequence at Kalambo Falls in Zambia (Clark 1974).

South of Ethiopia and the Horn of Africa, the lines between Holocene LSA, Neolithic, and Iron Age blur considerably. From about mid-Holocene times onward, stone tools, ceramics, and bones of domesticated cattle and sheep/goats occur in complex combinations. Such combinatory complexity increases when iron artifacts begin to appear in the region. Whether this complexity reflects actual human behavioral variability, "time-averaging" – distinct forager, herder, and farmer occupations taking place in such close succession at the same sites that archaeologists cannot tell them apart, or post-depositional stratigraphic mixing – requires a case-by-case assessment. Whatever the cause, for sites dating from about Mid-Holocene times onward archaeologists often either struggle to assign single-site levels to only one age-stage or they do not do so at all. Kenyan examples of such assemblages include Gabel's (1969) Kavirondo rockshelter sites, Gogo Falls (Robertshaw 1991), Deloraine, (Ambrose et al. 1984), Seitsonen's Kansyore (2010) sites, and Laikipia Horizons II-V (Siiriäinen 1984). Mahal Teglinos (Kassala) in Sudan (Phillipson 2017), Kessy's (2013) Kondoa (Tanzania) sites, Baura 1, Lusangi 1, and Markasi Lusangi 2 (Unit 3) fit into this category as well. So too do the later levels of Mlambalasi Rockshelter (Biittner et al. 2017) and Seronera (Bower 1973) (both in Tanzania), and Nsongezi Rockshelter, Levels I–IV (Nelson and Posnansky 1970) and Rangi Cave Levels II–III (Robbins et al. 1977) (both in Uganda). Stone tools from the uppermost levels of three Zambian cave sites, Kalemba (Miller 1969, Phillipson 1976), Mumbwa (Barham 2000), and Thandwe (Phillipson 1976), also fit uncomfortably in just one of the Eastern African later prehistory's traditional age-stages.

The Iron Age witnessed the formation of urban states, consolidation of regional trade networks, and large-scale population movements. Eastern African state formation – that is, regional polities centered on urban settlements – was largely a northern and coastal phenomenon. In northern Ethiopia, the Aksum Kingdom (sometimes also spelled Axum) flourished around 100–940 AD, influencing nearby societies economically, as well as spiritually, through the diffusion of Christianity. Along the Indian Ocean Coast, a series of towns arose along departure points for trade routes into the interior. Some of these towns, including Mogadishu, Shanga and Manda near Lamu, Gedi, Malindi, Zanzibar and Kilwa, developed into Swahili city-states. Islam arrived in Eastern Africa primarily through these city-states.

To the south, the Eastern African Iron Age's defining events included the spread of agro-pastoralism (especially cattle herding), ironworking, and distinctive regional ceramic traditions westward and south across the region, and beyond. Phillipson (2005: 249) unites these activities into a "Chifumbaze Complex," – although in doing so he emphasizes variability in their occurrence and the probability that they spread somewhat independently of one another. Archaeologists have long linked the Iron Age to dispersals of Bantu-speaking populations from the southern margins of the Sahara. Some sources refer to Iron Age polities in Uganda and adjacent territories as states, or even empires, but most might be more accurately termed chiefdoms – regional powers organized along religious and ethnic lines that draw power chiefly from trade networks. Actual multiethnic states/empires are largely historical phenomena.

UWAZI VALLEY TALES, EPISODE 4: ANCIENT ONES' CAVE

The rock-shelter, Pango Wa Kwale, occupied the south facing side of a gray rock outcrop. About a hundred meters of acacia-choked valley floor stretched from where we stood to the base of the rock-shelter on the opposite side of the valley. There remained about two meters' clearance between the cave's uppermost surface and its soot-blackened ceiling. A single narrow step trench cut down from the surface through about 20 meters of deposits. A half-meter-thick basalt layer projected outward about 10 meters from these deposits' lowest level. Beneath some trees off to one side, Aya sat at a plywood lab table set up on wooden sawhorses. Canvas tarpaulins provided shade for her and for a half dozen African laborers. Another half-dozen men and women perched at various points in the vertical trench, filling black plastic buckets with sediments.

Aya wore dark green cargo pants, canvas desert boots, and a partly unbuttoned blue chambray shirt with its sleeves rolled.

"Where's my co-director?" she asked as we approached.

"Went off after a leopard," said the Old Africa Hand.

"What?"

"It's OK, Joseph's with him," I said.

"That's worse!"

"He'll be fine, young lady," said the Old Africa Hand. "Pango Wa Kwale, eh? Interesting name, Ancient Ones' Cave."

Aya sighed. "Joseph led us here three years ago on the first field season. The name's a bit of a mouthful in Swahili, but it has a nice ring in English."

The Polymath and Joseph emerged from the trail unscathed and leopard-less. "The name has the further advantage of being accurate," said Joseph.

"Aya, how about a progress report for me and the Cook's Tour for our new colleagues, please?" the Polymath asked. He set down his daypack and took out his orange notebook. A tall, slender African woman approached. She wore khaki pants, a denim jacket, and a fleece vest. Under her arm, she carried an archaeology textbook.

"First things first," Aya said. "This is Endurance, our National Museum Representative."

She shook our hands.

"Are you studying archaeology in graduate school? I asked her.

"No, I work for the National Museum. I read whatever I can so that I can understand what you scientists do, so I can make the museum better for the people who visit it, especially the schoolchildren." She smiled, turned, and walked a short distance exchanging her sandals for hiking boots.

"Endurance, what a cool name," I said to the Polymath.

"Her parents named her Endurance after the explorer Sir Ernest Shackleton's ship," he said. "Good to read about Shackleton, Robin. His and his men's adventures in Antarctica help keep our 'fieldwork disasters' in perspective."

"Customarily, one names ships after women," the Old Africa Hand remarked. "Turnabout's fair play, I suppose."

Aya put on a broad-brimmed canvas hat, picked up her notebook, and led the five of us to the base of the excavation trench. Joseph remained behind, chatting with the workmen resting in the shade. Wooden stairs set off to one side of the cave led us up to a wider platform cut into the cave sediments about halfway up. Making room for us, the excavators gathered their buckets and descended to the shaded sediment-screening area below.

"Ancient Ones' Cave is a bit like Mumba and Nasera, those caves Mehlman excavated. We've got pretty much everything from Historic and Iron Age at the top of the sequence to earlier MSA down below on top of the Big Basalt Block."

(Author's note: A diagram of the Pango Wa Kwale stratigraphy and older sediments in the Uwazi Valley are among supplemental materials available on the Cambridge University Press website for this book.)

"What's the oldest date?" I asked.

"The Big Basalt Block, clocks in at 300 Ka, but the tuff directly overlying it dates to 250 Ka. Up top in Unit I, Level 1 we have historic glass beads, some broken bottle glass, and a few brass rifle bullet cartridges. Deeper down, we have Urëwe and Lelesu ceramics and a few stone tools. So, that's Historic and Iron Age. Not much for you there, Robin. The lithics are pretty sparse, but there's lot of animal bones, both wild species and domesticated sheep, goats, cattle. Radiocarbon clocks in about 0.5–2.5 Ka in calibrated years. Lot of ash and dung deposits."

"The early Anthropocene," said the Polymath.

"The Age of Goat Poop," said the Old Africa Hand, kicking the ground.

"A little lower in Unit I, we pick up lots of obsidian tools, sheep, goat, cattle bones, and Nderit pottery. At 3.5 Ka on average, Level 2 is some sort of ceramic Neolithic, perhaps Savanna Pastoral Neolithic, or something very closely related to it. You're going to wish you had a microscope, Robin. I've never seen stone tools so small."

"Level 3 is a bit sparser in fossils and artifacts. Standard early Holocene LSA stuff with a few scraps of pottery, dates running 5–12 Ka in sequence. Mostly obsidian and quartz tools and wild animal fossils. There's a lot more clay in these levels, so we think we've caught the mid-Holocene wet phase."

Aya continued, pointing to the level on which we stood. "Here, at the top of Unit II, we pick up more sandy deposits, so we think we're in one of the major Late Pleistocene arid episodes."

"Dates?" the Old Africa Hand asked.

"Radiocarbon gives us 13–35 Ka for Level 4 and 40 Ka to infinite ages for Level 5. But there's good news. The optically stimulated luminance (OSL) dates for Level 5 range between 42 and 65 Ka and in stratigraphic order."

"You trust OSL?" I asked.

"It's that new single-grain approach out of Australia. Very reliable," she said.

"Anyway, Level 4 is Later Stone Age (LSA). Only wild animals, as you'd expect. The stone tools are about an even mix of obsidian and quartz with the odd bit of chert and coarse volcanics. Level 5 looks like something transitional between Middle and Later Stone Age. This is where we need your help, Robin. I know the basics about stone tools, but I'm an archaeozoologist. My colleagues tell me you have a unique talent for stone tool analysis."

"This could be very important," The Polymath said to all of us. "Genuinely transitional MSA/LSA sequences are quite rare in Eastern Africa. People have been looking for evidence of an MSA/LSA transition analogous to the European Middle-Upper Paleolithic for decades. There's Mumba, Panga Ya Saidi, Kisese II, and now Ancient Ones' Cave."

"Let's not get ahead of ourselves," said Aya. "All we have so far are preliminary dates from a sounding trench. We need to refine the chronology and expand the trench laterally to capture some of the variability within levels. We're years away from testing hypotheses about the mode and tempo of the MSA/LSA transition here."

"Quite right, young lady," said the Old Africa Hand. "Quick is the enemy of good."

"But if there are all these other sites already excavated, why do we need to excavate this one?" I asked.

"Well, for one thing," Aya said. "Archaeologists excavated all but Panga Ya Saidi decades ago, and other research teams are currently working on those."

"The other thing, Robin," the Polymath spoke, "is that archaeology is an upside-down ecosystem."

"A what?" I asked.

"In a normal ecosystem, producers outnumber consumers," the Polymath answered. "Plants are more common than herbivores, herbivores more common than carnivores. In archaeology, a vast number of potential consumers depend on a small number of producers, or field scientists."

Aya interrupted, "If you want to make a big impact early on in your career and to assure your place in the profession, start a field project. Just be sure you can live without a fixed residence, a personal life, or sleep."

She shot a look at the Polymath, who studied the ground.

Aya resumed the tour. "Anyway, beginning in Unit III, Level 6 and continuing on down to Level 7, we see alternating layers of sand-silt-clay with layers dominated by aeolian sand. Bones are sparse, and the artifacts are 'classic' MSA. Level 6 is mostly smaller tools made of obsidian and quartz, but Level

7 has larger tools, more rhyolite and basalt and less obsidian. The OSL gives us a date of 75 Ka for Level 6, but nothing yet for Level 7. The good news, though, is we've matched the chemical signature of the tuff between 6 and 7 to one dated to 90 Ka up north in Ethiopia. So, with the White Tuff on top of the Big Basalt Block dating to 250 Ka, we can bracket Level 7 to 90–250 Ka."

"That's a pretty impressive sequence," I said.

"Indeed," said the Polymath. "The whole of the Later Pleistocene in one cave!"

"You're going to have your work cut out for you, Robin," said the Old Africa Hand.

"But wait, there's more." Aya continued. "As I am sure the Polymath told you, capstones of the Basal Basalt Block cover stone tool and fossil deposits downslope not far west of here."

"Ah, yes, quite eager to see them." said the Old Africa Hand.

The Polymath had not mentioned these other deposits to me.

He spoke: "We haven't done much with them yet, other than to sample the tuffs in them, but it looks like we may have Earlier Stone Age (ESA) deposits, Acheulian above and possibly Oldowan below them.

Aya addressed the Old Africa Hand directly: "We hoped we could interest you in having a look at them and assess potential sites for future excavations. After all, you've found more African ESA sites than anyone."

"Flattery will get you everywhere, young lady," the Old Africa Hand smiled, "but I'm still well short of Desmond Clark's record. I'll do it, but I haven't much time to write up field survey collections.

"Great, then!" said the Polymath. "Joseph and I will help you survey. Robin's dissertation can describe anything we find."

"Yeah, great," I feigned an eager smile. I had been starting to worry that describing stone tools from Ancient Ones' Cave would be too much for a single dissertation. Now, I would be dealing with the whole Stone Age sequence of Eastern Africa. I imagined myself in my seventies, still in graduate school.

CHAPTER 5

THE EASTERN AFRICAN LITHIC RECORD

This chapter reviews the Eastern African lithic record. Using stone tool evidence from more than 250 Eastern African archaeological lithic assemblages (Figures 5.1 and 5.2), it finds numerous mismatches between that evidence and archaeologists' assumptions about differences among age-stages. The chapter introduces the East African Stone Tool (EAST) Typology, a framework specifically designed to improve our understanding of stone tool variation.

ARTIFACT-TYPES AND INDUSTRIES

As do their colleagues in other regions, Eastern African archaeologists populate prehistoric age-stages with named industries defined in terms of lithic artifact-types. Table 5.1 lists the principal industries archaeologists currently recognize in each Eastern African age-stage, as well as some no longer widely used that appear in older literature. For brevity, the table omits named stone tool industries not in wide usage, such as those that occur at only one site or a few sites near one another in time and space.

Earlier Stone Age Lithic Technology

Most ESA lithic artifacts are short, thick flakes struck using hard-hammer percussion from pebbles, cobbles, clasts, tabular pieces, and other rocks. Such artifacts occur in every ESA assemblage (Shea 2010) (Figure 5.3). The most commonly recognized cores in earlier ESA assemblages are pebble-cores, choppers, discoids, and polyhedrons. Assemblages deposited after 1.7–1.8 Ma also preserve a variety of large (>100 mm) elongated retouched pieces. Archaeologists use a wide range of terms for these artifacts. This work follows precedent (Shea 2017b) and calls them long core-tools (LCTs). ESA stone-workers made LCTs in different ways. In some cases they selected rocks that were already elongated and relatively thin (Harmand 2007). In others, they shaped them from large flakes (Sharon 2010).

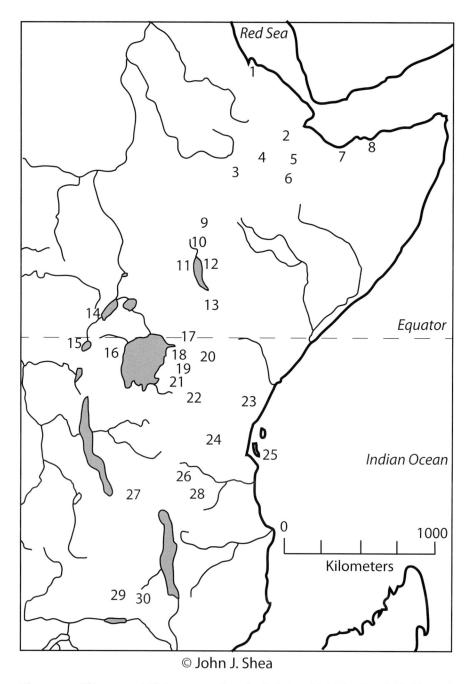

© John J. Shea

Figure 5.1 Pliocene and Pleistocene archaeological sites. (1) Abdur Reef; (2) Afar and
Middle Awash Sites (Gona, Hadar); (3) Central Ethiopia Rift Valley Sites (Melka
Kunture, Gadeb, Gademotta, Kulkuletti, K'one); (4) Hugub; (5) Meiso sites; (6) Porc
Epic Cave, Goda Buticha; (7) Las Geel Shelter 7; (8) Midhishi 2; (9) Mochena
Borago; (10) Lower Omo Valley and Environs Sites (Omo Shungura, Omo Kibish,
Fejej, Konso-Gardula); (11) West Turkana Sites (Lomekwi 3, Naiyena Engol 2,
Lokalalei 2, Kokiselei 4); (12) East Turkana sites (Koobi Fora, Ileret); (13) West Baringo

Archaeologists recognize a variety of LCT types (protobifaces, picks, handaxes, and cleavers), differentiating them by size, shape, and other criteria (Figure 5.4). The earliest LCTS are relatively large and thick, with sinuous worked edges that appear shaped solely by hard-hammer percussion. Younger specimens' sizes vary widely. Some Middle Pleistocene LCTs exhibit broad and deeply invasive flake scars characteristic of soft-hammer percussion. Large flakes with smaller-scale retouch appear around the same time, too, but archaeologists differ in what they call these artifacts, and whether they count them as LCTs. All these "large elongated retouched pieces" (LERPs) artifacts grade into one another. The archaeological consensus holds that LCTs, LERPs, and similar artifacts differ from older and penecontemporaneous ones in showing clear evidence for the patterned imposition of nonintrinsic shape: that is, shapes not predictable from raw material properties.

Also beginning around 1.8 Ma, ESA assemblages preserve more orthogonally retouched pieces (scrapers, truncations, backed pieces, notches, denticulates, awls, etc.) as well as artifacts shaped by extensive percussion (spheroids and subspheroids).

Since the 1960s, archaeologists have assigned ESA lithic assemblages dating between 1.7–2.5 Ma to the Oldowan Industry (see Figure 5.3). Recent years have seen the Oldowan joined by older Pre-Oldowan and Lomekwian industries. The earliest of these, the Lomekwian, features relatively large cobbles and flakes struck from them. Pre-Oldowan assemblages differ from Oldowan ones, mainly in displaying (subjectively assessed) inferior stoneworking skills, such as frequent occurrences of "stacks" and relatively large hinge- and step-terminated fractures. All these assemblages feature pebble-cores and flakes and stone percussors. Developed Oldowan and Early Acheulian (also spelled Acheulean) industries appear after 1.7–1.8 Ma. Developed Oldowan assemblages feature elongated discoids/protobifaces, spheroids, and retouched pieces. Acheulian assemblages feature these artifacts, too, but also LCTs (see Figure 5.4).

Observing that Developed Oldowan assemblages appeared earlier than Early Acheulian ones at Olduvai Gorge, Mary Leakey (1971) treated them as distinct and successive industries (sometimes calling them "cultures"). Subsequent research has closed the gaps between first-appearance dates for the two

Figure 5.1 (*cont.*) Kapthurin Formation Sites; (14) Matupi Cave; (15) Ishango II; (16) Nyabosusi; (17) Chesowanja, Muringa Rockshelter, Songhor; (18) Kanjera, Muguruk, Nyamita, Rusinga Island Sites, Simbi; (19) Enkapune Ya Muto, Lukenya Hill, Nasera, Mumba, Prolonged Drift, Nderit Drift; (20) Isenya, Olorgesailie, Kilombe, Kariandusi, Cartwright's Site, Prospect Farm; (21) Kirumi Isamburira; (22) Olduvai Gorge, Peninj, Lake Manuyara Makuyuni Sites; (23) Mtongwe, Panga ya Saidi; (24) Kisese II, Magubike; (25) Kuumbi Cave; (26) Isimila; (27) Kalambo Falls; (28) Mlambasi Rockshelter; (29) Twin Rivers, Mumbwa Cave; (30) Kalemba Cave.

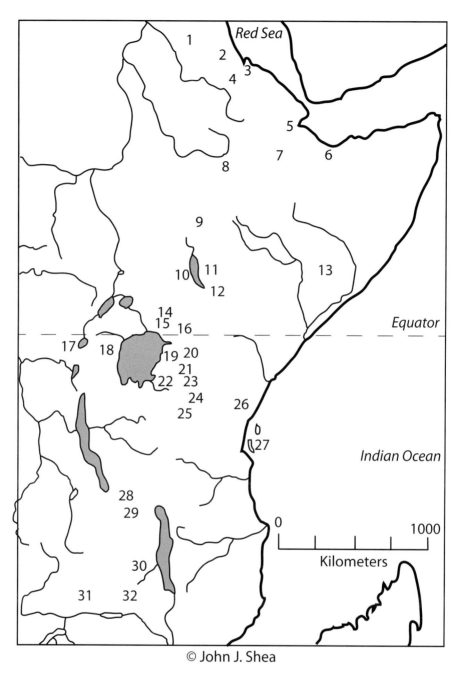

© John J. Shea

Figure 5.2 Holocene archaeological sites. (1) Mahal Teglinos (Kassala); (2) Sembel, Kokan; (3) Gehlalo, Misse East, Asfet; (4) Aksum, Baahti Nebait, Gobedra, Anger Baahti, Seglamen, Medogwe, Mai Agam; (5) Asa Kona, Wakrita; (6) Las Geel Shelter 7; (7) Goda Buticha, Lake Besaka; (8) Bulbula River Sites; (9) Mochena Borago; (10) Lothagam, Lopoy; (11) East Turkana Sites (GaJi 1, GaJi 11, GaJi 14, Dongodien, FwJi 5), Lowasera; (12) Kulchurdo Rockshelter; (13) Bur Hakaba, Bur Eibe; (14) Rangi; (15); Abindu, Agoro, Jawuoyo, Nyaidha, Randhore, Rangong, Haa, Usengi,

TABLE 5.1 *Eastern African named stone tool industries.*

Age-stage	Industry names still in use★	Industry names no longer used
Earlier Stone Age	Lomekwian (K)	Kafuan (R)
	Pre-Oldowan (R)	Chellean (R)
	Oldowan (R)	Chelles-Acheulean (R)
	Developed Oldowan (R)	Fauresmith (K)
	Acheulian (R)	Acheulo-Levalloisian (R)
Middle Stone Age	Sangoan (R)	Tumbian (U)
	Lupemban (R)	Levalloisian (KTU)
		Still Bay/Stillbay (R)
		Mousterian (KT)
		Nanyukian (K)
Later Stone Age	Tshitolian (UZ)	Magosian (KTU)
	Eburran Phases 1–4 (KT)	Wilton (KTU)
		Hargesian (H)
Neolithic	Elementeitan (KT)	Kageran (U)
	Savanna Pastoral Neolithic (KT)	Njoroan (K)
		Doian (H)
	Eburran Phase 5 (KT)	Wilton – Neolithic A/B (KTU)
		Kenya Aurignacian/Capsian (KT)
		Gumban A/B (aka "Stone Bowl Culture") (KT)

Note: This list excludes most industries that have been identified at only one site or a few sites located close to one another. Key: H = "Horn of Africa" (Eritrea, Ethiopia, Djibouti, Somalia), K = Kenya, R = Region-wide usage, T = Tanzania, U = Uganda, Z= Zambia.

industries, and they now overlap completely in time and space at regional scales. Archaeologists do not usually call assemblages younger than 1.0 Ma Developed Oldowan, but instead refer everything younger than this date up to 0.2–0.3 Ma as various kinds of regional "Acheulian" industries. Although Developed Oldowan is firmly entrenched in older literature (and among older researchers), one sees it less and less in recent literature.

Some archaeologists differentiate an Early Acheulian industry featuring picks and other thick LCTs, a Middle Acheulian featuring thinner cleavers and

Figure 5.2 (*cont.*) Wadh Lang'o; (16) Deloraine, Laikipia; (17) Ishango II; (18) Nsongezi; (19) Gogo Falls, Narosura, Ngamuriak, Lemek, Oldorotura, Sugenya; (20) Maasai Gorge Cave, Gable's Cave, Tunnel Rock Shelter, Hyrax Hill, Salasun, Ngamuriak, Njoro River Cave, Ndabibi, Ilkek (Gilgil); (21) Enkapune ya Muto, Seronera, Nasera, Mumba, Jangwani, Prolonged Drift, Nderit Drift, Ngorongoro; (22) Kirumi Isamburira; (23) Luxmanda; (24) Baura, Lusangi, Markasi Lusangi; (25) Mlambasi, Kwa Mwango-Isanzu, Kadanga; (26) Tsavo, Panga ya Saidi; (27) Kuumbi Cave; (28) Kalambo Falls; (29) Mwela Rockshelter (30) Thandwe Cave; (31) Gwisho; (32) Mumbwa Cave, Kalemba Cave, Makewe Cave.

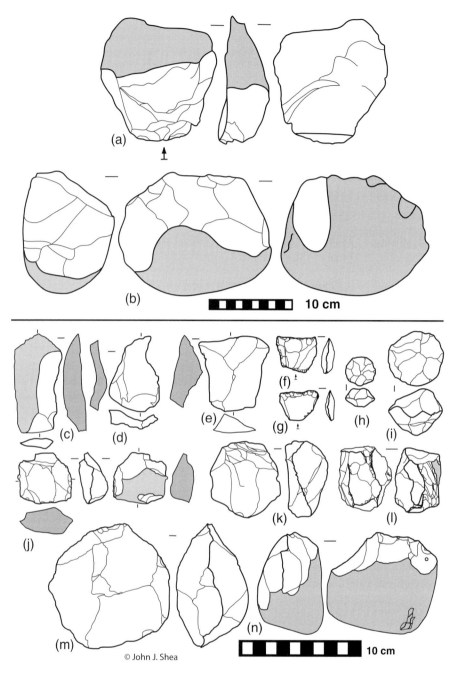

Figure 5.3 Earlier Stone Age Lomekwian (a–b) and Oldowan (c–n) artifacts. Large flake (a), large unifacial chopper (b), flakes (c–g), retouched pieces (f–g), micro-core/ discoid (h–i), bifacial hierarchical cores (j–k), polyhedron (l), discoid (m), bifacial chopper (n). Sources: Lomekwi 3, Kenya (a–b), KBS Formation Sites, East Turkana, Kenya (c–e, j) and Olduvai Gorge, DK Site in Bed I (f, g, k–n) and BK Site in Bed II (h–i). Note differences in scales above and below the horizontal line. References: Harmand, et al. (2015), Isaac and Isaac (1997), Leakey (1971)

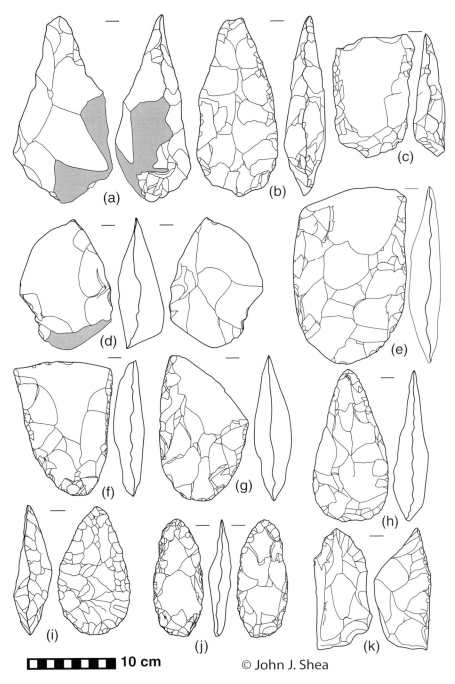

10 cm © John J. Shea

Figure 5.4 Earlier Stone Age large elongated retouched pieces. Pick (a), handaxes (b, h, i), cleavers (c, e, f), large backed/thinned piece (d), knife (g), lanceolate (j), core-axe (k). Sources: Olduvai Gorge, Tanzania (a–c), Kalambo Falls, Zambia (d–h, j–k), Kariandusi, Kenya (i). References: Leakey (1931), Leakey (1965), Clark (2001)

handaxes with an "S-twist" edge-profile, and a Later Acheulian with smaller and more sharply tipped "Micoquian" handaxes (Sahnouni et al. 2013). Micoquian handaxes (named for the French site, La Micoque) feature concave convergent lateral edges.

The older literature describes minimally modified pre-Acheulian stone tools as belonging to a "Kafuan" Industry. Archaeologists recovered few Kafuan tools from controlled excavation, and many appear to be naturally fractured rocks. The term "Kafuan" has largely faded from use.

When archaeologists describe ESA tools, they often use Mary Leakey's (1971) typology for Olduvai Gorge or Bordes' (1961) typology for European Lower and Middle Paleolithic artifacts (Debénath and Dibble 1994).

Middle Stone Age Lithic Technology

Middle Stone Age lithic technology differs from its ESA precursor in several ways (Clark 1988). Large LCTs continue to be made and discarded, but they appear mainly in older (>100 Ka) assemblages (see Figures 5.5 and 5.6). Small LCTs (Micoquian handaxes) persist into later MSA contexts. These range between short, wide, and thick pieces that recall ESA protobifaces and narrow, thin, and elongated ones that grade into lanceolates and foliate points. MSA assemblages feature many "prepared" cores and flakes struck from them. These prepared cores are relatively flat in cross-section. A series of shorter flakes struck from one side of its edge allow stoneworkers to detach broader and more deeply invasive flakes from the other. The more invasive flakes usually feature facetted striking platforms. Some MSA assemblages preserve evidence for prismatic blade core reduction. Prismatic blade cores are cores from which stoneworkers have detached a series of blades. Blades are relatively long flakes with parallel lateral edges and dorsal flake scars aligned parallel the flake's long axis. Distinctively MSA retouched pieces include core-axes, foliate points, and flake-points. Core-axes are elongated and feature a convex retouched edge at one end. Foliate points are extensively, bifacially, and invasively retouched pieces. Flake-points are triangular flakes with convergent distal retouch. These two point types grade into one another and with smaller LCTs. A few assemblages preserve backed and truncated pieces much like Later Stone Age microliths, only larger. Some MSA assemblages feature "grindstones" – tabular rocks and other stones with flat-abraded surfaces but little or no other evidence of shaping. Pitted stones, rocks damaged from focused percussion on small areas of their surface, occur as well. Although textbook illustrations of MSA artifacts emphasize larger and more extensively retouched artifacts, small (<30 mm long) cores, flakes, and retouched pieces appear in many if not most Eastern African MSA lithic assemblages. It is not yet clear whether such miniaturized artifacts are more common in recent MSA assemblages than they are in older ones or, indeed, among their ESA antecedents.

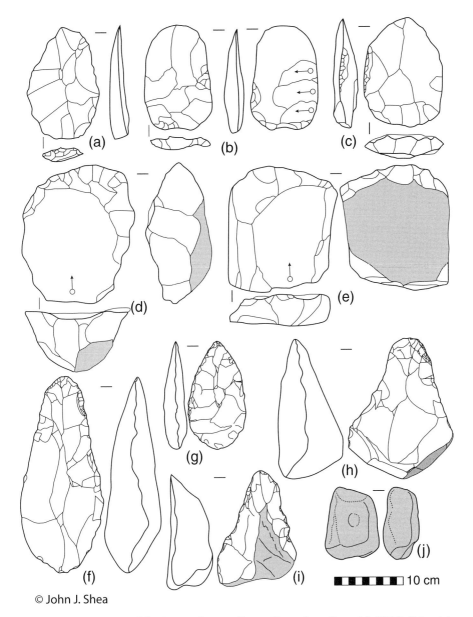

© John J. Shea

Figure 5.5 Large Middle Stone Age artifacts. Central preferential BHC flake (a), Dorsally and basally thinned piece (b), Central preferential BHC flake/sidescraper (c), Preferential bifacial hierarchical core (d), Recurrent unidirectional laminar bifacial hierarchical core (e), Bifacially retouched celt (f), Handaxe (g), Wedge-shaped core-axes (h–i), Tabular surface percussor/ "pitted stone" (j). Sources: Kapthurin Formation, Lake Baringo, Kenya (a–e), Kalambo Falls, Zambia (f–j). References: Clark (2001), Tryon, et al., (2005)

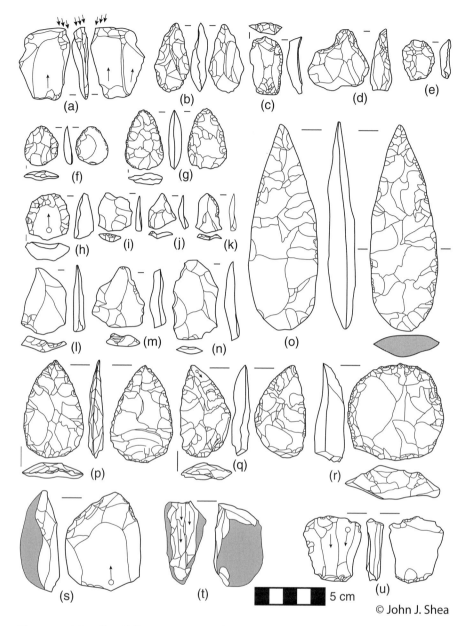

Figure 5.6 Small Middle Stone Age artifacts. Burin on a bipolar flake-core (a), Foliate points (b, g, o, p, q,) Scrapers (c, d, e, r), Dorsally and basally thinned piece (f), Bifacial hierarchical cores (h, s), Flakes struck from bifacial hierarchical cores (i–n), Unifacial hierarchical core (t), Core-on-flake (u). Sources: Mumba Rockshelter, Tanzania (a–e), Aduma Sites, Middle Awash Valley, Ethiopia (f–g), Lower Omo Valley, Kibish Formation, Ethiopia (h–o), Gademotta, Ethiopia (p–u). References: Mehlman (1989), Yellen, et al., (2005), Shea (2008), Wendorf and Schild (1974)

Archaeologists consider the Sangoan Industry transitional between the ESA and MSA. Quintessentially Sangoan stone tools include large picks and thick core-axes. Prominent numbers of picks, core-axes, core-scrapers, and other relatively large "heavy-duty" core-tools among Sangoan assemblages, such as those from Sango Bay, Uganda, and Kalambo Falls, Zambia, led many early prehistorians to think this industry reflected a forest adaptation marked by intense woodworking. Although this remains a possibility, these Sangoan tools' actual functions remain unknown.

Stone tools of the Lupemban Industry typically follow Sangoan ones, but only a few Lupemban assemblages come from secure stratigraphic contexts (Taylor 2016). Diagnostic Lupemban stone tools include large, elongated, and bifacially worked "lanceolate" points. Archaeologists assign MSA assemblages younger than 100 Ka to a variety of local named stone tool industries. These "later MSA" assemblages' composition varies widely with little obvious geographic or chronological patterning (Blinkhorn and Grove 2018). Few named MSA industries appear at more than one site or site complex located more than 50 km apart from one another.

Some older works identify an MSA/LSA "transitional" industry called the Magosian (after Magosi Springs, Uganda). Since the original Magosian assemblage was shown to be a geological mixture of MSA and LSA artifacts, the term has largely dropped from use.

When Eastern African archaeologists describe MSA artifacts, they typically do so using English-equivalent terms for artifact-types in Bordes' typology (1961, see Debénath and Dibble 1994).

Later Stone Age Lithic Technology

Later Stone Age (LSA) assemblages preserve more evidence for prismatic blade core reduction than MSA assemblages, but relatively flat discoidal cores remain common. Blades with plain, dihedral, and abraded striking platforms replace facetted-platform flakes. Retouched artifacts include many tools with steep orthogonal retouch, such as backed knives and truncations (Figures 5.7 and 5.8). Many of the ways in which LSA artifacts differ from MSA ones involve systematic small stone tool production. Such lithic miniaturization is most obvious in the enormous numbers of geometric microliths and small bipolar cores-on-flakes (aka "scaled pieces"/*outils écaillées*) that occur in virtually every LSA assemblage, as well as Neolithic and, to a lesser extent, Iron Age ones. Some LSA assemblages feature groundstone artifacts with evidence of use-related abrasion and some degree of purposeful shaping, as well as grooved and perforated stones.

Eastern Africa has very few named regional-scale LSA stone tool industries. As in the later MSA, named LSA industries are mostly local rather than regional phenomena. Tshitolian assemblages come mainly from sites in the

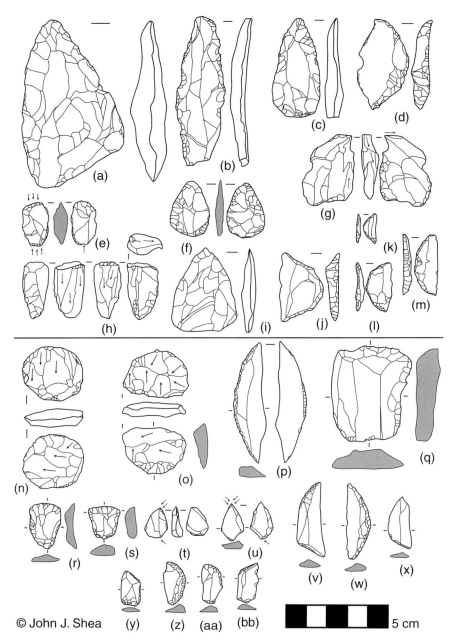

© John J. Shea

5 cm

Figure 5.7 MSA/LSA (a–m, above line) and Pleistocene Later Stone Age (l–bb, below line) flaked stone artifacts. Thinned biface (a f, i)), Double scraper (b), Convergent scraper (c), Backed/truncated piece/microlith (d, j–m, p, v–bb), Bipolar core (e), Burin (g, t–u), Bladelet core (h), Discoidal/radial core (n–o), Endscraper (q–s). Sources: Mumba Rockshelter, Tanzania (a–d, g, i–m), Nasera Rockshelter, Tanzania (e–f, h), Enkapune Ya Muto, Kenya (n–bb). References: Ambrose (1998), Mehlman (1989)

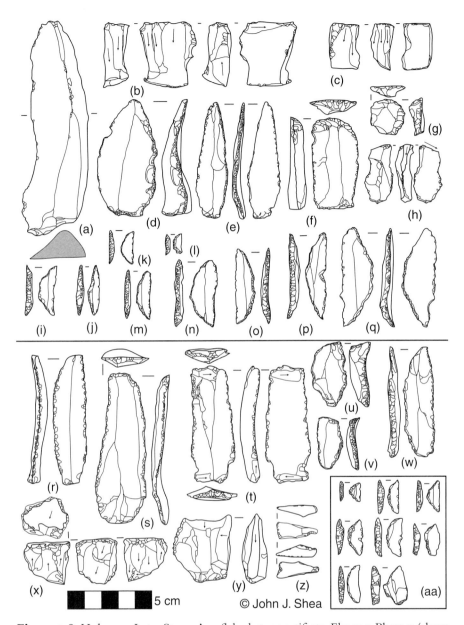

Figure 5.8 Holocene Later Stone Age flaked stone artifacts, Eburran Phase 2 (above line), Elementeitan (below line). Large blades with lateral edge damage and/or distal retouch (a, r), Burin/blade cores on flakes (b, c), Backed flakes/blades (d, e, w), Endscrapers (f–g, s, u–v), Burin on flake/blade (h, t, y), Backed/truncated pieces/geometric microliths (i–q, aa), Bladelet core (x), Blade segment (z). Source: Maasai Gorge Rockshelter, Kenya. References: Ambrose (1985)

Congo. LSA industries from the Kenyan and Tanzanian Rift Valley deserve a short comment for historical reasons, and because their terminology has undergone major reorganization. In his first synthesis of the Kenyan Stone Age, Louis Leakey (1931) named several MSA and LSA stone tool industries by attaching the prefix "Kenya" to names of industries known from other regions, such as the Aurignacian (France), the Still Bay ("Stillbay" in some sources), and the Wilton (both from South Africa). During the 1940s, he renamed the Kenya Aurignacian the "Kenya Capsian" after a north African industry. In place of the Kenya Aurignacian/Kenya Capsian, Eastern African archaeologists now use the term "Eburran Industry" for the stone tool assemblages in the core area around Mt. Eburru in western Kenya (Wilshaw 2016). Neither Kenya Stillbay nor Kenya Wilton enjoys much use any longer.

Some researchers working in Kenya and Tanzania highlands describe LSA assemblages as phases of an Eburran Industry (Ambrose 1984). Assemblages described as Eburran Phases 1–4 date from early to mid-Holocene times (ca. 12–6 Ka Cal. BP). These earlier phases contain variable numbers of long and short backed/truncated pieces ("crescents"), and the typological differences among them remain less than clear. Phase 4, dating to around 6–7.5 Ka Cal. BP witnesses a reduction in these artifacts' sizes and increased use of the term "microlith" for them. Phase 5 assemblages are Neolithic (see below).

When archaeologists describe LSA stone tools, many incorporate aspects of Tixier's (1963) North African typology and the typology in Nelson's unpublished doctoral dissertation (1973, see also Merrick 1975). Mehlman's (1989) unpublished doctoral dissertation presents a thorough discussion of LSA artifact types and a table attempting a concordance among different typologies.

Neolithic Stone Tools

Neolithic ceramic wares are more chronologically diagnostic than Neolithic stone tools. As a result, archaeologists group Neolithic assemblages (and the Iron Age ones that follow them) based on their ceramics rather than their lithic assemblage characteristics (Phillipson 1977b, Ashley and Grillo 2015).

Neolithic flaked stone tools differ little from their LSA precursors. Many of the same types of scrapers, backed/truncated pieces, and microliths and cores that appear in LSA assemblages continue to appear in Neolithic contexts (see Figure 5.6). The most novel features of Neolithic stone technology include abraded-edge celts, stone vessels, and grinding slabs (Figures 5.9 and 5.10).

Researchers working in Kenya and Tanzania recognize three named Neolithic stone tool industries: the Elementeitan Industry, the Savanna Pastoral Neolithic, and the Eburran Phase 5 (sometimes divided into Phases 5A and 5B) (Ambrose 1983). All of these assemblage-groups preserve evidence for blade production, microlithic backing/truncation, scrapers, burins, scaled pieces (bipolar cores on flakes), and stone vessel production. All appear together with

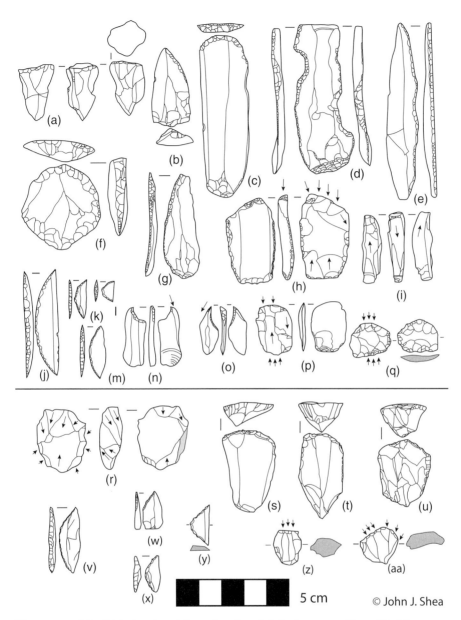

Figure 5.9 Neolithic (a–q) and Iron Age (r–aa) flaked stone artifacts. Bladelet cores (a, z–aa), Backed pieces/microliths (b, e, g, j–m, v–y), Endscrapers (c, f, s–u), Bipolar cores/scaled pieces (h–i, p–q), Microburins (n–o). Sources: Ngamuriak, Kenya (a–d, f–I, k–m, o–q), Hyrax Hill, Kenya (e, j, n), Goda Buticha, Ethiopia (r–aa). References: Robertshaw (1990b), Leakey et al. (1943), Leplongeon, et al. (2017)

ceramics and other evidence for pastoralism. They also differ in habitat preferences. Elementeitan and Eburran Phase 5 assemblages occur above 1,900 meters above sea level in forest and woodland/savanna ecotones. Savanna Pastoral Neolithic assemblages are found at lower elevations and in open grassland habitats.

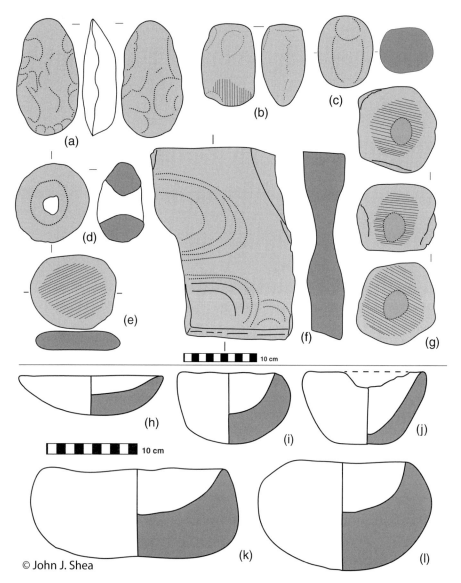

Figure 5.10 Later Stone Age, Neolithic, and Iron Age groundstone artifacts. Groundstone celts (a–b), Pestle-rubber (c), Perforated stone (d), Grindstones/querns (e–g) Stone bowls (h–l). Sources: Kalambo Falls, Zambia (a), Gwisho B, Zambia (b, f–g), Hyrax Hill, Kenya (c), Mumba Rockshelter,Tanzania (d), Ngamuriak, Kenya (e), Njoro River Cave, Kenya (h–l). References: Clark (1974), Fagan and van Noten (1971), M. Leakey and L. Leakey et al. (1943, Leakey and Leakey 1950), Mehlman (1989), Robertshaw (1990b)

Elementeitan assemblages appear mainly in the western Rift Valley between 1.3–2.5 Ka cal. BP. They feature long, broad, punch-struck blades segmented by bipolar percussion on their dorsal and ventral surfaces. Geometric microliths are generally smaller and less variable than in LSA assemblages. Many blades feature irregular retouch.

Savanna Pastoral Neolithic assemblages date to 1.3–3.3 Ka Cal. BP in the highlands and 3.3–5.3 Ka cal. BP in the lowlands. They feature short, broad blades and flakes and somewhat larger geometric microliths than Elementeitan assemblages. Backing and truncation are more formal (i.e., standardized and symmetrical) than in the Elementeitan.

Eburran Phase 5 assemblages preserve long, narrow blades and flakes and long, narrow microliths/backed pieces. Many endscrapers feature narrow ("carinated") retouched edges. Unlike in Elementeitan and Savanna Pastoral, Neolithic, Eburran Phase 5 assemblages preserve evidence for blade segmentation using the microburin truncation technique. Flakes and blades feature relatively large striking platforms with extensive facetting.

Iron Age and Historic Stone Tools

One has to look assiduously for published accounts of Iron Age excavations that include detailed descriptions of flaked stone tools. Archaeologists often describe flaked stone tools from Iron Age sites as possibly intrusive from older deposits.

Eastern Africa's Iron Age boasts few stone tools unique to that period alone. Much Iron Age stoneworking appears to have been opportunistic and not clearly patterned in time or space. Scrapers continued to be made (see Figure 5.9), but geometric microliths are uncommon. Archaeologists do not take variation among stone tools into account in formulating Iron Age cultural entities. Instead, in Ethiopia, Eritrea, and along the Red Sea coastline, archaeologists reference known historical polities, such as Aksum, its predecessors and its contemporaries. In interior Kenya, Tanzania, and adjacent regions, archaeologists define the principal cultural entities in terms of ceramic wares. The earliest of these include the Urewe (Lake Victoria Basin and western Kenya), the Kwale (eastern Kenya and Tanzania), and the Lelesu (interior southern Kenya and western Tanzania). Tana ceramics occur in the foundational levels of many coastal sites, attesting to indigenous African involvement in the formation of Swahili coastal towns and cities.

Stone tools remained in wide use up to about 1000 AD, but afterward, as iron production increased, metal implements seem to have replaced stone tools. By the time European powers established colonies in the region during the nineteenth and early twentieth centuries, stone tool production had largely ceased in all but the most remote areas. Louis Leakey's (1977) ethnography of the turn-of-the-century Kikuyu people of Kenya does not list stone tools among their material culture. Leakey's autobiography, *White African* (1937), further notes that the Kikuyu, among whom he grew up, did not recognize obsidian tools eroding from archaeological sites as artifacts.

Ethiopian hide-workers continue to use hafted flaked stone scrapers to this day (Gallagher 1977, Brandt and Weedman 1997, Weedman 2006, Weedman

Arthur 2010, 2018), but other than this, ethnographic Eastern African flaked stone tool use seems largely opportunistic and latent. That is, people know they can make a stone cutting tool when the need for one arises, but they rarely do so when metal knives are available.

THE EASTERN AFRICAN PREHISTORIC STONEWORKING SURVEY

Materials: The Sample Assemblages

How well does the account of the Eastern African lithic record, recounted above, compare with the actual evidence for change and variability in prehistoric stoneworking? To answer this question, this work compiles data on the more than 250 Eastern African lithic assemblages, hereafter the Eastern African Prehistoric Stoneworking Survey (EAPSS, see Appendix 1). Because the EAPSS is far too large to print in this work, Cambridge University Press has posts it on its website for *Prehistoric Stone Tools of Eastern Africa*. Table 5.2 lists all the assemblages included in this comparative study, together with information about their ages and published references.

The overwhelming majority of the data in the EAPSS and Table 5.2 come from published works (monographs and peer-reviewed journal papers), but they include a few from doctoral dissertations available online from ProQuest™ and similar sources. That these are only works in English, French, and German reflects the author's linguistic limitations. The EAPSS does not include assemblages comprised solely of surface collections, but it accepts most arguments for linking surface collections to excavated artifacts at particular sites.

The EAPSS generally takes published dates and attributions to age-stages at face value. Dates for these assemblages listed in the EAPSS arise from a variety of sources, including radiopotassium, radiocarbon, Uranium-series, optically stimulated luminance, obsidian hydration, and stratigraphic correlations. Blank spaces in the older/younger ages columns indicate age estimates based on unclear evidence or artifact typology. For sites dating to 40 Ka and younger, the EAPSS converts all dates to calibrated calendar years before the present (using CalPal Online Version 1.5). In spite of all precautions and efforts to make the data in the EAPSS representative, it remains a judgmental sample. Statistics derived from it have to be treated cautiously.

Figures 5.1 and 5.2 indicate locations of all the source sites for the lithic samples in the EAPSS. Ethiopian, Kenyan, and Tanzanian assemblages account for fully (81%) of these samples (Table 5.3). This probably reflects the early start and sustained pace of archaeological research in these countries and their relative political stability.

In selecting sites to include in the sample, one sought rough numeric parity among different age-stages (Table 5.4). The EAPSS divides the Earlier Stone

TABLE 5.2 *Stone tool assemblages in the EAPSS and included in this comparative study.*

Age-stage and Country	Sample	Date Ka BP	Reference
EARLY ESA			
Ethiopia	Fejej FJ-Ia	1900	Asfaw et al. (1991), Barsky et al. (2011)
	Gona (Afar Dist.)	2300–2600	Semaw et al., (2009)
	Gona (Busidima Formation)	2500–2600	Semaw et al., (2009)
	Hadar (Afar Dist.)	2300	Kimbel et al., (1996), Goldman-Neuman and Hovers (2012)
	Hadar, Afar (AL 894)	2600	Hovers (2009)
	Melka Kunture >1.6 Ma	1600–2000	Chavaillon and Piperno (2004)
	Omo Shungura Formation Member F	2200–2400	Merrick and Merrick (1976) Howell et al., (1987), Delagnes et al., (2011), de la Torre (2004)
Kenya	East Turkana/Koobi Fora Formation, KBS Member Burgi Fmn.	1600–1800	Isaac (1997)
	Kanjera	2000	Plummer et al. (1999)
	Kanjera South	2000	Bishop et al. (2006)
	West Turkana Lomekwi 3	3300	Harman, et al. (2015)
	West Turkana Naiyena Engol 2	1700–1800	Roche et al. (2018)
	West Turkana Lokalalei 1	2300–2400	Kibunjia (1994)
	West Turkana Lokalalei 2C	2300–2400	Delagnes and Roche (2005)
Tanzania	Olduvai Gorge Bed I and Lower Bed II	1860	Leakey (1971), Leakey and Roe (1994), Blumenschine et al. (2003), Domínguez-Rodrigo et al. (2007)
Uganda	Nyabosusi NY 18	1500–2000	Texier (1995)
LATER ESA			
Ethiopia	Gadeb 8D–F	700	Kurashina (1978), de la Torre (2011)
	Gadeb 2B, C, E	700–1500	Kurashina (1978), de la Torre (2011)
	Hugub	500–600	Gilbert et al. (2016)
	Konso-Gardula	100–1600	Beyene et al. (2013)
	Konso-Gardula KGA6-A1 Locus C	1600–1800	Beyene et al. (2013)
	Melka Kunture <1.6 Ma	700–1600	Chavaillon and Piperno (2004)
	Middle Awash Bouri A1 (BOU-A1)	1000	Schick and Toth (2017)

(continued)

TABLE 5.2 *(continued)*

Age-stage and Country	Sample	Date Ka BP	Reference
	Middle Awash Hargufina A4 (HAR-A4)	500	Schick and Toth (2017)
	Mieso Sites 7 and 31	200–800	de la Torre et al. (2014)
Kenya	Chesowanja Chemoigut Fmn.	1400–1600	Gowlett et al. (1981)
	Chesowanja Chesowanja Fmn.	500	Gowlett et al. (1981)
	East Turkana, Koobi Fora Formation, Okote Member	800–1600	Isaac (1997)
	Isenya Units V and VI	900–100	Roche et al. (1988)
	Kariandusi	900–1100	Shipton (2011)
	Kilombe EH and AH	≥700	Gowlett (1993)
	Olorgesailie, Olorgesailie Formation Mbrs. 1–14	500–1200	Isaac (1977), Potts et al. (1999)
	West Lake Baringo lower K3 GnJh 42, 50	500	Johnson and McBrearty (2010)
	West Turkana Kokiselei 1, 5–6	1760	Lepre et al. (2011)
	West Turkana Kokiselei 4	1760	Lepre et al. (2011)
	West Turkana Nadung'a 4	700	Delagnes et al. (2006)
Tanzania	Isimila Sands 1–3	≥260	Howell et al.(1962)
	Makuyuni sites, Lake Manyara	400–600	Giemsch et al. (2018)
	Olduvai Beds III–IV	700–1200	Leakey and Roe (1994)
	Olduvai Mid-Upper Bed II	1200–1600	Leakey (1971)
	Peninj, EN & ES sites	1200–1500	Domínguez-Rodrigo et al. (2009)
	Peninj, ST Site Complex	1200–1500	de la Torre and Mora (2009)
Zambia	Kalambo Falls, Final/Late ESA	250	Clark (2001)
ESA/MSA TRANSITION			
Kenya	Muguruk Member 2	200–300	McBrearty (1981a)
	Muguruk Member 4	200	McBrearty (1981a)
	West Lake Baringo Komilot Locus 1 and 2	200–300	Tryon et al. (2005)
	West Lake Baringo upper K3 -LHA, GnJh17	300–500	Tryon et al. (2005)
Zambia	Kalambo Falls, Sangoan	200–250	Clark (2001)
	Twin Rivers	170–266	Bartham (2000)
MIDDLE STONE AGE			
Eritrea	Abdur Reef Limestone Complex	125	Bruggemann et al. (2004)

(continued)

TABLE 5.2 (*continued*)

Age-stage and Country	Sample	Date Ka BP	Reference
Ethiopia	Gademotta (ETH-72)	104–276	Wendorf and Schild (1974), Sahle et al. (2014), Douze and Delagnes (2016).
	Gademotta GDM 7, 10	≥183	Sahle et al. (2014)
	K'one	>40–<200	Kurashina (1978)
	Kulkuletti (ETH 72-9)	104–276	Wendorf and Schild (1974)
	Middle Awash Aduma Ardu Beds	80–100	Yellen et al. (2005)
	Middle Awash Upper Herto Formation	154–160	Clark et al. (2003)
	Omo Kibish Members 1–3	104–195	Shea (2008)
	Porc Epic Cave	60–80	Pleurdeau (2005)
Kenya	Cartwright's Site	440–557	Waweru (2002, 2007)
	East Turkana FwJi 1	>30?	Kelly (1996)
	East Turkana FwJi 2	>30?	Kelly (1996)
	East Turkana FwJi 3	>30?	Kelly (1996)
	East Turkana FxJj 61	>30?	Kelly (1996)
	East Turkana FxJj 66	>30?	Kelly (1996)
	East Turkana GaJj 17	>30?	Kelly (1996)
	Enkapune Ya Muto Levels GG/GL	≥50	Ambrose (1998)
	Lukenya Hill (GvJm 22) Occ G.	>47	Tryon et al. (2015)
	Lukenya Hill (GvJm 22) Occ. F	26–46	Merrick (1975), Gramly (1976), Tryon et al. (2015)
	Mtongwe Upper Group	5–40	Omi (1988)
	Muringa Rockshelter Levels 9–10	Typol	Sutton (1973)
	Olorgesailie, Oltulelei Formation	295–325	Deino, et al. (2018: Supplementary Information)
	Panga Ya Saidi Levels 13–16	59–62	Shipton et al. (2018)
	Panga Ya Saidi Levels 17–19	73–77	Shipton et al. (2018)
	Prolonged Drift (GrJi 11)	>30?	Merrick (1975)
	Prospect Farm Spit 16	>30?	Merrick (1975)
	Prospect Farm Spits 22–23	>30?	Merrick (1975)
	Prospect Farm Spits 9–11	>30?	Merrick (1975)
	Rusinga Island, Nyamita Main Site	36–49	Blegen et al. (2017)
	Rusinga Island, Wakondo Beds, Bovid Hill Site	69	Jenkins et al. (2017)
	Simbi	40–200	McBrearty (1992)
	Songhor	>40–<300	McBrearty (1981b)

(*continued*)

TABLE 5.2 (*continued*)

Age-stage and Country	Sample	Date Ka BP	Reference
	West Baringo Kapthurin Formation, Sibiloi School Road Site (GnJh 79)	200	Blegen (2017)
	West Lake Baringo, Kapthurin Formation, upper Member K3, GnJh 17, GnJh 33	300–500	Leakey et al. (1969), Cornellison (1992), Tryon et al. (2005)
	West Lake Baringo, Kapthurin Formation, upper Member K4 Komilot (GnJh-74) Locus 1 and 2	300–500	McBrearty (2005), Tryon et al. (2005)
Somalia	Midhishi 2	>40–<300	Gresham (1984)
Tanzania	Kisese Rockshelter II Units XXII–XXVII	45	Tryon et al. (2018)
	Mumba Cave Unit VI-A (Kisele Industry)	64	Mehlman (1989) Marks and Conard (2008), Gliganic et al. (2012)
	Mumba Cave Unit VI-B (Sankazo Industry)	≥64	Mehlman (1989) Marks and Conard (2008), Gliganic et al. (2012)
	Nasera Rockshelter Levels 12–25	56–73	Mehlman (1989), Tryon and Faith (2016)
	Olduvai Ndutu Beds	50–200	M. Leakey et al. (1972), Eren et al. (2014)
Zambia	Kalambo Falls, MSA-Lupemban	50–200	Clark (2001)
	Kalemba Cave, Unit G	35	Phillipson (1976)
	Mumbwa Cave, Unit IX	170	Barham (2000), Clark (1942)
	Mumbwa Cave, Unit VII–VIII	105–130	Barham (2000), Clark (1942)
	Mumbwa Cave, Unit X–XIV	171	Barham (2000)
MSA/LSA TRANSITION			
Ethiopia	Goda Buticha	25–63	Leplongeon et al. (2017)
	Mochena Borago Lower T-Group	48–50	Brandt et al. (2017)
	Mochena Borago R-Group	37–43	Brandt et al. (2017)
	Mochena Borago S-Group	44–46	Brandt et al. (2017)
	Mochena Borago Upper T-Group	48–49	Brandt et al. (2017)

(*continued*)

TABLE 5.2 (*continued*)

Age-stage and Country	Sample	Date Ka BP	Reference
Kenya	Enkapune Ya Muto Levels RBL 4.1-4.2	39–50	Ambrose (1998), personal communication May 22, 2018
	Panga Ya Saidi Levels 10–12	49–51	Shipton et al. (2018)
Tanzania	Nasera Rockshelter Levels 6–7	25–37	Mehlman (1989), Tryon and Faith (2016)
	Nasera Rockshelter Levels 8/9–11	50–56	Mehlman (1989), Tryon and Faith (2016)
	Kalambo Falls, MSA-LSA Polungu Industry	10–20	Clark (1974)
Zambia	Kalemba Cave, Units H–K	24–25	Phillipson (1976)
	Mumbwa Cave, Unit V	40	Bartham (2000)
LATER STONE AGE			
DR Congo	Ishango II ZB (Holocene)	≤13	Mercader and Brooks (2001)
	Ishango II, NT–NFP (Late Pleistocene)	20–25	Mercader and Brooks (2001)
	Matupi Cave "Matupi Industry"	12–21	Van Noten (1982)
Eritrea	Asfet F	5–6	Beyin (2010)
	Gehlalo NW	7–8	Beyin (2010)
	Misse East	8	Beyin (2010)
Ethiopia	Baahti Nebait Levels 1–2	4	Finneran et al. (2000a)
	Baahti Nebait Levels 4–6	11–12	Finneran et al. (2000a)
	Bulbula River Late Pleistocene	33–34	Ménard et al. (2014)
	Bulbula River Pleistocene/ Holocene	11–14	Ménard et al. (2014)
	Gobedra Rockshelter Unit II b	4–5	Phillipson (1977a)
	Gobedra Rockshelter Unit III	5–7	Phillipson (1977a)
	Gobedra Rockshelter Units IV–VI	7–10	Phillipson (1977a)
	Goda Buticha	6–8	Leplongeon, et al. (2017)
	Lake Besaka, Brandt Period 1	19–22	Brandt (1982)
	Lake Besaka, Brandt Period 2	12	Brandt (1982)
	Lake Besaka, Brandt Period 3	4–11	Brandt (1982)
	Lake Besaka, Brandt Period 4	4	Brandt (1982)
	Mochena Borago SD1, SD3	1–5	Ménard (2015)

(*continued*)

TABLE 5.2 (*continued*)

Age-stage and Country	Sample	Date Ka BP	Reference
Kenya	East Turkana GaJj 1	8–9	Barthelme (1985)
	East Turkana GaJj 11	4–8	Barthelme (1985)
	Enkapune Ya Muto Levels BS 1A–RBL 2	3–6	Ambrose (1998)
	Enkapune Ya Muto Levels DBL 1.2–1.3	19–39	Ambrose (1998)
	Enkapune Ya Muto Levels RBL 2.2–3.1	6–7	Ambrose (1998)
	Gamble's Cave 2, Level 12	4–6	Leakey (1931), Ambrose (1984), Frahm and Tryon (2018)
	Gamble's Cave 2, Level 14 lower	8–9	Leakey (1931), Hivernel (1974), Ambrose (1984), Frahm and Tryon (2018)
	Gamble's Cave 2, Level 14 upper	6–8	Leakey (1931), Hivernel (1974), Ambrose (1984), Frahm and Tryon (2018)
	Lopoy	1–2	Robbins (1980)
	Lothagam Lokam	8–11	Robbins (1974), Goldstein et al. (2017)
	Lowasera	3–5	Phillipson (1977c)
	Lukenya Hill (GvJm 22) Occupation E	23–24	Merrick (1975)
	Lukenya Hill (GvJm 62) Unit A	20–21	Kusimba (2001)
	Maasai Gorge Spits 1–2	9–10	Ambrose (1985)
	Maasai Gorge Spits 12–18	2–3	Ambrose (1985)
	Maasai Gorge Spits 3–10	6–7	Ambrose (1985)
	Mtongwe Lower Group	40–200	Omi (1988)
	Muringa Rock Shelter, Levels 4–8	Typol	Sutton (1973)
	Nderit Drift (GsJi 2/T) LSA	14	Merrick (1975)
	Panga Ya Saidi Levels 1–4	1–8	Shipton (2018)
	Panga Ya Saidi Levels 5–7	15	Shipton (2018)
	Panga Ya Saidi Levels 8–9	23–33	Shipton (2018)
	Tunnel Rockshelter Layers 5–11	2–3	Sutton (1973)
Somalia	Bur Harkaba, Rifle Range Site Layer D	Typol.	Clark (1954)
	Bur Harkaba, Rifle Range Site Layer F	Typol.	Clark (1954)
	Gur Warbei/Bur Eibe "Doian"	Typol.	Clark (1954)
	Gur Warbei/Bur Eibe "Magosian"	Typol.	Clark (1954)

(*continued*)

TABLE 5.2 (*continued*)

Age-stage and Country	Sample	Date Ka BP	Reference
	Gur Warbei/Bur Eibe "Magosio-Doian"	Typol.	Clark (1954)
	Las Geel Shelter 7 Unit 708	13	Gutherz et al. (2014)
	Las Geel Shelter 7 Units 703–702	5	Gutherz et al. (2014)
	Las Geel Shelter 7 Units 709–711	13–42	Gutherz et al. (2014)
Tanzania	Baura 1 Units 1–4	3	Kessy (2013)
	Kirumi Isumbirira Levels 13–15	3	Masao (1979)
	Kirumi Isumbirira Levels 5–13	$\geq$0.2	Masao (1979)
	Kisese II Rockshelter Units III–X	18–20	Tryon et al. (2018)
	Kisese II Rockshelter Units XI–XXI	22–45	Tryon et al. (2018)
	Kuumbi Cave Phase 2	12–13	Sinclair et al. (2006), Shipton et al. (2016)
	Kuumbi Cave Phase 3	17–20	Sinclair et al. (2006), Shipton et al. (2016)
	Kwa Mwango-Isanzu	4	Masao (1979)
	Lusangi 1 Unit 1 LSA	1	Kessy (2013)
	Magubike Rockshelter	40–100	Werner and Wiloughby (2017)
	Markasi Lusangi 2 Unit 3	1–5	Kessy (2013)
	Mlambalasi Rockshelter LSA	15–20	Biittner et al. (2017)
	Mumba Cave Lower Bed III (Nasera Industry)	37	Mehlman (1989) Marks and Conard (2008), Gliganic et al. (2012)
	Mumba Cave Unit V (Mumba Industry)	49–57	Mehlman (1989) Marks and Conard (2008), Gliganic et al. (2012)
	Mumba Cave Upper Bed III (Oldeani Industry)	1–12	Mehlman (1989) Marks and Conard (2008), Gliganic et al. (2012)
	Nasera Rockshelter Level 3B	12–16	Mehlman (1989), Tryon and Faith (2016)
	Nasera Rockshelter Levels 4–5	16–24	Mehlman (1989), Tryon and Faith (2016)
	Olduvai Naisusu Beds	17	M. Leakey, et al. (1972)
Zambia	Gwisho Site A	Typol.	Gabel (1965)
	Gwisho Sites B and C	4–6	Fagan and van Noten (1971)
	Kalambo Falls, LSA-Kaposwa Industry	4–10	Clark (1974)

(*continued*)

TABLE 5.2 *(continued)*

Age-stage and Country	Sample	Date Ka BP	Reference
	Kalemba Cave, Levels 5–6	10–22	Miller (1969)
	Kalemba Cave, Levels 8–10	22–24	Miller (1969)
	Kalemba Cave, Lower Level 2	3	Miller (1969)
	Kalemba Cave, Lower Level 4	10	Miller (1969)
	Kalemba Cave, Units L–N	11–14	Phillipson (1976)
	Kalemba Cave, Units O–Q	4–6	Phillipson (1976)
	Kalemba Cave, Upper Level 4	4	Miller (1969)
	Makwe Cave, Levels 2–5	1	Phillipson (1976)
	Mumbwa Cave, Unit II–III	6	Barham (2000), Clark (1942)
	Mwela Rockshelter Level RBSD	7	Miller (1969)
LSA/NEOLITHIC			
Tanzania	Kadanga A9	0.2–4	Masao (1979)
	Kirumi Isumbirira Levels 1–4	0.2	Masao (1979)
NEOLITHIC			
Djibouti	Asa Koma	3–5	Gutherz et al. (2015)
	Wakrita	4–5	Gutherz et al. (2015)
Ethiopia	Anqer Baahti (Aksum) Context 13	4–6	Finneran et al. (2000b)
Kenya	East Turkana Dongodien (GaJj 4)	4	Barthelme (1985)
	East Turkana Ileret Stone Bowl Site (FwJj 5)	4	Barthelme (1985)
	Enkapune Ya Muto Levels ELM	3	Ambrose (1998)
	Gamble's Cave 2, Level 6	1–3	Leakey (1931), Ambrose (1984), Frahm and Tryon (2018)
	Hyrax Hill, Site I	5–6	Leakey (1943), Sutton (1998)
	Ilkek (Gilgil)	2	Brown (1966)
	Laikipia Horizon I	≥3	Siiriäinen (1984)
	Lemek NE (GuJf 13)	2	Robertshaw (1990b)
	Lemek NW (GuJf 92)	3	Robertshaw (1990b)
	Lemek West (GuJf 14)	2	Robertshaw (1990b)
	Marula	1–3	Odney-Obul (1996)
	Narosura	3	Odner (1972)
	Ndabibi	1–2	Odney-Obul (1996)
	Nderit Drift Units 25 and 13	4	Ambrose (1984)
	Ngamuriak (GuJf 6)	2	Robertshaw (1990b)
	Njoro River Cave	3	Leakey and Leakey (1950)

(continued)

TABLE 5.2 (*continued*)

Age-stage and Country	Sample	Date Ka BP	Reference
	Oldorotua 1 (GuJe 4)	1–2	Robertshaw (1990b)
	Oldorotua 3 (GuJf 66)	1–2	Robertshaw (1990b)
	Olopilukunya	2	Robertshaw (1990b)
	Prolonged Drift (GrJi 11), Formation C	2–3	Nelson (1973), Bower et al. (1977), Larson, (1986)
	Salasun	1–3	Bower et al. (1977), Ambrose (1984)
	Sambo Ngige (GuJf 17)	1–2	Robertshaw (1990b)
	Sugenya	2–3	Goldstein (2018)
	Tsavo Wright's PN sites	1–6	Wright (2005)
Tanzania	Luxmanda	2–3	Grillo, et al. (2018)
	Nasera Rockshelter Level 3A	1–4	Mehlman (1989), Tryon and Faith (2016)
	Ngorongoro Burial Mounds	2	Leakey (1967), Sassoon (1968)
LSA/NEOLITHIC/ IRON AGE			
Kenya	Abindu Rockshelter	2	Gabel (1969)
	Agoro Rockshelter	2	Gabel (1969)
	Deloraine	1–2	Ambrose et al. (1984)
	Gogo Falls, Trench I	3–7	Robertshaw (1991)
	Gogo Falls, Trench II	2	Robertshaw (1991)
	Gogo Falls, Trench III	2	Robertshaw (1991)
	Gogo Falls, Trench V	2	Robertshaw (1991)
	Haa H1	>4.5	Seitsonen (2010)
	Haa H2	1–2	Seitsonen (2010)
	Jawuoyo Rockshelter	2	Gabel (1969)
	Laikipia Horizons II–V	0.5–3	Siiriäinen (1984)
	Nyaidha Rockshelter	2	Gabel (1969)
	Randhore Rockshelter	1	Gabel (1969)
	Rangong Rockshelter	3	Gabel (1969)
	Usengi 1-K	>5	Seitsonen (2010)
	Usengi 3-K	3	Seitsonen (2010)
	Usengi 3-U	>5	Seitsonen (2010)
	Wadh Lang'o 1	4	Seitsonen (2010)
	Wadh Lang'o 2	2	Seitsonen (2010)
Sudan	Mahal Teglinos (Kassala) [Sudan]	4	Phillipson (2017)
Tanzania	Baura 1 Units 1–4	0.4	Kessy (2013)
	Lusangi 1 Unit 1 LSA and Iron Age	1	Kessy (2013)
	Markasi Lusangi 2 Unit 3	1	Kessy (2013)
	Mlambalasi Rockshelter LSA/Iron Age	Typol.	Biittner et al. (2017)
	Seronera	1	Bower (1973)
Uganda	Nsongezi Rockshelter, Levels I–IV	0.5	Nelson (1970)

(*continued*)

TABLE 5.2 (*continued*)

Age-stage and Country	Sample	Date Ka BP	Reference
	Rangi Cave Levels II–III	0.5	Robbins et al. (1977)
Zambia	Kalemba Cave, Units R–S	0.5	Phillipson (1976)
	Kalemba Cave, Upper Level 2	1	Miller (1969)
	Mumbwa Cave, Unit I	<2	Bartham (2000)
	Thandwe Cave	1–2	Phillipson (1976)
IRON AGE			
Eritrea	Kokan Rockshelter	2	Brandt et al. (2008)
	Sembel (Asmara)	2–3	Teka and Okubatsion (2008)
Ethiopia	Aksum Site D	2–3	L. Phillipson (2009) Fattovich et al. (2012)
	Aksum Site D	1	L. Phillipson (2009) Fattovich et al. (2012)
	Aksum Site K	1	L. Phillipson (2009) Fattovich et al. (2012)
	Gobedra Rockshelter Unit I a	<3	Phillipson (1977a)
	Goda Buticha	1–2	Leplongeon et al. (2017)
	Mai Agam SU 2	2	Phillipson and Sulas (2005)
	Medogwe, Workshop Locality	1–3	Capra (2017)
Kenya	Hyrax Hill, Site II	1–2	Leakey (1943), Sutton (1998)
	Kulchurdo Rockshelter Levels 1–2	0.5	Phillipson and Gifford (1981)
	Maasai Gorge Spits 19–21	0.5–1.0	Ambrose (1985)
Tanzania	Jangwani I		Mehlman (1989)
	Kuumbi Cave Phase 1	0.5–0.6	Sinclair et al. (2006), Shipton et al. (2016)
	Malambasi Rockshelter Iron Age	0.5–1.0	Biittner et al. (2017)
Zambia	Kalambo Falls, Iron Age	0.3–2.0	Clark (1974)

Age into earlier and later phases around 1.6–1.7 Ma. Doing so follows Eastern African archaeologists' common practice of distinguishing older ESA assemblages – Oldowan, Pre-Oldowan, Lomekwian, and the like – from younger Acheulian and Developed Oldowan ones. Assemblages listed as ESA/MSA, and MSA/LSA are ones their references assign to transitional periods. Earlier ESA assemblages and Neolithic ones might appear underrepresented, but this is not actually the case. Some Plio-Pleistocene site complexes (e.g., Olduvai Gorge, East Turkana, Melka Kunture) preserve numerous assemblages from separate

TABLE 5.3 *Sample sites by country.*

Country	N	%
Djibouti	2	0.7
Democratic Republic of the Congo	3	1.1
Eritrea	6	2.2
Ethiopia	51	19.0
Kenya	119	44.6
Somalia/Somaliland	9	3.3
Sudan	1	0.4
Tanzania	45	16.9
Uganda	3	1.1
Zambia	29	10.9
Grand Total	268	100.0

TABLE 5.4 *Sample sites by age-stages.*

Age-stage	N	%
early ESA	17	6.3
later ESA	27	10.1
ESA/MSA	6	2.2
MSA	46	17.2
MSA/LSA	12	4.5
LSA	81	30.3
LSA/Neolithic	2	0.7
Neolithic	30	11.2
LSA/Neolithic/Iron Age	31	11.6
Iron Age	16	6.0
Grand Total	268	100

localities within the same geological or chronostratigraphic level that differ little from one another. Rather than listing each such site individually, and unnecessarily lengthening the EAPSS, this work combines them. Neat and tidy distinctions between Later Stone Age (LSA), Neolithic, or Iron Ages become problematical among lithic assemblages dating to mid-Holocene and onwards, <3–5 Ka. When it was not possible to attribute a lithic assemblage to only one of these age-stages (or when the reporting reference declined to do so clearly), the EAPSS assigns them to a composite LSA/Neolithic/Iron Age sample.

Methods: Stoneworking Modes A–I

To organize observations, the EAPSS uses Stoneworking Modes A–I, a framework the author has used elsewhere for surveys of the global stone tool evidence (Shea 2017a, 2017b). Stoneworking Modes A–I describe strategies

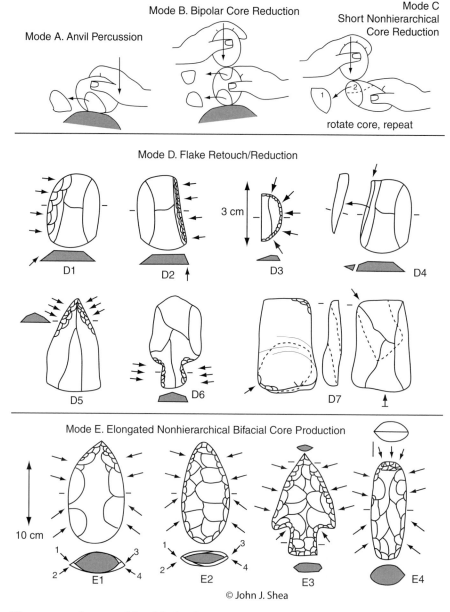

Figure 5.11 Stoneworking Modes A–E.

for modifying lithic artifacts observed among living humans and nonhuman primates, as well as those reverse-engineered from archaeological evidence (Figures 5.11 and 5.12). Stoneworking Modes A–I is not an artifact typology but a standardized set of terms for diagnosing stoneworking strategies. A strategy is one among different ways of accomplishing the same objective. To run an errand some short distance away, for example, one could either walk, ride a bicycle, or drive an automobile. Each of these strategies has

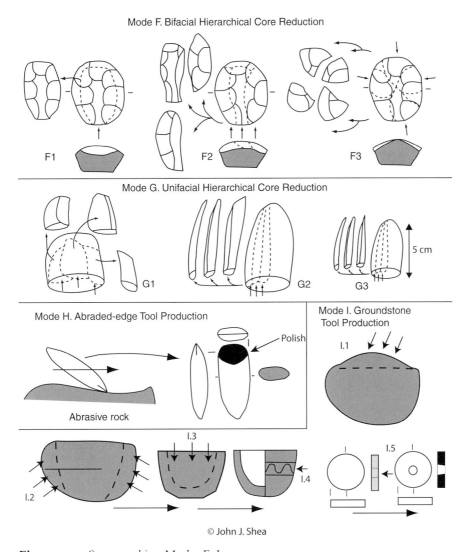

© John J. Shea

Figure 5.12 Stoneworking Modes F–I.

different associated costs (time spent, prior ownership of a bicycle or car) and
benefits (time saved, the ability to carry more things).

Current archaeological approaches to strategic variation in stoneworking
often divide this subject into techniques and methods. Techniques are different
strategies for modifying stone mechanically, such as by soft- versus hard-
hammer percussion. Methods are different sequences of operations performed
in modifying stone, such as different ways of detaching flakes from one or
another side of a worked edge or different ways of sequentially detaching flakes
from a core surface. Lithic operational chains are sequences of stoneworking
methods.

The distinctions among stoneworking Modes A–I emphasize differences in
stoneworking methods. As in the American Psychiatric Association's *Diagnostic*

and Statistical Manual (2013), some symptoms (artifact-types) indicate specific diagnoses (modes). To recognize significant differences among similar strategies, Modes A–I identifies "submodes" (indicated by Arabic numerals). Except in two cases (discussed below) Stoneworking Modes A–I do not take artifact size into account.

Mode A, *anvil percussion*, involves throwing or striking a core against another rock or some other hard substrate, such as a bedrock exposure. Diagnostic artifacts include stone percussors, hammerstones.

Mode B, *bipolar core reduction*, creates fractures by striking the uppermost surface of a core or flake that rests on a hard substrate. Diagnostic artifacts include bipolar cores, scaled pieces.

Mode C, *short nonhierarchical core reduction*, involves sequential and relatively large (>2 cm long) nonhierarchical flake removals from nonelongated clasts (rounded rocks) or angular rock fragments. Diagnostic artifacts include bifacial choppers, discoids, and polyhedrons.

Mode D, *flake retouch*, detaches relatively small (≤20 mm long) flakes from the edge of a flake or flake fragment. Such retouch can be either hierarchical or nonhierarchical. Characteristic artifacts include retouched pieces.

Submode D1, *orthogonal retouch*, creates an edge that is relatively acute in cross-section by removing a continuous series of flakes at right angles to the edge of a flake/flake fragment. Diagnostic artifacts include scrapers, notches, and denticulates.

Submodes D2 and D3 both refer to *backing/truncation*, retouch along an edge that results in edges that are relatively steep in cross-section (>70°). Submode D2, *macrolithic backing/truncation*, creates artifacts longer than 30 mm. Submode D3, *microlithic backing/truncation* results in artifacts ≤ 30 mm long. Diagnostic artifacts include backed and/or truncated pieces, geometric microliths. This size-based distinction follows common Old World archaeological practice in recognizing the production of relatively small backed/truncated pieces ("microliths") and allied tool forms as distinct from manufacturing larger backed/truncated pieces. The strongest theoretical justification for this D2/D3 distinction is that even novice stoneworkers can create small backed-truncated pieces in mere seconds (often by recourse to bipolar percussion along an edge), whereas backing/truncating larger and longer pieces requires a greater, if imprecisely quantifiable, degree of skill (Shea 2015).

Submode D4, *burination*, propagates a fracture roughly perpendicular to a flake's dorsal or ventral surface. Diagnostic artifacts include burins, burin flakes, tranchet flakes. Burin flakes grade into elongated flakes struck from cores-on-flakes (discussed below).

Submode D5, *convergent retouch*, brings together retouched edges that intersect at acute angles in both plan and profile views. Diagnostic artifacts include points, awls, and convergent scrapers.

Submode D6, *concave proximal retouch*, creates one or more symmetrically positioned concavities near a flake's striking platform. Diagnostic artifacts include tanged pieces.

Submode D7, *flake-core reduction*, detaches relatively large flakes (>20 mm long) from flake fragments. Diagnostic artifacts include cores-on flakes. As noted above, burins grade into cores-on-flakes and vice versa.

Mode E, *elongated nonhierarchical bifacial core reduction*, involves nonhierarchical flake detachments from an elongated piece of stone (a core, flake, or tabular rock fragment) in such a way that flakes propagate roughly perpendicularly to the core's long axis.

Submode E1, *long core-tool (LCT) production*, creates bifacial cores with width/ thickness ratios usually less than 3 to 1. Diagnostic artifacts include handaxes, cleavers, picks. Note: LCTs made from large flakes count as both Submode E1 and D7.

In Submode E2, *thinned biface production*, flakes struck from the edges of the core propagate relatively far across the core surface, reducing the core's thickness with minimal correlated reduction in its circumference. "Thinned bifaces" have width/thickness ratios greater than 3 to 1. Diagnostic artifacts include lanceolates and foliate points.

Submode E3, *tanged biface production*, is proximal concavity retouch applied to an elongated bifacial core. Diagnostic artifacts include tanged bifacial points (but see discussion below).

Submode E4, *celt production*, involves making a sharp cutting edge at the distal end of an elongated bifacial core. Archaeologists have used the term "celt" for such artifacts since the nineteenth century, but some Africanist archaeologists use the terms "adze" or "axe" instead. Celts' steeply retouched lateral edges give these artifacts relatively low width/thickness ratios, 2 to 1 or less.

Mode F, *bifacial hierarchical core (BHC) reduction* detaches relatively short flakes from one side of a worked edge and longer flakes from the other side of that same edge. Ridges separating the shorter fracture scars ("faceting") create a convexity that concentrates percussor force onto a small area, propelling fracture propagation farther than would otherwise be the case. Levallois cores are BHCs, but Mode F also includes BHCs that some archaeologists do not routinely classify as Levallois cores.

Preferential BHC reduction (Submode F1) detaches a single relatively large flake from the fracture propagation surface.

Recurrent laminar BHC reduction (Submode F2) detaches overlapping series of large flakes parallel to one another.

In *recurrent radial-centripetal BHC reduction* (Submode F3), an overlapping series of flake scars converge with one another from multiple points around the core's circumference. Diagnostic artifacts include Levallois discoidal cores, pseudo-Lavallois points.

Mode G, *unifacial hierarchical core (UHC) reduction*, entails a stable hierarchy of fracture initiation and fracture propagation surfaces in which the fracture initiation surface is roughly planar and maintained at nearly a right angle to the curved and convex fracture propagation surface. *Platform core reduction*, Submode G1, detaches relatively short flakes (length $<$ 2$\times$ width) from tabular or roughly hemispherical cores. Submode G2, *blade core reduction*, detaches relatively large ($>$5cm long) and elongated flakes (length $\geq$ 2$\times$ width) parallel to one another. Submode G3, *microblade core reduction*, utilizes cores 50 mm or shorter and creates blades/flakes less than 10 mm wide. Diagnostic artifacts include unifacial choppers, core-scrapers, blade/bladelet/ microblade cores, and blades/bladelets/microblades.

As with Submodes D2 and D3, the size-based distinctions among Submodes G1–G3 are a nod to archaeological practice (the distinction between blades, bladelets, and microblades), but they also recognize that detaching relatively small laminar flakes/blades calls for a greater measure of skill than simply detaching short, thick flakes from one side of a core's worked edge.

Abraded-edge tool production, Mode H, creates a cutting edge by abrading one or both sides of an edge. Diagnostic artifacts include abraded/polished-edge celts, and knives.

Mode I, *groundstone artifact production*, creates convex, planar, or concave surfaces, and/or perforations by percussion and abrasion (or "pecking and grinding"). This work recognizes five submodes of Mode I based on the shapes imposed on groundstone artifacts: namely, *flat surfaces* (I.1), *concave surfaces* (I.2), *convex surfaces* (I.3), *grooved surfaces* (I.4), and *perforated surfaces* (I.5). Characteristic artifacts include querns, mortars, handstones, pestles, and perforated stones.

Modes A–I is not encyclopedic. It does not track all the various methods by which humans modify stone. Nor does it track variation in stoneworking techniques (i.e., hard- versus soft-hammer percussion, pressure-flaking, indirect percussion, and the like).

Modes A–I works best as an aid to synthesizing stoneworking variation among large numbers of archaeological lithic assemblages (e.g. Shea 2013a, Shea 2017b), and this work uses it for that purpose.

Identifying Modes The EAPSS records presence/absence of evidence for specific modes. It notes whether evidence for particular modes is either rare or unclear, but it does not provide artifact counts. Doing this might seem to sacrifice detail, but it actually enhances accuracy. Archaeologists' disagreements about what constitutes a point or a microlith, for example, could result in widely diverging statistics for points and microliths in a given assemblage. Presence/ absence is less controversial, and where in-text descriptions of artifacts are ambiguous, inspecting artifact illustrations can often settle the issue. Determining whether an assemblage preserved evidence for one or another mode or submode was, for the most part, fairly straightforward. Nevertheless, there were some recurring problems worth reviewing briefly for those who want to replicate this study.

- Identifying bipolar core reduction (Mode B) occasionally proved problematical. Some sources (mainly Francophone ones) use the term "bipolar core" for cores with bidirectional-opposed fracture propagation scars. Anglophone sources use the term more narrowly for cores damaged by bipolar percussion. Beyond these linguistic differences, there also appears to be considerable variation in how individual archaeologists recognize and identify wear from bipolar core reduction.

- Many sources fail to distinguish between backed/truncated pieces and microliths (Submodes D2 and D3). One could usually assess Submodes D2 and D3 presence from illustrations and/or statistical presentations of measurements.

- Multiple burins (Submode D4) and bladelet cores made on flakes (Submode G3) grade into one another. Archaeologists' distinctions among them often appear arbitrary. This study counted flakes with single burin removals on one flake edge or fracture propagation surface as burins. It counted pieces with multiple parallel removals along the fracture propagation surface as flake-cores.

- "Points" often commingle unifacially retouched and bifacially retouched/thinned specimens that simultaneously met criteria for Submodes D4, D5, E2, and E3. Such points' presence nearly always required verification by inspecting illustrations.

- Sources report cores-on-flakes inconsistently. Some identify them as such if the artifact retains its striking platform; others do not, or they use other criteria. Many EAPSS identifications reflect identifications from illustrations; thus, this survey may underestimate cores-on-flake actual occurrences.

- The EAPSS treats large flakes shaped into LCTs and other large elongated retouched pieces as cores-on-flakes, and as evidence for Submode D7, if their flake scars exceeded 30 mm in length.

- Identifying bifacial hierarchical cores (BHCs) encountered several problems. First, some sources describe BHCs as "formal cores," "prepared cores," or some other such term. Second, Eastern African archaeologists use the European-derived term "Levallois," for these artifacts, mainly for MSA artifacts, and different terms for ESA or post-MSA occurrences. Finally, sources vary in how they describe BHCs with radial-centripetal preparation that lack large preferential flake scars. Some call them Levallois cores, others do not. (Use of the term, "Levallois," seems correlated with Francophone research.)

- Many sources do not distinguish blades from bladelets or blade cores from bladelet cores. This makes it difficult to tell if Submodes G2 or G3 were present. Fortunately, one could usually assess size variation among these artifacts from measurements and illustrations.

Variation among the Sample Assemblages

Table 5.5 lists the number of samples from each age-stage at which diagnostic artifacts for Stoneworking Modes A–I occur. Instances where evidence for one or another stoneworking mode is present are scored as one (1) and tabulated accordingly. Table 5.5 omits cases where sources report evidence as "rare" (indicated with an "r" in the EAPSS) and cases where than evidence is unclear (indicated with a question mark, "?"). I did this to provide summary data with the least possible ambiguity.

How well do traditional age-stages correlate with Stoneworking Modes A–I? Not very well at all. Except at its Pliocene dawn and its recent twilight, every phase of Eastern African prehistory preserves evidence for wide stone-working variation and for complex variability. Eastern African stoneworking strategies do not follow the kinds of stage-wise changes those strategies seem to exhibit in other regions, such as Europe, the Mediterranean Basin, or southern Africa. Stoneworking strategies traditionally viewed as characteristic of one prehistoric age-stage or another routinely appear in multiple age-stages. Products of Modes B, C, and G1, the pebble-cores and core-scrapers that supposedly distinguish the earliest phases of the ESA, occur in all age-stages.

Handaxes and other long core-tools associated with Submode E1 supposedly distinguish the later ESA. In fact, they appear in nearly all later periods of Stone Age prehistory. The commonplace perception that elongated core-tools of this sort rarely appear in MSA contexts probably reflects variable standards for distinguishing "handaxes" from larger foliate points. (One suspects but cannot prove beyond a few cases that such artifacts' "absence" from Neolithic and Iron Age contexts is an artifact of taxonomy, of archaeologists using different terms for stone tools dating to different periods.)

Similar problems afflict efforts to identify "points." Some archaeologists use this term inclusively for any and all convergently retouched pieces. Others parse it more narrowly for triangular pieces with convergent retouch at their distal end. Still others reserve the term for bifacially thinned "foliate points." The archaeological literature provides few explicit criteria for distinguishing these larger foliate points from handaxes and allied artifacts. In any event, sufficient numbers of these artifacts appear in LSA contexts to reject the longstanding view that points (however defined) are quintessentially MSA artifacts.

Products of Mode F, bifacially hierarchical cores (BHCs), are not restricted to the Middle Stone Age as conventional wisdom has it. BHCs with large preferential removals appear in ESA (or ESA/MSA) contexts in the Kapthurin Formation in West Baringo (Kenya) (Tryon et al. 2005). However, BHCs with radial-centripetal preparation first appear around 1.8–2.0 Ma, at Kanjera South and Naiyena Engol 2 (both in Kenya) and Nyabosusi NY 18 (Uganda) (Texier 1995, Bishop et al. 2006, Roche et al. 2018). Such radial-centripetal BHCs

TABLE 5.5 *Occurrences of Stoneworking Modes A–I among age-stages.*

Modes	Early ESA	Later ESA	ESA/ MSA	MSA	MSA/ LSA	LSA	LSA/ Neol.	Neolithic	LSA/N/ Iron	Iron Age	Total
A. Unipolar percussion	9	17	6	21	4	27	0	10	18	2	113
B. Bipolar percussion	8	5	2	15	6	49	1	23	28	5	142
C. Short nonhierarchical core reduction	17	20	6	37	8	49	0	21	17	10	184
D. Flake retouch	10	19	5	42	12	76	2	29	31	14	240
D1. Orthogonal retouch	10	16	5	38	9	69	1	26	25	14	213
D2. Macrolithic backing/truncation	4	3	2	14	7	60	2	18	17	11	138
D3. Microlithic backing/truncation	0	0	1	6	5	69	2	27	29	12	151
D4. Burination	1	4	2	9	7	41	2	21	15	4	106
D5. Convergent retouch	2	8	3	28	5	39	2	16	8	0	111
D6. Concave proximal retouch	0	0	0	0	0	7	0	0	0	0	7
D7. Flake-core reduction	1	4	1	10	1	20	2	16	1	2	58
E. Elongated nonhierarchical bifacial core reduction	1	20	5	26	8	16	0	0	2	2	80
E1. Long core-tool production	1	20	4	12	1	4	0	0	0	1	43
E2. Thinned biface production	0	2	2	19	7	11	0	0	1	0	42
E3. Tanged biface production	0	0	1	1	1	3	0	0	0	0	6
E4. Celt production	0	1	2	2	1	2	0	0	1	1	10
F. Bifacial hierarchical core (BHC) reduction	3	6	5	41	8	22	0	2	4	4	95
F1. Preferential BHC reduction	0	1	5	22	6	7	0	1	1	1	44
F2. Recurrent laminar BHC reduction	0	0	1	17	6	5	0	0	0	1	30
F3. Radial/centripetal BHC reduction	3	5	3	27	9	15	0	0	2	2	66
G. Unifacial hierarchical core reduction	10	14	5	29	11	67	1	24	29	11	200

(continued)

TABLE 5.5 (*continued*)

Modes	Early ESA	Later ESA	ESA/ MSA	MSA	MSA/ LSA	LSA	LSA/ Neol.	Neolithic	LSA/N/ Iron	Iron Age	Total
G1. Platform core reduction	10	13	5	26	10	29	1	15	23	5	136
G2. Blade core reduction	0	1	2	21	8	33	0	18	4	5	92
G3. Microblade core reduction	0	0	1	9	7	31	0	12	15	7	82
H. Abraded-edge production	0	0	0	0	0	8	0	3	1	1	13
I. Groundstone (GS)	0	1	1	5	2	32	2	14	11	5	73
I.1. Flat GS	0	1	1	5	2	25	2	4	10	4	54
I.2 Concave GS	0	0	1	0	0	7	0	12	4	2	26
I.3. Convex GS	0	0	1	2	0	13	0	6	3	2	27
I.4. Grooved GS	0	0	1	0	0	0	0	2	2	1	6
I.5. Perforated GS	0	0	0	0	1	11	1	6	2	1	22
N samples	17	27	6	46	12	81	2	30	31	16	268

persist into the LSA, indeed up into the Iron Age at Gobedra Rockshelter and Goda Buticha, both in Ethiopia (Phillipson 1977a, Leplongeon et al. 2017) (see Figure 5.9 r).

Evidence for prismatic blade and bladelet core reduction (Submodes G2–G3), purportedly diagnostic of the European Upper Paleolithic age-stage, appear from Later ESA times onward. The oldest claimed occurrence of blade core reduction appears ca. 0.5 Ma in West Lake Baringo (Kenya) (Johnson and McBrearty 2010).

Small backed/truncated pieces, or microliths (Submode D3), occur in ESA/MSA, MSA, LSA, Neolithic, and even Iron Age samples. Holocene microliths appear to be smaller on average than Pleistocene ones, and the most recent (Iron Age) ones less well made and less consistently retouched than their precursors (Tryon and Faith 2013).

Abraded-edge tools (Mode H), signature artifacts of the Eurasian Neolithic and early agriculture, first appear in LSA samples. Groundstone artifacts (Mode I) have a deep Pleistocene antiquity.

Plainly, much remains to be discovered about what caused change and variability in the Eastern African lithic record. For testing hypotheses about those sources of change and variability, Eastern African archaeology needs a stone tool typology that can describe the lithic evidence from all time periods. The next section introduces a typology specifically designed for this purpose.

THE EASTERN AFRICAN STONE TOOL TYPOLOGY: AN INTRODUCTION

The Eastern African Stone Tool (EAST) Typology recognizes more than 200 artifact-types (See Appendix 2). It arranges these artifact-types into 11 major categories, Groups I–XI. These include cores and core-tools (Groups I–III), flakes (Groups IV–VII), retouched pieces (Groups VIII–IX), percussors (Group X), and groundstone artifacts (Group XI). The typology divides each group into morphologically and technologically homogeneous artifact-types. Rather than assigning numbers to each artifact-type, as most traditional archaeological type-lists do, the EAST Typology uses a hierarchy of letters and numbers. Doing this allows expansion or contraction of the typology's categories in conjunction with different researchers' analytical goals. To discriminate single endscrapers from double endscrapers, one can do so with types IX.A.1.a and IX.A.1.c, respectively. One can also tabulate occurrences of more inclusive categories, such as scrapers (IX.A.1) or retouched pieces (Group IX). The EAST Typology's nested hierarchy easily accommodates newly recognized artifact-types. A new scraper type, for example, could be added as (IX.A.1.l) without requiring the renumbering of all artifact-types that follow it in the list and without placing that scraper at the end of the list, apart from other scraper types.

Although one can use the EAST Typology as a homotaxial framework (i.e., one term for each artifact type), it can also be adapted for use as a polytaxial system. For example, one can describe a multiple notch (IX.A.2.b) made on a lateral bifacial hierarchical core repair flake (VII.B.2) as "IX.A.2.b/VII.B.2," with names listed in the order of certainty about identification. That is, one knows that the artifact is a multiple notch, but because retouch has removed some portion of its original mass one can only conjecturally identify its original condition. Such conjecture could be indicated with a question mark (?): e.g., "IX.A.2.b/VII.B.2?" Long sequences of Roman numerals, Latin letters, Arabic numbers, and so on will be difficult to learn and to remember. Therefore, to make the EAST Typology as user-friendly as possible, it retains some traditional artifact-type names.

Developing the EAST Typology also presents an opportunity to do some much-needed taxonomic "housecleaning." Specifically, the EAST Typology sinks a few long-used artifact names. It retires some terms that fail to accurately describe how the artifacts in question actually appear as well as those implying unproven functions, such as "sinew frayers," "fabricators," "digging stick weights," and "tortoise core" (Leakey 1931, Hromnik 1986). It does not do this for all such terms because some of these (e.g., scraper, point, and burin) are so deeply established in worldwide archaeological terminology that replacing them would create more problems than it solves.

Most terms referencing discovery sites, such as Still Bay point, Mousterian point, Levallois core/flake, and the like, have been renamed using more clearly descriptive terms. The EAST Typology retains a few such place-name-based terms, such as Nubian core, Kombewa flake/core, and Victoria West core, because they enjoy wide and fairly consistent usage among Eastern African archaeologists.

Chapters 6–9 review the EAST Typology in detail. Each chapter begins with guidance about how to measure artifacts and then turns to classifications and current taxonomic issues. (This work does not dwell on past taxonomic debates now largely settled.) When the text in Chapters 6–9 first mentions an EAST artifact-type, parentheses enclose the EAST type number. These chapters are fairly technical but abundantly illustrated with schematic diagrams of artifacts, including sketches reconstructing how stoneworkers created particular artifacts. Readers are urged to follow in-text prompts to view these figures for they clarify ambiguities in the text. For ease of reference, figures show the EAST type numbers for artifacts in italics next to the illustration themselves, rather than in the captions. (Anticipating that some readers may find some of this book's figures too small for easy viewing, the author has posted enlargeable digital versions online.)

No artifact typology can be all-inclusive. Readers will encounter artifacts that do not fit easily into the EAST Typology's categories. Using discrete categories to partition continuously variable phenomena inevitably produces observations that do not fit into one or another category. This is not a compelling reason against using a typology. (One does not disavow using whole integers because the value of *pi* (π) is neither 3 nor 4.) However, to be useful, a good artifact typology should have a mechanism for improvements and for accommodating new observations. So that the EAST Typology will remain a "living document" after this work's publication, the author invites proposals to recognize new artifact-types. Such proposals must be accompanied by the following:

1. A sound theoretical justification for such recognition, such as linkages to specific behaviors or demonstrable chronostratigraphic or culture-historical values.

2. References from peer-reviewed literature to at least three occurrences of the artifact-type at different archaeological sites. Those occurrences must be from excavated contexts that have well-constrained geochronometric age-estimates.

3. Illustrations of no fewer than three such artifacts showing plan, profile, and section views accompanied by a metric scale.

One invites those identifying new artifact-types to propose names for them, but those names must be descriptive rather than historical: that is, their names should reference, first and foremost, the artifacts' appearance. Names should not reference inferred functions, conjectured relationships to other artifacts, specific archaeological sites, stone tool industries, geographic regions, or individuals. Admittedly, and unavoidably, the EAST Typology includes some well-established artifact-type names with these characteristics, but there is no reason to enlarge their number. Changes to the EAST Typology will be posted on a webpage devoted to this purpose on the author's personal website (https://sites.google.com/a/stonybrook.edu/john-j-shea/).

UWAZI VALLEY TALES, EPISODE 5: QUESTIONS AND LESSONS

Two weeks later, I was in the field laboratory discussing the stone tool sequence with Aya. Located in a room in the old cinder-block mission schoolhouse, my lab bench sat next to the large windows along one wall. This allowed me to examine artifacts in bright afternoon sunlight. Plastic boxes of stone tools labeled by field season and level sat on wooden shelves against one recently whitewashed wall. Against the wall opposite my lab bench, I had arranged a plywood "display table." Strips of blue masking tape delimited columns marking excavation levels at Ancient Ones' Cave. In separate rows, also marked with tape, I had positioned representative cores, flakes, retouched pieces, and other artifacts. Aya and I stood by the table as Endurance and Joseph entered. Both took seats.

"The Iron Age stuff looks very simple and unorganized," I said. "It's as if they forgot how to make stone tools but rediscovered stoneworking from time to time."

"What about the Neolithic?"

"Lots of small blade cores on flakes and microliths. You were right about needing a microscope. I've never seen *outils écaillées* so small."

"What's that?"

"*Outils écaillées*. . ., err, bipolar cores. Yeah, I'm having a bit of a problem with these things."

"How so?"

"Well, when archaeologists write about such tools, they use two French terms, *piéces esquillées* and *outils écaillées*, and eight English ones, wedges, scaled pieces, cores-on-flakes, truncated-facetted pieces, rods, bipolar pieces, micro-cores, and, of course, bipolar cores. Some list them as cores, others as retouched pieces, still others as a stand-alone artifact category. A few references use more than one of these terms, but they don't explain how they distinguish them from each other. Older books and papers sometimes don't even mention them. That makes me think they just didn't recognize them at the time."

"Sounds like quite a mess," Aya said. "In archaeozoology, we have just one name for each kind of bone, femur, scapula, and so on."

"I'll manage," I said, "I like a challenge. Just don't ask me about scrapers, or burins, or points, or microliths."

"Why lithics, Robin? What's the appeal?" Aya stepped back.

"Back home, when we hiked and camped, my parents and I would look for animal tracks and signs. Sometimes we'd find stone tools, too. I enjoyed that, and for me, trying to "read" stone tools is a bit like tracking. When I found a stone tool, it felt like the person who made it spoke to me. 'I was once where you are now.'"

"*Et in arcadia, ego,*" Aya said.

"Exactly. Finding a stone tool was like starting a conversation between the present and the past. After I learned how to make reproductions of prehistoric tools, stoneworking became a fun hobby. How about you? Why bones?"

"As kids, we had lots of pets: dogs, cats, birds, rabbits, even a tortoise. When I went to college, I thought I'd study to be a veterinarian. The Polymath's daughter Susan and I were lab partners in the animal physiology class, and we were both on the track team. Susan and two other students from the team were in the Polymath's lab sorting bones from older excavations. They had fun doing it, so I signed up, too, and I got hooked immediately."

"Why?"

"Bones are cool. There's the aesthetics, form and function integrated. You're from the Southwest. You've seen Georgia O'Keeffe's paintings of sheep skulls?"

I had, and long admired them and her other works.

"There's also the detective story. You have a splinter of bone and you ask: 'what can I learn from this piece of a once-living thing?' You have an advantage with the stone tools, Robin."

"Oh?"

"When you were in college and you showed people the stone tools you made, they thought they were cool, right?"

"Well, yes." I had given many away, even sold a few reproductions to collectors.

"When I showed other students the animal bone collection in my dorm room, they reported me to Campus Counseling Services."

We laughed.

"So, is there a picture emerging on the display board over here?"

"Kind of, but it's still murky."

"In what way?" Aya asked.

"Each of these major age-stages, Neolithic, LSA, and MSA, are supposed to have characteristically different stone tools. At least that's the textbook version." I pointed at Endurance's archaeology book. "But here instead we have the same range of core, flake, and retouched piece types in all periods."

"What about Level 5? MSA, LSA, or something else?" Aya asked.

"I can't tell yet. It depends on the criteria one uses, and those criteria differ among researchers."

"Maybe the age-stages are the problem," Endurance spoke. "This textbook says that archaeologists originally defined the LSA and MSA in southern Africa and the Neolithic and Iron Age in Europe. Maybe it is like you are trying to use field guides to the birds of Europe and southern Africa to identify Eastern African birds."

I remembered the Polymath's guidebook to Eastern African birds from the drive here.

"If you have geochronology, why use age-stages?" she asked.

"Well, some sites don't have firm geochronology," I said. "Using age-stages helps us be sure that when we compare assemblages from different sites, we are comparing things of similar age."

"But here in Eastern Africa, consecutive age-stages overlap with one another for thousands of years," said Endurance.

Joseph spoke, smiling, "Imagine a man of my great-grandfather's time, a hunter. The man wakes up and needs to repair an arrow, but his son has borrowed his iron knife. So, he uses a sharp obsidian flake instead. The man goes hunting and shoots an antelope. He knows he can exchange the animal in town for other things, so the man goes to town and trades the antelope for *ugali* (maize meal) and a ceramic bowl for his friend. On the way home, the man gives the bowl and the *ugali* to his friend. Back in camp, his son returns his metal knife. Our man went from the Stone Age to the Neolithic and then to the Iron Age in the same day."

"It doesn't work that way, Joseph," I said. "Once you are in the Iron Age, you can't leave it. It's like reading. Once someone's literate, they cannot become illiterate."

The two ladies laughed. "Robin's clearly not read much academic writing!" said Endurance.

Aya leaned over to her, "Nor graded many term papers!"

"OK, so the age-stages aren't perfect guides to chronology. That's why, within age-stages, we identify stone tool industries, groups of assemblages with similar characteristics. We assume people living at the same time had similar needs for stone tools and ideas about how to make then, so we group similar sets of tools into named industries. Each age-stage has a sequence of named stone tool industries."

"Nasty things, those named stone tool industries," Aya said.

"But are you sure the things archaeologists call the same industries are the same and different industries different?" Endurance asked. "If they have so many different terms for individual artifact types, like your bipolar cores, you'd expect more, not less, variation in their terms for groups of artifacts."

"That's true, and there is a pattern. Many industries appear at only one site, or at sites the same person excavated. The numbers of archaeologists working on sites dating to that time period seem to correlate with the number of named stone tool industries in a given age-stage."

"So, said Endurance, "it's not clear whether you're seeing variation in the evidence or variation in how archaeologists describe that evidence."

"Probably a bit of both," I admitted.

"So why use them at all?" she asked.

"When archaeologists describe what they think happened in prehistoric times, they use these industries as stand-ins for groups of people," I said. "It's like in a play or a TV show. They describe the characters or industries they think are important in a great detail and give them specific and distinctive names like Eburran, Elementeitan, or Lomekwian. Less import-ant industries often just get generic names, 'Typical MSA' or 'Middle Acheulean'. It's like in the cast credits at the end of a movie, Policewoman #2 or Terrorist #5."

"Sign of lazy screenwriting," Aya said.

"But stone tools aren't people," said Joseph. "Imagine our man, again. He needs more stone for carving a wooden bow. He has stone at camp, but only very little. The man remembers that the other day out hunting he saw obsidian tools eroding from a riverbank near a big tree. So he goes there.

The stones on the surface are all small and too dull to use. So he digs up some big, fresh stones, and breaks pieces from them to bring home to camp. Now, this man, he knows that little children could get up to no good with sharp obsidian. There, next to the tree, he buries pieces of obsidian he brought from camp together with pieces he made but that he does not want to bring back to camp. A long time later, you *wazungu* excavate next to the tree. If you name an industry for what you found, that combines our man's tools with those of people who lived there many years ago."

"But we'd be able to detect that intrusive deposit from the disturbed stratigraphy," I said, tentatively.

"Perhaps, Robin, but I did not say our man only did this once. I did not say he was the only one who did this. Maybe the people whose tools our man found had done the same thing at the same place hundreds of years earlier, and other people did the same thing there, thousands of years before that. Maybe even earlier not-men did it too."

"Hominins, Joseph, or hominids," said Endurance.

"Well," I said, "when we find stone tools from the same industry in the same place, we assume people did broadly similar things, even if they recycled them sometimes."

"But these stone tools," said Joseph, "they are like a *panga*, what you Americans call a machete. If you are strong and clever, you can do pretty much anything you want with it: dig, carve wood, scrape hide, butcher animals, cut firewood. Why carry different stone tools for each activity, when one will do? Stone tools are heavy. The more you carry, the more you are likely to lose. The more you know, the less you need. Look around, how many people in Uwazi Valley do you see carrying more than one *panga*?"

One *did* rarely see anyone carrying more than one *panga*.

"You make a good point, Joseph," I said, "several of them, actually."

"I have one more for you, Robin. Why do you think we call the cave Ancient Ones' Cave rather than Ancient Ancestors' Cave?" Joseph asked.

"Why?"

"Because everyone who comes to the valley uses the cave. When they hunted and gathered near here, my people sometimes stayed here overnight, other times for a few weeks. The herders sometimes camped in the valley and penned their goats up there at night to keep them safe from lions and leopards. Other times, during the rainy season, the people stayed in the cave and penned the cattle below in the valley and set watchmen over them. Some German soldiers camped there during World War I. Later, the *wazungu* settlers and farmers took picnics there. All the things we and they left behind, and older things, too, are in Level 1. So if you call what you find in Level 1 an industry, we know it contains traces of people doing many different things for a very long time."

"But people and things have changed so much more here recently than in the past. . ."

Joseph cut me off, "Every generation thinks that way. Things always change. They always have, and they always will. If you archaeologists know that the ways you group together things from your excavations today mix together things that different people made at different times and for different reasons, shouldn't you assume you are doing so with things from the past, and not the other way around?"

"Why assume either one thing or the other?" Endurance added. "Why not develop 'multiple working hypotheses' and then work hard to test each of them. My fiancée is a police inspector, and this is what he and his colleagues do. They don't just arrest the first man accused of a crime. They gather evidence, identify suspects, and try to winnow them down before arresting anyone."

"When you eliminate the impossible, only the truth remains," said Joseph.

"A saying among your people, Joseph?" I asked.

"Sherlock Holmes," he smiled, "or rather his creator, Sir Arthur Conan Doyle."

"If age-stages cannot predict age, and if industries do not tell you who made the stone tools or why, what good are they?" Endurance asked. "In the National Museum, we changed how we organize our exhibits to match the message we want the visitors to understand. During Colonial times, the exhibits showed our different tribes and ethnic groups more or less the same way they showed different kinds of birds or mammals. After Independence, we wanted to emphasize national unity over ethnic differences, so we changed the exhibits to show different people in their professions – farmer, engineer, policeman, teacher, and so on – all working for the common good. We do not mention their tribe or ethnic group."

Joseph said, "Maybe you archaeologists would be better off without these industries and age-stages. All humans tell tales that explain their past. Endurance's book says we humans first evolved here in Eastern Africa. So we Eastern Africans have been explaining our past to each other longer than the *wazungu* or anybody else. We don't use age-stages or industries to explain our past. We tell stories, of course, but often we just compare things. How were things in my grandparents' time different from today? We ask how things differ before we try to explain why they differ."

"My head hurts," I said. I looked out to the Gentlemen's Smoking Lounge, where the Old Africa Hand and the Polymath had taken their places.

"Robin, you need a break," Aya said. "Tomorrow the other senior staff are surveying in the Lower Valley. Go with them. Clear your head a bit."

CHAPTER 6

CORES AND CORE-TOOLS

Chapter 6 reviews conventions for measuring, describing, and classifying cores and core-tools. These include EAST Typology Group I, short nonhierarchical cores; Group II, hierarchical cores; Group III, other cores; and Group IV, elongated core-tools. It also answers common questions about cores and core-tools.

MEASURING CORES AND CORE-TOOLS

When measuring cores and core-tools, most archaeologists measure length (longest axis), width (longest dimension perpendicular to length), and thickness (longest dimension perpendicular to the plane formed by the intersection of length and thickness). However, archaeologists have different conventions for measuring different kinds of cores and core-tools (e.g., Brézillon 1977). For example, some measure width and thickness at the midpoint of length rather than the maximum thickness value. Where one measures width or thickness doesn't really matter, but since they can give different values for the same object, one should specify which measurements one uses. Because mass is a proxy measure for potential tool utility, core and core-tool one should always measure mass.

Core cortex coverage and counts of fracture scars help to estimate the degree to which stoneworkers altered a core or core-tool from its original condition. In principle, higher core cortex coverage values indicate less modification from original rock sources. Archaeologists differ in how finely they divide such holistic cortex coverage estimates. Minimally, cortex coverage ought to to be estimated as a percentage of the entire core surface: e.g., no cortex, or <50% cortex, or >/= 50% cortex.

Also, in theory, the number of fracture scars should increase with continued core modification, but this relationship can vary among different core reduction strategies. When archaeologists count fracture scars on cores, they usually do so using a size threshold: e.g., "fracture scars longer than 25 mm."

This threshold can differ among lithic analysts, but it is usually somewhere between 10 and 30 mm.

The EAST Typology divides cores into nonhierarchical cores (EAST Group I), hierarchical cores (Group II), other/miscellaneous cores (Group III), and elongated nonhierarchical core-tools (Group IV). In nonhierarchical core reduction, stoneworkers detach more than one flake of roughly equal length from either side of a core's worked edge. In hierarchical core reduction, stoneworkers treat opposite sides of a worked edge differently, typically detaching longer flakes from one side than from the other. A single core can have both hierarchical and nonhierarchical worked edges.

SHORT NONHIERARCHICAL CORES (GROUP I)

Short nonhierarchical cores (Group I) have roughly equal lengths and widths. On such cores, stoneworkers treat worked edge fracture initiation and propagation surfaces interchangeably. Consequently, both sides of their worked edge preserve similar fracture scars. Nonhierarchical cores include unipolar cores, bipolar cores, and pebble cores (Figure 6.1).

Unipolar Cores

Unipolar cores (EAST Type I.A) feature one or a few large fracture scars propagating away from a single focal point of percussion, (Figure 6.1a), but their surfaces lack other fracture scars. Several different activities can create unipolar cores. Modern-day stoneworkers often "test" stones' fracture properties and interior appearance by striking a few flakes from them. A stoneworker may only need one or two cortical flakes, and, having obtained them, abandon the core with only those fracture scars on it. Hammerstones can resemble tested stones when overly forceful percussion causes a large fracture scar to propagate away from the percussor's working surface.

Bipolar Cores

Bipolar cores (I.B) feature large fracture scars and crushing damage on opposite points on their circumference (Figure 6.1b). Their fracture scars extend to half their length or further. As their name implies, this kind of damage can result from bipolar percussion, but anvil percussion applied to different places along a core's circumference could mirror this effect. Applied to rounded stones, bipolar percussion can result in bipolar cores on pebbles (I.B.1) (Figure 6.1b) or in split pebble/cobbles (See Chapter 7, Figure 7.3a). On tabular rocks and angular rock fragments (I.B.2), bipolar percussion often detaches thin, flat flakes with irregular edge shapes (Figure 6.1c). Most illustrations of bipolar

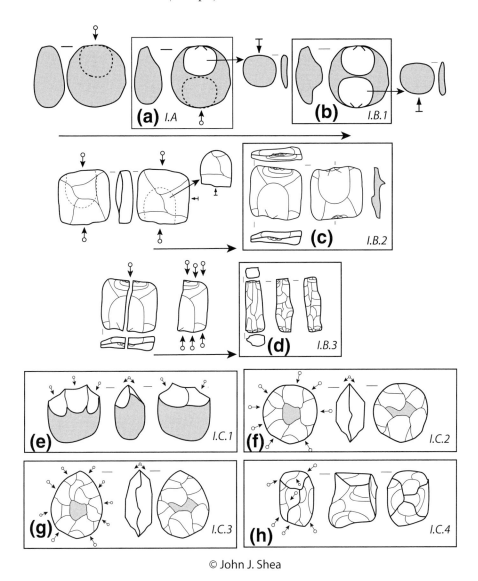

© John J. Shea

Figure 6.1 Nonhierarchical cores. (a) Unipolar core, (b) Bipolar core on pebble/cobble, (c) Tabular bipolar core, (d) Cylindrical bipolar core, (e) Chopper, (f) Discoid, (g) Protobiface/elongated discoid, (h) Polyhedron. Note: Text in italics indicates an artifact's EAST Typology identification number.

cores show *tabular bipolar cores* (I.B.2), but they can take many forms. If a stoneworker rotates a bipolar core horizontally or vertically, it can feature two or more paired sets of crushing/comminution. If the bipolar core splits in two, continued bipolar percussion along the same axis can create *cylindrical bipolar cores* (I.B.3) (Figure 6.1d).

The EAST Typology treats bipolar cores made on flakes that retain some of their original flake surfaces as *scaled pieces* (IX.G.3), a kind of retouched piece.

Short Bifacial Cores

Short bifacial cores (I.C.1–3) include clasts (rounded rocks) and angular/tabular rock fragments whose bifacially flaked worked edge runs for at least one eighth of their circumference. Short bifacial cores' most commonly recognized morphological variants include *choppers, discoids, protobifaces,* and (arguably) some *polyhedrons* (Figure 6.1e–h). These artifact-types differ mainly in the extent of their worked edge(s).

A *chopper's* (I.C.1) worked edge runs for least one fourth of its circumference (Figure 6.1e). The worked edge on a *discoid* (I.C.2) encompasses its entire circumference, or very nearly so (Figure 6.1f). Where to draw the line between choppers and discoids is an arbitrary choice. Most archaeologists seem to set that boundary between 50% and 75% of the circumference. They nearly always classify as choppers nonhierarchical cores with worked edges running for less than 50% of their circumference. Those whose worked edges run for more than 75%, are usually classified as either discoids or partial discoids.

Rather than making such arbitrary distinctions, a better approach could be to divide chopper and discoid circumference into a series of polar coordinates (segments of an arc bounded by lines radiating outward from a central point) and then record the distribution of worked edge(s) across those polar coordinates. Archaeologists who do this typically use somewhere between four and eight such polar coordinates. In principle, one could measure these polar coordinates in terms of degrees and minutes (English measurements) or grads and radians (metric), but such precision requires more time to make the measurement.

Archaeologists working in the later phases of Eastern African prehistory often recognize a kind of nonhierarchical core called "discs" or "disc cores." These terms describe discoids with a relatively flat cross-section (i.e., a high ratio of width to thickness) and invasive fracture scars on both sides. Some of these discs may owe their flatness to having started out as flakes, rather than clasts or tabular rocks. Most illustrations of discs/disc cores lack evidence of their origin as a flake (i.e., residual flake ventral surfaces or striking platforms). Any that do, however, should be classified as either cores-on-flakes (III.B) or as thinned pieces (IX.D). Inasmuch as discoids and discs/disc cores grade into one another, the EAST Typology does not maintain separate categories for them. If a research question requires one to distinguish between discoids and discs/disc cores, this can be done simply by measuring their width/thickness ratios and setting the theoretically justified dividing line between them.

Protobifaces (I.C.3) are moderately elongated discoids (length $\geq 1.3 \times$ width) (Figure 6.1 g). The name "protobiface" reflects early archaeologists' theory that the activities that created these artifacts eventually led stoneworkers to manufacture bifaces and other LCTs. Jones (1994) argues that some protobifaces are merely heavily resharpened LCTs.

Polyhedrons

Polyhedrons (I.D) feature either multiple unifacial and bifacial nonhierarchical worked edges or combinations of both (Figure 6.1h). Archaeologists disagree over whether prehistoric stoneworkers shaped polyhedrons for a specific purpose. That polyhedrons often appear among cores that novice stoneworkers discard (Shea 2015) suggests that many archaeological polyhedrons are simply failed cores – cores that prehistoric stoneworkers abandoned when percussion no longer yielded useful flakes. With regard to polyhedrons, archaeologists recognize them mainly on the basis of their overall blocky or cuboid shape rather than on specific technological criteria. Some may be bifacial cores, others not.

Short nonhierarchical cores grade into one another, making hard and fast categorical distinctions among them somewhat arbitrary. Many of their morphological differences may reflect greater or lesser amounts of core reduction (Figure 6.2)

Note: although the illustrations in Figures 6.1 and 6.2 show nonhierarchical bifacial cores with residual cortex on them, such artifacts can lack cortex. For such artifacts, cortex is an inessential attribute (present in some cases) rather than an essential one (present in a plurality of cases) or a key attribute (present in all cases) (Clarke 1978).

HIERARCHICAL CORES (EAST GROUP II)

The EAST Typology divides hierarchical cores (EAST Group II) into bifacial hierarchical cores (BHCs) and unifacial hierarchical cores (UHCs).

In doing this, the typology tries to fix some terminological problems afflicting these artifacts. Many archaeologists describe bifacial hierarchical cores and some of the flakes detached from them as "Levallois" cores/flakes, after the Paris suburb where nineteenth-century excavations first brought these artifacts to archaeologists' attention. An alternative term, "tortoise core," appears in some older references, apparently because these cores reminded archaeologists of tortoises with their head and legs retracted. Many archaeologists also describe elongated unifacial hierarchical cores as either "blade cores" or "prismatic blade cores." The EAST Typology does not use either of these terms for two reasons. First, archaeologists working in Eastern Africa, and in sub-Saharan Africa more generally, use the terms Levallois and blade inconsistently. Second, and more importantly, these terms imply facts not in evidence: namely, that stoneworkers reduced these cores mainly to procure certain kinds of flakes/blades and not others. This renaming will probably not settle archaeologists' various long-running debates about whether or not an artifact is "really" Levallois or a blade core. Both terms have larger culture-historical implications and affiliations with one or another research tradition that encourage their use, but renaming them will refocus debate on these artifacts observable properties.

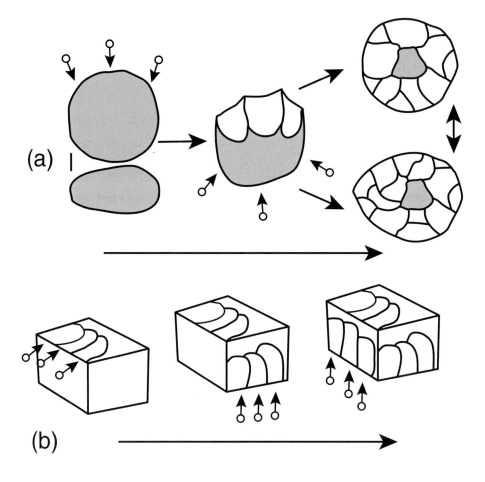

Figure 6.2 Effects of core reduction on short nonhierarchical bifacial core morphology. (a) Clast to chopper to discoid/protobiface. (b) Tabular piece to polyhedron (one among many possible scenarios).

Bifacial Hierarchical Cores

Bifacial hierarchical cores (BHCs) (II.A) are relatively long and wide with variable thicknesses. BHC length and width may be equal or unequal, but both are usually greater than thickness. BHCs feature at least two fracture propagations surfaces. The more invasively fracture-scarred surface is called the "upper" surface (an arbitrary designation). These scars propagate near to or beyond the point on the core surface where length and width axes intersect with one another. BHCs' "lower" surface features less-invasive fracture scars. Patches of cortex often remain visible at the lower surface's center, beyond where its relatively shorter flake scars terminated. Upper and lower surfaces intersect

EAST Group II.A Preferential Bifacial Hierarchical Cores

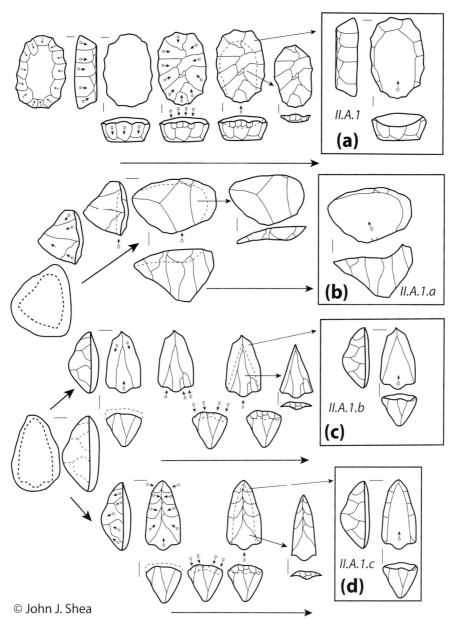

© John J. Shea

Figure 6.3 Preferential bifacial hierarchical cores. (a) preferential BHC, (b) Victoria West core, (c) Beaked/Nubian core Type 1, (d) Beaked/Nubian core Type 2.

with one another at relatively high angles (>70 degrees). Archaeologists divide BHCs into products of preferential versus recurrent core reduction based on patterned variation in the alignment of flakes scars on their upper surface (Boëda 1995, Chazan 1997) (Figure 6.3).

Preferential bifacial hierarchical cores (II.A.1) feature at least one relatively large fracture scar on their upper surface (Figure 6.3a). These scars typically extend to at least the midpoint of core length, as measured from the fracture initiation point. Naming these cores and the flakes struck from them as "preferential" in no way implies that other flakes struck from these cores were unused or unintended core reduction products. These central removals may reflect efforts to create a central concavity from whose lateral margins stoneworkers detached flakes with one steep lateral edge that afforded a safe grip and another acute cutting edge opposite (Sandgathe 2004).

The EAST Typology recognizes three preferential BHC subtypes: Victoria West cores and two varieties of beaked/Nubian cores.

Named for a South African town, *Victoria West cores* (II.A.1.a) are relatively large (>200–300 mm long) preferential BHCs (Sharon and Beaumont 2006) (Figure 6.3b). These cores are elongated and roughly plano-convex in cross-section. Their relatively flat upper surface features one large (>100–200 mm long) flake scar running more or less perpendicularly to the core's long axis. Many such flakes appear to have been retouched to make large elongated retouched pieces, especially knives and cleavers (discussed later in this chapter). Some archaeologists view Victoria West cores as part of a larger phenomenon, an Acheulian Large Flake/Giant Core Technological Complex, distributed across Africa and southern Asia (Sharon 2010).

Beaked or Nubian cores (II.A.1.b–c) are preferential BHCs whose upper surfaces preserve a large, often triangular, central fracture scar (Figure 6.3c–d). These upper surfaces are usually triangular in plan view, their distally converging edges creating the "beak" to which one of their names refers. Archaeologists recognize two major types of these cores. *Beaked/Nubian Type 1 cores'* (II.A.1.b) upper surfaces have bidirectional-opposed preparation (Figure 6.3c). Stoneworkers predetermined the preferential triangular fracture scar trajectory by laminar removals at the core's distal and proximal ends. *Beaked/Nubian Type 2 cores'* (II.A.1.c) upper surfaces feature radial convergent preparation (Figure 6.3d). The predetermining fracture scars intrude from the upper core surface's lateral edges. Earlier researchers described these artifacts as "beaked" cores. Over time, they have become widely known as Nubian cores. Early finds of these artifacts did occur at sites in what is now Sudan, formerly Nubia, (Guichard and Guichard 1968, Van Peer 1991), but archaeologists have also identified Nubian cores in the East Mediterranean Levant (Goder-Goldberger et al. 2016), the Arabian Peninsula (Usik et al. 2013), and South Africa (Will et al. 2015). One suspects that they appear in many other parts of the world, too, but either under different artifact-type names or unrecognized as distinctive artifact-types.

Recurrent bifacial hierarchical cores (II.A.2) preserve multiple deeply invasive fracture scars on their upper surfaces (Figure 6.4). Usually similar to one another in size and/or shape, these scars' propagation trajectories align with one another in various ways. The EAST Typology recognizes four types of recurrent BHCs

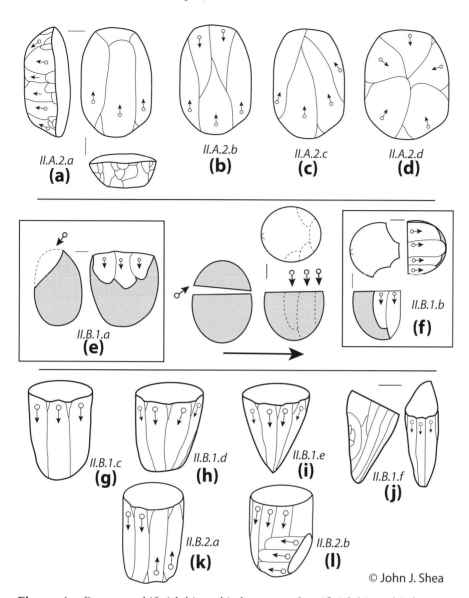

Figure 6.4 Recurrent bifacial hierarchical cores and unifacial hierarchical cores. (a) Recurrent unidirectional BHC, (b) Recurrent bidirectional-opposed BHC, (c) Recurrent convergent BHC, (d) Radial-centripetal BHC, (e) Unifacial chopper, (f) Split platform core, (g) Single-platform blade core, (h) Convergent single-platform blade core, (i) Pyramidal/cone-shaped convergent single-platform blade core, (j) Narrow-fronted single-platform blade core, (k) Distal opposed-platform blade core, (l) Orthogonal opposed-platform blade core.

based on these alignments. *Recurrent unidirectional BHCs* (II.A.2.a) feature two or more elongated fracture scars that propagate parallel with one another and in the same direction (Figure 6.4a). *Recurrent bidirectional-opposed BHCs* (II.A.2.b) preserve elongated fracture scars that propagate parallel and toward one another from opposite sides of the upper surface (Figure 6.4b). *Recurrent convergent BHCs* (II.A.2. c) have fracture scars that converge at or beyond the midpoint of the core's upper surface (Figure 6.4c). On the upper surfaces of *recurrent radial-centripetal BHCs* (II.A.2.d), fracture scars propagate toward the center of the core's upper surface, but they do not extend much further than this (Figure 6.4d).

Unifacial Hierarchical Cores

Unifacial hierarchical cores (UHCs) (II.B) have a worked edge on one side of which relatively long (>10 mm) fracture scars propagate approximately parallel to one another and more orless perpendicularly to the worked edge. The EAST Typology recognizes two major groups of UHC types, single-platform cores (II.B.1) and multiple-platform cores (II.B.2).

Single-platform cores (II.B.1) feature a series of flake scars initiated mainly from one side of a single, continuous worked edge. The EAST Typology recognizes six single-platform core types.

Unifacial choppers (II.B.1.a) are UHCs that preserve a worked edge with fracture scars on one side only (Figure 6.4e). The fracture initiation surface is unmodified and/or cortical.

Split platform cores (II.B.1.b) feature a worked edge preserving a single large fracture scar on one side that served as the fracture initiation surface for multiple fracture scars propagating away from the other side of that edge (Figure 6.4f). Older works refer to split platform cores as "core-scrapers," "heavy duty scrapers," or even "*rabots*" (from the French term for push-planes, a kind of carpentry tool).

A *parallel single-platform core* (II.B.1.c) features one relatively broad worked edge from which elongated fracture scars extend parallel to each other (Figure 6.4g). "Elongated" flake scars are generally longer than they are wide.

Convergent single-platform cores (II.B.1.d) have elongated flakes scars with convergent trajectories spreading from a relatively broad and arched worked edge (Figure 6.4h).

A *pyramidal/cone-shaped convergent single-platform core* (II.B.1.e) features a worked edge that makes a complete circuit around the core (Figure 6.4i). Elongated fracture scars extend from one side of that edge and converge at the core's distal end.

Narrow-fronted single-platform cores (II.B.1.f) have relatively narrow (medio-laterally thin) fracture propagation surfaces (Figure 6.4j). Fracture scars may be parallel or convergent. Stoneworkers often made such cores by detaching flakes from under the edge of a flake or a biface fragment. Such cores grade into burins (see Chapter 8).

A *bidirectional-opposed-platform core* (II.B.2.a) features two separate worked edges aligned roughly parallel with one another (Figure 6.4k). The flakes detached from these edges may appear on the same or different sides of the core.

Orthogonal opposed-platform cores (II.B.2.b) have two separate worked edges aligned roughly perpendicular with one another (Figure 6.4l). One or more of the core's sides may preserve such flakes.

These core-types appear in many descriptions of Eastern African stone tool assemblages dating after 50–60 Ka BP), although sometimes having different names than those used here. Southwest Asian prehistorians use these core types (Rollefson 1994, Shea 2013b), as do colleagues working elsewhere in Africa (Tixier 1963). While they are common, fairly simple, and straightforward ways to classify cores, one has to remain alert to the possibility that the ways that prehistoric stoneworkers detached flakes from cores immediately prior to discarding them may have differed profoundly from how they modified cores in earlier phases of core reduction. To detect such strategic variation, one should compare frequencies of "terminal" core scar patterning with variation in flake dorsal scar patterning among flakes of varying sizes.

Many archaeological typologies, as well as Stoneworking Modes A–I, divide unifacial hierarchical cores into blade cores (>50 mm long), bladelet cores (<50 mm long), and microblade cores (<20–30 mm long). This practice and the size thresholds used to distinguish such blade cores from other unifacial hierarchical cores vary among research traditions and between individual archaeologists. Rather than trying to reconcile irreconcilable differences among archaeological systematics, researchers interested in the degree to which unifacial hierarchical cores retain "laminarity" (elongation) when they were discarded can simply measure and compare the cores' cardinal dimensions (i.e., length, width, and thickness).

OTHER CORES (GROUP III)

The EAST Typology Group III combines several other core types: mega-cores, micro-cores, and cores-on-flakes. Although most of these match technological or morphometric criteria for other core types, archaeologists often distinguish them from those other core categories based on their size (Figure 6.5). The EAST Typology does not intend for mega-cores, micro-cores, or cores-on-flakes to be "stand alone" artifact identifications. Rather, one should pair them with other more specific artifact-types. The EAST Typology retains mega-cores, micro-cores, and cores-on-flakes mainly to indicate the "scaling up" or "scaling down" of core designs and artifact discard thresholds.

Mega-Cores

Mega-cores (III.A) are boulders featuring one or more flake scars longer than 100 mm (Figure 6.5a). These cores differ from Victoria West cores (see above) and similar hierarchical cores recognized elsewhere in Africa in that flakes have been detached from them without much prior preparation of fracture initiation and fracture propagation surfaces.

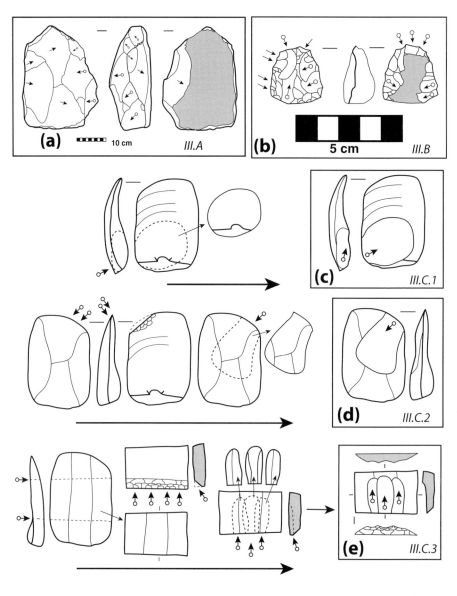

© John J. Shea

Figure 6.5 Other cores. (a) Mega-core, (b) Micro-core, (c) Core- on-flake ventral surface (aka Kombewa core), (d) Core–on- flake dorsal surface, (e) Flake segment core. Sources: (a) Gesher Benot Yaacov, Israel, (b) Omo Kibish KHS (Shea 2017b)

Micro-Cores

Just as there are mega-cores made on boulders, archaeologists recognize small (<30 mm long) cores, or *micro-cores* (III.B) (Figure 6.5b). Micro-cores' small size, and the fact that those found in Eastern Africa are often made of quartz, can make it difficult to assign them to either hierarchical or nonhierarchical core groups.

Cores-on-Flakes

Cores-on-flakes (III.C) are flake fragments featuring at least one flake removal at least half the piece's length. These flake detachments usually originate from a naturally steep edge or a backed or truncated portion for the core-on-flake's circumference. Cores-on-flakes grade into other core types, such as BHCs and UHCs, and even into retouched pieces, such as burins.

Eastern African archaeologists often use the term, *Kombewa cores* (III.C.1) for cores-on-flakes on which a relatively large fracture scar has removed all or most of the bulb of percussion from the ventral surface (Figure 6.5c). The name Kombewa references a Kenyan village.

East African typologies have no specific names for cores-on-flakes preserving flake detachment scars on their dorsal surface (III.C.2) (Figure 6.5d). Calling them *flake dorsal surface cores* seems a simple solution to this need for an artifact-type name. *Flake segment cores* (III.C.3) are truncated flake fragments from which small blades have been detached by fractures propagating under dorsal scar ridges (Figure 6.5e). Newcomer and Hivernell-Guerre (1974) document and illustrate a rich series of such artifacts from Gamble's Cave 2 in Kenya.

ELONGATED CORE-TOOLS (GROUP IV)

Elongated core-tools (Group IV) have uneven length-to-width dimensions. Most are elongated along one major morphological axis and feature relatively large and invasive flake scars. Their edges may be modified hierarchically, nonhierarchically, or both. Elongated core-tools differ from other cores mainly in having straight, sharp, and symmetrical retouched edges. Archaeologists ascribe this edge modification to both purposeful shaping of straight, mechanically efficient cutting edges, to accommodations to prehension and hafting, and to resharpening use-dulled edges. The EAST Type-List recognizes three major categories of elongated core-tools: long core-tools, foliate points, and celts/core-axes.

Long Core-Tools

Long core-tools, or LCTs (IV.A), include elongated and bilaterally symmetrical core-tools with unequal length, width, and thickness dimensions (length > width > thickness). Shaped from elongated clasts, tabular pieces of rock, and large flakes, LCTs range from relatively small pieces only a few centimeters long to massive objects of more than 300 mm.

Archaeologists' terms for LCTs vary widely. The EAST Type-List uses the term "long core-tool" because LCTs are elongated (thus "long"), most feature flake scars longer than 20–30 mm (thus "cores"), and they are indisputably artifacts (thus "tools"). Alternative terms in wide usage include handaxes, bifaces, and large cutting tools, but each of these terms has problems. "Handaxe" refers to the specific subset of long core-tools featuring retouched convergent tips. Using it as a catchall general term conflates the specific and the general, much as would using "chimpanzee" for all African apes. "Biface" is inadequate because it references invasive bifacial flake scars that not all LCTs feature. The term biface describes other bifacially flaked retouched pieces, such as foliate points (discussed below). "Large cutting tool" is doubly problematic. Most LCTs are not particularly large. They are, on average, about the size of an adult human hand with its fingers extended. Little or no direct evidence shows that LCTs were systematically used as cutting tools. Some undoubtedly were used to cut things, but archaeologists more often assume their cutting function than they can empirically demonstrate it. Few African LCTs preserve diagnostic wear traces or residues uniquely referable to cutting.

The EAST Typology's principal LCT subtypes include handaxes, cleavers, knives, picks, and lanceolates (Figure 6.6). The differences among these artifacts largely parallel those in Howell, et al., (1962).

Handaxes' (IV.A.1) retouched lateral edges converge to a sharp symmetrical distal point (Figure 6.6a–c). Near that point, or "tip", handaxes are usually medio-laterally symmetrical and lenticular (biconvex) in cross-section. Handaxes' proximal end shape can be thick or thin, rounded or angular, cortical or noncortical. European typologies recognized numerous kinds of handaxes defined in terms of their shape and to a lesser extent their size (Bordes 1961, Debénath and Dibble 1994). While experimental studies suggest greater handaxe size improves cutting performance (up to a point), shape seems to have little effect (Key and Lycett 2017). Differences among lithic materials demonstrably influence handaxe morphometric variation in Eastern Africa (Jones 1979) and elsewhere (Villa 1983). As of this writing there does not appear to be a compelling theoretical justification for recognizing further shape-based distinctions among handaxes.

Cleavers (IV.A.2) preserve an acute, broad, and unretouched edge at their distal end aligned more or less transversely to the tool's long axis (Figure 6.6d–e). Cleavers' lateral edges are usually retouched, but this varies. The lateral edges run more or less parallel to the cleaver's long axis. The EAST Typology distinguishes cleavers shaped from clasts or tabular pieces of rock as *core cleavers* (IV.A.2.a/Figure 6.6d) and those that retain evidence of their origin as large flakes, or *flake cleavers* (IV.A.2.b/Figure 6.6e). Cleavers of indeterminate origin should be classified using the more inclusive taxon, IV.A.2.

Some equatorial African sites preserve *flared cleavers* (IV.A.2.c) whose lateral edges expand laterally (or "flare") towards their (usually unretouched) distal edge (Figure 6.6f). Their lateral edges may be straight or moderately concave. These edges usually converge with one another at the end of the cleaver

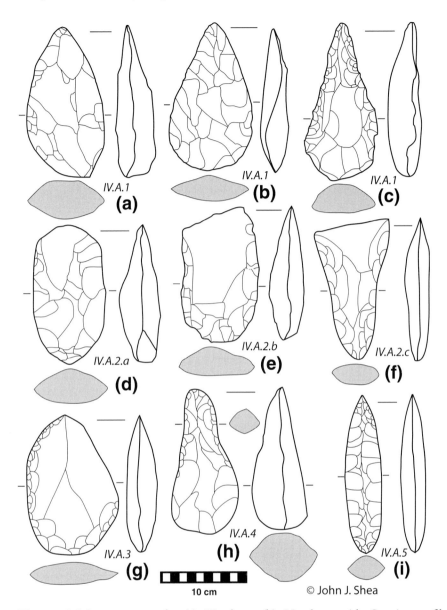

Figure 6.6 Long core-tools. (a) Handaxe, (b) Handaxe with S-twist profile, (c) "Refined" handaxe with intensely retouched tip, (d) Cleaver on core, (e) Cleaver on flake, (f) Flared cleaver, (g) Knife, (h) Pick, (i) Lanceolate.

opposite the unretouched edge. Older sources describe flared cleavers as "tranchet cleavers." This name misrepresents how stoneworkers produced these artifacts. Most flared cleavers simply retain an unretouched edge of a large flake. Actual tranchet axes are celts that have a sharp unretouched edge at one end created by a large "tranchet" flake detached perpendicular to its long axis (e.g., VIII.C.1, VIII.C.2).

A *knife* (IV.A.3) has a relatively long straight and unretouched edge near its distal end that intersects the tool's long axis at an oblique angle (Figure 6.6g). The edge opposite the unretouched edge is either naturally steep or steeply retouched. Retouch on other edges varies in extend and invasiveness. Many knives are large flakes with retouch along all but one of their edges. As such, they grade into various kinds of large elongated retouched pieces, including scrapers (IX.A.1), backed/truncated pieces (IX.B), and thinned pieces (IX.D).

Picks (IV.A.4) have a thick distal tip formed at the conjunction of two slightly concave lateral edges (Figure 6.6h). This tip's cross-section can be rectangular, plano-convex, or triangular. The East Typology recognizes *single-pointed picks* (IV.A.4.a) and *double-pointed picks* (IV.A.4.b).

Lanceolates (IV.A.5) are relatively long (>100 mm) LCTs with parallel and tapering retouched lateral edges (Figure 6.6i). These straight or shallowly convex edges converge to a point at their distal end and to either a rounded or pointed edge at their proximal end. Lanceolates are narrow (<100 mm) and thick (>20 mm). Like handaxes, their cross-sections are biconvex or plano-convex. They differ from double-pointed picks mainly in thinness (<30 mm). Lanceolates' name implies use as a hafted weapon tip, but little or no evidence supports this conjectural function.

Foliate Points

Foliate points ("leaf-like points," IV.B) are relatively small (<100 mm long) core-tools featuring at least one point formed by converging retouched edges and either wholly or partly bifacial flake scars around their circumference (Figure 6.7a–d). Flake scars that extend to or beyond the midpoint of their width suggest stoneworkers deliberately tried to reduce their dorsal-ventral thickness and, thus, their mass. Unlike small LCTs, foliate points preserve invasive "thinning" retouch scarring at their proximal end. These could be modifications for inserting this part of the tool into a handle; but not all foliate points preserve such basal thinning retouch. Many foliate points are so extensively retouched that one cannot determine whether they were originally a flake or, if so, what kind. Some foliate points retain cortex at or near their base or one of their other surfaces. Foliate points differ from convergently retouched flake-points (IX.C) in lacking a complete remnant striking platform (see Chapter 6).

The EAST Typology subdivides foliate points into five major groups along gross morphological lines. *Flat-based foliate points* (IV.B.1) have a flat or moderately concave retouched edge at their base (Figure 6.7a). *Convex-based foliate points* (IV.B.2) have a sharp point at one end and a convex edge at the other (Figure 6.7b). *Double-tipped foliate points* (IV.B.3) have converging retouched edges at both distal and proximal ends (Figure 6.7c). *Tanged foliate points* (IV.B.4) have retouched concavities near the proximal ends of their lateral edges that create a symmetrical projection, or "tang" (Figure 6.7d). *Concave-based foliate*

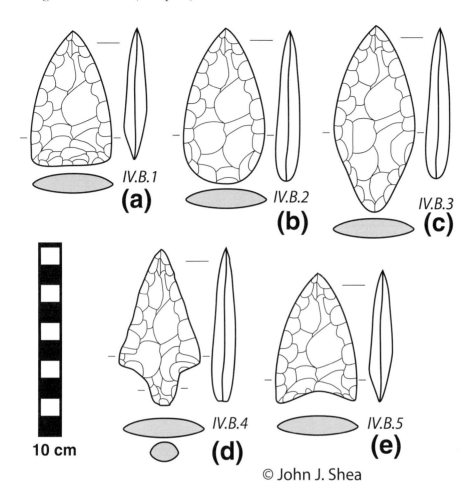

Figure 6.7 Foliate points. (a) Flat-based foliate point, (b) Convex-based foliate point, (c) Double-tipped foliate point, (d) Tanged foliate point, (e) Concave-based foliate point.

points (IV.B.5) have a concave indentation at their base (Figure 6.7e). As with handaxes, future research may justify more complex foliate point typology, but no reason for doing so exists today.

Eastern African archaeologists recognize a few foliate point types, such as Aduma points, Hargesian points, and Tshitolian points, but few of these have caught on more widely than among the sites and regions where archaeologists originally identified them. Published artifact illustrations suggest much overlap among foliate point types.

No archaeological consensus exists over where to draw the line between bifacially retouched LCTs (handaxes and lanceolates) and foliate points. Large-scale comparisons using some combined index of length versus cross-sectional area may reveal either patterns in archaeologists' diagnoses or "natural" breaks among archaeological specimens. One or the other of these could serve as a metric criterion for making a formal taxonomic distinction between LCTs and foliate points.

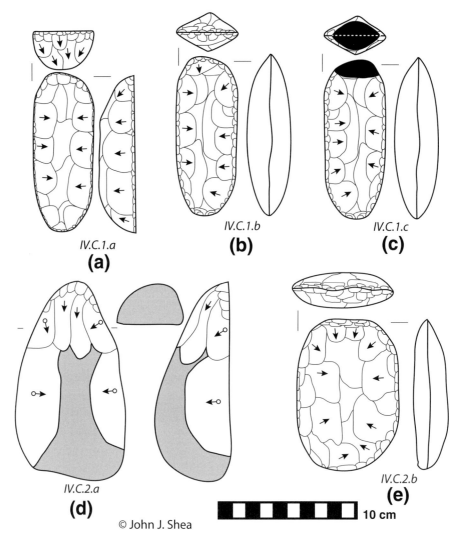

© John J. Shea

Figure 6.8 Celts and core-axes. (a) Unifacially retouched celt, (b) Bifacially retouched celt, (c) Retouched celt with abraded distal edge, (d) Wedge-shaped core-axe, (e) Flat core-axe.

Celts and Core-Axes

Celts and core-axes (IV.C) are elongated core-tools with a straight or convex retouched edge at their distal end.

Celts (IV.1) are elongated and roughly rectangular or trapezoidal in shape (Figure 6.8a–c). Their lateral edges may be straight, convex, or distally expanding. Celts' maximum width and thickness are located near the midpoint of their length or at their distal end. The EAST Typology recognizes three major celt types (IV.C.1.a–c): *unifacially retouched celts* (IV.C.1.a, Figure 6.8a), *bifacially retouched celts* (IV.C.1.b, Figure 6.8b), and *retouched celts with abraded distal edges* (IV.C.1.c, Figure 6.8c). It treats celts whose entire surfaces are abraded as groundstone artifacts (see Chapter 9).

The EAST typology recognizes two main variants of core-axes (IV.C.2). *Wedge-shaped core-axes* (IV.C.2.a) are roughly conical or wedge-like in overall shape. They have a broad proximal end and distally converging lateral edges. Their maximum width and thickness are near their proximal end (Figure 6.8d). Wedge-shaped core-axes grade into picks (IV.A.4), from which they differ only in distal edge shape. When such artifacts appear in younger contexts, archaeologists' names for them vary widely. *Flat core-axes* (IV.C.2.b) are relatively wide and thin with roughly parallel lateral edges (Figure 6.8e). Some such flat core-axes may be heavily resharpened celts approaching the end of their use-life.

Box 4 *Questions about cores and core-tools*

Were choppers actually used to chop things? Some ESA choppers (unifacially and bifacially retouched pebble-cores) have damage on their edges consistent with use as percussive cutting tools used on hard materials, such as wood or bone (Leakey 1971). This being said, many choppers are too small to have been used for such work.

Are there chronological trends in handaxe design and, if so, what do they mean? Handaxes were among the first stone tools proposed as evidence for human geological antiquity (Gamble and Kruszynski 2009). Archaeologists have been speculating about handaxes for more than 200 years with no end in sight (Wynn and Gowlett 2018). At the time prehistoric research began in Eastern Africa, European archaeologists thought that increased handaxe "refinement" (thinness, symmetry, small-scale retouch) over time tracked evolutionary progress among prehistoric hominins.

In his first synthesis of African Stone Age prehistory, Louis Leakey (1936) noted that handaxes from earlier Pleistocene contexts were large pieces with thick tips, large flake scars, and sinuous edge profiles. Middle Pleistocene handaxes were also large, but these handaxes and cleavers were also more symmetrical and extensively flaked, featuring straight or slightly curved edge profiles. Later Pleistocene handaxes were smaller, with concave edges forming more sharply convergent tips. These later pieces appeared not as well made as earlier handaxes, and so Leakey proposed that in Eastern Africa handaxe designs followed a recursive trend (Figure 6.9a). That is, earlier LCTs tracked progressive improvements in hominin toolmaking skills, but those skills declined toward the end of the Pleistocene.

Later studies analyzing large handaxes samples from Olorgesailie (Isaac 1977), Isimila (Kleindienst 1961), and Olduvai (Roe 1994) showed wide variation among handaxes from deposits of roughly the same age. Some archaeologists still equate handaxe "refinement" with some kind of progressive evolutionary trend, but most see handaxe shape variation as combining a core set of metric properties with considerable stochastic (randomly variable) shape variation (Crompton and Gowlett 1993). Early

Box 4 (*Cont.*)

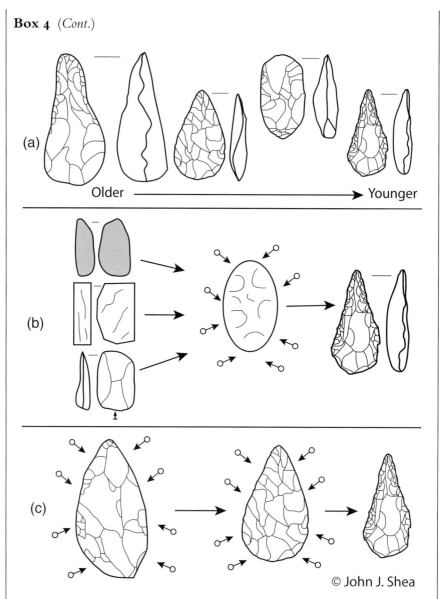

Figure 6.9 Models of long core-tool variation. (a) Progressive model, (b) Convergence model, (c) Curation model.

Pleistocene handaxes vary mainly in ways reflecting greater or lesser amounts of tip and edge resharpening, while Later Pleistocene ones reflect stoneworkers' imposing a specific shape on edges (McPherron 2007).

Convergence complicates archaeological hypotheses about handaxes. Put simply, one can shape an LCT from pretty much any starting point: a tabular piece of stone, a large clast, or a large flake (Figure 6.9b). Traces of these different origins may remain on less-extensively modified handaxes, but they may be invisible on more heavily flaked and retouched artifacts.

Box 4 *(Cont.)*

Resharpening poses further problems interpreting handaxe variation through time, because retouch alters lithic artifact size and shape. Continued use and retouch can cause larger and broader handaxes to become smaller and narrower (Figure 6.9c). This means that assemblages dominated by larger/broader or smaller/narrower handaxes may not necessarily reflect specific toolmaking traditions so much as variation in artifact discard thresholds (Jones 1994).

Does reducing hierarchical cores require more skill or intelligence than reducing nonhierarchical cores? Hierarchical core reduction requires someone to create and maintain functionally different sides of worked edges and to delay striking the edge until both fracture initiation and propagation surfaces have been adequately shaped. It follows that planning depth and impulse control are crucial skills for hierarchical core reduction (Wynn 1989). Bonobos that have been taught to make stone tools do not make hierarchical cores at all (Toth et al. 1993). Humans who learn to make stone tools usually make nonhierarchical cores first and hierarchical cores later (Shea 2015). These observations support the "more skill and impulse control" hypothesis, although one has to be cautious about equating these qualities with intelligence. Measuring intelligence among living humans is difficult enough (Gould 1981), let alone inferring it for extinct hominins from stone tools about whose production and use we know so little with any great certainty.

Why do archaeologists care so much about blade cores and blades? Occurrences of elongated unifacial hierarchical "blade" cores and prismatic blades in assemblages older than 40 Ka attract great popular and scientific notice (Bar-Yosef and Kuhn 1999). This attention reflects the history of archaeological research. In Europe and western Asia, where prehistoric research began, blade cores and prismatic blades became common in archaeological assemblages dating to around 30–45 Ka, appearing together with *Homo sapiens'* fossils, bone tools, and art (Mellars 1989). From this correlation, many archaeologists inferred that blades were hallmarks of human "behavioral modernity" (McBrearty and Brooks 2000). Some archaeologists considered, and still consider, occurrences of blade production in older contexts as evidence for the origins of "behaviorally modern" humans (Nowell 2010). Such claims often cite Leroi-Gourhan's (1964) assertion that blade core reduction recovered vastly more potentially useful cutting edge than alternative methods. In fact, bipolar core reduction yields more useful cutting edge per unit of stone and per unit of time than blade core reduction (Pargeter and Eren 2017). With early examples of blade core reduction currently dating to 0.5 Ma in Eastern and southern Africa (Johnson and McBrearty 2010, Wilkins and Chazan 2012), making blades now appears to be no "big deal" at all, just one of a battery of toolmaking strategies hominins deployed under varying circumstances from Middle Pleistocene times onward.

UWAZI VALLEY TALES, EPISODE 6: HANDAXES,
LCTS, AND LERPS

Morning found us standing in a *laga*, a dry streambed, looking up at a tall
vertical section of stratified clays, silts, sands, and tuffs. The Old Africa Hand
and I faced the Polymath, who described the stratigraphy.

"Immediately under these Big Basalt Block capstones lies Bed A. It contains
MSA much like in Level 7 in sands and silts. Under Bed A is the Brown Tuff. It
dates to 0.5 Ma."

The tuff was white, so I asked, "Why do you call it the Brown Tuff?"

"We named it in memory of Frank Brown, the geologist," the Polymath
said. "Under that, Bed B preserves fluvial deposits with handaxes and other
Acheulian tools in them. There's a few single-elephant and single-hippo
carcass sites with stone artifacts around them.

"Meat jackpot sites," I thought.

The Polymath continued, "The Gray Tuff separates Bed B from Bed C. It
dates to 1.7 Ma. Bed C contains mainly lakeshore and near-shore sediments
with small clusters of pebble-cores and flakes. So, we're thinking Oldowan or
pre-Oldowan.

"Any big stone tools, like the Lomekwian?" I asked the Polymath.

"Not so far. At any rate, lower Bed C sits on a massive basalt layer dating to
4.5 Ma."

The Polymath and the Old Africa Hand had put survey pins, colorful plastic
flags attached to metal wires, at various points along the edge of the *laga* where
they found stone tools or large vertebrate fossils concentrated.

We walked, tracing the Gray Tuff as it meandered across the *laga* walls. After
about half an hour the Old Africa Hand announced a discovery.

"Now, here's a beauty." He photographed a black stone artifact roughly the
size and shape of his hand, planting an orange flag next to it. He picked up the
artifact and dusted it off with a small whisk broom.

"A biface?" I asked.

"An Acheulian handaxe," the Old Africa Hand replied.

"A large cutting tool," said the Polymath at the same time.

"Archaeologists have names for these things like Eskimo have names for
snow," said the Old Africa Hand.

"Americans often call them bifaces, though not all of them have been
shaped bifacially," said the Polymath.

"Some of these artifacts are just big flakes with a bit of retouch here and
there. Others have been reduced from tabular pieces of stone," said the Old
Africa Hand.

"So, they're large, elongated retouched pieces," I said. Why not abbreviate them to LERPs?"

"That may be the worst acronym for stone tools I have ever heard," said the Old Africa Hand.

"It's accurate," I said.

"It lacks panache," the Old Africa Hand replied.

"That's just what the field needs, another name for these artifacts," said the Polymath.

"I wonder what the hominins who made them called them?" I said.

"Probably nothing, or at least nothing we could understand," said the Polymath. "These handaxes' makers, *Homo ergaster*, had a different upper respiratory tract than ours. They probably couldn't talk as we do."

"But all the same," said the Old Africa Hand, "there's more here than just opportunistic stoneworking or chimpanzee rock-smashing. There's this shape imposed in a patterned kind of way, a patterned imposition of non intrinsic shape. You can't deny this is culture of some kind?"

"Can you have culture without spoken language?" I asked.

"Our colleague, Famous Primatologist, argues that chimpanzees have culture," said the Polymath. "Chimpanzee groups differ in how they use tools and groom one another."

"Well, said the Old Africa Hand, "if you reduce your definition of culture to the lowest common denominator, then, yes, apes have culture, but by the same logic, anyone who's camped overnight in the woods can claim to be a 'wilderness survival expert' and anyone who's taken a dip in the ocean without drowning is a 'swimmer'. If apes have culture, then where is their Shakespeare, their Bach, their Vincent Van Gogh?"

"In her last television documentary, Famous Primatologist argued that if we taught chimpanzees and bonobos how to communicate using artificial symbols, they might create their own art, music, and literature," I said.

" 'Might' and 'will' are very different things, Robin," said the Old Africa Hand. "You can fit speculation to any theory, but you should only take seriously theories that make specific predictions."

"Maybe we need different terms for different kinds of cultures: one term for ethnographic ones, other terms for nonhuman primate ones, and another set for prehistoric hominins whose behavior we cannot observe directly," I said.

"That will never fly, Robin," said the Old Africa Hand. "Using different terms would undercut the publicity value of claiming to find evidence of culture among nonhuman primates or precociously early in the archaeological record. Never underestimate the power of the press release."

The Polymath spoke: "Human culture varies. These LCTs remain more or less unchanging, or minimally variable across vast areas for hundreds of thousands of years. They are virtually the *opposite* of culture. That lack of variability suggests they might not be cultural products at all. Maybe they're something else, something for which we have no close analogy among our own material culture."

"Something genetically programmed, like a birdsong or a bird's nest?" I suggested.

"Some have argued as much," the Polymath said.

"Has anyone systematically compared LCTs from *Homo ergaster* contexts to ones found together with *Homo sapiens*?" I asked. "I mean, if language and culture structure human stoneworking but not *Homo ergaster*'s stoneworking, then we ought to see differences in the way LCTs found with these hominins vary."

"McPherron compared early handaxes to ones found with *Homo heidelbergensis* and Neandertals in Europe and found some differences, but nobody's done a similar study for African handaxes found with early *Homo sapiens*. One of the problems for doing such a study is that we identify them by simple, visually assessed morphological analogy. That is to say, 'that looks like a handaxe,' rather than by objective measurements. The other problem is that they call your 'large elongated retouched pieces' by different names in different age-stages. Acheulian handaxes range from massive artifacts several times larger than this one to little ones not much bigger than your thumb. One calls those from MSA assemblages handaxes, but longer narrower ones are "lanceolates" and shorter ones 'foliate points.' Handaxes, lanceolates, and foliate points also grade into one another. They seem rather rare in LSA, Neolithic, and Iron Age assemblages, but that could be a bit of confirmation bias at work. When archaeologists find artifacts like handaxes in recent contexts, they often assume the artifacts were dislodged from older deposits. At any rate, archaeologists rarely call such things 'handaxes' or 'LCTs' when they find them in contexts younger than 40,000 years ago."

"The other problem, Robin," the Old Africa Hand said, "is that we have so few sites in which early *Homo sapien* fossils occur together with rich stone artifact assemblages – basically Herto in the Middle Awash and the sites near Kibish in the Lower Omo River Valley."

As if he were a father putting a baby in its cradle, the Old Africa Hand gently set the stone tool where he found it.

"Why did you put it back?" I asked.

"To preserve site visibility," said the Polymath.

"Damn things are heavy." The Old Africa Hand smiled, pointing his walking stick at other stone tools nearby. "Besides, if we took it, it might grow lonely and miss its companions."

Hours later, the Old Africa Hand and I walked together on the trail back up to camp. The Polymath and Joseph had spotted pangolin tracks and set off in hot pursuit.

"Tracking is the root of the scientific method!" the Polymath shouted as they set off.

"Last semester he taught us stoneworking was," I sighed.

"I'm going to have a problem comparing the stone tool from Beds A–C to those from the Ancient Ones' Cave," I said to the Old Africa Hand.

"What's the problem?" he replied, pausing.

"It's all of Eastern African stone tools systematics, the typologies, the age-stages, the industries. Basically, it's anarchy. Not like 'Friday night at the frat house' anarchy, but nineteenth-century utopian anarchy, a landscape of small self-governing communities and individuals. After talking with Aya, Endurance, and Joseph, yesterday, I'm not sure I can reconcile our evidence with the different definitions of age-stages or industries. I don't even know where to start trying to fix things."

"Look, Robin, if you're going to compare stone tools across wide ranges of time and space, don't waste your time on the age-stages and industries. Those things are antiques. Archaeologists mostly keep them around out of misplaced reverence for past practices. 'My professor taught me to do this, so I teach my students the same.' I only teach about age-stages and industries so that students will know what the terms mean when they read the older literature. With time, they will probably just fade from use. Someone will stop using them, others will follow their example."

"European archaeologists have used the same age-stages and industries for more than a century," I said.

"I didn't say it would happen overnight. Besides, maybe they suit their needs. You'll enjoy more success if you focus on the artifacts and the artifact-types. Each artifact is like a snapshot of human behavior. Patterned variation among snapshots parallels variation in their subjects. Most formal wedding pictures have an identifiable bride and a groom, though I gather that varies more and more these days. They differ from children's school photos, pictures in newspapers' sports pages, and images people post on social media when they're on vacations or out to dinner. Age-stages, industries – they're more like collages children put together from whatever photographs they can lay hands on. No two of them have the same organization."

He continued, "Like telling one kind of photograph from another, matching an individual artifact to an artifact-type still involves visually assessed morphological analogy. In principle, it ought to be less controversial than dealing with industries and age-stages. If you call a shoulders-up picture of a well-groomed child a school photo or some other kind of formal portrait, few will dispute that identification. Claims about collages are more controversial. One's own child's collage is a work of genius; those of other people's children, perhaps not so much. Start fresh. You'll make mistakes, but at least they will be your own mistakes, not someone else's. First, though, you'll need to show others the problems you've discovered. Do a little 'demonstrator project.'"

162

Cores and Core-Tools

"So, where to start?" I asked. "Handaxes?"

"You mean LERPS? No. Handaxes are iconic, but only a small number of archaeologists actually care about them. Fewer archaeologists work on the ESA than other age-stages."

"How about points?" I asked.

"Too complex. Archaeologists have argued over what to call these things for more than 50 years now. Back in the 1960s, François Bordes proposed determining what sorts of stone tools to call points by attaching replicas to spears and then having typologists hunt bears with them. He admitted that doing this would run down the supply of typologists."

A missed opportunity, I thought.

"Here in Eastern Africa points are mainly an issue for the MSA. It's a hot topic these days, but the audience remains small."

"Levallois tools?"

"Same thing, mainly relevant for the MSA and its chronological margins. But that's actually a success story. Criteria for identifying Levallois tools used to be a mess, but since Boëda's work redefining them, there's more consistency. People use the same criteria across different research traditions. Good to cite that in your work, Robin. It shows that reform can happen if people want it to, and if they push hard for it. Why don't you give microliths a go? They're common in recent age-stages. More archaeologists work on those time periods than the ESA or MSA."

"OK, but there's a lot of variation in the literature about microlith definitions and about how to measure them."

"There's the place to start, then: widest interest, maximum impact. Hunt elephants, not rabbits."

"Do you think we can reform Eastern African stone tool systematics?" I asked.

"Yes, but it won't be easy. The whole edifice is like a tree full of weaver-bird nests, their individual strands all tangled together, and no two nests alike."

"How about starting over from scratch. Just discard all the old terms and devise new ones."

"Burn down the tree, eh? A bit cruel to the weaver birds. Remember, archaeologists didn't purposefully design their stone artifact typologies to be mutually incomparable. The Devil did not make them do it, either. Their incomparability evolved from the history of archaeological research here in Eastern Africa. In other parts of Africa, Europe, and Asia people use the same typologies over vast areas."

"Besides," the Old Africa Hand continued, "calls for radical reform rarely succeed in archaeology. Whatever their politics, college professors are a conservative lot. Have you read much about Glynn Isaac's work?

"Just some papers about food-sharing and central place foraging among Plio-Pleistocene hominins."

"That's a pity. Much of his really innovative ideas have slipped below the "Academic Literacy Event Horizon"."

"What's that?"

"It's a kind of moving frontier that advances year by year toward the present. Nobody makes students read papers published before that year, and so they disappear from professional knowledge, much like matter does into the event horizon of a neutron star. Anyway, back in the 1980s, Glynn Isaac proposed scrapping all stone artifact-types other than cores, flakes, retouched pieces and percussors and then requiring anybody who wanted to recognize more specific artifact-types to provide sound and compelling theoretical justifications for doing so."

"How'd that work out?" I asked.

"Have you read many sound and compelling theoretical justifications for the artifact-types archaeologists recognize today?"

"Not one."

"Indeed. Archaeology self-governs by consensus. If you want things to change, you'll have to build a consensus for change. You'll have to promote your views, of course. Read papers at meetings, publish journal articles. It's a long game, though. Don't expect instant success. Just remember, old habits die hard; bad ideas have their own dark energy. Nothing spreads faster, lasts longer, or has more popular appeal than a bad idea. Good ideas need careful nurturing and tireless advocacy."

We came across some elephant tracks and paused to examine them.

"Professor, back at the university, people say you keep an elephant gun in your office. Growing up here, in Africa, did you hunt elephants?"

"Slaughter those majestic creatures so short-fingered vulgarians can buy carved ivory trinkets? No. Richard Leakey has the right idea. Shoot the poachers, burn the ivory, and throw the traffickers in prison. Besides, we owe the elephants a debt. How do you think humans and earlier hominins dispersed so far, so fast, and so widely here in Africa?

"Boats and rivers?"

"Possibly. We don't know when Africans started making boats, but we know they had feet. You won't get far walking through an acacia thorn woodland."

Acacias, or "wait-a-bit" bushes, would end up shredding the shoulders off many of my shirts that year.

"The paths elephants trampled through Africa's forests were the continent's original green highways. If you ever get lost or stranded out here, Robin, follow the elephants to water. Just give the mothers with calves a wide berth. They can hear and smell you long before you see them."

"How ironic that modern highways now bring poachers to the elephants," I said.

"Irony and tragedy are different things. Besides, those highways also bring food, medicine, education, and the rule of law. Roads are civilization's yardsticks. Do you know the story about the Roman Emperor Hadrian's visit to the Pyramids in Egypt?"

"No," I said.

"One of the Seven Wonders of the Ancient World, and even back then, tourists overran them. Hadrian's Egyptian hosts asked the Emperor what he thought. Hadrian said, 'Who are these fools who marvel at the tombs of bygone tyrants and ignore the new Roman roads on which they traveled here safely?'"

I nodded, and we walked on. Later, much later, I realized he had dodged my question about his elephant gun.

CHAPTER 7

FLAKES/DETACHED PIECES

This chapter reviews conventions for measuring, describing, and classifying flakes or "detached pieces." These include core-initiation flakes (EAST Typology Group V), core-exploitation flakes (Group VI), core-repair flakes (Group VII), and retouch flakes (Group VIII). The chapter answers common questions about flakes/detached pieces.

MEASURING FLAKES/DETACHED PIECES

Measurements archaeologists make on flakes can be technological measurements, morphological measurements, or some combination of both (Figure 7.1). *Technological measurements* are fixed in relation to the fracture initiation point located on the ridge between the ventral surface and the striking platform. Technological length originates at the fracture initiation point and extends perpendicularly from it across the ventral surface to the farthest point on that surface's distal edge. Many archaeologists measure technological width and thickness at the midpoint of technological length. Striking platform width originates and terminates at those two points where the dorsal surface, striking platform surface, and ventral surface intersect with one another. Striking platform thickness is measured from fracture initiation point to the nearest point on the ridge, dividing the striking platform from the rest of the dorsal surface. *Morphological measurements* of length, width, and thickness are usually maximum values – maximum length, maximum width perpendicular to length, and maximum thickness perpendicular to the dorsal/ventral plane. Morphological striking platform measurements also emphasize maximum values and maximum striking platform width and thickness.

Since no single standard set of measurements prevails among Eastern African archaeologists, it does not really matter whether one uses technological or morphological measurements. However, as with cores and core-tools (Chapter 6), it is crucially important that the choice of measurements used is clearly apparent when reporting measurements to colleagues. The author

Technological Measurements

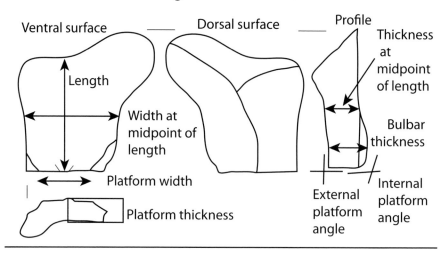

Morphological Measurements

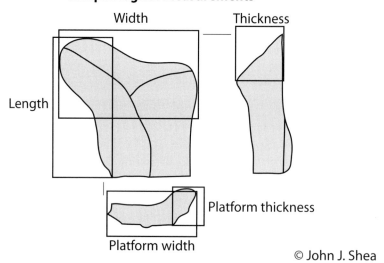

© John J. Shea

Figure 7.1 Continuous measurements for flakes.

prefers recording technological length, width at midpoint of length, thickness at midpoint of length, striking platform width, and striking platform thickness at the fracture initiation point. No evidence shows that such technological measurements are intrinsically more analytically valuable or replicable than morphological ones. One could very well measure both, if so inclined, and thereby increase the ease with which these observations could be compared with a larger number of lithic assemblages. In selecting measurements, such comparability has to be balanced with other factors, such as relevance to one's research question, of course, but also replicability (i.e., measurements that other researchers can reproduce).

Increasingly, archaeologists also measure either the internal or external *striking platform angle*. The internal striking platform angle (IPA) measures the angle at which the striking platform and flake ventral surfaces intersect. An external striking platform angle (EPA) measures the angle at which striking platform and flake dorsal surfaces intersect. These angles are roughly reciprocals of one another. In principle, high EPA/low IPA values indicate flakes struck from relatively steep worked edges, while low EPA/high IPA values indicate flakes struck from narrower worked edges. An external platform angle can be difficult to measure reliably, for it can vary widely along an edge. Platform crushing can also lead to ambiguous EPA values. Measuring an internal platform angle poses fewer such difficulties, and this variable's values are roughly inversely correlated with external platform angles. For a comparative study of different methods for measuring such angles, see Dibble and Bernard (1980).

Increasingly, many archaeologists also record flake mass. That they rarely did this in former times probably reflects the recent availability of inexpensive digital scales. Similarly, the availability of digital calipers has paralleled an increased use of measurement-based comparisons of intra and interassemblage variability. Nevertheless, *always measure flake mass*. It is the most replicable measurement of all the countless measurements archaeologists make on flakes or any other artifact.

Archaeologists do not do much, analytically, with flake fragments other than count and (sometimes) weigh them. Because proximal flake fragments retain parts of the original flake's striking platform, however, archaeologists often perform similar measurements on their striking platforms to those that they measure on complete flakes.

The most common discrete measurements of detached pieces include dorsal cortex coverage, dorsal flake scar count, striking platform morphology, fracture termination, and dorsal flake scar pattern (Figure 7.2).

Dorsal cortex coverage: As with cores, how much weathered exterior surface remains on a flake's dorsal surface (including the striking platform) can reveal whether stoneworkers detached a flake early or later in core reduction (Figure 7.2a). Archaeologists usually estimate flake cortex coverage as a range of percentage values. Most distinguish flakes with more than 50% cortex coverage from those with less. Others make finer distinctions, but doing so increases potential interobserver variation. The intervals 0, 1–10, 10–40, 40–60, 60–90, 90–99, and 100% seem a good balance between precision and replicability.

Fracture termination (Figure 7.2b) describes whether the distal end of a flake is sharply angular ("feathered"), steeply angled ("stepped"), dorsally recurved ("hinged"), or ventrally recurved ("plunging"). Flake scars left by stepped, hinged, and recurved fracture terminations create obstacles to further removals from core fracture propagation surfaces. Finding many such fracture terminations among flakes may indicate low stoneworker skill, but lithic material

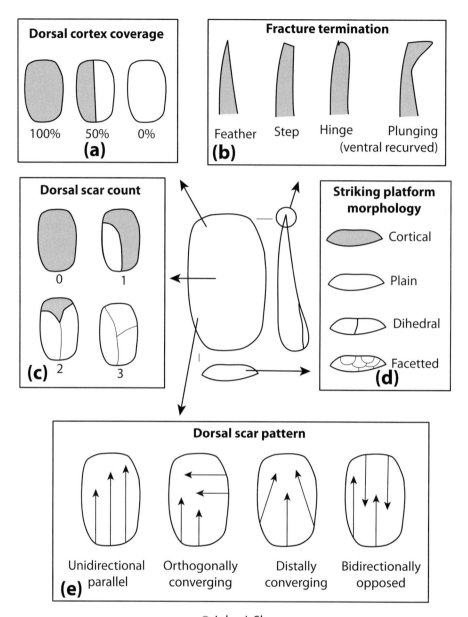

© John J. Shea

Figure 7.2 Discrete measurements for flakes. (a) Dorsal cortex coverage, (b) Fracture termination, (c) Dorsal scar count, (d) Striking platform morphology, (e) Dorsal scar pattern.

toughness may affect these values, too. Brittle rocks such as quartz and obsidian are more susceptible to postdetachment bending fractures. They may preserve high frequencies of step-terminated fractures for reasons unrelated to stoneworker skill. Ratios of feather- versus hinge-terminated flakes may be better measures of stoneworker skill (i.e., fewer hinge-terminated fractures indicates more skill).

In principle, *dorsal scar count* (Figure 7.2c) – how many flake detachment scars above a given size appear on a flake's dorsal surface – indicates whether a stoneworker detached a flake earlier or later in core reduction. Archaeologists usually set the lower length threshold for counting fracture scars somewhere between 10 and 30 mm. Whatever threshold one sets for this variable should be the same one used for counting flake scars on cores.

Striking platform morphology (Figure 7.2d) describes the extent of cortex and flake scars on a flake's striking platform. This attribute is usually recorded as cortical, plain, dihedral, or facetted. Cortical and plain striking platforms are thought to indicate flakes detached earlier on in core reduction than dihedral or facetted ones. Some sources also record absent, crushed, or partial striking platforms.

Dorsal scar pattern (Figure 7.2e) describes how the propagation trajectories of flake scars on a flake's dorsal surface align with one another. Such flake scar directionality is thought to reflect learned strategies for core initiation, exploitation, and repair. Archaeologists differ in how they infer values for this attribute and in how they record it. A minimal classification includes unidirectional parallel, orthogonally converging, distally converging, and bidirectionally opposed flake scars. Whatever categories one uses to record this variable, they should be the same or as close as possible to those used to describe core scar patterning. Doing this will allow one to detect changes in core surface preparation during the course of core reduction as well as differences between final, prediscard core preparation, and earlier core preparation strategies.

The EAST Typology divides flakes and other detached pieces into technological categories: core-initiation flakes (Group V), core-exploitation flakes (Group VI), core-maintenance flakes (Group VII), and retouch flakes (Group VIII).

CORE-INITIATION FLAKES (GROUP V)

Core-initiation removes naturally occurring obstacles to predictable flake detachment, such as cortex, concavities, ridges, and other rock surface features. Core-initiation flakes' dorsal surfaces preserve these features. Core-initiation flakes are usually relatively thick, preserving low ratios of cutting edge to either mass or volume. The EAST Typology recognizes four main kinds of core-initiation flakes: split clasts, clast initiation flakes, tabular initiation flakes, and crested flakes (Figure 7.3).

Split Clasts

A clast is a rock that abrasion has worn into a round shape. *Split clasts* (V.A) describe clast fragments that stoneworkers have split using shear fracture. Split clasts are usually round or oval in plan view and hemispherical or plano-convex in cross-section (Figure 7.3a).

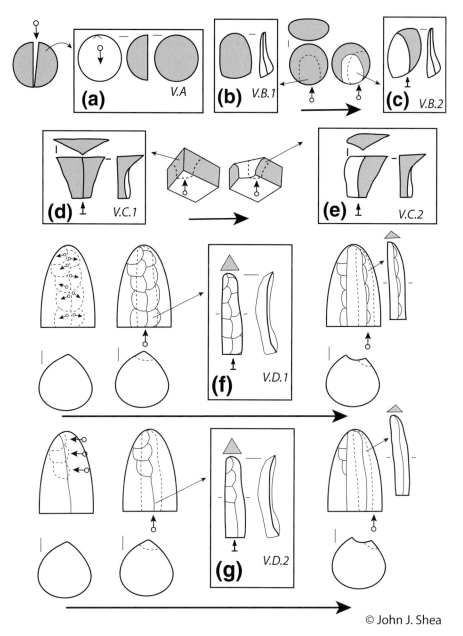

© John J. Shea

Figure 7.3 Core-initiation flakes. (a) Split clast, (b) Primary clast initiation flake, (c) Secondary clast initiation flake, (d) Primary tabular initiation flake, (e) Secondary tabular initiation flake, (f) Bifacially crested flake, (g) Unifacially crested flake.

Clast Initiation Flakes

Clast initiation flakes (V.B) result from Hertzian cone fractures initiated at the margins of a rounded rock. Clast initiation flakes differ from split clasts in preserving a striking platform, a ventral surface with a bulb of percussion, as well as variable amounts of weathering on their dorsal surface (Figure 7.3b–c). Their thickest point is usually at their proximal end, giving most clast initiation flakes a wedge-shaped profile. The EAST Typology recognizes primary and secondary clast initiation flakes. On *primary clast initiation flakes* (V.B.1), 50% more of their dorsal surface retains weathered/cortical (Figure 7.3b). On *secondary clast initiation flakes* (V.B.2), the cortex covers less than 50% of the dorsal surface (Figure 7.3c).

Tabular Initiation Flakes

Tabular initiation flakes (V.C) are detached from tabular stones (Figure 7.3d–e). Such tabular stones usually feature steep angular edges and extensive cortex. As a result, the first several flakes detached from them feature sharp projections at their distal end, which is often their thickest part. The EAST Typology recognizes primary and secondary tabular initiation flakes. *Primary tabular initiation flakes* (V.C.1) often have expanding lateral edges, while *secondary tabular initiation flakes* (V.C.2) have lateral edges skewed either right or left. Both kinds of tabular initiation flakes preserve cortex, with primary ones having 50% or more of their dorsal surface, secondary ones having less than 50%.

Crested Flakes

Crested flakes (V.D) have a shaped dorsal scar ridge ("crest") running parallel with their long axis from which shorter flake scars propagate more or less perpendicularly away from that ridge (Figure 7.3f–g). Crested flakes' thickest point lies beneath this ridge. They are usually triangular or trapezoidal in cross-section. The EAST Typology recognizes two crested flake types. On *bifacial crested flakes* (V.D.1), fracture initiations appear on both sides of the flake's central ridge (Figure 7.3f). On *unifacial crested flakes* (V.D.2), fracture initiations appear on one side of the crest only Figure 7.3g). Either kind of crested flake may feature cortex on its dorsal surface.

As Figure 7.3 shows, detaching a crested flake can remove convexities from fracture propagation surfaces and it can straighten a ridge on a fracture propagation surface. Crested flake detachment can leave behind the two relatively straight flake scar ridges that help stoneworkers to create the first in a series of elongated and symmetrical core-exploitation flakes.

Archaeologists associate bifacial crested flakes with unifacial hierarchical core reduction, especially prismatic blade/bladelet core reduction. Yet other tool-making activities can create them, too. Efforts to reestablish convexities at the flake propagation surfaces' lateral margins during recurrent laminar BHC reduction create crested flakes similar to those from UHC reduction.

CORE-EXPLOITATION FLAKES (GROUP VI)

Stoneworkers detach core-exploitation flakes (Group VI) in order to recover useable sharp cutting edges, to produce flakes of one or another predetermined shape, and to impose shape on a core. Inasmuch as these needs can vary through time and space and even occur simultaneously, core-exploitation flakes encompass a wide range of artifact morphological and metric variation. Most core-exploitation flakes have relatively high ratios of circumference to mass, and many are also symmetrical. These qualities enhance cutting effectiveness, ease of use, and prehension, as well as potential for resharpening and reuse. Group VI recognizes five groups of core-exploitation flakes: bipolar flakes (VI.A), biface thinning flakes (VI.B), bifacial hierarchical core exploitation flakes (VI.C), unifacial hierarchical core exploitation flakes (VI.D), and other core-exploitation flakes (VI.E).

Bipolar Flakes

Bipolar flakes (VI.A) result from bipolar percussion applied to either a clast or a flake. Their defining features include concentrations of overlapping incompletely propagated flake scars near their points of fracture initiation (Figure 7.4a). Bipolar flakes may preserve more than one such patch of comminution at opposite ends of a flake's circumference. Because bipolar flakes often result from shear fracture, their ventral surfaces can lack a distinct bulb of percussion. Instead, they may feature deep concentric ripples radiating away from the point(s) of fracture initiation. Bipolar flakes are relatively thin in relation to their length and width.

Biface Exploitation Flakes

Biface exploitation flakes (VI.B) detach from the edge of elongated nonhierarchical bifacial cores, or "bifaces" (Figure 7.4b–c). The fractures that create such flakes usually propagate at a relatively low angle to the core's surface and, as a result, they have low external platform angles (and correspondingly high interior ones). Viewed from the side, biface exploitation flakes' ventral surfaces are relatively flat or slightly concave. Their shape in plan view and their dorsal surface topography can vary widely. When stoneworkers detach them using soft-hammer percussors or pressure, biface exploitation flakes' ventral surfaces may lack a Hertzian cone and a prominent bulb of percussion. Their striking platforms are often either facetted or dihedral. Some archaeologists use the term "lipping" for these striking platforms' broad and convex border with the ventral surface.

Smaller biface exploitation flakes grade into biface retouch flakes (see below). Those who wish to retain a distinction between these artifact types

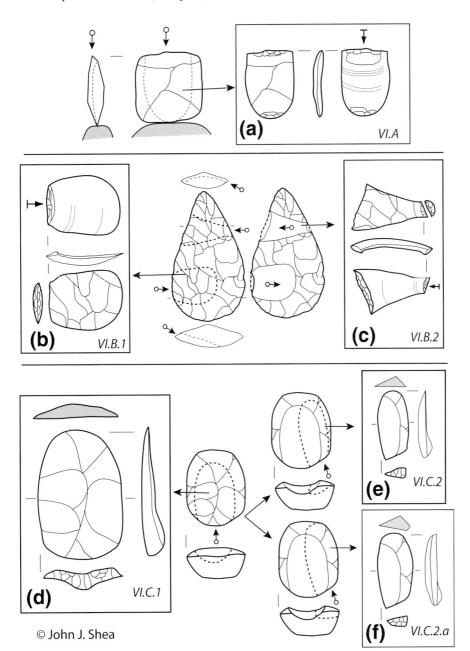

Figure 7.4 Core-exploitation flakes. (a) Bipolar flakes, (b) Biface exploitation flake, (c) Biface-overshot flake, (d) Central preferential BHC flake, (e) Lateral preferential BHC flakes, (f) Central preferential BHC flake, (g) Lateral preferential and worked edge BHC flake.

ought to set an explicit size cutoff. Inasmuch as larger biface exploitation flakes recovered from excavation are often broken, that size cutoff should not be based on overall artifact length, width, or thickness but on striking platform dimensions. A platform width threshold of >5 mm will seemingly sort most larger biface exploitation flakes from smaller biface retouch flakes, but as with so many other artifact-types, the best course of action would be to measure all these artifacts in the same way and compare/contrast them statistically.

Depending on how far they have propagated under a core surface, biface exploitation flakes may have preserved the distal ends of fracture scars propagating from the opposite side of the core. The EAST Typology recognizes two kinds of biface exploitation flakes: *Biface-thinning flakes* (VI.B.1) incorporate all the features enumerated in the preceding paragraph (Figure 7.4b). *Biface-overshot flakes* (VI.B.2) retain a portion of the worked edge from the opposite side of the core at their distal end (Figure 7.4c).

Bifacial Hierarchical Core Exploitation Flakes

Bifacial hierarchical core (BHC) exploitation flakes (VI.C) are relatively long, broad, and thin with convex facetted striking platforms and high external platform angles. Much as with BHCs, some archaeological sources describe these artifacts using the adjective "Levallois."

Central preferential BHC flakes (VI.C.1) are subrectangular or oval in plan view and relatively flat and thin in profile view. Their dorsal surfaces feature the distal ends of flake scars whose propagation trajectories converge at or near the center of the flake's dorsal surface (Figure 7.4d). Their striking platforms are facetted, have steep external platform angles (~70 degrees), and project outward from the center of the flake. Some typologies call these artifacts "typical Levallois flakes."

Lateral preferential BHC flakes (VI.C.2) undercut the lateral margins of preferential flake scars and for this reason they are moderately medio laterally asymmetrical (Figure 7.4 e): that is, one edge will be acute, the other relatively steep. Their dorsal flake scars usually juxtapose short partial flake scars on one edge with at least one larger partial flake scar on the opposite or adjacent edge. Lateral preferential BHC flakes do not detach significant amounts of core worked edge on their lateral edges. Those that do, the EAST Typology groups among core-repair flakes and recognizes as *lateral preferential and worked edge* BHC flakes (see below). Older typologies often use the term, atypical Levallois flake, for *Lateral preferential BHC flakes.*

A persistent mistranslation of the French term, *atypique* (asymmetrical) into English as "atypical" has created a widespread misperception that such artifacts are rare in comparison with so-called typical forms. This is not the case, or at least not universally. In some African lithic assemblages, atypical Levallois flakes can outnumber typical ones (e.g., Shea 2008).

The relatively large (>150–200 mm long) BHC flakes that some African archaeologists distinguish as *Victoria West flakes* Africa (VI.C.1.a) are either central preferential BHC flakes or lateral preferential BHC flakes, depending on the particular nature of their shape in plan view and their fracture termination.

BHC triangular flakes (VI.C.3), often called Levallois points, are symmetrical flakes with converging lateral edges (Figure 7.5a–c): that is, their width at the midpoint of their length is significantly less than their striking platform width. In plan view, most resemble either isosceles or scalene triangles. BHC triangular flakes vary widely in length and in dorsal flake scar patterning. Many have a symmetrical "inverted Y-shaped" or "lambda (λ)-shaped" dorsal flake scar pattern (Figure 7.5a). Eastern African archaeologists often distinguish two "Nubian" variants of BHC triangular flakes. On *Nubian Type 1 points* (VI.C.3.a), diverging and proximally propagating fracture scars form a central ridge near the point's distal end (Figure 7.5b). On *Nubian Type 2 points* (VI.C.3.b), medio-laterally converging fracture scars form a central ridge near the point's distal end (Figure 7.5c).

BHC blades (VI.C.4) are elongated rectangular flakes with parallel lateral edges and dorsal flake scars (Figure 7.5d). These artifacts are symmetrical in their medio-lateral and proximal-distal axes. Their width at the midpoint of their length is about the same as their striking platform width. Traditional European typologies often call BHC blades "atypical" Levallois flakes or Levallois blades. Some of these typologies also distinguish BHC blades with pointed distal ends as "elongated Levallois points" (Debénath and Dibble 1994). The EAST Typology combines such artifacts with BHC blades.

BHC radial flakes (VI.C.5) are short triangular or trapezoidal flakes whose morphological long axis aligns diagonally to their technological long axis (Figure 7.5e). As their name implies, they comprise common products of recurrent radial-centripetal BHC core reduction. Confusingly, some typologies call BHC radial flakes "pseudo-Levallois points" (Bordes 1961, Debénath and Dibble 1994).

Unifacial Hierarchical Core Exploitation Flakes

Unifacial hierarchical core exploitation flakes (VI.D) vary in their distinctiveness. Few flakes detached from unifacial hierarchical cores are referable solely to UHC reduction. Many resemble flakes detached by other stoneworking methods. Flakes detached from elongated unifacial hierarchical cores are more plausibly referable to blade or bladelet core reduction. All these artifacts (VI.D.1–5) are "prismatic blades" in the traditional sense – their length is greater than or equal to their width. They have straight and parallel lateral edges. Their dorsal flake scars align parallel to each other and with the flake's axis of fracture propagation (Figure 7.5f–i). *Noncortical blades* (VI.D.1) lack cortex on their dorsal surface (Figure 7.5f). *Laterally cortical blades* (VI.D.2) have cortex on one of their lateral edges (Figure 7.5g). *Distally cortical blades* (VI.D.3) preserve cortex at their distal end but not along their lateral edges (Figure 7.5h). *Laterally and distally cortical blades* (VI.D.4) preserve cortex at their distal end and along one lateral edge (Figure 7.5i). For other kinds of blades,

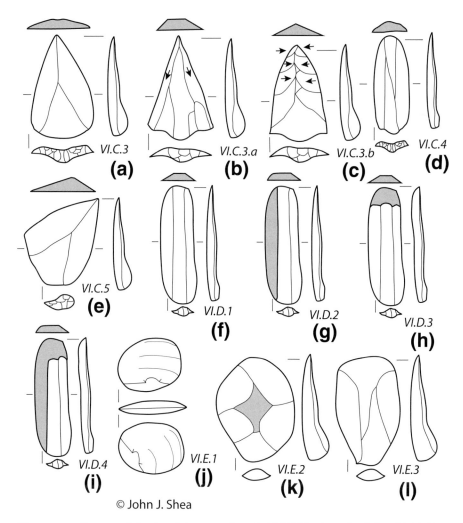

© John J. Shea

Figure 7.5 Core-exploitation flakes, continued. (a) BHC triangular flake, (b) Nubian Type 1 BHC triangular flake, (c) Nubian Type 2 BHC triangular flake, (d) BHC blade, (e) BHC radial flake, (f) Noncortical blade, (g) Laterally cortical blade, (h) Distally cortical blade, (i) Laterally and distally cortical blade, (j) Flake ventral surface flake (Kombewa flake), (k) Medial residual cortical flake, (l) Noncortical flake.

the EAST Typology retains a fifth residual *other prismatic blade category* (VI.D.5). The EAST Typology treats prismatic blades with plunging distal terminations as core-repair flakes (VII.C.1, see below).

Archaeological typologies for other regions recognize different kinds of prismatic blades based on their length and/or their width (Tixier 1963, Shea 2013b). These typologies commonly recognize as *bladelets* prismatic blades shorter than 50 mm and less than 12 mm wide. *Microblades* are prismatic blades less than 20–30 mm long. This practice varies, however, and archaeologists differ over specific size cutoffs separating blades, bladelets, and microblades. Some apply these terms solely to noncortical pieces, while others are more inclusive. Rather than endorsing one or another such practice, the EAST Typology groups all prismatic blades together. As with cores, researchers interested in variation among prismatic blades can measure these artifacts and describe their variation statistically. It may well be that blades versus bladelets sort out from one another "naturally" as they do in other regions (Tixier 1963), but this is something needs to be demonstrated, not something assumed in advance.

Increasingly, archaeologists working in southern Africa use Soriano and colleagues' (2007) framework for describing blades and blade-core-reduction products. The EAST Typology retains some of these distinctions; many others seem unnecessarily specific outside the context of research questions narrowly focused on variation in blade core reduction.

Other Core Exploitation Flakes

Other core exploitation flakes (VI.E.) include flakes resulting from core exploitation but not referable specifically to one core-exploitation strategy. *Flake ventral surface flakes* (VI.E.1) result when a stoneworker detaches a flake from the ventral surface of other flakes (Figure 7.5j). These flakes, which African archaeologists often call "Kombewa flakes," appear to have two ventral surfaces and two points of fracture initiation. (European archaeologists sometimes call such artifacts "Janus flakes" after the Roman god with two faces.) *Medial residual cortical flakes* (VI.E.2) group together flakes whose dorsal surfaces feature a relatively small patch of cortex that does not extend to the flake's edges (Figure 7.5k). *Noncortical flakes* (VI.E.3) lack cortex on their dorsal surface, and they do not match the criteria for any of the other core-exploitation flakes (Figure 7.5 l).

CORE-REPAIR FLAKES (GROUP VII)

Core-repair removes obstacles to fracture propagation and flake detachment that form during core reduction and artifact shaping/maintenance. These obstacles are usually more than a centimeter from the worked edge, but this property can vary with core size. Such obstacles come in three major forms: (1) "stacks" of step-terminated flake scars (see Chapter 3); (2) large flake scars that end in a hinge- or step-termination; and (3) worked edges and core surfaces that have become too steep or too convex to allow further fracture detachments. Core-repair flakes undercut these and other obstacles to fracture propagation, thereby restoring a flake propagation surface's potential usefulness. Calling these artifacts "core-repair flakes" uncomfortably combines observation with inference. The best defense for this choice is that such flakes do indeed remove obstacles to a core's continued use. Moreover, as an inclusive term, "core-repair flake" fits better in the EAST typology than alternatives, overshot flake (implies an error), core-trimming flake (imprecise), or core rejuvenation flake (awkward metaphor for inanimate objects). Readers and others who use the EAST Typology should not dismiss the hypothesis that prehistoric stoneworkers detached core-repair flakes for purposes other than those their name implies.

Group VII recognizes *biface repair flakes* (VII.A), *BHC repair flakes* (VII.B), and *UHC repair flakes* (VII.C). For other core-repair flakes, the EAST retains a residual category, *other concavity/convexity removal flakes* (VII.D).

Biface Core-Repair Flakes

On bifacial nonhierarchical cores (either short or elongated), fractures that terminate short of the distal end of fracture propagation surface can create adjacent concavities, convexities, and stacks that prevent subsequent fractures from passing beyond them (Figure 7.6a).

A *proximal biface core-repair flake* (VII.A.1) removes concavities/convexities from a bifacial core surface by directing an undercutting fracture from the same direction as the fracture scars that created the concavity/convexity (Figure 7.6b). The most successful such flakes are offset somewhat from the concavity/convexity. For this reason, many proximal biface repair flakes are medio-laterally asymmetrical (one edge convex, the other concave). A *distal biface core-repair flake* (VII.A.2) removes concavities/convexities from a bifacial core surface by projecting an undercutting fracture from the distal end of the flake scar (Figure 7.6c). An *orthogonal biface repair flake* (VII.A.3) undercuts the concavity at approximately a right angle to its fracture propagation trajectory (Figure 7.6d). When distal and orthogonal biface repair flakes terminate in a concavity, they may exhibit expanding lateral edges and/or a concave distal end.

Bifacial Hierarchical Core-Repair Flakes

Over the course of core reduction, BHCs' more invasively flaked upper surfaces accumulate convexities at their distal end and along their lateral margins. *Bifacial hierarchical core-repair flakes* (VII.B) remove these convexities by undercutting them (Figure 7.6e). Distinctions among BHC core-repair flakes in the EAST Typology focus on the location of the portions of BHC worked edge preserved on the flake's circumference. Many otherwise Anglophone references describe these artifacts as *éclats débordants* (border flakes).

Proximal-lateral BHC repair flakes (VII.B.1) include part of the core's lateral worked edge (Figure 7.6f). Such a flake's thickest point is at or near its striking platform, but this point may be offset several centimeters either to the left or the right of the fracture initiation point. Such relatively short, thick flakes are often wedge-shaped in both proximal–distal and medio-lateral cross-section.

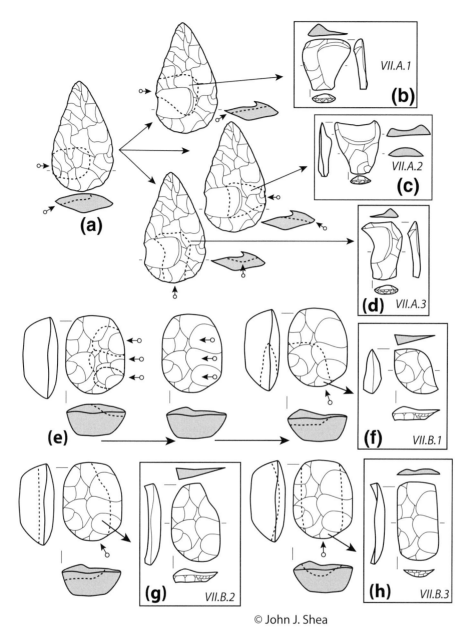

© John J. Shea

Figure 7.6 Core-repair flakes. (a) Concavity formation and repair on a bifacial nonhierarchical core, (b) Broximal biface repair flake, (c) Distal biface repair flake, (d) Orthogonal biface repair flake, (e) Convexity formation BHC, (f) Proximal-lateral BHC repair flake, (g) Lateral BHC repair flake, (h) Distal BHC repair flake.

On *lateral BHC repair flakes* (VII.B.2), the worked edge extends beyond the fracture initiation point along the lateral edge and to at least part of the flake's distal end (Figure 7.6g). This distal remnant worked edge distinguishes lateral BHC repair flakes from lateral preferential and worked edge BHC flakes (VI.C.2.a).

Distal BHC repair flakes (VII.B.3) preserve remnant worked edge at their distal end but not on their lateral edges (Figure 7.6h). Distal worked edge flakes' thickest point is usually at their distal end.

Unifacial Hierarchical Core-Repair Flakes

Unifacial hierarchical core (UHC) reduction creates concavities/convexities that need to be removed to maintain a fracture propagation surface (Figure 7.7a). Because UHC core reduction concentrates fracture initiations close to one another along an edge, small-scale edge damage can cause that edge to become increasingly steep. When the edge reaches about 90 degrees of steepness in cross-section, stoneworkers encounter difficulties initiating fractures that propagate more than a few millimeters. (It is not impossible to detach flakes from a 90-degree edge, but it is difficult to do other than by using pressure flaking or indirect percussion.) The EAST Typology recognizes three categories of UHC core-repair flakes: plunging flakes, core-tablet flakes, and core-platform flakes.

A *UHC plunging flake* (VII.C.1) removes concavities/convexities at a fracture propagation surface's distal end by projecting a flake underneath them that spreads more or less parallel with the UHC's long axis and parallel with the surface on which the concavity/convexity appears (Figure 7.7b). Often long and narrow for much of their length, such flakes flare in width and/or thickness at their distal ends. UHC plunging flakes can grade into burin retouch flakes (VIII.B), discussed below. Although the EAST Typology groups UHC plunging flakes among core-repair flakes, plunging flakes often result from stoneworker errors.

UHC tablet flakes (VII.C.2) can remove concavities located near the worked edge. They likely reflect stoneworkers' attempts to reestablish a less than 90-degree convergence on a worked edge by undercutting that edge laterally (Figure 7.7c). UHC tablet flakes can be either triangular or rectangular in profile or section, but most are relatively thick. Their most distinctive feature is a ridge on their dorsal surface running more or less with parallel their axis of fracture propagation on which there are multiple points of fracture initiation and associated small-scale fracturing and abrasion. UHC tablet flakes can grade into unifacially crested flakes (V.D.2).

UHC platform flakes (VII.C.3) result from fractures initiated orthogonally (perpendicular to the fracture propagation surface) that undercut much of the UHC fracture initiation surface (Figure 7.7d). UHC platform flakes preserve part of the worked edge fracture propagation surface on their striking platform rather than on the other parts of their dorsal surface. Like UHC tablet flakes, UHC platform flakes likely reflect efforts to reestablish a narrow worked edge, but in this case locally, along one small part of the edge, rather than by removing the entire worked edge, as a UHC tablet flake does.

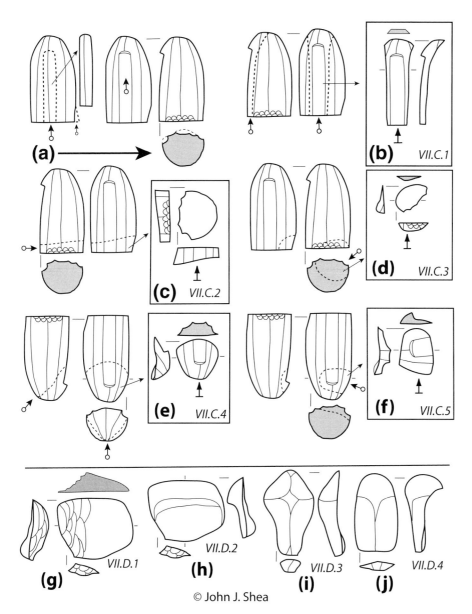

Figure 7.7 Core-repair flakes, continued. (a) Distal convexity formation on a unifacial hierarchical core (UHC), (b) UHC plunging flake, (c) UHC tablet flake, (d) UHC platform flake, (e) UHC distal concavity removal flake, (f) UHC orthogonal concavity removal flake, (g–j) Other concavity/convexity removal flakes.

Superficially viewed, small UHC platform flakes can resemble backed/ truncated pieces. Unlike most such retouched pieces, UHC platform flakes preserve a fracture initiation point on the ventral surface adjacent to the seemingly "retouched" edge.

UHC distal concavity removal flakes (VII.C.4) eliminate step/hinge fractures by undercutting them from the distal end of a fracture propagation surface

(Figure 7.7e). These flakes propagate more or less parallel, and in the opposite direction, to that of the fracture that created the step/hinge fracture. Consequently, that step/hinge fracture scar's distal end aligns perpendicularly to the flake's fracture propagation axis.

UHC orthogonal concavity removal flakes (VII.C.5) remove step/hinge fractures by undercutting them from the side of a fracture propagation surface (Figure 7.7f). Because these flakes propagate more or less perpendicularly to the fracture that created the step/hinge fracture, that step/hinge fracture scar's distal end aligns parallel to the flake's fracture propagation axis.

Other Concavity/Convexity Removal Flakes

Core geometries and topography vary so widely that exhaustively listing core-repair flakes referable to them would needlessly inflate the already long list of artifact-types in the EAST Typology. To supplement the core-repair types previously discussed, the EAST Typology recognizes *other concavity/convexity removal flakes* (VII.D) (Figures 7.7g–j). Most such flakes' thickest point is neither the bulbar eminence nor the striking platform but some point at or beyond the midpoint of their length or near their distal end. The EAST Typology recognizes four major variants of other concavity/convexity removal flakes: *stack removal flakes* (VII.D.1), *single step/hinge scar removal flakes* (VII.D.2), *medial convexity removal flakes* (VII.D.3), and *distal convexity removal flakes* (VII.D.4). Should there be a compelling reason to do so, stack removal flakes and single step/hinge scar removal flakes could be subdivided further, in terms of how their axis of fracture propagation aligned with their specific obstacles.

RETOUCH FLAKES (GROUP VIII)

Retouch changes artifact surface topography within a centimeter or so of a worked edge. Group VIII recognizes three major retouch flake categories: edge-retouch flakes (VIII.A), burin flakes (VIII.B), and tip-removal flakes (VIII.C). A fourth residual category, flake fragments (VIII.D), encompasses artifacts that may result from retouch or from other processes (Figure 7.8).

Edge-Retouch Flakes

Edge-retouch flakes (VIII.A.) originate from fractures initiated orthogonally (perpendicularly) to tool edges. They propagate more or less perpendicularly from that edge onto the artifact's dorsal or ventral surface. Edge-retouch flakes differ from the other flakes previously discussed in this chapter mainly in their relatively short length (<20–30 mm). The EAST Typology recognizes *unretouched edge-retouch flakes* (VIII.A.1), *unifacial edge-retouch flakes* (VIII.A.2), and *bifacial edge-retouch flakes* (VIII.A.3) (Figure 7.8a–c).

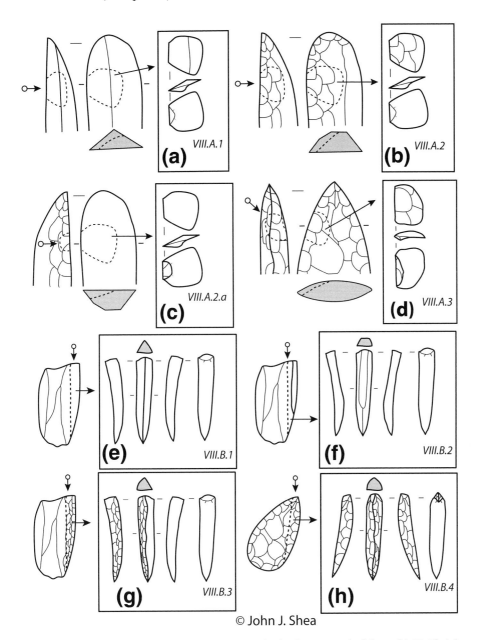

© John J. Shea

Figure 7.8 Edge-retouch flakes. (a) Unretouched edge-retouch flakes, (b) Unifacial edge-retouch flake, (c) Inverse unifacial edge-retouch flake, (d) Bifacial edge-retouch flake, (e) Unretouched burin edge flake, (f) Multiple burin edge flake, (g) Unifacially retouched edge burin flake, (h) Bifacially retouched edge burin flake.

Unretouched edge-retouch flakes (VIII.A.1) are small flakes that result from fracture initiations along unretouched edges. As such, they may feature either a plain or cortical striking platform (Figure 7.8a). Most unifacial edge-retouch flakes' dorsal surfaces are former flake dorsal surfaces. In such cases, cortex, arrisses, and portions of flake scars appear on their dorsal surface.

Unifacial edge-retouch flakes (VIII.A.2) result from fracture initiations along unifacially retouched edges. Such flakes may have plain and noncortical striking platforms, but either their dorsal or ventral surface will feature damage from fracture initiations (Figure 7.8b). As with unretouched edge-retouched flakes, fractures initiated on an unretouched surface detached most unifacial edge-retouch flakes. Nevertheless, nearly every large lithic assemblage preserves some *inverse unifacial edge-retouch flakes* (VIII.A.2.a), flakes detached by fractures initiated on the retouched side of an edge (Figure 7.8c). (In many typologies, "inverse" retouch is that located on flake ventral surfaces.) Inverse unifacial edge-retouch flakes can look very similar to backed/truncated pieces (see Chapter 8). They differ from backed/truncated pieces in preserving a point of fracture initiation adjacent to the apparent "retouch."

Small-scale fracture initiations along bifacially retouched edges create *bifacial edge-retouch flakes* (VIII.A.3). Such flakes preserve damage from fracture initiations on both sides of that portion of the worked edge preserved on their striking platform (Figure 7.8d).

Burin Flakes

Burin flakes (aka "burin spalls," VIII.B) are long, narrow, and relatively thick in proportion to their width. Stoneworkers mostly initiated burin flakes on projections rather than on edges, although this varies. Burin flakes vary widely in length. Some burin flakes are very small (<30 mm), but others can run a flake's full length. Long and narrow, burin flakes break easily. Excavations rarely recover complete specimens.

The EAST Typology recognizes four kinds of burin flakes based on dorsal surfaces that can be identified on burin flake fragments (Figure 7.8e–g). *Unretouched burin edge flakes* (VIII.B.1) are propagated under an unretouched flake edge. As such, their dorsal surface preserves at least one partial flake ventral surface and one partial dorsal flake scar (Figure 7.8e). They are usually triangular in cross-section. *Multiple burin edge flakes* (VIII.B.2) spread under an edge that has had at least one burin detached from it previously. The fracture scar from this prior removal gives multiple burin edge flakes either rectangular, trapezoidal, or polyhedral cross-sections (Figure 7.8f). *Unifacially retouched edge burin flakes* (VIII.B.3) undercut an unifacially retouched flake edge. Their dorsal surface features a ridge one side of which preserves multiple fracture initiation scars propagating more or less perpendicular to the burin flake's fracture propagation axis (Figure 7.8g). *Bifacially retouched edge burin flakes* (VIII.B.4) propagated under a bifacially retouched edge. Their dorsal surface preserves a ridge with multiple partial fracture scars propagating more or less perpendicular to the burin's fracture propagation axis (Figure 7.8h).

Much as unretouched edge burin flakes can grade into prismatic blades, both unifacially retouched and bifacially retouched edge burin flakes can grade into *crested flakes* (V.D.1–2).

Tip-Removal Flakes

Archaeologists often distinguish flakes that remove the tip (distal end) from elongated artifacts, such as bifacial LCTs, points, and celts, as well as the distal ends of scrapers and other unifacially retouched pieces. The EAST Typology recognizes three major groups of such tip-removal flakes: *biface point tip-removal flakes* (VIII.C.1), *biface celt tip-removal flakes* (VIII.C.2), and *scraper tip-removal flakes* (VIII.C.3) (Figure 7.9a–d).

In principle, each of these tip-removal flakes could be subdivided further into specimens detached orthogonally (by fractures initiated on their dorsal or ventral surfaces) and specimens detached laterally (by fractures initiated on their worked edges). Figure 7.9 illustrates such differences, but incorporating them into the EAST Typology without some prior question-driven research goal would needlessly enlarge that typology. Prehistoric Eastern African stoneworkers modified the tips of LCTs, foliate points, and other convergently retouched pieces using laterally directed fractures. Archaeologists recognize flakes detached in this way using a variety of terms. The EAST Typology recognizes such artifacts as *biface tranchet flakes* (VIII.C.1.a).

Some tip-removal flakes may result from tool breakage during use rather than from deliberate artifact repair. Archaeologists generally accept that finding tip removal flakes that refit to artifacts in the same assemblage indicates artifact repair, but the absence of such refits has little probative value. They may be genuinely absent, remain in an unexcavated portion of the site, have been re used/recycled to the point where one can no longer recognize them, or may have simply escaped archaeologists' notice.

Flake Fragments

Flake fragments (VIII.D) are portions of formerly whole flakes that fractures propagating more or less perpendicularly to the flakes' dorsal/ventral surfaces have detached from one another. These fractures may be bending fractures or Herztian cone fractures. Retouch can create such fractures, but so too can trampling, sediment compaction, bending pressures during fracture propagation, and excavation-related damage. Because of this equifinality (getting the same result from different causes), archaeologists tabulate flake fragments separately from complete detached pieces (whole flakes) and from retouched pieces.

The EAST Typology recognizes two major groups of flake fragments: *unretouched flake fragments* (VIII.D.1) and *retouched flake fragments* (VIII.D.2) (Figures 7.9e–f and g–h, respectively). It further divides each of these categories

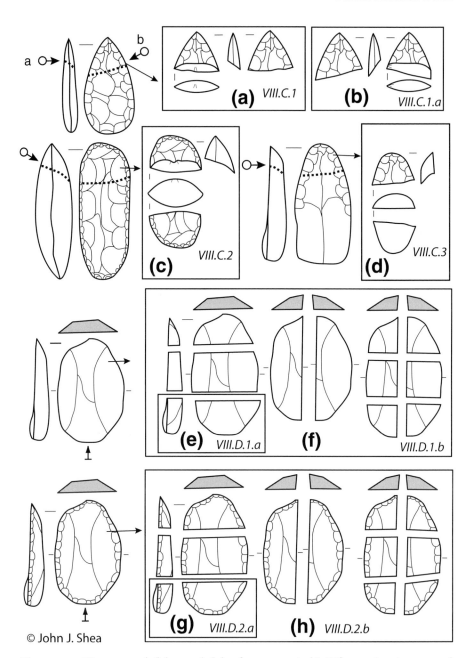

© John J. Shea

Figure 7.9 Tip-removal flakes and flake fragments. (a–b) Biface point tip-removal flakes, (c) Biface celt tip-removal flake, (d) Scraper tip-removal flake, (e) Unretouched proximal flake fragment, (f) Other unretouched flake fragments, (g) Retouched proximal flake fragment, (h) Other retouched flake fragments.

into *unretouched/retouched proximal flake fragments* (VIII.D.1.a and VIII.D.2.a) and other flake fragments. Since many retain their striking platforms, archaeologists consider proximal flakes more informative about core reduction than other flake/retouched piece fragments. Some archaeologists distinguish medial, distal, and lateral flake fragments as well as combinations of these categories (Sullivan and Rozen 1985), but even if they record them, few Eastern African archaeologists actually use these more detailed flake fragment categories for analytical purposes.

Box 5 *Questions about flakes*

What are "end-struck" and "side-struck" flakes? These are older terms for flakes, now rarely used. End-struck flakes' longest dimension lies parallel to the plane of fracture propagation: that is, the striking platform is at one end of its morphological long axis. In technological terms, an end-struck flake is longer than it is wide. Side-struck flakes' longest dimension is perpendicular to the plane of fracture propagation. A side-struck flake is wider than it is long.

Were core-initiation, core-repair, and retouch flakes used as cutting tools? Most core-initiation, core-repair, and tool-retouch flakes feature sharp cutting edges. Microwear and residue analysis demonstrate that core-initiation, core-repair, and retouch flakes were used as cutting tools in much the same way that core exploitation flakes were. Indeed, having partly cortical dorsal surfaces that resist slippage or a steep lateral edge against which tool-users could safely rest their thumb or their index finger during use might have made some core-initiation and core-repair flakes more desirable handheld cutting tools than some core-exploitation flakes.

How big or complete must a flake be for one to measure it? All archaeologists employ a length threshold for flake measurement. This threshold varies among individual researchers, but most use a length value between 10 and 30 mm. Unretouched flakes shorter than this are usually just counted and/or weighed. This size threshold reflects archaeologists' assumption that such flakes are too small to have been used as cutting tools. While this assumption may be correct for very small tools, i.e., ones <5–10 mm long, ethnographic humans demonstrably used flakes <30 mm long as cutting tools, often by embedding them in mastic and/or by attaching them to handles. In summarizing stone tool measurements, one should always explicitly state what minimum size cutoff one used.

Why are there so many more flakes than cores or retouched pieces in archaeological lithic assemblages? Unretouched flakes and flake fragments dominate nearly every known archaeological lithic assemblage. It seems vanishingly improbable that this pattern reflects any one cause. Nevertheless, several such causes suggest themselves. Experiments show stone tool edges become

Box 5 (*Cont.*)

blunt quickly (Key et al. 2018). Perceiving such loss of functionality, prehistoric stone tool users might have discarded unretouched cutting tools at far more rapid rates (that is, at relatively low discard thresholds) than either recent humans who tend to use retouched stone tools attached to handles or than archaeological experimenters unaccustomed to detecting declines in stone tool functionality.

Alternatively, prehistoric stoneworkers anticipating future needs for cutting edges might have made stone flakes in bulk at strategically "provisioned places," such as prominent landscape features, crossroads along habitual pathways, or other sites near places where resources requiring stone tool use occur predictably (Potts 1988, Kuhn 1995).

If prehistoric humans shaped stone tools as some recent craft/hobby stoneworkers do (Toth et al. 1992, Whittaker 2004), then many of these flakes may be byproducts of shaping "finished" tools of one kind or another. Some modern-day stoneworkers' workshops and residences preserve accumulations of worked stone so vast that removing them requires backhoes and bulldozers (Whittaker 2004). Lacking such machines, earlier humans might have either segregated stoneworking activities away from preferred habitation sites and areas with high foot traffic, discarded stoneworking debris in middens and other designated dumping areas or shifted their habitation sites and footpaths away from dense stoneworking deposits. None of these strategies are mutually exclusive and, as such, all may affect lithic assemblage composition.

Finally, one needs to be alert that the amount of time over which most prehistoric lithic assemblages accumulated remains unknown. What to archaeologists' eyes appears to be intensive, in-bulk stone tool production may be the aggregate of many separate short-term artifact-discard episodes.

UWAZI VALLEY TALES, EPISODE 7: THE THREE WISEGUYS' VISIT

Joseph met us at the edge of camp, calling out. "The three wiseguys are here."

The Polymath had invited four colleagues to visit us in the field: the Transatlantic Ethnographer, the Continental Biological Anthropologist, the American Geologist, and the Famous Primatologist. Two men and a woman sat in the Gentlemen's Smoking Lounge with Aya and Endurance.

"Wiseguys! You hear that?" the Transatlantic Ethnographer asked the other guests in a nasal New York accent. A slender, dapper man with bright red hair, the Ethnographer sported a tailored suit jacket with extraordinarily wide lapels, a blue Oxford cloth shirt, and pressed blue jeans.

"Yeah, that's us, me and my crew here. Fuhgettaboutit!"

Aya laughed.

The Ethnographer stood up, leaned over Aya, and wrinkled his brow. "Oh, you think I'm funny? Funny how? Do I amuse you?"

"I think Joseph meant the Three Magi," said a calm, French-accented woman's voice. "The Three Wise Men, but then, he spoke about you, Ethnographer, so maybe not." The Continental Biological Anthropologist wore an immaculately tailored khaki pantsuit, a large greenstone necklace, a floral print kerchief, and enormous black designer sunglasses. Except for a pith helmet perched on her knee, the Biological Anthropologist could have been sitting in a Paris café. She smoked a Galois cigarette. "And, remember that Martin Scorsese wants his royalties for each time you use his 'Do I amuse you?' routine from *Goodfellas*. Besides, Mr. Pesci did it better."

A third voice boomed, male, distinctively Californian. "Dudes, great to see you again! These two have been at each other like this since we got off the plane. I need a cold beer and ear plugs." Tall and rangy, the American Geologist was tanned even more deeply than the Polymath. Wearing a Hawaiian print shirt, knee-length board shorts and sandals, the Geologist looked like he'd just wandered in from Malibu Beach. Decades of sun and saltwater had bleached his shoulder-length hair.

"Folks, welcome to Uwazi Valley," said the Polymath. "Where's the Famous Primatologist?"

"Her fieldwork permit got delayed at the museum, so her agent sent her on a book tour in South Africa for the next week," said the Biological Anthropologist.

"But her graduate students came in on the same flight we did," said Aya. "They've been at their field site up in the mountains for weeks."

"They'll be fine," said the Polymath. "They all passed the "fieldwork survival skills" course."

"That lot?" The Old Africa Hand harrumphed, "It's probably *Lord of the Flies* there already."

"I'll ask Endurance to give the museum a call on the satellite phone," Aya sighed.

The Polymath, the Old Africa Hand, and I went to our tents and to wash up before dinner. Afterward, we all gathered in the Gentlemen's Smoking Lounge. A small fire flickered. We sat in a semi-circle facing a pastel orange sunset. One by one planets, then stars, flickered into view.

"Want more wood on the fire, Joseph?" I asked.

"No, Robin, this is an African fire, not *wazungu* fire. Just bright enough to see faces and the stars above."

The Polymath stood. "Folks, Robin has this idea about how to study stone tools. Let's run it up the flagpole and see who salutes."

"Or, which peasants run for their pitchforks and torches," said the Biological Anthropologist looking at the Ethnographer, who smiled and raised an eyebrow.

"I love you, Toots," he said.

"OK," I started, "and I really am thankful for your advice. Most of the time, when archaeologists compare stone tools among sites in Eastern Africa, they do so horizontally, within specific time periods. But I want to do something new with the stone tools from the Ancient Ones' Cave and from the older sites down in the Uwazi Valley. We have here a sequence running from Historic times all the way back to the Plio-Pleistocene. It's not continuous, of course, but it does allow us to control for geography a bit when we ask what changed in terms of how people and earlier hominins lived here over the last two million years. So, here's my problem. For each major time period, archaeologists describe stone tools differently. If I describe MSA tools from here, I can compare them to a few other MSA assemblages elsewhere, but not so well to older ESA ones or younger LSA ones. English archaeologists use one typology, Americans another, French yet a different one."

"This is simple," said the Biological Anthropologist. "Use the one the French archaeologists use."

"Remind me again for whom chauvinism is named?" the Ethnographer asked, his accent suddenly upper-class British.

"But even the French archaeologists use different typologies and different measurement conventions," I said. "For the MSA, some use Bordes' typology, others use Laplace's, still others use typologies they devised themselves."

"Also, simple," said the Biological Anthropologist. "Use Bordes' typology."

The Polymath leaned over to me. "Bordes was one of her professor's professors."

The Ethnographer laughed, "Robin, don't listen to her. Just because someone's done something for a long time doesn't mean they're the best at it, or even very good. It just means nobody's seriously challenged them, yet. It's Evolution 101. When you relax selective pressure, you get increased variability. Every street corner thug and wannabe wiseguy thinks he's Tony Soprano or Walter White, until he meets the real deal, a John Gotti or a Whitey Bulger."

"You Americans have no respect for tradition," the Biological Anthropologist blew cigarette smoke at him. "Peasant!"

"Tourist!"

"Dudes, chill," said the Geologist.

"It's neither a French problem nor an American one; neither a Kenyan one nor a Tanzanian one," I said. "It affects every archaeologist who wants to compare one stone tool to another. So, rather than trying to correlate all their different typologies, I am developing a new typology that I can use to describe stone tools from all prehistoric periods. It will be hierarchical, so categories can be expanded or combined as needed. It will be polytaxial. Classifications can be combined if a single artifact matches more than one of them. Also, it will standardize measurements across the board so that when we compare cores and flakes from down in the Uwazi Valley to those in Ancient Ones' Cave, we compare like with like."

"And, when Robin finds differences," Aya added, "they will be differences among the stone tools, not differences in analytical methods."

"Best of all, I don't need to get hung up over definitions of age-stages and industries. In fact, I don't even need to mention them."

"So, what's the problem?" the Ethnographer asked. "A hundred years ago, anthropologists classified people as savages, barbarians, and civilized folk. After we realized culture was more complex than those stereotypes, we started identifying and defining ethnographic cultures. Nowadays, we anthropologists understand that people construct their social identities dynamically. So we no longer write about 'definitive article cultures,' *the* Maya, *the* Maasai, or *the* Aranda. We investigate the dynamic process of how culture forms, not its transient static products. Real cultures only remain unchanged in books about them."

"Yes, the same in my field, too," said the Biological Anthropologist. "Long ago we tried to identify different human races. Early anthropologists defined races based on things like skin color or hair texture or skull shapes. Eventually, we realized there was more variation within these races than between them. Now, if we want to study, say, red hair, we look at its genetic basis, its geographic distribution, and then we test hypotheses about selective pressures for and against red hair. Or, for the Ethnographer, we check the hair dye bottle in his bathroom."

"Ouch," said the Ethnographer. "Do you really want to go there, my dear?"

The Old Africa Hand touched the Ethnographer's arm, "A gentleman would not."

"Same in earth sciences, said the Geologist. "Early geologists thought there had been just one Ice Age, but pretty quickly they recognized from glacial moraines and river terraces there had been more than one. So, from the early twentieth century onward, we organized the Pleistocene Epoch in terms of Alpine Glacial Stages or, here in East Africa, Pluvial Periods. Then, from the 1960s onward, we also started dividing time in terms of marine oxygen-isotope stages. Now we have many accurate geophysical methods to establish exact ages and climate conditions. Rather than describing all glacial periods as uniformly cold and interglacial ones as uniformly warm, we reconstruct specific levels of humidity and temperature for radiometrically measured time periods."

"You see the pattern, Robin?" the Polymath said. "New questions lead to new measurements, new ways to organize observations. Thomas Kuhn called these correlated changes 'paradigm shifts.'"

"So, is archaeological stone tool analysis undergoing a paradigm shift?" I asked the Polymath.

"Hard to know. Nowadays, claiming to found a new paradigm can just be an academic strategy for attracting attention, 'journalist bait.' Historically, scholars recognize paradigm changes in hindsight. But a universally applicable typology that did not require age-stages or industries – like what you describe – could make obsolete much of what archaeologists have written about stone tools over the last hundred years, not just here in Eastern Africa but everywhere."

"You say that like it's a bad thing," said Aya.

"No, just a warning."

The Old Africa Hand chimed in. "Robin, none of us here care much about age-stages, industries, or artifact-types. Just remember, though, other archaeologists do. They have been writing about stone tools using these terms and concepts for decades. They have grown comfortable with age-stages and industries, and their own typologies because they make unfamiliar stone tools seem like familiar things. You will get a lot of resistance if you tell them it was all for naught."

The Biological Anthropologist spoke. "I disagree. We biological anthropologists have been debunking 'race' for decades. And yet, it persists, but so do we, for the struggle is worth it. As a young professor, I once had a colleague throw a pitcher of water at me because I objected to his proposed degree program in 'race studies.'"

"Yikes!" I exclaimed. "What happened?"

"My hero, here," she nodded at the Ethnographer, "he blocked it with his head."

The Ethnographer touched a long scar on his forehead. "Anything for you, Doll," (New York accent again).

"What happened to the professor who threw the pitcher?" I asked the Ethnographer.

"He had an unfortunate accident. Look, it took us social anthropologists a while to get rid of 'primitive cultures'; but some popular anthropology books and television programs still speak about 'pristine' cultures untouched by modern life."

"Brooklyn?" asked the Biological Anthropologist, arching an eyebrow at the Ethnographer.

"Paris," the Ethnographer replied, leaning back in his chair, winking and grinning.

"I've lost count of how many times I've given media interviews explaining that there were more than one Ice Age and that it is not over," said the Geologist. "My own brother can now surf-cast off his back porch into what used to be his lawn, and he still thinks global warming is a hoax."

"Old habits die hard, Robin," said the Old Africa Hand, pipe smoke rising. "If you want to improve how archaeologists describe stone tools here in Eastern Africa, then you need to create selective pressure against the habits, not against the people who practice them. Both push and pull. Show them both the problems with current practices and the advantages of changing them, but do so in a measured way."

"A tall order," I said.

"Yes, it is," said the Old Africa Hand. "I hope you enjoy a challenge."

I went to my tent shortly thereafter to read a bit and to write some notes. A few hours later, a loud commotion woke me. It came from one of the tents and sounded like wild animals. I stepped outside my tent, found the Old Africa Hand, the Polymath, Aya, and the Geologist sitting close to one another next to the fire's dying embers, all smirking at each other.

"Lions fighting?" I asked.

"No," said the Old Africa Hand.

"Hyenas mating?"

"Nope," said Aya, covering a smile with her hand.

"Warmer," laughed the Polymath. "Travel is a liminal state; it loosens inhibitions and arouses the passions. You'd never know the Ethnographer and the Biological Anthropologist have been married to each other for 20 years."

"You didn't ride out here in the car with them," said the Geologist.

CHAPTER 8

RETOUCHED PIECES

This chapter reviews conventions for measuring, describing, and classifying retouched pieces (EAST Typology Group IX). These artifacts include scrapers, notches, and denticulates, backed/truncated pieces, convergently retouched pieces/flake points, thinned pieces, burins, flake segmentation products, and other retouched pieces. The chapter also answers common questions about retouched pieces.

MEASURING RETOUCHED PIECES

Conventions for measuring retouched pieces follow closely those for cores. Length, width, and thickness are usually morphological or maximum values. When retouched pieces preserve striking platforms or enough dorsal or ventral surfaces to indicate their origins as flakes, some archaeologists anchor measurements to the fracture initiation point as they would technological measurements for flakes. No prior theory recommends one approach versus another to measuring retouched pieces, but one should explicitly state which protocols one uses. To measure retouched pieces that preserve no identifiable flake landmarks, many archaeologists treat the more extensively retouched surfaces as the dorsal surface and the wider end of such pieces as the proximal end. This practice varies, however, and if followed, it (or a different set of procedures) should be noted in any publications.

As with cores and flakes, for retouched pieces, most archaeologists characterize dorsal cortex extent, dorsal flake scars' number and orientation, and striking platform morphology. Because one can use mass as a proxy measurement for the amount of potential utility remaining in a retouched piece when a stone tool user discarded it, and thus a measure of discard threshold variation, one should always measure retouched piece mass.

In characterizing retouch, archaeologists increasingly supplement holistic classifications of retouched artifact-types with measurements of retouch itself. Many archaeologists measure the retouched edge steepness, or "edge angle."

Dibble and Bernard (1980) tested a variety of methods for measuring edge angle, finding the combination of "calibrated calipers" most reliable. This approach involves measuring edge thickness some set distance from the edge (2–3 mm) and then employing a trigonometric function to calculate the edge angle. Researchers faced with analyzing large numbers of retouched tools should consider using Bisson's (2000) framework for measuring retouch variation by sectors along an artifact's circumference. Kuhn (1990), Clarkson (2002), and Eren and colleagues (2005) discuss the pros and cons of competing retouch invasiveness measurement.

RETOUCHED PIECES (GROUP IX)

The EAST Typology groups all retouched pieces other than core-tools together in Group IX. Within Group IX, it recognizes six major subgroups: scrapers/notches/denticulates, backed and truncated pieces, convergently retouched pieces/retouched flake points, thinned pieces, burins, flake segmentation products, and a seventh residual "other retouched pieces" category.

Scrapers, Notches, and Denticulates

Scrapers, notches, and denticulates (SNDs) are flake fragments whose edges preserve a sharp unifacially retouched cutting edge, usually one less than 60–70 degrees in cross-section (Figure 8.1).

Scrapers (IX.A.1) have at least one retouched edge. Retouch scars on this edge run at least 10 mm along the edge and extend onto the tool surface for more than 2–3 mm. These retouch scars usually occur on the flake fragment's dorsal side, but this varies. The EAST Typology lists 12 major scraper types.

Endscrapers feature retouch at their distal end. *Single endscrapers* (XI.A.1.a) have a single relatively narrow retouched edge at that distal end (Figure. 8.1a). That edge is not much wider than the artifact's width at the midpoint of its length (hereafter "midpoint width"). *Transverse scrapers* (XI.A.1.b) are endscrapers whose retouched edge is wider than the tool's midpoint width (Figure 8.1b–c). The EAST Typology recognizes two sub-types: *symmetrical transverse scrapers* (XI.A.1.b.i), on which this transverse edge is aligned more or less perpendicularly to the piece's fracture propagation axis (Figure 8.1b), and *asymmetrical transverse scrapers* (XI.A.1.b.ii), on which this edge is aligned diagonally to the piece's fracture propagation axis (Figure 8.1c). *Double endscrapers* (XI.A.1.c) have retouched scraper edges at both their distal and proximal ends (Figure 8.1d). On *platform scrapers* (XI.A.1.d) a flake's striking platform ("butt" in older works) has been retouched away (Figure 8.1e). (Much to the chagrin of undergraduate students everywhere, archaeologists no longer describe platform scrapers as "butt scrapers.")

Sidescrapers feature retouch on their lateral edges. A *single sidescraper* (XI.A.1.e) features one retouched lateral edge (Figure 8.1f). *Double sidescrapers*

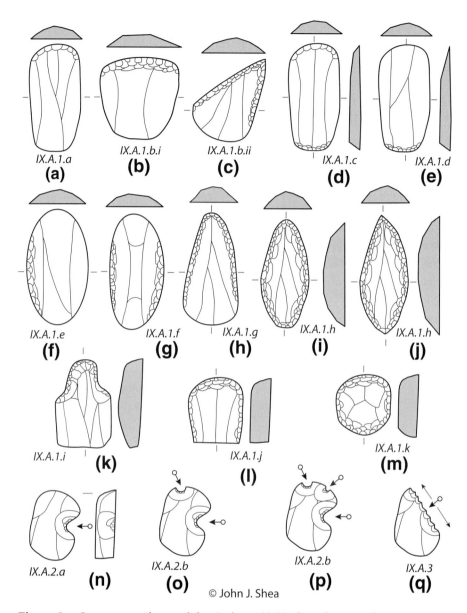

Figure 8.1 Scrapers, notches, and denticulates. (a) Single endscraper, (b) Symmetrical transverse scraper, (c) Asymmetrical transverse scraper, (d) Double endscraper, (e) Platform scraper, (f) Single sidescraper, (g) Double sidescraper, (h) Single convergent scraper, (i–j) Double convergent scrapers, (k) Carinated scraper, (l) Thumbnail scraper, (m) Disc scraper, (n) Single-notched tools, (o–p) Multiple-notched tools, (q) Denticulate.

(XI.A.1.f) feature two retouched lateral edges that do not converge with one another (Figure 8.1g). On *single convergent scrapers* (XI.A.1.g), the retouched lateral edges converge with one another at one end of the tool (Figure 8.1h). These edges are more or less equal in length and symmetrical about the piece's long axis. *Double convergent scrapers* (XI.A.1.h) feature convergently retouched edges at both distal and proximal ends (Figure 8.1i–j). (Some older references describe double convergent scrapers as a *limace*, French for slug.)

Carinated scrapers (XI.A.1.i), also known as "beaked" or "nosed" scrapers, are relatively thick pieces with a series of elongated flake scars on their scraper edges (Figure 8.1k). This artifact-type grades into relatively small unifacial hierarchical cores (II.B). Some typologies distinguish the two based on the fracture scars at their distal end, treating those with several parallel laminar scars as cores and those lacking such flake scars as scrapers. Africanist archaeologists differ widely over whether or not they recognize carinated scrapers as a distinct artifact type and over whether and how they distinguish them from unifacial hierarchical cores. Carinated scrapers have considerable importance in Eurasian Later Pleistocene prehistory, where they distinguish the Early Upper Paleolithic Aurignacian culture (Belfer-Cohen and Grosman 2007). Whether or not archaeologists working in Eastern Africa recognize them and how they treat them (i.e., as scrapers, cores, or both) seems to correlate with prior training and experience in Eurasian prehistory.

Thumbnail scrapers (XI.A.1.j) are short (<30 mm long) pieces on which retouch extends over lateral and distal edges (Figure 8.1l). Their name references these artifacts' usually small size, not their assumed function. *Disc scrapers* (XI.A.1.k) are round or oval pieces with scraper retouch around their entire circumference (Figure 8.1m). Larger and thicker thumbnail and disc scrapers can grade into platform cores. One recommends identifying as thumbnail/disc scrapers only artifacts less than 50 mm long and less than 20 mm thick.

More than with any other artifact, the author wanted to "sink" the name, scraper, but an informal poll of colleagues suggested that efforts to replace this term with another would be futile. The EAST Typology therefore retains "scraper" for this reason only.

Notches (XI.A.2) have at least one relatively large retouched concavity on their edge (Figure 8.1n–p). The notches often consist of one large flake scar enclosing a cluster of several smaller flake scars. The EAST Typology distinguishes single-notched and multiple-notched tools (XI.A.2.a–b). Older works sometimes refer to pieces with a single large and invasive notch as a "Clacton notch" after the archaeological site at Clacton-on-Sea (England), where archaeologists first identified such artifacts.

Denticulates (XI.A.3) have at least one edge preserving many small concave removals (Figure 8.1q). These removals may be unifacial or bifacial. Denticulates' concavities differ from those on notches mainly in being relatively small and minimally invasive.

While some of the differences between and among SNDs could reflect task-specific edge designs, others may result from resharpening (Figure 8.2). Rolland (1981) suggests that efforts to resharpen a use-dulled flake edge by repeated cycles of denticulate retouch result in scraper retouch. Dibble (1987, 1995)

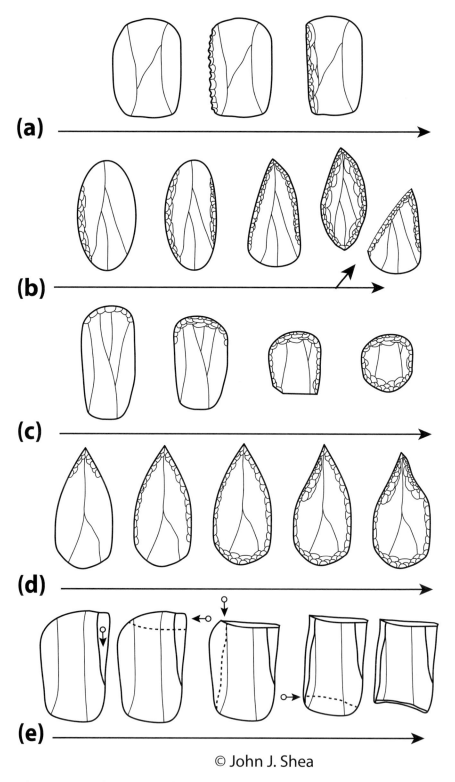

© John J. Shea

Figure 8.2 Resharpening effects. (a) Denticulate to scraper, (b) Sidescraper to convergent scrapers, (c) Single endscraper to disc scraper, (d) Flake points, single burin to multiple burins.

argues that resharpening can cause side scrapers to grade into convergent and transverse scrapers. Reuse and resharpening may cause similar variation among endscrapers, points, burins, and many other retouched tools.

Backed/Truncated Pieces

Backed/truncated pieces (IX.B) have one or more steeply retouched edge. These edges are between 70 and 90 degrees in cross-section. Truncation retouch runs perpendicular or obliquely to the artifact's long axis. Backing retouch runs along an edge parallel the artifact's long axis. Archaeologists generally view backing/truncation as strategies for either blunting an edge to make it safe to grip while cutting or for shaping a tool so that it fits into a handle. Many typologies distinguish longer truncations and backed/truncated pieces from smaller "microliths" and "geometric microliths." The metric criteria by which they assign artifacts to backed/truncated pieces versus microliths vary widely, but the length threshold usually lies between 30 and 50 mm. Subtypes of backed/truncated pieces often emphasize the alignment of the retouched edge to the piece's long axis (parallel versus transverse versus oblique), that edge's shape in plan view (convex, concave, straight), and the mode of retouch (unifacial, bifacial, etc.). Microliths/geometric microlith types usually only register artifact shape in plan view.

Archaeological "conventional wisdom" holds that microliths from recent periods are smaller than Pleistocene-age microliths, but one does not have to look too long among many such Pleistocene lithic assemblages to find microliths no larger than those dating to Holocene LSA and Neolithic contexts (Ambrose 2002). Rather than perpetuate these categorical distinctions to no obvious purpose, the EAST Typology combines these artifacts in a single "backed/truncated pieces" artifact category. Researchers interested in size variation among them can investigate this property by simply by measuring them (as they have been doing for decades). The EAST Typology retains shape-based distinctions among these backed/truncated pieces, simplifying them for ease of use (Figure 8.3). It recognizes five major shape-based types (crescents, triangles, rectangles, trapezoids, convergently- backed pieces) and an "other" category for artifacts that do not fit into these types.

Crescents (IX.B.1) combine one straight unretouched edge with a retouched one that is convex (Figure 8.3a–d). Other parts of either edge may be concave, straight, or recurved. Following precedent in other typologies, the EAST Typology distinguishes *short* and *elongated crescents* (IX.B.1.a and b, respectively). Elongated crescents preserve length/width ratios greater than or equal to 2.0. It also recognizes as *shouldered crescents* (IX.B.1.c) pieces with a concave retouched edge opposite its unretouched edge. *Notched crescents* (IX.B.1.d) have a retouched concavity at one end of their straight edge. Some archaeologists also call crescents "lunates."

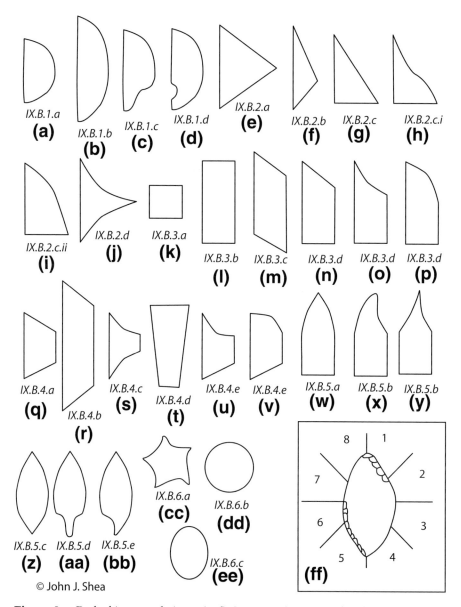

Figure 8.3 Backed/truncated pieces. (a–d) Crescents, (e–j) Triangles, (k–p) Rectangles, (q–v) Trapezoids, (w–bb) Convergently backed pieces, (cc–ee) Other backed/truncated pieces, (ff) Polar coordinate framework for orienting and measuring backed/truncated pieces.

Triangles (IX.B.2.) feature at least two straight edges that converge with one another (Figure 8.3e–j). The EAST Typology recognizes *isosceles*, *scalene*, and *right triangles* (IX.B.2.a–c), as well as other types of right triangles on which one edge is either concave or convex (IX.B.2.c.i and ii, respectively), and double-concave triangles (IX.B.2.d).

Rectangles (IX.B.3) feature four convergent edges about their circumference (Figure 8.3k–p). Rectangles include artifacts whose plan view outlines are square, elongated rectangles, parallelograms, and partial parallelograms, but they exclude trapezoids, which most researchers recognize as a distinct artifact-type.

Trapezoids (IX.B.4) are rectangles with no right-angle edge convergences (Figure 8.3 q–v). Regular trapezoids (IX.B.4.a) have short straight edges. *Elongated trapezoids* (IX.B.4.b) have two longer edges. *Hollow trapezoids* (IX.B.4.c) feature either one or two concave edges. *Flared trapezoids* (IX.B.4.d) feature one pair of short parallel edges and another pair of converging/diverging ones. *Partial trapezoids* (IX.B.4.e) include pieces with one straight oblique edge and either a concave or a convex edge opposite it.

Convergently backed/truncated pieces (IX.B.5) feature either one or two points/projections formed by pairs of converging truncated edges (Figure 8.3w–bb). *Single convergently backed pieces* (IX.B.5.a) preserve a medio-laterally symmetrical point at one end formed by either straight or convex edges. *Backed/truncated awls* (IX.B.5.b) feature points formed by pairings of concave retouched edges or convex and concave retouched edges. *Symmetrical double convergently backed pieces* (IX.B.5.c) have medio-laterally symmetrical points at opposite ends of the artifact and aligned parallel to one another (albeit in different directions). *Tanged symmetrical double convergently backed pieces* (IX.B.5.d) have two projections, one with straight/convex edges at one end, the other formed by symmetrically positioned concavities at the other. *Asymmetrical double convergently backed pieces* (IX.B.5.e) have one or more medio-laterally asymmetrical points at one or both ends.

Other backed/truncated pieces (IX.B.6) subsume artifacts that do not fit into one or another of the artifact-types enumerated above. Such artifacts include multiple backed/truncated awls, circles, and ovals, (Figure 8.3cc–ee). *Multiple backed/truncated awls* (IX.B.6.a) feature two or more convergently retouched projections formed by adjacent concave or convex backing/truncation retouch. Multiple awls' projections do not align parallel with one another. *Circles* and *ovals* (IX.B.6.b and c) differ from disc scrapers (discussed above) in being relatively broad and flat and in lacking invasive retouch (i.e., retouch fractures propagating more than 2–3 mm onto either dorsal or ventral surfaces).

One could argue that the EAST Typology oversimplifies variation among these artifacts, that it sacrifices detail for ease of use. This argument fails close critical examination. Archaeologists working in other parts of the world divide backed/truncated pieces not just in terms of their shape but also based on the distribution of retouch about their circumference and morphological variation in that retouch. They do this because research in those regions shows variation among these variables has chronostratigraphic and culture-historical value (Elston and Kuhn 2002, Shea 2013b). Put simply, if you show an archaeologist from Europe or Southwest Asia a backed/truncated piece, they have a reasonably good chance of being able to correctly place it in a major age-stage or assign it to a named stone tool industry. It remains unclear that Eastern African archaeologists can do this with any great precision. Absent such demonstrations, one cannot justify retaining overly complex classifications for backed/truncated pieces. Nor does any evidence show that archaeologists make distinctions among backed/truncated pieces consistently, either over the course of their individual careers or between individuals working independently of one another. Since backed/truncated pieces are so common in LSA and Neolithic assemblages, and because so many more archaeologists work on these later prehistoric periods, interobserver variation probably affects backed/truncated pieces far more than any other retouched pieces.

What to do? To measure variation among backed/truncated pieces, researchers should assign each artifact to one of the artifact-types described above, then place the artifacts in a polar coordinate grid divided into sectors, and finally record values of retouch morphology in each sector in which it occurs (Figure 8.3ff). How many such sectors one uses is a matter of individual preference. (The author prefers eight.) Advances in digital scanning technology may eventually make it possible to characterize retouch distribution in either degrees or grads. To standardize measurements, artifacts should be placed and oriented on the polar coordinate grid using the same alignments shown in Figure 8.3: namely, their long axis should be aligned with coordinates 8/1 at one end 4/5 at the other. The line dividing coordinates 6/7 and 3/4 should intersect at the midpoint of the artifact's morphological length.

Convergently Retouched Pieces/Retouched Flake Points

Convergently retouched pieces or *retouched flake points* (IX.C) include triangular flakes whose distal end features sharp and converging retouched edges. Just what to call these artifacts has long vexed archaeologists (Bordes 1961). The EAST Typology uses the term *retouched flake point* for retouched pieces on which portions of original flake dorsal and ventral surfaces remain visible. It recognizes *unifacially retouched flake points* (IX.C.1) (Figure 8.4a–e) and *bifacially retouched flake points* (IX.C.2) (Figure 8.4f–i). The Typology further subdivides both point categories based on retouch location and distribution (distal retouch only, distal and lateral retouch only, distal and proximal dorsal, distal and proximal ventral retouch). For flake points exhibiting a mix of different retouch patterns, it retains a third category, *unifacially and bifacially retouched point* (IX.C.3).

For convergently retouched pieces that feature steep (>60°) retouch and concave edges, the EAST Typology uses the term, *awl* (IX.C.4). Awls differ from backed/truncated awls in retaining their striking platforms. As with notched tools, with which awls can grade, the typology recognizes single awls (IX.C.4.a) and multiple awls (IX.C.4.b) (Figure 8.4j–k).

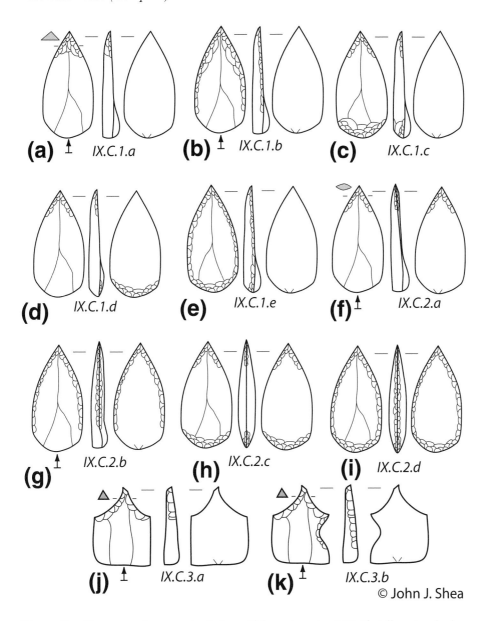

Figure 8.4 Convergently-retouched pieces/flake points. (a–e) Unifacially retouched flake points, (f–i) Bifacially retouched flake points, (j) Single awl, (k) Multiple awl.

Thinned Pieces

Thinned pieces (IX.D) describe flakes other than points that have deeply invasive flake scars on their dorsal and/or ventral surface. Pluralities of these flake scars extend to at least the center of one or the other surface. The EAST Typology recognizes three kinds of thinned pieces. *Dorsally thinned pieces* (IX.D.1) retain their striking platform and bulb of percussion but feature invasive thinning fracture scars on their dorsal surface (Figure 8.5a). *Basally thinned pieces* (IX.D.2) have only been

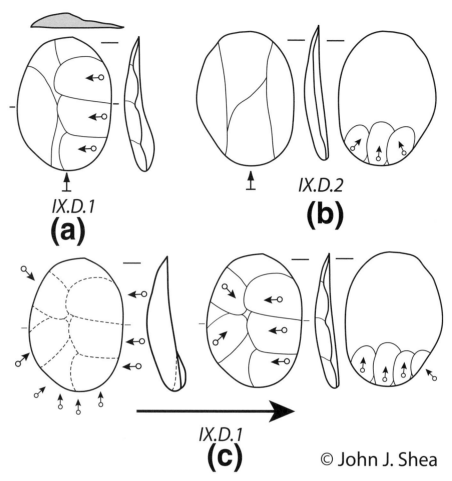

Figure 8.5 Thinned pieces. (a) Dorsally thinned piece, (b) Basally thinned piece, (c) Dorsally and basally thinned piece.

modified around their proximal end (Figure 8.5b). Their striking platform and/or bulb of percussion are missing. *Dorsally and basally thinned pieces* (IX.D.3) have had flakes detached from their dorsal surface and from that part of their ventral surface near their striking platform (Figure 8.5c). On such pieces, stoneworkers removed the striking platform entirely, as well as the bulb of percussion.

The EAST Typology does not make size-based distinctions among thinned pieces. Thus, this artifact category could encompass both very large pieces and very small flakes. Those using those types to should supplement such characterizations with measurements.

Burins

A *burin* (IX.E) is a flake fragment from which a flake has been struck that propagates parallel to an edge and more or less perpendicularly to the plane formed by the intersection of flake dorsal and ventral surfaces (Figure 8.6) (also see earlier discussion of burin flakes). Points or projections on a flake's circumference serve as striking platforms for these fractures. Stoneworkers often initiated burin removals by backing/truncating the end of a tool, or by simply bending and snapping it, and then striking that newly fractured surface near its lateral edge (Figure 8.6a–b). To control the distance that a burin fracture propagates under an edge, one can place a notch perpendicular to the intended fracture trajectory. This notch will cause the burin fracture to terminate at that point (Figure 8.6c).

The EAST Typology recognizes three major and three minor burin types (Figure 8.6 d–h). *Single burins* (IX.E.1) have a burin scar running parallel to one of their lateral edges or their distal end (Figure 8.6d). Most burin scars align more or less perpendicularly to the dorsal/ventral plane of the flake on which they appear. The *transverse and oblique burin* (IX.E.1.a), in contrast, propagates at oblique angles to this plane, leaving behind an acute edge (Figure 8.6e). *Dihedral burins* (IX.E.2) preserve two burin scars propagating in opposite directions from the same point (Figure 8.6f). *Multiple burins* (IX.E.3) feature more than one burin scar, either ones originating from the same point in the same direction (IX.E.3.a) or from separate points on a tool's circumference (IX.E.3.b) (Figure 8.6g–h).

Burin is French for a metal chisel. English equivalents, such as "graver" or "engraving tool," carry the same implied function – that prehistoric humans used these tools to carve things. And yet archaeological analyses show that stoneworkers used burin removals to shape and resharpen cutting edges and to modify artifact shape for hafting and other purposes. All of the same reasons for "sinking" and for retaining the term "scraper" (see above) apply to burin, too. It is equally too deeply embedded in lithics systematics to be replaced.

Flake Segmentation Products

Flake segmentation products (IX.F) result from modifications that split a flake medio-laterally. The EAST Typology recognizes two major categories of such artifacts: *orthogonal truncation-related pieces* (Figure 8.6i–n) and *microburins* (Figure 8.7). Although one could argue for treating these artifacts as retouch flakes, this work treats them as retouched pieces.

Orthogonal truncation-related pieces (IX.F.1) result from fractures initiated near the middle of the flake's dorsal or ventral surfaces. These artifacts differ from flake fragments that are due to bending fractures by featuring Hertzian cones or shear fracture damage on their freshly fractured surface. The EAST Typology recognizes *distal, medial, and proximal varieties of orthogonal truncation-related pieces* (IX.F.1.a–c).

Microburins (IX.F.2) are not small burins. Rather, they are products of the microburin truncation technique, a strategy for truncating blades by making

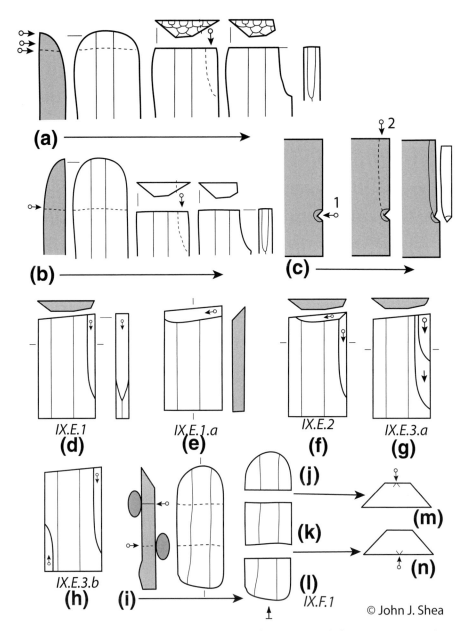

Figure 8.6 Burins and flake segmentation products. (a) Single burin on a truncation, (b) Single burin on a break, (c) Using a notch to predetermine burin termination, (d) Single burin, (e) Transverse and oblique burin, (f) Dihedral burin, (g–h) Multiple burins, (i) Flake segmentation by orthogonal truncation, (j) Distal orthogonal truncation-related piece, (k) Medial orthogonal truncation-related piece, (l) Proximal orthogonal truncation-related piece, (m) Segmentation scar on dorsal-initiated truncation, (n) Segmentation ventral-initiated truncation.

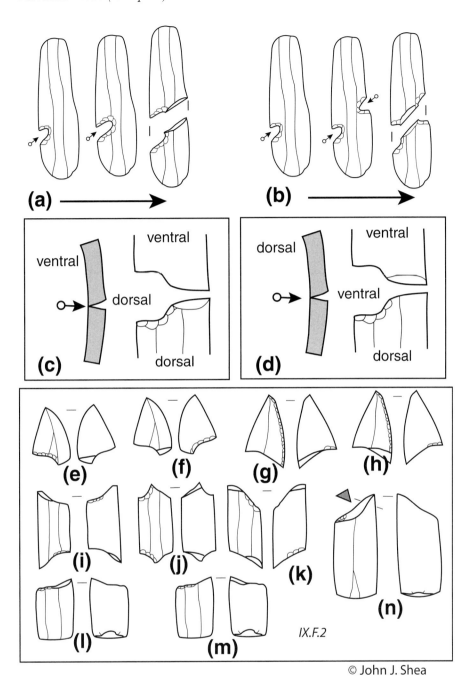

Figure 8.7 Microburin-related pieces. (a) Microburin formation using a single notch, (b) Microburin formation using two notches, (c) Microburin truncation from ventral pressure, (d) Microburin truncation from dorsal pressure, (e–n) Various kinds of microburin products on blades (g–h are "Krukowski microburins").

one or more notches on that artifact's lateral edges and then either making further notches or by bending or striking the pieces so that a fracture forms and propagates medio-laterally (Figure 8.7a–b). The "burin" to which the artifact-type name refers results from a bending fracture. Its location in relation to the notch or notches varies depending on how stoneworkers applied force at the moment of fracture initiation (Figure 8.7c–d).

Possibly because early archaeologists thought that microburins were functional "finished tools," they devised many named types for them. The truncated distal flake fragments shown in Figure 8.7g–h, for example, are called "Krukowski microburins." No compelling reason justifies retaining this or any other taxonomic distinction among microburin products. If such reasons arise the EAST Typology can accommodate them by adding distal, medial, and proximal subtypes along the lines shown in Figure 8.7e–n.

Other Retouched Pieces

The EAST Typology retains an "other retouched pieces" subgroup (IX.G). This subgroup includes four artifact categories: rods, tanged pieces, scaled pieces, and combination tools (Figure 8.8).

Rods, or *retouched cylinders* (IX.G.1), are long and narrow pieces with retouched lateral edges and roughly equal width/thickness ratios (Figure 8.8a–b). Most such pieces are bifacially retouched, but some specimens feature trihedral retouch. When rods/cylinders preserve convergent retouched edges at one or both ends, some sources call them "points," but this practice varies. Some rods/retouched cylinders preserve extensive abrasive damage on their tips and edges, suggesting use as drill bits. In Eastern Africa, rods/retouched cylinders often accompany other evidence for rotary drilling, such as stone, bone, or shell beads with deep cylindrical perforations.

Borers (IX.G.2) are pieces on which stoneworkers have retouched an elongated, narrow, parallel-edged projection (Figure 8.8c). Their tip may be pointed or blunt. In other parts of the world, such as the Middle East and North America, such implements are often interpreted as drill bits, but as with all surmises about stone tool functions, an open mind needs to be kept about this. Some "rods" (see earlier) may be pieces of borers fractured medio-laterally during use.

Tanged pieces (IX.G.3) are flakes on which retouched concavities at their proximal end have created thick, symmetrical projection (Figure 8.8d). This retouch can be either unifacial, bifacial, or a mix of both. While the artifact name suggests a particular function (a knife's "tang" is the part enclosed by its handle), such artifacts may have had other functions. For example, ceramics-using people in many parts of the world repair cracks in their pottery by carving holes on either side of the crack and then binding it closed with cordage. Tanged pieces might have been used to drill and ream out (enlarge) such holes.

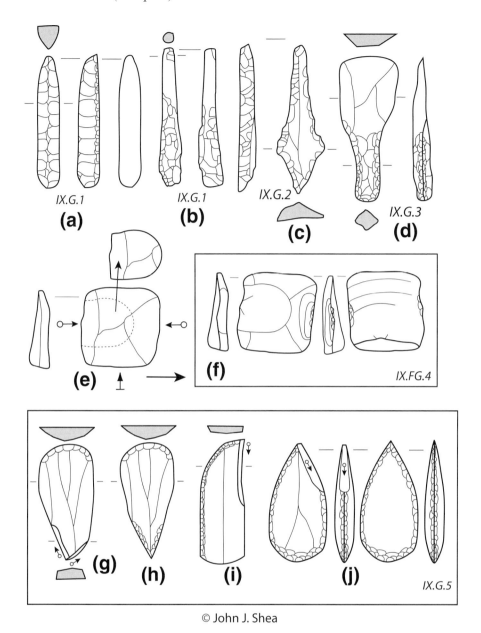

© John J. Shea

Figure 8.8 Other retouched pieces. (a–b) Rods/retouched cylinders, (c) Borer, (d) Tanged piece, (e) Scaled piece formation, (f) Scaled piece, (g–j) Selected combination pieces (see text).

Scaled pieces (IX.G.4) are flake fragments preserving extensive, if shallow, flake scars extending less than half of their length (Figure 8.8e–f). These flake scars' large ripples and overlapping patterns create the "scaled" appearance from which the artifact-type takes its name. Concentrations of crushing damage and bending fracture initiations on opposite edges of scaled pieces suggest that these artifacts result from bipolar percussion. Some of these artifacts may be flakes recruited for use as bipolar cores that retain enough of their original dorsal and ventral flake surfaces that one can recognize them. Scaled pieces' characteristic scarring could also result from some cutting or wedging task. Some typologies describe them as "wedges."

Combination tools (IX.G.5) have retouched edges that separately match the criteria for different retouched pieces. For example, one end may have a scraper edge, the other a burin or a convergently retouched edge (Figure 8.8g–h); or a backed piece or a flake point may have a burin removal (Figure 8.8i–j). Rather than inflating its list of artifact-types by listing all these artifact-types' potential combinations, the EAST Typology recommends dealing with them by combining other retouched pieces' names/numbers. If, for example a tool combines features of an endscraper and a dihedral burin (Figure 8.8 g), it would be called an endscraper-dihedral burin (IX.A.1.a/IX.E.2).

UWAZI VALLEY TALES, EPISODE 8: BEFORE THE CONFERENCE

"So, we have a plan," Aya leaned back in her canvas chair as I approached the Gentlemen's Smoking Lounge. Our guests had left two weeks ago. When he returned, our driver brought news. The National Museum Director had announced a one-day conference in the Capitol. He required all expeditions to send emissaries to read progress reports.

"I'll stay here to make sure the excavation continues to run smoothly," Aya continued. "The bones coming out of Level 5 are among the best preserved of any MSA/LSA context in Eastern Africa. If we conserve them right, this will be huge, like cover-of-*Nature* huge."

"We have the later afternoon slots, three papers, right after four o'clock tea break," she said. "I had to ask Endurance to call in a favor at the Museum Director's Office, but we're good to go."

"That late in the afternoon, we won't have to worry about the audience succumbing to the 'post-lunch food coma'," said the Polymath.

Aya turned to me. "Our senior colleague, the Old Africa Hand, goes first. He will read the 'big picture/broad perspective' paper."

"'The Uwazi Valley's Importance for Eastern African Prehistory: A Broad Perspective on the Big Picture,'" said the Old Africa Hand.

"Next, your advisor will read the report for last year."

The Polymath spoke. "'Excavations at Pango Wa Kwale (Ancient Ones' Cave), Uwazi Valley: An Interim Report.' I'll read it, but we're all co-authors,

---

Box 6 *Questions about retouched pieces*

Do retouched pieces' names indicate their actual functions? Some of the names early archaeologists gave to retouched pieces imply particular modes of use, such as scraper (orthogonal cutting), knife (longitudinal cutting), burin (engraving), awl (perforating), or point (weapon armature). These names reflect archaeologists' guesses about tool function based on morphological analogies with Industrial Era metal implements. Few of these names are demonstrably false, but they systematically underestimate stone tools' functional variability. Archaeological reconstructions of stone tool function based on microwear and residue analysis routinely indicate additional functions not implied by traditional artifact-type names. Experiment and experience using stone tools show that with enough strength and ingenuity one can make pretty any stone tool perform any cutting task, and Ancestral Africans were both strong and ingenious. They were, after all, the people who "invented inventing."

Why did Later Stone Age and Neolithic people make so many kinds of small backed/truncated pieces? Later Stone Age and Neolithic sites contain vast numbers of small backed/truncated pieces, or "geometric microliths." Surface exposures of such sites can contain dozens of such artifacts per square meter, yet only small proportions of these artifacts preserve evidence of use. More recent archaeological explanations for geometric microlith production focus on their ease of manufacture, their durability, and their functional versatility (Elston and Brantingham 2002). While these surmises may be true and shed some light on why stoneworkers made microliths, they do not explain microliths' morphological diversity.

Mass-producing distinctively shaped geometric microliths and littering habitation sites with them could have been an energetically inexpensive territory-marking strategy. Novice stoneworkers can learn how to make microliths in minutes, and experienced stoneworkers can make several such artifacts per minute (Shea 2015). Left at habitation sites, these artifacts would have sent persistent messages to newcomers in a region about past and present inhabitants' social identities (as indeed much archaeological stone tool analysis assumes they do).

---

as are the field staff and the lab technicians who ran the radiometric dates from last season."

"Is that normal?" I asked. I hadn't written a word.

"Eskimo seal hunting, Robin," the Old Africa Hand drew in on his pipe. Aya and the Polymath, both sighed, leaning back in their chairs.

The Old Africa Hand continued, "In my day, anyone named as an 'author' was supposed to have actually written a substantial part of the work and to be able to explain it. Nowadays anybody who has contributed to the work insists on being listed as an author."

"Why?" I asked.

"Well," Aya sat up, "academics have become so specialized that few people understand publications in one another's disciples. So, when you come up for promotion and tenure, some administrators just count how many papers you have published, whether they appear in prestigious journals, and how often your colleagues cite you."

"Really?" I asked.

"Not exactly," the Polymath said. "Aya's a bit anxious, like most junior faculty. Some of us read outside our specialty, but most don't. Busy college administrators often lack the expertise to evaluate technical papers in fields other than their own. This creates incentives for 'bean counting,' for evaluating candidates for promotion, such as Aya here, in terms of mere numbers of publications and citation indices. That in turn creates pressure on people to insist on authorship credit who are not authors in the traditional sense of the word, such as lab and field assistants, technicians, and colleagues who share data with one another."

"Shouldn't' those other people get rewarded for their work?" I asked the Polymath.

"Lab assistants, field staff, and technicians are employees and employees get paid," the Old Africa Hand grumbled. "Real scholars thank one another in acknowledgements. I once heard of this professor who accepted authorship credit for knapping a few flakes from a core for an experiment. Author – never a good thing to have the same name for two different things."

"Naming superfluous 'authors' costs nothing," Aya interjected, "so author lists just keep growing and growing. Last year three of us put together an outline at a break during the Society for Africanist Archaeology meetings. Three months later, when we submitted it to a journal, we had eight co-authors. Two of them I had neither met nor even heard of before. One of them, I know for a fact, doesn't even understand English."

The Polymath said, "As Chair of Anthropology, I proposed that for promotion and tenure we divide credit for faculty publications by the number of authors."

"How did that work?" I asked.

"Exactly as planned; he's no longer Chair," said Aya.

"So, Eskimo seal hunting?" I asked the Old Africa Hand.

"Among the Eskimo who hunt seals out on ocean ice, whoever touches a seal carcass before it reaches solid land has "helped" to kill the seal and thus deserves a share of its liver, a prized, iron-rich delicacy. So, when a hunter kills a seal, he conceals that fact until he can sprint for land. The moment he starts running, dragging the seal carcass behind him, all the other hunters nearby drop their spears and race off in pursuit, hoping to touch the seal before it reaches land. It's the perfect metaphor for academic authorship."

"Touching the seal. Nice. I'm going to use that someday," I said.

"Anyway," Aya rolled her eyes and continued, "you'll read your own paper on the stone tools. This idea about how to change stone tool analysis for the better is your idea. A stand-alone podium presentation at the end of the day will give you the best opportunity to make your point. Your paper will be fresh in the audience's minds for the day's final questions."

"Thank you, Aya," I said.

"Thank Endurance," she said.

"Be careful, Robin," the Old Africa Hand said, pouring whiskey into four shot glasses. "A lone baboon is a dead baboon. Yours is the last paper. Don't run over your time. It's bad form, and you're the only thing between the audience and cocktail hour. People are going to get impatient, and impatient people get testy. When you make a claim about problems with stone tool systematics, back that claim up with overwhelming evidence. Always keep a few such, for want of a better word, "trump card" slides in reserve for the questions you can anticipate your audience asking you."

"So, my paper's title?" I asked.

"Easier to say what not to use," said the Polymath.

"Remember 'My Pestle-Rubber is Bigger than Your Pestle-Rubber,'" said Aya. "That went over well."

"Anything with 'materiality' or 'agency' in the title," the Polymath said, sipping his drink. "Those are universally recognized signals for audience members to head for the restrooms or the hotel bar."

The Old Africa Hand chuckled, "Remember that absurd young fellow who changed the letters from upper- to lower-case alternatingly? 'The materiality of agency in pre-aksumite Ceramics,' and so on. Every bloody slide. Must have been dropped on his head at a young age."

"He never did answer when you asked him about that, or afterward in faculty meetings" said the Polymath.

Aya leaned over to me. "Just so you know, he's now Dean Absurd Fellow."

The Old Africa Hand sat up. "'Finding Clarity: A New Approach to Stone Tools from the Uwazi Valley.'"

"Nice," said Aya.

"Bravo!" said the Polymath.

"Good, good as done," I said, jotting the title in my notebook.

"To a successful meeting," the Polymath raised his glass.

"Any meeting you can walk away from is a good meeting," said Aya.

"Indeed." said the Old Africa Hand. "All things are ready if our minds be so."

"An old African proverb?" I asked.

"Shakespeare," said Joseph.

CHAPTER 9

PERCUSSORS AND GROUNDSTONE ARTIFACTS

This chapter reviews conventions for measuring, describing, and classifying percussors/hammerstones (EAST Typology Group X) and groundstone artifacts (Group XI). The latter include abraded-edge tools, perforated artifacts, abrading tools, pulverizing tools, and stone vessels. The chapter also answers common questions about percussors and groundstone tools.

This chapter treats percussors and groundstone artifacts together because these artifacts are usually made of different rocks than flaked-stone artifacts. They were also shaped and used in different ways than cores, flakes, and retouched pieces. Although it treats percussors and groundstone artifacts separately, these two artifact groups grade into one another in complex ways. Percussors often feature evidence for abrasive tasks. Groundstone artifacts and tool fragments frequently show comminution damage indicating reuse/recycling for percussive tasks. Each of these artifact categories exhibits such wide metric and morphological variation, both within and between samples from different sites, that the EAST Typology's classifications are "minimalist." Specific research questions ought to guide more complex groundstone artifact typologies.

MEASURING PERCUSSORS AND GROUNDSTONE ARTIFACTS

When archaeologists recover groundstone artifacts intact, most of their conventions for measuring percussors and groundstone artifacts are essentially the same as those for cores and core tools. They measure maximum length, width, thickness, and mass. Stone vessels and perforated artifacts enjoy a wider range of measurements specific to those artifact-types.

PERCUSSORS (GROUP X)

The EAST Typology recognizes three percussor categories: round percussors, tabular percussors, and ad hoc percussors. Archaeologists' terms for stone tool use vary widely, but one increasingly sees the terms "active" and "passive" employed for moving versus stationary components of tools used in percussive tasks. Many older works use the term "anvil" for stationary/passive percussors.

Round Percussors

Round percussors (X.A) are spherical or subspherical rocks (pebbles, cobbles, or boulders) featuring percussion damage. Major types include hammerstones, subspheroids, and spheroids (Figure 9.1). These artifacts range widely in size, from objects 50–100 mm in diameter that could easily have been held in one hand for percussive tasks to larger objects that would have to have been held in both hands while used or rested on the ground and struck with other objects.

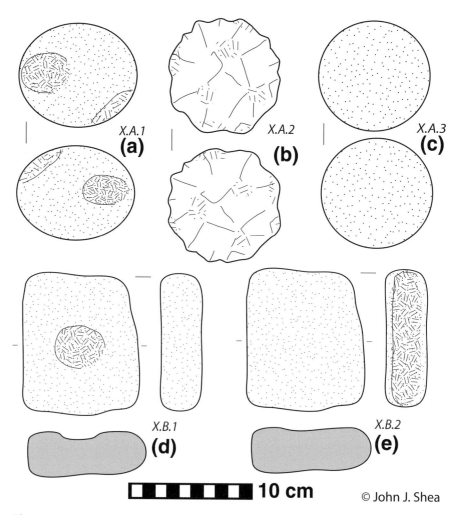

Figure 9.1 Percussors. (a) Hammerstone, (b) Subspheroid, (c) Spheroid, (d) Tabular surface percussor, (e) Tabular edge percussor.

Hammerstones (X.A.1) feature at least one concentration of comminution damage on their surface (Figure 9.1a). Many feature several such concentrations. These artifacts are usually made of tough rocks with poor fracture qualities, such as limestone, quartzite, and various dense, tough igneous and metamorphic rocks.

Subspheroids (X.A.2) combine features of both cores and percussors. They feature ridges and concavities from flake removals, as cores do, but they also feature extensive comminution and/or abrasion on many of those ridges and other projections (Figure 9.1b). Some subspheroids may be cores used as percussors.

Spheroids (X.A.3) preserve percussion damage on their entire surface, or very nearly so (Figure 9.1c). Subspheroids and spheroids from Plio-Pleistocene contexts in Eastern Africa and elsewhere are often made of rocks with weak conchoidal fracture properties, such as limestone, quartz, quartzite, and basalt (Willoughby 1985).

Tabular Percussors

Tabular percussors (X.B) are angular rock fragments that preserve percussion damage. The EAST Typology recognizes surface percussors and edge percussors, although many such artifacts combine features of both. On *tabular surface percussors* (X.B.1), percussion damage appears near the center of a flat surface (Figure 9.1d). If extensive, this damage can create a "pit" or concavity a few centimeters in diameter. Archaeologists call such artifacts "pitted stones" or "anvils."

The "anvil" hypothesis views *tabular surface percussors* as immobile hard substrates on which prehistoric humans split or crushed objects by placing them on the rock surface and then striking from above. Their characteristic pits could be either a consequence of prolonged use or a feature excavated into the rock surface to keep hard objects immobile during percussion. Although the anvil hypothesis is probably the most popular among archaeologists, smaller tabular percussors could have been used as active (moving) percussors, too.

On *tabular edge percussors* (X.B.2), percussion damage is concentrated around the object's circumference (Figure 9.1e). This damage may occur in patches or it may make a full circuit around the artifact. Archaeologists generally view tabular edge percussors as active percussors.

Ad Hoc Percussors

Ad hoc percussors (X.C) are cores, core-tools, detached pieces, and retouched pieces that preserve evidence for secondary use as percussors or pressure flakers. Other than being made of stone and featuring such damage, ad hoc percussors potentially co-occur among all core, flake, and retouched artifact types, as well as among groundstone artifacts. Louis Leakey (1931) identified a variety of flakes as "fabricators" that preserved damage on their edges consistent with use as percussors and/or pressure flakers. This term seems to have passed from common usage.

Although much of what archaeologists write about stone percussors seems to assume they were engaged in stoneworking, ethnographic humans use stone percussors for many other purposes. Such tasks can include food preparation (pulverizing seeds, nuts, roots, tubers, even dried meat), fiber extraction from plant tissues, preparing mineral pigments, even carpentry tasks. Archaeologists working on more recent time periods, in particular, ought to remain alert to the possibility of recovering organic residues from percussors, and only wash these artifacts after sampling them for such residues.

GROUNDSTONE ARTIFACTS (GROUP XI)

Groundstone artifacts' surfaces preserve abrasive wear, including striations and polishing. This fine abrasive wear, however, is often only the most recent transformation of an artifact previously shaped by cycles of percussion and coarse abrasion. The EAST Typology recognizes seven major groups of groundstone artifacts: abraded-edge tools, perforated tools, abrading tools, stone beads, pulverizing equipment, stone vessels, and pigments.

Abraded-Edge Tools

Abraded-edge tools feature a cutting edge shaped and maintained by abrasion (XI.A). In Eastern Africa, *groundstone celts* (XI.A.1) are the most commonly reported abraded-edge tools (Figure 9.2). Groundstone celts differ from flaked-stone abraded-edge celts (IV.C.1.c) in lacking fracture scars on their surfaces other than those referable to use. The EAST Typology recognizes five major groundstone celt types. *Flared groundstone celts* (XI.A.1.a) have a wide, flared edge and parallel, mildly convex, or tapering lateral edges (Figure 9.2a). On *lugged/bossed groundstone celts* (XI.A.1.b), the artifact's proximal end expands and features lateral convexities ("lugs" or "bosses"), a central concavity, or both (Figure 9.2b). *Grooved groundstone celts* (XI.A.1.c) feature one or more linear concavities that make either a full or partial circuit around the artifact (Figure 9.2c). *Biconvex groundstone celts* (XI.A.1.d) feature outwardly curving lateral edges whose maximum width occurs at about the midpoint of their length (Figure 9.2d). *Double-edged groundstone celts* (XI.A.1.e) preserve abraded edges at opposite ends of their long axis (Figure 9.2e).

Archaeologists sometimes describe celts as "polished axes." While many may have been hafted and used in this way, while hafted in the matter of an axe or an adze, others retain traces of percussion-related battering at the end opposite the worked edge. Such damage suggests they may also have seen

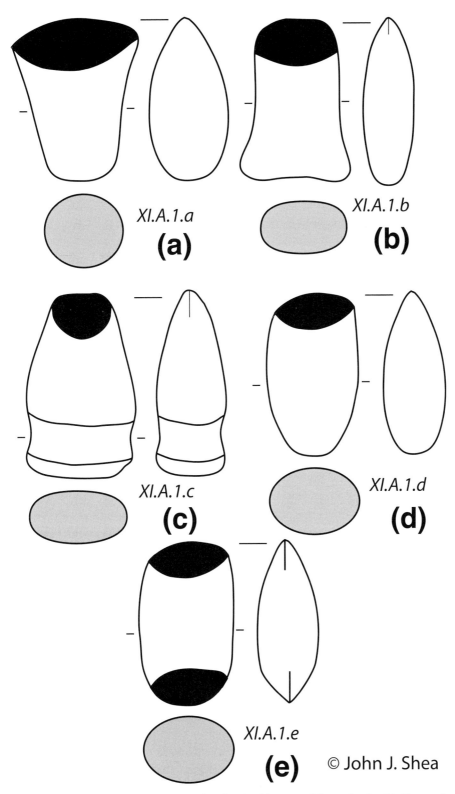

Figure 9.2 Groundstone celts. (a) Flared celt, (b) Lugged/bossed celt, (c) Grooved celt, (d) Biconvex groundstone celt.

use, unhafted, as wedges for splitting wood. Lugged/bossed celts' lugs/bosses may have been intended to increase accuracy in striking the ends of such wedges.

Abraded-edge knives and other cutting tools appear in many parts of the world, including the Nile Valley, but they are rarely reported from prehistoric contexts in Eastern Africa. The EAST Typology maintains an *other abraded-edge tool* category (XI.A.2).

Grooved Abrading Stones

Grooved abrading stones (XI.B) are artifacts used to shape other durable materials by concentrated linear abrasion. *Single-grooved abrading stones* (XI.B.1) preserve one carved linear concavity (Figure 9.3a), while *multiple-grooved abrading stones* (XI.B.2) feature more than one such groove (Figure 9.3b). The uses to which these artifacts were put remain unclear. Some might have been used to sharpen the tips of wood or bone points, to smooth the shafts of cylindrical artifacts, such as arrows. They might also have been used to shape beads. Some African ethnographic beadmakers smoothed ostrich eggshell beads' edges by stringing them tightly together and then dragging them back and forth through a groove carved in abrasive rocks (Orton 2008).

Perforated Artifacts

Perforated artifacts (XI.C) preserve at least one artificial perforation. Most such artifacts in the archaeological literature feature only one. The EAST Typology recognizes four main types. For perforated discs and beads, it retains terms in common usage. For larger ring-shaped objects (those longer than 50 mm in any dimension), it uses the term *torus* (plural = tori) . Although archaeologists rarely use the word, "torus" is a concise and well-established geometric term that lacks the overt functional connotations of many older archaeological alternatives.

A *symmetrical torus* (XI.C.1) has its volume distributed more or less symmetrically around the radius of its central perforation (Figure 9.3c). Symmetrical tori enjoy a variety of archaeological interpretations. In sub-Saharan Africa, they are often identified as "digging stick weights" – artifacts slipped onto digging stick shafts to add mass to the tool. However, actual ethnographic documentation of this practice is surprisingly scarce (Hromnik 1986, Waldron 1987). In the Nile Valley and the Middle East, larger examples are often called "mace heads," and viewed as weapons (Rosenberg 2010). Such mace heads vary, but many have their mass unevenly distributed around their central perforation. Some also have ridges or flanges carved into their circumference. So few such artifacts occur in Eastern Africa that one need not propose additional artifact-types. Archaeologists working in or near the Nile Valley,

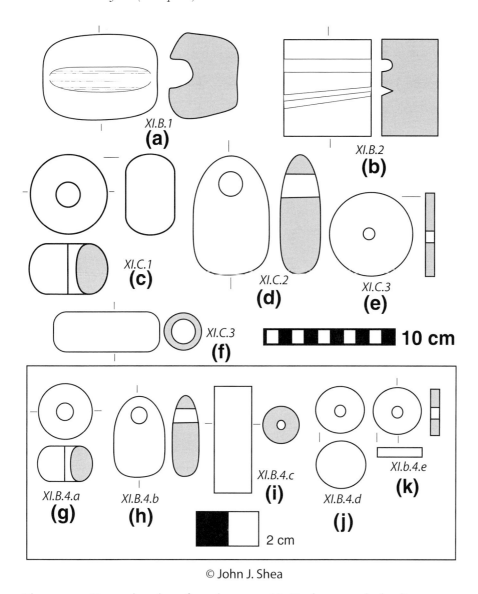

© John J. Shea

Figure 9.3 Grooved and perforated stones. (a) Single-grooved abrading stone, (b) Multiple-grooved abrading stone, (c) Symmetrical torus, (d) Symmetrical torus, (e) Perforated disc/plate, (f) Stone tube, (g–k) Stone beads, (g) Flat torus, (h) Pendant, (i) Cylinder, (j) Sphere, (k) Disc.

on the other hand, may wish to do so. Smaller perforated artifacts are sometimes interpreted as spindle whorls used in textile production. In some parts of the world, *symmetrical tori* are pulverizing tools (Wright 1992). They have a short shaft set through their perforation, and then one rolls them, wheel-like, over objects that need to be crushed. Symmetrical tori might also have been used as weights on the shafts of "pump-drills" (see https://primitivetechnology .wordpress.com/2016/01/22/cord-drill-and-pump-drill/).

An *asymmetrical torus* (XI.C.2) has its mass unevenly distributed around the radius of its central perforation (Figure 9.3d).

A *perforated disc/plate* (XI.C.3) is a relatively flat symmetrical torus (Figure 9.3e).

A *perforated tube* (XI.C.4) is a cylinder (length greater than or equal to its width) with a perforation running parallel to its long axis (Figure 9.3f).

Stone beads (XI.C.5.a–e) are perforated artifacts whose longest dimension is 50 mm or less. The EAST Typology recognizes five major bead types: the flat torus bead, the pendant bead, the cylinder bead, the sphere bead, and the disc bead (Figure 9.3g–k). As with other artifact categories, the EAST Typology offers a minimalist classification. Beck's (1928) *Classification and Nomenclature of Beads and Pendants* remains the "classic" work on this subject and a guide to its more generally recognized terminology and typology.

Pulverizing Tools

Pulverizing tools (XI.D) group together artifacts used in pairs to crush other objects by percussion and abrasion (Figure 9.4). These artifacts combine a mobile "handstone" together with a stationary "pulverizing surface stone." The EAST Typology lists these two artifact categories separately (XI.D.1 and XI.D.2), but for clarity this chapter discusses them together as two toolkits: mortar/pestle and grinding slab/handstone.

Pestles (XI.D.1.a) are solid cylinders with abrasion and percussion damage concentrated at one or both ends (Figure 9.4a). They are used together with *mortars* (XI.D.2.a), stones that have deep, narrow hemispherical or cone-shaped concavities (Figure 9.4f). The mortar/pestle combines compressive and shearing forces. The working end of the mortar crushes particles at the bottom of the mortar's working surface, pushing them upward onto the walls of that surface, where a twisting motion applied with the pestle shears them into smaller particles (Kraybill 1977). Ethnographic mortars vary widely. Some are small portable tools used to crush a variety of media, such as pigments, seeds, roots and tubers, even tobacco in ethnohistoric sites. Others are large stationary objects, even bedrock outcrops.

Handstones and *grinding slabs* work mainly by shearing forces. Particles are placed on the grinding slab's surface and are crushed between that surface and a handstone (Kraybill 1977). The EAST Typology recognizes three main kinds of handstones. *Conical handstones* (XI.D.1.b) are cone-shaped objects whose abrading surface lies at their base (Figure 9.4b). These contrast with *hemispherical handstones* (XI.D.1.c) (Figure 9.4c), whose abrading surface aligns more or less parallel with the plane defined by the artifact's length and width. Hemispherical handstones are usually plano-convex in cross-section. *Cylindrical handstones* (XI.D.1.d) feature abrasion-worn surfaces along their sides with striations aligned perpendicular to the tool's long axis (Figure 9.4d). After

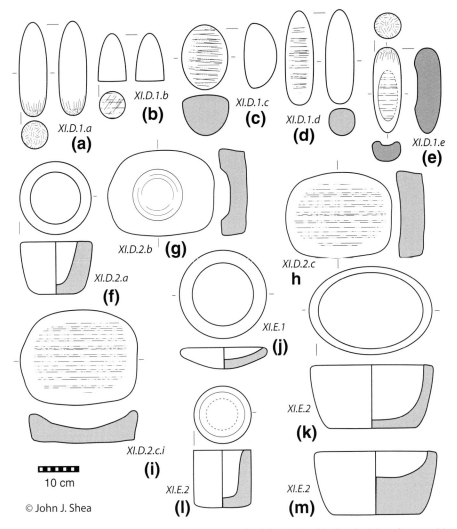

Figure 9.4 Pulverizing tools and stone vessels. (a) Pestle, (b) Conical handstone, (c) Hemispherical handstones, (d) Cylindrical handstone, (e) Pestle-rubber, (f) Mortar, (g) Rotary grinding slab, (h) Linear grinding slab, (i) Concave grinding slab, (j–m) Stone vessels (j) Platter, (k–m) Bowls.

prolonged use, cylindrical handstones can become oval or plano-convex in cross-section. *Pestle-rubbers* (XI.D.1.e) (Figure 9.4e) describe objects with percussion damage at one or both ends and either flat or shallow concave abrading surfaces on one or more sides.

Archaeological terms for grinding slabs diverge between research traditions. The EAST Typology retires the term "quern" because archaeologists use it inconsistently and for so wide a range of artifacts. *Rotary grinding slabs* (XI.D.2. b) preserve abrasive wear from rotary motion (Figure 9.4g). *Linear grinding slabs* (XI.D.2.c) preserve abrasive wear from linear motions (Figure 9.4h). *Concave grinding slabs* (XI.D.2.c.i) (formerly known as "saddle querns") are linear grinding slabs with deeply concave surfaces (Figure 9.4j). These concavities may reflect purposeful shaping, use-related wear, or some combination of both.

The EAST Typology registers grinding slabs and handstones whose abraded surfaces feature percussion-related concavities as combination grinding slabs/handstones and tabular surface percussors/pitted stones.

Stone Vessels

Stone vessels (XI.E) are cylinders, hemispheres, or truncated cones into which stoneworkers excavated a concavity (Figure 9.4j–m). Stone vessels vary widely in size, from objects the size of teacups to specimens more than 200–300 mm long, weighing several kilograms. Stoneworkers shaped them from a variety of rocks, including basalt, limestone, sandstone, and steatite. Following conventions for naming ceramic vessels, archaeologists describe stone vessels in terms of relatively broad and shallow *platters* (XI.E.1) and deeper *bowls* (XI.E.2) (compare Figure 9.4j versus Figure 9.4k–m). Platters and bowls can grade into one another. In southwest Asia, where such vessels are relatively common, archaeologists call platters "shallow vessels" whose ratio of rim diameter to height is greater than 3.0 and call "bowls" those vessels with lesser rim diameter/height ratios (Wright 1992).

Surveys and excavations often recover stone vessel fragments, but other than in funeral and (presumed) votive deposits, such as the Njoro River Cave in Kenya (Leakey and Leakey 1950), complete stone vessels rarely appear at habitation sites in Eastern Africa. Some of these artifacts have traces of ochre on them as well as carbon and other evidence of thermal damage.

Other Abrading/Abraded Stones

Many archaeological assemblages also contain artifacts with large-scale use-related abrasive wear. The EAST Typology recognizes pigment stones, stone cylinders, pottery-abrading stones, digging stones, and grindstones. These artifacts differ from other groundstone artifacts in that their abrasion appears to have resulted from use rather than purposeful shaping.

Pigment stones (XI.F.1) are pieces of red ochre (hematite/iron oxide), chalk, or other rocks that exhibit abrasion in their surfaces. Pigment stones are often conical, but they vary so widely that one gains little by listing all their possible morphological configurations unless some overriding research goal requires it.

Pottery-abrading stones (XI.F.2) are flaked-stone artifacts potters use to smooth ceramic vessel surfaces prior to firing. The resulting wear patterns, which can occur on edges, fracture scar ridges, and tool surfaces, feature numerous striations and polished surfaces. L. Phillipson (2013) describes these artifacts as "pot formers." Defined as they are in terms of use-related wear, pottery-abrading stones can take many forms, including any of the other artifact-types listed in the EAST Typology.

Although Phillipson (2013) uses a single term, "pot formers," for flaked stone and groundstone artifacts, it is wiser to distinguish them based on their morphology than to unite them based on their assumed function. Therefore, the EAST Typology groups otherwise unmodified artifacts with such abrasive wear among grindstones (XI.F.5, discussed below).

Digging stones (XI.F.3) appear mainly in Later Pleistocene and Holocene lithic assemblages, such as at Matupi Cave (Noten 1982). These are relatively large, elongated artifacts with one or more pointed ends. One or both such ends preserve large-scale striations and polish. Fractures may appear as well. Archaeologists usually interpret this damage as having formed when prehistoric humans used these tools to dig through hard sediments.

Groundstone cylinders (XI.F.4) are solid (i.e., unperforated) pieces with abraded sides and ends. It remains unclear whether the abrasion on them reflects shaping, use, or some combination of both. Ethnographic analogy suggests some groundstone cylinders may have been personal adornments, such as earrings or labrets, but one cannot rule out other possible uses.

Grindstones (XI.F.5) are rocks that preserve abrasive wear on one or more surfaces but no other evidence of purposeful shaping. Stones from Iron Age contexts preserving wear and other traces of use as whetstones would fall into this category, as would pottery-abrading stones made of materials other than flaked stone.

These artifact-categories do not exhaust the range of prehistoric stone artifacts featuring substantial use-related abrasion. Future researchers will almost certainly recognize additional such artifact-types.

Box 7 *Questions about percussors and groundstone artifacts*

What were spheroids? Archaeologists have long speculated about these "stone balls" (Willoughby 1985), with much of the debate focusing on whether stoneworkers shaped them deliberately, or if their shape was the result of use. Louis Leakey (1960) conjectured that spheroids might have been wrapped individually in leather or fabric pouches and tied together with strings to make *bolas* (a hunting weapon). J.D. Clark (1955) proposed that they could have been wrapped in leather and lashed to sticks to make the striking ends of clubs like a Maasai *rungu* (truncheon). Schick and Toth (1994) contend spheroids are not actually "finished artifacts" intended for particular uses but hammerstones discarded at the point where their spherical shaped began to imperil their users' fingers. Using an angular hammerstone made of softer rocks, such as quartzite and rotating it periodically to use undamaged surfaces, can eventually create a spheroid.

Box 7 (*Cont.*)

Spheroids seem to show excess tool production effort to no obvious improvement in tool function as well as control of symmetry. These are exactly the same qualities that led some researchers to propose handaxes were products of "costly signaling" in sexual selection (Kohn and Mithen 1999). That both handaxes and spheroids begin to appear regularly around the same time, ca. 1.6 Ma, could suggest spheroid production reflects a costly signaling strategy.

Alternatively, spheroids may owe their shape to the one thing they irrefutably did, which is to make noise. Striking one rock with another creates a loud short-lived report that carries over great distances. Comminution (crushing damage) from repetitively striking the same part of a stone dampens percussive noise. Rotating a percussor after one or more blows would have kept noises loud and, over time, created spherical objects covered with percussion damage. What purpose might such noisemaking have served? One possibility might be as aids to musical performances. Spheroids become common around 1.6 Ma, about the same time as first-appearance dates for larger-brained hominins, such as *H. ergaster* and *H. erectus*. Among primates, larger brains correlate with larger social groups, and as Dunbar (2016) argues, these hominins may have been among the first to deploy singing, music, and other rituals to extend social networks beyond physical grooming.

Rhythmic percussion might also have been a strategy by which hominins sent auditory signals to one another through dense vegetation or in low-light conditions. Brains are expensive tissues (Aiello and Wheeler 1995), and as hominin brain sizes grew larger, their foraging ranges likely increased as well. Repetitive rhythmic percussion might have been a strategy that hominins used in low-light conditions to help direct individuals back to nightly refuges.

Finally, we should not dismiss the percussive stones' potential roles in antipredator defense. Increasing dependence on hunted or scavenged meat and fat would have brought hominins into frequent and predictable contact with large carnivores, such as lions and hyenas. Guidebooks to wilderness survival routinely recommend making loud noises by striking objects against one another as a way to disperse carnivores. If this strategy fails, then throwing a stone projectile could clarify the "hominins + noise = pain" equation.

None of these ideas about spheroids are mutually exclusive. Still, one hesitates to call them hypotheses, because it is not clear that archaeologists will ever acquire the kinds of evidence they would need to refute them.

Box 7 (*Cont.*)

Why did Neolithic humans make stone pulverizing tools? Until recently, many ethnographic humans used stone mortars and grinding slabs to process domesticated cereal grasses' hard seeds (Adams 2014, Shoemaker et al. 2017). Understandably, archaeologists interpret increases in groundstone pulverizing tools as evidence for the onset of cereal agriculture. And yet, ethnographic hunter-gatherers often use such pulverizing tools to process wild grass seeds. They also use them to crush nuts, roots, and tubers, and to prepare mineral pigments. They often use carved wooden implements for the same purposes. Wooden mortar and pestle combinations grace countless equatorial African villages. Inasmuch as such perishable wooden pulverizing tools rarely preserve well enough for archaeologists to recover them, it may be a mistake to view first appearances of stone pulverizing tools as marking watersheds in human plant-processing technology and/or dietary change. Such changes may have occurred centuries or even millennia earlier and involved wooden pulverizing tools.

Making a groundstone mortar or grinding slab requires considerable labor. Unlike wood, which one can shape fairly swiftly by cyclical "charring and scraping," every particle of a groundstone artifact must be forcefully excavated. What factors might have tipped the cost/benefit ratio in favor of carving stone pulverizing tools? No one conducts fieldwork in Eastern Africa without noticing termites' impressive abilities to consume wood. Axe handles, table legs, chairs: nothing made of wood and left on the ground overnight eludes their attention or their appetite. When Eastern Africans became less residentially mobile, incentives for devising termite-impervious stone pulverizing tools could have increased accordingly.

Groundstone artifacts were probably no less multifunctional than any other stone tools. The handstones archaeologists reflexively interpret as aids to seed-grinding and pigment preparation are very much like stone tools Ancestral Native Americans used as abrasive stones to make high-quality leather garments (Hayden 1990). Lithic microwear and residue studies will shed light on this issue.

For what were stone bowls used? Calling these artifacts "stone bowls" conjures up images of them being placed directly on fire to cook food, much like a contemporary "Dutch oven." However, porous rocks like basalt and limestone readily absorb and retain moisture. Exposed to intense heat, differences in moisture and temperature between the vessel surface and its interior cause water absorbed in these rocks to expand at different rates. Such differential expansion can cause the rock itself to fracture, even to explode violently. If Ancestral Africans used stone bowls as aids to food consumption, they likely heated them slowly while dry and empty and

Box 7 (*Cont.*)

then placed in them food that cooked on contact with them. Using stone bowls in this way could have recovered fats that would otherwise be burnt by cooking over an open fire or lost by placing foodstuffs on a bed of heated rocks. Stone vessels might also have been used to parch or roast nuts and seeds.

Finally, we cannot reject the argument that stone bowls were expressions of "conspicuous consumption," labor-intensive carved-stone versions of mundane vessels intended to signal their owners' prestige and power. That so many Neolithic stone bowls have been recovered from mortuary contexts suggests they had symbolic functions beyond mere food preparation. Periodically interring stone vessels in mortuary rituals could have been a strategy for preserving the status-signaling value of those artifacts remaining in circulation.

UWAZI VALLEY TALES, EPISODE 9: AFTER THE CONFERENCE

Four full shot glasses and an open whiskey bottle sat on the stump before us in the Gentlemen's Smoking Lounge. Pipe smoke billowed around the Old Africa Hand. Endurance and Joseph each sipped a cup of tea.

"Well, how did the meeting go?" Aya asked me.
  I looked down. "Not well."
  "What happened?" she asked.
  "Well, I read the paper and kept to my time limit. The first audience question asked whether the tools from Level 5 are MSA, LSA, or MSA/LSA Transitional."

The Polymath chuckled, "Our young colleague, Robin, announced that these age-stages and transitions are – and I quote, 'nineteenth-century nonsense that outlived their usefulness a hundred years ago.'"

"They also asked me what LSA industries are represented in Levels 3 and 4."

The Old Africa Hand laughed. "I quote, 'Industries are both figments and failures of the archaeological imagination.'" He sipped at his glass and reignited his pipe. "Well put, Robin."

"They asked me how I defined microliths."
  "And?" Aya asked.
  "I told them that I used the four different microlith definitions each of the senior professors in the front row had published. Then, I projected a slide with a graph showing how each gave conflicting results for the tools from Level 5."

"Well played, Robin," said the Old Africa Hand.

"That must have gone over well," Aya sipped at her glass.

"Shame I sat in the back," said the Polymath, "I would have loved to have seen the looks on their faces."

"Yeah, that was a pretty picture," I said to the Polymath. "Should I fill out the application for truck-driving school before or after I get back to the university?"

I continued, "One professor told me I need to go back to school and spend some time in the library. Another professor said I was right about industries and age-stages, but that she had thought of it first decades ago, and that I should cite her."

"Those two," said the Old Africa Hand. "You'll find no books by him in any library, and her – the last thing she published she wrote in cuneiform on a clay tablet."

"She might have meant it as a peace offering," the Polymath said. "Some academics cite more or less like apes pick bugs off one another: to establish alliances, express affiliation, or to curry favor. 'Grooming citations,' one could call them."

"It did not sound like a peace offering," Endurance said.

"So, how did it end?" Aya asked.

"The four in the front all started arguing about how to define microliths," said Endurance. "There was a pause, and then our senior colleague stood up, started clapping, and everyone else joined in. The Museum Director woke up, took the stage, thanked everyone for coming, and invited them to the reception in the Main Exhibit Hall."

"Look, Robin," the Old Africa Hand set his glass on the table, "when colleagues give you a rough time, just remember your elephant gun."

Endurance and Aya spoke together, "Don't get mad, get even!"

The Polymath interrupted, "Shooting colleagues won't make your problems go away, Robin, but it will give you a whole different set of problems to worry about!"

The Old Africa Hand cleared his throat. "The elephant gun's a metaphor. Nobody ever solved a problem by shooting anyone."

He leaned forward, "Back in the old days, the few of us working here in Africa all knew each other well. If this one had a track record of good ideas and he or she proposed something new or controversial, we gave them a fair hearing. If we knew this other one was barking mad, we either ignored them or took what they told us with a grain of salt. Nowadays, there are so many of you young people in the field, so many pressures to publish and to make your mark," he glanced sideways at Aya, "that everyone is skeptical when a young person they do not know claims a game-changing discovery, and all the more so when the discovery is something intangible, like an innovation in method and theory, rather than, say, a fossil or some artifacts they found."

"So, what you're saying," the Polymath interjected, "is that archaeologists have turned from being novelty-seeking, like primates, to novelty-avoiding, like rodents. From neophilic talking monkeys to neophobic talking rats."

"Every college professor thinks they are a misunderstood genius." The Old Africa Hand looked over at the Polymath. "When you claim a new way of thinking about something, it's only human nature for others to wonder why, if the idea is so great, they themselves didn't think of it first."

The Polymath spoke up. "As Thomas Huxley said on learning of Darwin's theory of evolution by natural selection, 'How extremely stupid not to have thought of that.'"

"You think you are right," the Old Africa Hand continued, ignoring the Polymath. "They don't. Not yet, anyway. Telling them what they are doing is wrong won't convince them. Archaeologists aren't fools. They know full well what they have been doing with stone tools for the last century will not help them answer the big questions the next century will throw at them. They're whistling past the graveyard. You need to show them what one can do with what you propose. That's the work of a lifetime, Robin, not something you can do in a conference presentation, in a journal paper, or even in a book. Nor is it something you can do alone. Persuade others to join you. A lone baboon is a dead baboon."

"So, you think I will have a career in archaeology?"

"You are a born teacher," said Endurance.

"It is written," said Joseph.

"Nobody's born anything, and nothing is written." The Old Africa Hand leaned forward and turned eyeball-to-eyeball with the Polymath, who sobered instantly. "What did I tell you on your first day in my class?"

"Always w-work as h-hard as you c-can and n-never quit," the Polymath stammered.

"And what did you tell Aya on her first day in your class?"

She answered for him. "Always work as hard as you can and never quit."

"My parents have told me that since I was a little girl," Endurance said.

"As said our elders to all of us," said Joseph. "Words to keep you on the path, Robin."

"I will always work as hard as I can, and I will never quit," I said.

"Now you have your elephant gun," the Old Africa Hand sat back in his chair.

"Those words slay bigger and better game than elephants, Robin," said Aya.

The Polymath piped up, "Maybe, when you're older, Robin, you can write a book about stone tools, and explain your ideas about them in short fictional vignettes with characters based on us.

"Oh, be serious," Aya laughed.

"No, Robin, use humor," said Joseph. "The shortest distance between two people is laughter, for humor is truth."

"Well, OK, then. Just remember that any resemblance to actual events or persons, living or dead, is entirely intentional," I said.

"Indeed." The old Hand's pipe smoke coiled with the mist rising up from the Uwazi Valley.

CHAPTER 10

CONCLUSION

This chapter considers major questions about the Eastern African lithic record. It also argues for changes in archaeological practice that can improve the stone tool evidence.

BIG QUESTIONS ABOUT STONE TOOLS

Archaeologists have many questions about stone tools. We ask how to define a specific artifact-type, or lithic industry, or whether people did different things with stone tools at one site than at others. Stone tools have much more to offer archaeology, anthropology, and allied scholarly fields, such as biological anthropology, cognitive sciences, and history. This chapter examines three such "synergistic" questions that the Eastern African lithic record is uniquely poised to answer, namely:

- How did hominin stoneworking first evolve?
- Are language evolution and stone tool variability related to one another?
- Why did people stop making stone tools?

Reforming East African stone tool systematics along lines the EAST Typology proposes will help us answer these questions.

Early Evolution of Hominin Stoneworking

How did hominin stoneworking first evolve? Archaeologists currently seek stone cutting tools' evolutionary origins among sediments dating to the Pliocene Epoch, ca. 2.6–5.3 Ma. The oldest-known modified stone cutting tools, those from Lomekwi, Kenya, date to around 3.4 Ma (Harmand et al. 2015), and the hunt is now on throughout the region for older artifacts there and elsewhere. Credible claims for stone tool cut-marks on bone date to around the same time, ca. 3.5 Ma, at Dikika, in Ethiopia (McPherron et al. 2010). Stone tools become common and widespread in Africa after 1.8 Ma with the rise of the

Genus *Homo*. One of the major questions archaeologists ask about this early evidence is whether early hominin stoneworking comprises an adaptive strategy with a significant socially learned component transmitted over space and time, as using such terms as Lomekwian, Pre-Oldowan, Oldowan, and Acheulian industries implies. Or, if instead, it reflects a "latent" strategy, one that individual hominins' devised on their own when a need for cutting tools arose (Tennie et al. 2017) and one that appeared independently among multiple hominin lineages (Shea 2017a).

How will reforming stone tool systematics improve research into hominin stoneworking's origins? First, archaeologists need to develop empirical criteria for recognizing social learning in the stone tool evidence (Tostevin 2012, Eren et al. 2015). This is a tall order, but enough archaeologists are currently working on this problem to suggest that if such criteria can be found, they will be (Ranhorn, et al., 2020). The first step will involve detailed studies of individuals (humans and nonhuman primates) learning stoneworking techniques similar to those we infer for Plio-Pleistocene hominins. The next step will require large-scale comparisons among Plio-Pleistocene lithic assemblages seeking evidence for social learning. Fortunately, museums in Ethiopia, Kenya, and Tanzania preserve thousands of excavated stone tools that could be incorporated into such large-scale comparisons. Unfortunately, the archaeological research projects that documented Plio-Pleistocene lithic artifacts used, and continue to use, different systematics. Anyone who wants to conduct such a large-scale comparison will have to examine the original artifacts and measure them. If, as in the past, these comparisons rely on either stone tool systematics from only one archaeological research tradition or ones devised uniquely for this comparison, their observations will have severely limited value. Redescribing samples of these Plio-Pleistocene assemblages using the EAST Typology will not only enable comparisons among previously incomparable Plio-Pleistocene assemblages, it will also facilitate comparisons with lithic samples from more recent periods in which the habitual and obligatory nature of hominin stoneworking is more firmly established (Shea 2017a, 2017b).

Language Evolution and Stoneworking Variability

Are language evolution and stone tool variability related to one another? Language is among our species' most distinctive derived evolutionary characteristics. The consensus among linguists holds that quantal speech accompanied by the use of symbolic artifacts was not in place among human ancestors 500 Ka, but that it was present among all humans living less than 35 Ka (Lieberman and McCarthy 2014). Linguists disagree over whether human language evolved suddenly in one place and at one time and spread outward or if it instead evolved gradually and cumulatively (Lieberman 2015).

In *Stone Tools in Human Evolution* (Shea 2017b: 84–107) I proposed that increasingly complex spatial and chronological patterning in the stone tool evidence ("quasi-linguistic" patterning) beginning around 200–300 Ka resulted from a major change in linguistic abilities among later Middle Pleistocene *Homo*, and specifically the origins of quantal speech among *Homo sapiens*. Eastern Africa offers a unique opportunity to test this hypothesis in detail using an archaeological record associated with *Homo sapiens* and our immediate evolutionary ancestors, and not with other hominins. That Eastern African chimpanzees might have fractured stone in the course of cracking open nuts remains a possibility (McGrew 1992), but thus far the practice seems restricted to chimpanzee populations living far to the west and since 4,300 years ago (Mercader et al. 2007).

The main obstacle for testing hypotheses about human language evolution in Eastern Africa is the diversity of stone tool systematics archaeologists use for evidence dating to 35–500 Ka. Spread out as it is over Earlier, Middle, and Later Stone Ages, the relevant stone tool evidence exists in a "perfect storm" of lithics systematics anarchy. Archaeologists are working to standardize measurements and other systematics for the entire African MSA (Will et al. 2019), but the MSA covers only the latter half of the period of interest for language emergence. Using the terms and measurements the EAST Typology proposes for Eastern African stone tools dating between 35 and 500 Ka will help archaeologists test hypotheses about language evolution that we cannot currently test.

Stoneworking's Decline

Why did people stop making stone tools? Of all the questions archaeologists ask about stone tools, why people stopped making them seems the easiest one to answer, but it is actually the most difficult one to understand. That people abandoned stone tools almost instantly when they acquired more durable and mechanically efficient metal tools is the most widely accepted answer to this question. Indeed, this scenario accurately characterizes the end of the Stone Age in the Americas, Australasia, and the Pacific over the last few centuries. Eighteenth–twentieth-century European factories turned out finished metal tools in far greater quantities and at lower costs than in earlier times. Transport innovations, such as railways and ocean-going cargo vessels allowed manufacturers to ship metal tools in bulk from European factories to the opposite side of the planet in a matter of months or less. These conditions differ starkly from stoneworking's decline in southwest Asia over the Bronze and Iron Ages (Rosen 1996, 1997). There, stone tools continued in use alongside metal implements for millennia. Nor does "instant abandonment" accurately characterize the "end" of the Stone Age in Eastern Africa. The archaeological consensus holds that early iron metallurgy originated in equatorial Africa and spread east and southward over the last two millennia (Phillipson 2005). Stone tools remained in use for centuries after the first evidence for iron production appears (Phillipson 2017).

If mere knowledge of metallurgy does not explain the "end" of the Eastern African Stone Age, then what does? To understand stone tools' decline in Eastern Africa, archaeologists need to learn more about stone tool use during the early Iron Age and Historic periods. In the Horn, Aksumite stone tools grow increasingly well documented (Phillipson 2017), but we know much less than we should about stone tool production and use in Eastern Africa's interior. Many reports on Iron Age and historic archaeological sites describe groundstone artifacts adequately, but flaked stone tools less so, or at least in far less detail than for prehistoric sites.

How will reforming stone tool systematics along the lines the EAST Typology proposes improve research on stoneworking's decline in Eastern Africa? Of all the more than 250 lithic samples compiled for this work, conventions for describing stone tools varied more among Iron Age sites than in any other age-stage. One has far less difficulty comparing Earlier Stone Age artifacts made a million years apart than comparing Iron Age stone assemblages made within a century or two of each other. This hypervariability is not an intrinsic property of the Eastern African Iron Age archaeological record. Iron Age ceramics and other evidence were and remain sufficiently organized that archaeologists published regional and continental syntheses of the Iron Age evidence (Oliver 1975, Phillipson 1977b) during the same period that archaeologists stopped writing regional syntheses of the Stone Age evidence. Two possible explanations for Eastern African Iron Age lithics systematics' hypervariable state suggest themselves.

First, stone tools are not that common at many Iron Age sites. Lacking familiarity with them, archaeologists describing these artifacts may either use unfamiliar typologies or ad hoc ones they develop themselves. One assumes archaeologists excavating Iron Age sites in Eastern Africa receive routine training in lithic artifact identification, but this is an assumption. After all, few archaeologists who excavate Pleistocene Stone Age sites have formal training in recognizing and describing ceramics and metal tools.

A second possibility might be simple neglect. Iron Age lithic evidence remains unorganized because archaeologists do not consider it all that important, or at least not as important as ceramics, beads, architecture, metal tools, and other artifacts. Tellingly, not one named stone tool industry enjoys wide usage among Iron Age archaeologists.

Although the EAST Typology might seem first and foremost as an aid to Stone Age prehistory, it may actually have greater potential transformative value for Iron Age archaeology. One of Iron Age prehistory's major questions concerns population movements, particularly the so-called "Bantu migrations." L. Phillipson (2017) has made a case for tracking Iron Age population movements around northern Ethiopia from the stone tool evidence. Closer examination of stone tools from the interior parts of Kenya, Tanzania, and adjacent countries may discover lithic evidence for later prehistoric and historic population movements, too. One cannot predict what form such lithic evidence might take, but one can predict that we will never find such evidence unless we start looking for it.

Nor is the EAST Typology's potential limited to testing hypotheses about population movements. While many iron artifacts, glass beads, and other trade goods were made locally (Kusimba et al. 1994, Dussubieux et al. 2008/2010), significant quantities arrived from abroad. These commodities had to have been exchanged for things procured and produced in Eastern Africa. What those things were and how they varied remains to be discovered. Changes in the Iron Age stone tool evidence could provide insights into the larger economic changes at work as Eastern Africa became integrated into a global exchange network. A large-scale comparative study and synthesis of Eastern Africa's Iron Age lithic record must be a priority for twenty-first-century archaeology.

PROPOSALS FOR THE FUTURE

Archaeology has a poor record for self-reform. The participants at the 1965 Wenner-Gren Foundation Symposium, "Systematic Investigation of the African Later Tertiary and Quaternary" unanimously called for abandoning the terms Earlier, Middle and Later Stone Ages (Bishop and Clark 1967: 896–7, Kleindienst 1967), but archaeologists continue using them, showing little inclination to abandon them. Unlike some other sciences, archaeology lacks a governing body to adjudicate disputes about terminology or to settle conflicts about professional practices. This is not entirely a bad thing. Archaeology benefits by attracting people who like to think differently and to "color outside the lines." Unlike most other behavioral sciences, however, archaeologists deal with a limited resource. Ethological populations and ethnographic subjects renew themselves, but only so many archaeological sites date to any given age. Erosion, construction, and excavations daily reduce their number. For this reason, we have to think deeply about ways to do archaeology better. This section goes beyond changes in stone tool systematics to propose changes to archaeological practice that could make the Eastern African stone tool evidence more useful to prehistory and to paleoanthropology.

Searching for the Oldest Stone Tools

Lomekwi 3 in Kenya currently preserves the oldest stone tools, but sound reasons lead one to expect that older lithic artifacts will turn up either in Eastern Africa or elsewhere. So many different primates use tools that the capacity for doing so must be deeply evolutionarily primitive. By the time any behavioral change leaves a trace in fossil morphology, the selective pressures favoring that morphological change must have been at work for a very long time. If we accept that shaped stone cutting tools are essentially artificial teeth and nails, then our search for selective pressures inspiring stone cutting tool production ought to focus on evolutionary forces driving reductions in ancestral hominine dentition. Fingernails and hands seem less likely to be informative. Fingernails do not preserve, and bonobos manage to make stone tools even though their hands lack distinctively hominin fingertip to thumb opposability (Christel 1994, Marzke and Wullstein 1996, Marzke 2013). The need to compensate for reduced canines and incisors, the most likely selective pressure leading to stone tool production, probably began in earnest during later Miocene times, ca. 5–10 Ma, at or around the time ancestral hominins and African apes diverged from one another. Pliocene hominin fossils such as *Ardipithecus*, *Australopithecus*, *Paranthropus*, and *Kenyanthropus* already have significantly less prognathic faces and smaller canine teeth than living apes and their Miocene precursors (Fleagle 2013).

To learn why Pliocene hominins made stone tools, we need to search older, specifically Miocene, sedimentary deposits for stone objects bearing traces of percussion, fracture, and abrasion that differ from those natural forces create. This will take considerable work. Fossiliferous Miocene sediments are patchily preserved in Eastern Africa. Most paleontologists who search for Miocene and Pliocene fossils lack formal training in how to recognize stone tools. If one wonders how many credible examples of Miocene hominine stoneworking may have been overlooked, history offers an instructive lesson. Fifty years ago, Louis Leakey (1968) reported finding a percussion-damaged pebble in Miocene contexts at Fort Ternan in Kenya that he claimed was a stone tool. The paleoanthropological consensus rejected Leakey's claim (Pickford 1986); but surely it is no accident that among the paleontologists scouring such ancient deposits at that time, Leakey was the only one with experience at finding, recognizing, and interpreting stone tools. That number has not increased much since. Scientists and their staff prospecting for Pliocene and Miocene-age fossils must receive formal training in how to recognize stone artifacts. Properly taught, such lessons should take no more than a few hours. Such minor training investments might yield important insights into hominin stoneworking's evolutionary origins.

In archaeology, the search for the earliest anything carries with it great rewards, but it also consumes disproportionate resources, resources all too easyily squandered defending what turn out to be indefensible claims about the oldest stone tools. Paleoanthropologists searching for Miocene and Pliocene stone tools would do well to remember and use the criteria for recognizing human agency in stone tool production developed for dealing with chronological outliers in more recent contexts (*now*, see Table 3.1). Stone tools that would not pass muster as legitimately anthropogenic chronological outliers in, say, pre-20 Ka contexts in the Americas or pre-60 Ka contexts in Australia, will probably not gain much traction if they come from Miocene or Pliocene sites in Eastern Africa.

Stone Tools and Excavation: Hit-and-Runs, Orphans, and Mines

To improve the stone tool evidence from Eastern Africa, archaeologists need to change how we excavate and how we publish our findings. Currently, no small number of archaeological field projects cluster around three extremes: hit-and-runs, orphans, and mines. "Hit-and-runs" are field projects that dig one or more test trenches into a site, describe their findings superficially, and then end. "Orphans" are larger sites whose substantial lithic collections languish unstudied. "Mines" are larger-scale projects that run on for a decade or more without comprehensive syntheses of their findings.

The circumstances and selective pressures that create hit-and-runs, orphans, and mines vary. Some hit-and-runs began as projects for graduate students whose post-graduate interests led them to other pursuits. Many orphans remain undocumented because the archaeologists in charge of them moved on to other field projects or died before completing their work. Mines persist at least in part because high-quality field excavation takes a lot of time and because those directing such projects, mostly foreigners, conduct fieldwork seasonally, in-between their duties at overseas colleges and universities.

Hit-and-runs, mines, and orphans limit what we know about stone tool variability. To reduce their number, institutions overseeing archaeological research, funding agencies, and archaeologists themselves must ensure that research proposals include incentives for timely publication as well as penalties for failing to do so. One strategy by which to accomplish this would be for Eastern African museums to place a statute of limitations on access to artifact collections gathered under research permits. Permit holders could enjoy exclusive access to the collections only for a set period of time (five to seven years seems about right) after which anyone could examine those collections and publish their findings about them.

Archaeologists' proposals for fieldwork should include "study seasons" during which they do not excavate or conduct other fieldwork but instead produce publishable interim reports and a final monographic publication. Published abstracts of papers and posters presented at professional meetings or documents prepared for museums, funding agencies and for institutional purposes must not count as such interim or final reports. In making decisions about faculty promotion and tenure, colleges and universities generally disregard such nonpeer-reviewed "gray literature," and so too should those administering archaeological heritage. Research permit renewals ought to require evidence of prompt publication.

Finally, archaeologists need to turn off the "money spigot" to excavations that persist for a decade or more without either significant findings or well-documented conclusions published in the professional literature. A "mine" excavation can persist for several reasons. Executing a complex and large-scale research project can take a lot of time. They can also persist because the evidence discovered cannot answer the original research question; because investigators have added new research questions while fieldwork was in progress ("mission creep" in military/diplomatic slang); due to investigator incompetence; or due to some combination of these factors. A thorough review should clarify this uncertainty, and if necessary, permits revoked and funding terminated. The argument that an underdocumented excavation must continue in order to train students carries no weight. Anyone unwilling or unable to publish their findings promptly ought not be in the business of training future archaeologists.

Working with Older Collections

The time has long passed when a graduate student could excavate an archaeological site on their own and write it up as their doctoral dissertation. Excavating and documenting an irreplaceable archaeological site is too much to ask of students just learning their craft. It virtually guarantees the worst possible research outcomes.

On what should aspiring Eastern African archaeologists write their dissertations?

Future research on Eastern African prehistory will benefit from increased efforts to reexamine and reanalyze previously described lithic assemblages and to publish unpublished lithic collections. This is not necessarily a path of least effort (or greatest convenience). Gaining access to such collections requires permissions. Permission is always required from the museums curating artifact collections, but some institutions also require permission from the collections' original excavators. Most professional archaeologists grant such permissions when other scholars request them. Still, such requests can be controversial. Some archaeologists view such requests as challenges to their own published findings. Custodians of unpublished collections may see such requests as preempting research that they plan to do in the future. Still others may have promised the "rights" to describe an unpublished collection to a colleague or a student. Some students may be reluctant to undertake research on published collections out of concern that they will not discover anything new and publishable. And yet, as currently practiced, archaeological lithic analysis involves so much subjective, visually assessed, morphological analogy that they will assuredly find differences. Indeed, a reanalysis that found no such differences should be a cause for concern.

The EAST Typology offers a solution to this problem. Reorganizing and re-documenting already published lithic assemblages in terms of the EAST Typology will make older collections comparable to other Eastern African stone tool assemblages in ways that are currently impossible. Using the EAST Typology to describe undescribed collections will bring those collections "in from the cold" and to the attention of wider scholarship. By any reasonable standard, doing either of these things constitutes an original contribution to knowledge that justifies conferring a doctoral degree.

Teaching and Training

Eastern Africa is the best place to investigate Eastern African prehistory, but the best places to study the subject and to receive professional training in archaeology today are at universities located outside the region. European, Asian, and American universities have more resources available for archaeology than their Eastern African counterparts. Aspiring indigenous Eastern African archaeologists face an enormous "buy-in" cost, the expense of attending university abroad. Some manage this, but they remain few in number. This needs to change. With limited funds available for archaeology, does it really make sense to annually fund expensive airfares and hotel bills so that foreign researchers can travel to field sites at which they work, at most, for a few months in between academic semesters in North America and Europe? Would archaeology not get better returns by funding researchers permanently based in Eastern Africa? With funding for research dwindling even in countries where it once abounded, archaeologists need to find ways to deliver instruction in stone tool analysis at Eastern African institutions of higher learning competitive with what students acquire at foreign universities.

Scientific Meetings versus Conferences

Papers and posters about Eastern African archaeology appear prominently at international scientific meetings, including those for the Society for Africanist Archaeologists (SAfA) and the Pan-African Congresses on Prehistory. The region even has its own East African Association for Palaeoanthropology and Palaeontology (EAAPP). However, for such meetings to lead to reform in stone tool systematics and improvements in connecting the lithic evidence to major issues, archaeologists need to restore professional scientific meetings' original functions.

   In former times, scientific meetings *invited* only paying members of professional societies. These experts met face-to-face, announced major discoveries, debated important matters, and voted on binding resolutions. Today's scientific meetings, in contrast, are open to all who can pay the membership and registration fees. They are first and foremost opportunities to do professional networking in the service of career advancement. Rather than a meeting's podium papers announcing major discoveries, journal editors and institutional media relations departments issue press releases. The more papers and posters presented at scientific meetings, the more meeting organizers and their hosts gather in registration fees. To cram more papers into the program, meeting organizers eliminate time formerly spend on questions, discussions, and open debate. Relaxing selection increases variability and, as a result, audiences endure inferior papers that contribute nothing of consequence to major debates. Such "debate" as occurs at these meetings all too often consists of little more than shameless self-promotion and "gotcha" questions delivered to academic rivals. This all makes amusing theater, a kind of "live" version of Internet comment threads, but it is virtually the opposite of the conditions needed to promote meaningful reform in archaeology and, as a result, the science suffers.

Since selective pressures within academia have made scientific meetings the way they are, any call to restore "the good old days" is not likely to succeed. (From the standpoint of systematically underrepresented women and indigenous African researchers, those old days weren't that good in the first place.) Nevertheless, Eastern African archaeology needs forums at which experts can meet regularly to discuss and resolve issues about stone tool systematics, lithic analysis, and allied issues. For such meetings to have lasting effect, any resolutions they pass must be binding ones. If, for example, meeting participants vote that the terms "pestle-rubber" or "Neolithic" should be sunk or replaced by new terms, then those in attendance should pledge to abide by that resolution themselves, encourage nonattending colleagues to do so too, and reject journal papers, book manuscripts, and grant proposals that flout that resolution. Otherwise, archaeologists will ignore those resolutions, much as they have previous calls for reform.

Will this work? History offers up an illustrative example. In 1927, at roughly the same point in time that prehistoric research in Eastern Africa began (and mere miles from where I write these words), Alfred Vincent Kidder convened the first Pecos Conference at Pecos Pueblo in New Mexico. Meeting at Pecos, and elsewhere in subsequent years, archaeologists working in the U.S. Southwest and northern Mexico shared their findings and correlated their systematics for ceramics and other artifacts. That greater Southwestern archaeology today operates at an extraordinary level of scientific sophistication is not due to the Pecos Conferences alone, of course. Nevertheless, these and similar such conferences played important roles in making this happen (Mills and Fowles 2017). As the 2011 Pecos Conference website aptly puts it:

> To make progress with objective science and with other cultural matters, books and journal articles are important, but one still must look colleagues in the eye and work out the details of one's research in cooperative and contentious forums. (www.swanet.org/2011_pecos_conference)

Similar conferences in Eastern Africa devoted to archaeological systematics (not just stone tools) could have equally productive results. Such conferences should not take place online but at a physical setting. If the conferences occur in a remote location near a convenient transportation hub, then the shared experience of traveling there will encourage collaboration among participants. Face-to-face meetings encourage prosociality, our evolved skills for seeking out contact with others and working together with them towards a common purpose.

Emulating Kidder's original Pecos Conference strategy, such events should be restricted to experts and active researchers, excluding students, inactive researchers, and various "hangers-on." Some will object that this proposal is elitist, that it excludes younger less well-established researchers who are so often the font of new ideas and older scholars who can put proposed changes in historical perspective. This objection conflates exclusivity with elitism. The conferences I propose are unashamedly exclusive, for we have all seen what "open-to-all comers" does to scientific meetings, but they are not elitist. Properly overseen, they would be open to any person with a good idea to contribute.

Such conferences should not take place as symposia within professional societies' meetings or at the Pan-African Congresses. Too much goes on at such meetings for conference participants to focus on the matters at hand. Stand-alone conferences held every five years or so ought to be about right. Such intervals will ensure the issues under consideration are nontrivial, that proposals for changes have had a fair chance to develop on their own, and that resolutions can be shared widely.

Most importantly, these conferences' formal resolutions need to be widely disseminated. The traditional conference publication format, the edited book, no longer works well for this purpose. Compiling edited books takes considerable effort and time, commodities of which most active archaeologists have little to spare. Moreover, the market for such books is so small that traditional publishers find them unattractive prospects. Publishing conference papers and resolutions as special issues of academic journals might work, but the necessity of peer review would delay publication and introduce (as peer reviewers) the views of persons not invited to the conferences. Furthermore, journal subscriptions erect a financial barrier between this information and its most important audience: scholars and students at Eastern African museums and institutions of higher learning. The best publication strategy would be to post and archive conference proceedings, resolutions, and conference papers online in an open-access forum on some institutional host's servers, combining this with some means for print-on-demand publishing.

All of what I propose above will cost money, but the Pecos Conferences, the Wenner-Gren Conferences, and more recently, the Turkana Basin Institute's Human Evolution Workshops offer models for how motivated individuals can make such events happen.

FINAL THOUGHTS

Relaxing selective pressure increases variability, and Eastern African stone tool systematics have suffered from relaxed selective pressure for a very long time. Up to now, archaeologists working in Eastern Africa have been able to organize their observations of the stone tool evidence pretty much any way they wanted to without consequence. Things need to change. With millions of dollars invested in Eastern African archaeology, the profession and the public deserve better returns on their investments.

When a student asks their professor on what they should write their doctoral dissertation, master's thesis, or research paper, their professors often encourage them to describe a stone tool collection. As Mehlman (1989: 120) noted long ago, that student-researcher faces a choice. They can either:

1. Devise a new typology and suite of measurements specifically for those stone tools or,
2. Use an older, established typology and suite of measurements.

Option 1 simply increases Eastern Africa's lithics systematics anarchy. At best, Option 2 merely perpetuates it; at worst, it increases it. As Louis Leakey (1931) observed in *The Stone Age Cultures of Kenya Colony*, few archaeologists who use stone artifact typologies have actually examined the original artifacts on which those typologies are based.

The EAST Typology offers a "third way," one engaging selective pressure. The EAST Typology facilitates comparisons of the stone tool evidence across the full sweep of Eastern African prehistory. Bearing in mind that academics value citations more or less like normal human beings value air, water, and food, any student-researcher should ask themselves, "Which among Options 1, 2, and the EAST Typology will most likely garner the most citations?" The EAST Typology will. Researchers will be far more likely to cite publications they can simply and straightforwardly compare to their own work and less so ones that require them to either reorganize their own artifact descriptions or make comparisons only in terms of "lowest common denominator" typology.

After learning my plans for this book, several colleagues voiced their objection, "But I like my own typology!" If that typology helps you answer the questions for which you originally obtained research funding, you should continue using it. It's your choice, but choices have consequences. Your colleagues now know about the EAST Typology and its potential to facilitate large-scale and long-term interassemblage comparisons. They also know (for no few have pointed it out) that the EAST Typology can easily be adapted for use in adjacent regions in Africa, or even farther afield. Those colleagues will take a dim view of grant proposals, book manuscripts, and journal papers whose stone tool systematics only permit comparisons with evidence that their author excavated themselves. Archaeologists do not own the things we find. We hold them in trust for all humanity.

In archaeology's early years, when scholars worked largely on their own and in isolation from one another for prolonged periods, the profession could tolerate wide differences in how individual archaeologists organized their observations. Those days are long gone. The big questions twenty-first-century archaeologists will need to answer require that we compare evidence broadly, that we collaborate with colleagues, and that we find ways to share data that do not sacrifice detail. If this book serves its best hoped for purpose, it will help Eastern African archaeologists to follow multiple "trails" for longer intervals and to compare them more effectively. Doing this, we will more clearly see where we have been and more clearly see where we are going.

UWAZI VALLEY TALES, EPILOGUE

I last glimpsed the Uwazi Valley receding into clouds in the Land Rover's rearview mirror. Writing my dissertation took the customary blood, sweat, and tears, but in the end, Big American University conferred my doctoral degree.

The United States' National Science Foundation awarded Aya a six-figure grant for five more years of work at Uwazi Valley. That grant and Aya's publications resulting from it earned her promotion with tenure.

The Polymath retired shortly after Aya's promotion. He and his wife moved away to be closer to their son and his family.

The Old Africa Hand vanished a few years later, and his whereabouts remain unknown. The custodial staff cleaning out his office did not find an elephant gun.

Ten years after the events described here, Endurance became National Museum Director. She instituted many of the reforms proposed in this chapter.

Joseph remains in the Uwazi Valley. His grandchildren delight in his tales of the *wazungu* who excavated the Ancient Ones' Cave.

APPENDIX 1

THE EASTERN AFRICAN PREHISTORIC
STONEWORKING SURVEY

The Eastern African Prehistoric Stoneworking Survey is too large to print in this book. It can be found at www.cambridge.org/PSToEA. Updated versions of the EAPSS will also appear on the author's personal website: https://sites.google.com/a/stonybrook.edu/john-j-shea/

APPENDIX 2

THE EASTERN AFRICAN STONE TOOL (EAST) TYPOLOGY

GROUP I. SHORT NONHIERARCHICAL CORES

   A.   Unipolar core
   B.   Bipolar cores
       1. Bipolar core on pebble
       2. Tabular bipolar core
       3. Cylindrical bipolar core
   C.   Short bifacial cores
       1. Bifacial chopper
       2. Discoid
       3. Protobiface
   D.   Polyhedrons

GROUP II. HIERARCHICAL CORES

   A.   Bifacial hierarchical cores (BHCs)
       1. Preferential BHCs
          a. Victoria West core/large, wide, and preferential BHC
          b. Type 1 Beaked/Nubian core (distal-proximal preparation)
          c. Type 2 Beaked/Nubian core (medio-lateral preparation)
       2. Recurrent BHCs
          a. Recurrent unidirectional laminar BHC
          b. Recurrent bidirectional-opposed BHC
          c. Recurrent convergent BHC
          d. Radial-centripetal BHC
   B.   Unifacial hierarchical cores (UHCs)
       1. Single-platform cores
          a. Unifacial chopper
          b. Split-platform core

      c. Parallel single-platform core

      d. Convergent single-platform core

      e. Pyramidal/cone-shaped convergent single-platform core

      f. Narrow-fronted single-platform core

   2. Multiple-platform unifacial hierarchical cores

      a. Bidirectional-opposed-platform core

      b. Orthogonal opposed-blade core

GROUP III. OTHER CORES

A. Mega-core

B. Micro-core

C. Cores-on-flakes

   1. Kombewa core/flake ventral surface core

   2. Flake dorsal surface core

   3. Flake segment core

GROUP IV. ELONGATED CORE-TOOLS

A. Long core-tools (LCTs)

   1. Handaxe

   2. Cleaver

      a. Core cleaver

      b. Flake cleaver

      c. Flared cleaver

   3. Knife

   4. Pick

      a. Single-pointed pick

      b. Double-pointed pick

   5. Lanceolate

B. Foliate points

   1. Flat-based foliate point

   2. Convex-based foliate point

   3. Double-tipped foliate point

   4. Tanged foliate point

   5. Concave-based foliate point

C. Celts/core-axes

   1. Celts

      a. Unifacially retouched celt/massive scraper

      b. Bifacially retouched celt

      c. Retouched celt with abraded distal edge

2. Core-axes
   a. Wedge-shaped core-axe
   b. Flat core-axe

GROUP V. CORE-INITIATION FLAKES

A. Split clast
B. Clast initiation flakes
  1. Primary clast initiation flake
  2. Secondary clast initiation flake
C. Tabular initiation flakes
  1. Primary tabular initiation flake
  2. Secondary tabular initiation flake
D. Crested flakes
  1 Bifacial crested flake
  2. Unifacial crested flake

GROUP VI. CORE-EXPLOITATION FLAKES

A. Bipolar flake
B. Biface exploitation flakes
  1. Biface thinning flake
  2. Biface overshot flake
C. Bifacial hierarchical core (BHC) exploitation flakes
  1. Central preferential BHC flake
    a. Victoria West core flake
  2. Lateral preferential BHC flake
    a. Lateral preferential and worked edge BHC flake
  3. BHC triangular flake
    a. Nubian point Type 1
    b. Nubian point Type 2
  4. BHC blade
  5. BHC radial flake
D. Unifacial hierarchical core (UHC) exploitation flakes
  1. Noncortical blade
  2. Laterally cortical blade
  3. Distally cortical blade
  4. Laterally and distally cortical blade
  5. Other blades
E. Other core exploitation flakes
  1. Flake ventral surface flake (Kombewa flake)
  2. Medial residual cortical flake
  3. Noncortical flake

GROUP VII. CORE-REPAIR FLAKES

A. Biface core-repair flakes
1. Proximal biface core-repair flake
2. Distal biface core-repair flake
3. Orthogonal biface core-repair flake
B. Bifacial Hierarchical Core-(BHC) repair flakes
1. Proximal-lateral BHC repair flake
2. Lateral BHC repair flake
3. Distal BHC repair flake
C. Unifacial Hierarchical Core-(UHC) repair flakes
1. UHC plunging flake
2. UHC tablet flake
3. UHC platform flake
4. UHC distal concavity removal flake
5. UHC orthogonal concavity removal flake
D. Other concavity/convexity removal flakes
1. Stack removal flake
2. Single step/hinge scar removal flake
3. Medial convexity removal flake
4. Distal convexity removal flake

GROUP VIII. RETOUCH FLAKES AND FLAKE FRAGMENTS

A. Edge-retouch flakes
1. Unretouched edge-retouch flake
2. Unifacial edge-retouch flake
    a. Inverse unifacial edge-retouch flake
3. Bifacial edge-retouch flake
B. Burin flakes/burin spalls
1. Unretouched edge burin flake/spall
2. Multiple burin edge flake /spall
3. Unifacially retouched edge burin flake/spall
4. Bifacially retouched edge burin flake/spall
C. Tip-removal flakes
1. Biface point tip removal flake
    a. Biface tranchet flake
2. Biface celt tip-removal flake
3. Scraper tip-removal flake
D. Flake fragments
1. Unretouched flake fragment
    a. Unretouched proximal flake fragment
    b. Other unretouched flake fragment

2. Retouched flake fragments
   a. Retouched proximal flake fragment
   b. Other retouched flake fragment

GROUP IX. RETOUCHED PIECES

A. Scrapers/notches/denticulates
   1. Scrapers
      a. Single endscraper
      b. Transverse scraper
         i.   Symmetrical transverse scraper
         ii. Asymmetrical transverse scraper
      c. Double endscraper
      d. Platform scraper (aka "butt-scraper")
      e. Single sidescraper
      f. Double sidescraper
      g. Convergent scraper
      h. Double convergent scraper
      i. Carinated scraper
      j. Thumbnail scraper
      k. Disc scraper
   2. Notches
      a. Single-notched tool
      b. Multiple-notched tool
   3. Denticulate
B. Backed/truncated pieces
   1. Crescent
      a. Short crescent
      b. Elongated crescent
      c. Shouldered crescent
      d. Notched crescent
   2. Triangle
      a. Isosceles triangle
      b. Scalene triangle
      c. Right triangle
         i.   Concave right triangle
         ii. Convex right triangle
      d. Double concave triangle
   3. Rectangle
      a. Square
      b. Elongated rectangle
      c. Parallelogram
      d. Partial parallelogram

4. Trapezoid
    a. Regular trapezoid
    b. Elongated trapezoid
    c. Hollow trapezoid
    d. Flared trapezoid
    e. Partial trapezoid
5. Convergently backed/truncated piece
    a. Single convergently backed piece
    b. Backed/truncated awl
    c. Tanged symmetrical double convergently backed piece
    d. Asymmetrical double convergently backed piece
6. Other backed/truncated piece
    a. Multiple backed/truncated awl
    b. Circle
    c. Oval
C. Convergently retouched pieces/retouched flake points.
    1. Unifacially retouched flake points
        a. Distal retouch only
        b. Distal and lateral retouch only
        c. Distal and proximal dorsal
        d. Distal and proximal ventral
        e. Circumferentially retouched
    2. Bifacially retouched flake points
        a. Distal retouch only
        b. Distal and lateral retouch only
        c. Distal and proximal retouch only
        d. Circumferentially retouched
    3. Unifacially and bifacially retouched point
    4. Awl
        a. Single awl
        b. Multiple awl
D. Thinned pieces
    1. Dorsally thinned piece
    2. Basally thinned piece
    3. Dorsally and basally thinned piece
E. Burins
    1. Single burins
        a. Transverse and oblique burin
    2. Dihedral burin
    3. Multiple burins
        a. Multiple burin – single point of origin
        b. Multiple burin – separate points of origin

    F.   Flake segmentation products
- 1. Orthogonal truncation-related piece
  - a. Distal orthogonal truncation-related piece
  - b. Medial orthogonal truncation-related piece
  - c. Proximal orthogonal truncation-related piece
- 2. Microburins

    G.   Other retouched pieces
- 1. Rod/retouched cylinder
- 2. Borer (elongated narrow convergent truncation)
- 3. Tanged piece
- 4. Scaled piece
- 5. Combination piece

GROUP X. PERCUSSORS

    A.   Round percussors
- 1. Hammerstone
- 2. Subspheroid
- 3. Spheroid

    B.   Tabular percussors
- 1. Tabular surface percussor (anvil, pitted stone)
- 2. Tabular edge percussor

    C.   Ad hoc percussor

GROUP XI. GROUNDSTONE ARTIFACTS

    A.   Abraded-edge tools
- 1. Groundstone celts
  - a. Flared groundstone celt
  - b. Lugged/bossed groundstone celt
  - c. Grooved groundstone celt
  - d. Biconvex-sided groundstone celt
  - e. Double-edged groundstone celt
- 2. Other abraded-edge tool

    B.   Grooved abrading stone
- 1. Single-grooved stone
- 2. Multiple-grooved abrading stone

    C.   Perforated artifacts
- 1. Symmetrical torus (digging stick weight, mace, grinding wheel)
- 2. Asymmetrical torus (pendant, loom weight)
- 3. Perforated disc/plate

4. Stone tube
5. Bead
   a. Flat torus bead
   b. Pendant bead
   c. Cylinder bead
   d. Perforated sphere bead
   e. Perforated disc bead
D. Pulverizing tools
   1. Handstones
      a. Pestle
      b. Conical handstone
      c. Hemispherical handstone
      d. Cylindrical handstone
      e. Pestle-rubbers
      f. Abraded cone
   2. Pulverizing surfaces
      a. Mortar
      b. Rotary grinding slab
      c. Linear grinding slab
         i. Concave grinding slab (saddle quern)
E. Stone vessels
   1. Platter
   2. Bowl
F. Other abrading/abraded stones
   1. Pigment stones
   2. Pottery-abrading stone
   3. Digging stone
   4. Groundstone cylinder
   5. Grindstone

GLOSSARY

Abrasion Wear resulting from one stone tool surface sliding against another surface.

Actualistic observations Direct observations of stone tool production, use, and discard.

Age/Age-stage Archaeological time period defined in terms of variation in assemblages.

Anthropocene Recently proposed and not yet formally recognized geological epoch marked by global-scale human impacts on the environment.

Anthropogenic 1. Made by humans or other hominins, 2. Related to human origins.

Arris (plural **arrisses**) Ridge separating fracture/flake scars on artifact surfaces.

Archaeological primatology Research focused on tool use among living nonhuman primates.

Archaeological site Location where archaeologists have identified artifacts on the surface or in sedimentary deposits.

Archaeological site complex Location where multiple spatially discrete archaeological sites occur near one another.

Artifact An object whose shape, appearance, and/or composition result from human activity.

Artifact-type A group of stone tools defined in terms of shared technological and/or morphological characteristics.

Assemblage Artifacts and other remains recovered from the same sedimentary deposit.

Assemblage-group A group of stone tool assemblages sharing similar artifact-type inventories (see also industry, stone tool).

Awl A relatively short, steep-edged, and convergently retouched piece.

Backed/truncated piece Retouched piece with steep orthogonal retouch on lateral edges (backed pieces) or distal/proximal edges (truncated pieces).

Backing/truncation retouch Orthogonal retouch that creates a steep edge.

Basalt Igneous rock largely comprised of plagioclase with pyroxene and olivine.

Bead Relatively small and symmetrical torus-shaped perforated groundstone artifact.

Beaked core See **Nubian core**.

Behavioral modernity Putatively distinctive behavioral characteristics of *Homo sapiens* defined in terms of the derived features of the European Upper Paleolithic Period (ca. 12,000–45,000 years ago).

Behavioral variability Simultaneously deploying multiple solutions to the same problem; arguably a shared primitive characteristic of the Genus *Homo*, and among living primates, a distinctive characteristic of *Homo sapiens*.

Bending fracture Fracture that forms due to bending stresses at a point separate from where loading occurs (aka "remote fracture").

BHC Acronym for bifacial hierarchical core.

Bipolar core Core preserving by bidirectionally opposed fracture scars and comminution.

Bipolar flake Flake detached by bipolar percussion (aka "scaled piece").

Blade Elongated flake (length ≥ twice its width) with straight lateral edges and arrisses aligned parallel to one another and to the flake's axis of fracture propagation.

Blade core Unifacial hierarchical core preserving elongated fracture scars that indicate a series of blade removals.

Bladelet Blade less than 50 mm long.

Blank An unretouched flake detached from a hierarchical core. (Term not used in this volumn)

Bored stone See **tTorus**.

Bowl, Stone Deeply concave carved stone vessel.

Brittle Mechanical property of materials that fail under loading by forming a cleavage plane/fracture.

Bulb of percussion Convex area on flake ventral surface adjacent to the fracture initiation point.

Bulbar concavity Concave area adjacent to the fracture initiation point on a flake scar surface.

Bulbar convexity Synonym for bulb of percussion.

Burin Retouched piece modified by burination.

Burin flake Flake detached by burination (aka "burin spall").

Burination (Submode D4) Detaching a flake from a flake in such a way that it propagates parallel to a flake's edge.

Celt Elongated core-tool, roughly cylindrical in shape, with retouched or abraded worked edge at one or both ends (aka "axes" or "adzes").

Chaîne opératoire See operational chain.

Chert Sedimentary silicate rock comprised of detrital quartz.

Chronostratigraphy Arranging archaeological deposits in chronological order

Clark Modes 1–5/6 J.G.D. (Grahame) Clark's framework for global-scale technological complex variation.

Clast A rock rounded by physical weathering.

Comminution Multiple overlapping and incompletely propagated fractures that result from percussion.

Conchoidal fracture Failure property of brittle, isotropic, and cryptocrystalline solids (e.g., glass).

Confirmation bias The tendency to seek out, prefer, and recall information in ways that support one's preexisting hypotheses or other views.

Confounding variability Variability that obscures cause–effect relationships between other variables.

Constellation Groups of stone tools whose fractured surfaces conjoin to one another.

Contextual observations Observations arising from the archaeological record and interpreted following generally accepted principles from other scientific fields.

Convergently retouched piece See **Flake point**.

Core A rock featuring one or more fracture scars longer than 10 mm (aka "flaked piece").

Core-axe Roughly conical or wedge-shaped core-tool featuring a broad proximal end and distally converging lateral edges.

Core-initiation flake Flake that removes naturally occurring obstacles to predictable flake detachment.

Core-exploitation flake Relatively large flakes detached during core reduction.

Core-repair flake Flake that removes obstacles to predictable flake detachment created during core reduction (aka "core-trimming elements" and "core rejuvenation flakes").

Core-tool Core with a retouched edge or edges.

Core-on-flake Flake fragment featuring at least one flake removal at least half the piece's length.

Cortex Weathered external rock surface.

Craft/hobby stoneworkers Modern-day stoneworkers who manufacture stone tools for sale or for recreation.

Cryptocrystalline A property of rocks whose component particles are too small to be seen without artificial magnification.

Culture, Archaeological Assemblages from the same region and time period featuring similar lithic and/or nonlithic artifact-type inventories.

Culture-Historical archaeology Archaeological research focusing on normative patterns of human behavior change.

Culture-Historical Period (of prehistoric research in Eastern Africa) From 1947 to 1965.

Curation Transporting and/or modifying a stone tool to prolong its utility.

Débitage 1. Collective term for flakes and flake fragments, 2. French term for "flaking," commonly use in Anglophone literature for core reduction aimed at producing flakes for use as cutting tools.

Debris Small <20–30 mm and unretouched flakes and flake fragments.

Denticulate Piece with numerous small retouched concavities along an edge.

Derived A morphology or behavior that occurs uniquely among some but not all organisms descended from a common ancestor.

Desert varnish Polishing that results from stone surfaces exposed to numerous and prolonged collisions with airborne sand.

Detached piece See **Flake**.

Dibble's Rule Actual stone tools always crosscut archaeologists' artifact typologies.

Digger's Delusion The erroneous assumption that experience excavating stone tools confers expertise in archaeological lithic analysis.

Digging stick weight Former term for a relatively large stone torus.

Discard threshold The point at which the costs for curating an artifact exceed the benefits for doing so.

Double patination Differences in surface weathering on stone tools that were discarded, weathered, and then reused after prolonged periods of time.

Earlier Stone Age (ESA) >250,000 years ago. Diagnostic implements include pebble cores and (after 1.7 million years ago) long core-tools.

EAST (Eastern African Stone Tool) Typology Taxonomic framework for describing stone tools from Eastern Africa that divides such artifacts into eleven "groups" that it further subdivides hierarchically. (For definitions of individual EAST Groups and artifacts, see Chapters 5–8.)

Group I. Nonhierarchical cores

Group II. Hierarchical cores

Group III. Other cores

Group IV. Elongated core-tools

Group V. Core-initiation flakes

Group VI. Core-exploitation flakes

Group VII. Core-repair flakes

Group VIII. Retouch flakes and flake fragments

Group IX. Retouched pieces

Group X. Percussors

Group XI. Groundstone artifacts

Ecofact Naturally shaped object found together with artifacts and other evidence of human/hominin activity.

Ecotone A place where several distinct biotic communities conjoin to one another.

Edge angle Angle at which two sides of an edge converge.

Edge-retouch flake A (usually small) flake detached by retouch.

Elongated core-tool Core-tool with uneven length and width dimensions.

Embedded procurement Collecting tool materials during routine foraging activities or other daily work.

End-struck flake A flake whose longest dimension is parallel the plane of fracture propagation.

Endscraper Scraper with orthogonal scraper retouch at its distal end.

Epoch, Geological Time period defined in terms of changes in rocks, fossil assemblages.

Equifinality Obtaining the same result from different causes.

Ethnoarchaeology Cross-cultural research on living humans conducted by archaeologists and focused specifically on material culture and other tangible behavior residues.

Ethnography Cross-cultural research on living humans (aka social anthropology, cultural anthropology).

Ethology Research on (nonhuman) animal behavior.

Expedient/Expediency Making a stone tool for immediate needs and discarding it without further use.

Exploratory Period (of prehistoric research in Eastern Africa) Before 1947.

Fabricator Former term for various retouched and edge-damaged pieces.

Façonnage See **Shaping**.

Feather (terminated) fracture Fracture that terminates at an acute angle to the fracture propagation surface.

Finished Artifact Fallacy Assuming that the forms in which lithic artifacts appear are those that prehistoric toolmakers intended them to be, unaffected by reuse and recycling.

Flake Piece of stone fracture has detached from another rock (aka "detached piece").

Flake point/Convergently retouched piece Retouched piece with relatively acute, converging edges that preserves portions of its original flake dorsal and ventral surfaces.

Flake scar Concavity fracture detachment has left on a tool surface.

Flaked piece See **Core**.

Flaked-stone artifact Artifact shaped or substantially damaged by anthropogenic fracture.

Flaking 1. Detaching flakes from another rock, 2. Core reduction with the goal of producing flakes intended for use as tools (aka *débitage*).

Flintknapper 1. Industrial Era craft specialists who manufactured gunflints from the eighteenth century onward , 2. Modern-day craft/hobby stoneworkers.

Flintknapper's Fantasy The erroneous assumption that modern-day experience making and using stone tools confers expertise in archaeological lithic analysis.

Foliate point Relatively small (<100 mm long) pointed core-tools that feature either wholly or partly bifacial flake scars around their circumference.

Fracture Cleavage plane that forms when loading causes brittle rocks to fail.

Fracture initiation point The point along the edge of a flake ventral surface and its striking platform where a fracture initiated.

Fracture initiation surface That side of a worked edge on which fractures initiate.

Fracture propagation surface That side of a worked edge under which a fracture propagates and terminates.

Fracture scar See **Flake scar**.

Frison Effect Use-related changes to artifact morphology.

Geofact An object modified by natural sources of abrasion, fracture, and/or thermal alteration that superficially resembles a stone artifact.

Geometric microlith See **Microlith**.

Grindstone An otherwise unmodified rock preserving use-related abrasive wear.

Grinding slab Relatively flat and horizontally extensive pulverizing tool, the stationary component of a grinding stone/handstone pulverizing toolkit.

Grooming citations Citing colleagues' and their publications because they agree with you and/or to curry favor with them.

Groundstone Artifact shaped or substantially damaged by abrasion.

Haft A handle to which stoneworkers attach a stone tool.

Hafting Attaching a stone tool to a handle.

Hammerstone A stone percussor.

Handstone Pulverizing tool, typically plano-convex in cross-section, the mobile component of a grinding stone/handstone pulverizing toolkit.

Hard-hammer percussion Initiating a fracture by forcefully striking a rock with another stone or a metal implement.

Hertzian cone fracture Fracture due to compressive stress in an expanding half-cone directly below the point of loading.

Hierarchical core Core preserving substantially different flake scars on opposite sides of worked edge.

Hierarchical core reduction. Core reduction in which opposite sides of a worked edge have flakes detached from them in systematically different ways.

Hinge (terminated) fracture Fracture that terminates recursively above the plane of fracture propagation, i.e., toward the nearest core surface.

Holocene Geological epoch dating from 11,700 years ago to the present.

Hominin Bipedal primates.

Human *Homo sapiens*.

Igneous rock Rock that formed as the result of heat (e.g., obsidian, rhyolite, basalt).

Index fossil Stone tool thought distinctive of a particular time period, industry, or archaeological culture.

Indirect percussion Initiating fracture on stone by striking an intermediary object (a "punch") placed on the tool's surface.

Industrial complex See **Technological complex**.

Industry Assemblages from the same region and time period sharing similar lithic artifact-type inventories.

Invasiveness How far flake scars, retouch, microwear, residues, or other phenomena extend from a given tool edge onto an artifact surface.

Iron Age Cultural period, ca. 500–2000 years ago in Eastern Africa, during which archaeological sites preserve evidence for indigenous iron production and/or iron implement use.

Isotropy/isotropic Mechanical property in which a given material resists loading equally in any direction.

Jelinek's Transparency Principle That one should present one's observations in such a way that others can evaluate them independently of one's interpretations of them.

Knapping/knapper Craft specialist stoneworking/stoneworker.

Ka Thousands of years ago.

Ka cal. BP Thousands of years before "the present" (i.e., AD 1950) based on calibrated radiocarbon dates.

Kombewa core/flake Core-on-flake from which a relatively large fracture scar has removed the bulb of percussion. The resulting Kombewa flake appears to have two ventral surfaces.

Large elongated retouched piece (LERP) A retouched flake or core-tool longer than 100 mm.

Latent behavior A behavior observed among multiple organisms that is thought to have evolved spontaneously and independently, rather than having been inherited from a common ancestor.

Later Stone Age (LSA) less than 50,000 years ago to ca. 2,000 years ago or less, depending on the region. Diagnostic implements include prismatic blades and geometric microliths, rare pottery.

LCT Acronym for **long core-tool**.

LERP Acronym for **large elongated retouched piece**.

Levallois core, flake, etc. European term for bifacial hierarchical cores, flakes.

Lithic Stone artifact.

Lithic miniaturization Systematic production of small stone tools.

Long core-tool/LCT Elongated and bilaterally symmetrical core-tool with unequal length, width, and thickness dimensions.

Ma Millions of years ago.

Manuport A relatively large an exogenous unmodified stone found together with archaeological remains.

Mastic Glue or other adhesive substance.

Mega-core Boulders featuring one or more relatively large >100 mm long flake scars.

Metamorphic rock Rock that formed due to a combination of heat and pressure (e.g., quartzite, steatite, marble).

Micro-cores Cores less than 30 mm long.

Microburin Flake fragment with a bending fracture scar resulting from truncation using the microburin technique.

Microburin technique Technique for segmenting blades by making ever-more-invasive concavities until a bending fracture splits the artifact in two.

Microlithization Systematic production of microliths and other small backed/truncated stone tools.

Microwear Small-scale fractures, striations, and polish on stone tools.

Middle-range theory Hypotheses based on either actualistic or contextual evidence that link observations and measurements to inferences about behavior.

Microlith Small (<50 mm long) backed/truncated piece (aka "geometric microlith").

Middle Stone Age (MSA) 50,000 years ago–250 Ka. Diagnostic implements include bifacial hierarchical cores and foliate points.

Mining 1. Systematically extracting stone tool materials from bedrock deposits. 2. Excavating archaeological sites for years without publishing a synthesis of the findings.

Miocene Geological epoch ca. 5,300,000–23,000,000 years ago.

MIS Marine oxygen-isotope stage.

Morphological variables Shape and/or size-related artifact properties that vary independently of manufacturing techniques and that archaeologists think reflect cultural differences among stoneworkers.

Mortar Relatively deep and narrow pulverizing tool, stationary component of a mortar/pestle toolkit.

Neolithic Period during which there is evidence for agriculture and pastoralism but not metallurgy. Circa 2000–>6000 years ago in Eastern Africa, but dates vary widely within the region.

Nonhierarchical core Core preserving similar flake scars on opposite sides of its worked edge.

Nonhierarchical core reduction Core reduction in which opposite sides of a worked edge have flakes detached from them in the same ways.

Notch Retouched piece with one or more large concavities.

Nubian core Bifacial hierarchical core prepared distally to allow a triangular preferential flake removal (aka "beaked core").

Obsidian Volcanic glass.

Operational chain The series of actions performed on stone from raw material procurement, production and use, to discard and recycling.

Orientation Conventions for positioning artifacts before measuring, drawing, or photographing them.

Orthogonal retouch Retouch applied at right angle to an edge's dorsal/ventral plane.

Outil écaillé French for "scaled piece," synonym for bipolar flake/core.

Overdesign Labor-costly artifact modifications to no obvious functional benefits; ostensibly made for symbolic purposes or to enhance their value as trade goods.

Paleolithic Archaeological periodization of North African and Eurasian Pleistocene prehistory.

Panin African apes, i.e., chimpanzees, bonobos, and gorillas.

Paradigm shift Within a scientific discipline, an across the board change in epistemology (questions asked) and practice (what measured).

Neolithic Period dating ca. 2,000–4,000 years ago in Eastern Africa featuring evidence of domesticated sheep, goats and cattle, but not iron metallurgy.

Pareidolia A capacity for recognizing patterns in unpatterned evidence (e.g., animal shapes in clouds).

Patina/Patination Chemical staining on a rock surface.

Patterned imposition of nonintrinsic shape Recurring artifact designs that reflect imposition of shapes neither intrinsic to, nor predictable from, unaltered raw materials (e.g., a nail forged from iron ore).

Pecking and grinding Shaping stone by alternating cycles of percussion and abrasion.

Pebble core Former term for relatively short nonhierarchical cores.

Pendant Relatively small and asymmetrical perforated groundstone artifact.

Percussor Rock damaged from or shaped by repeated percussion (aka hammerstone).

Percussion Shaping stone by striking it forcefully, thereby initiating fracture.

Pestle Relatively long and narrow pulverizing tool damaged at one or both ends, mobile component of a pulverizing toolkit.

Platform angle The angles at which a worked edge's fracture initiation and fracture propagation surfaces intersect. On flakes, the intersection of the striking platform and ventral surface (internal platform angle, IPA), and the intersection of striking platform and the dorsal surface (external platform angle, EPA).

Platform core Relatively short unifacial hierarchical core.

Platter Shallowly concave or flat stone vessel.

Pleistocene Geological epoch dating 11,700–2,600,000 years ago.

Plio-Pleistocene The later Pliocene and Early Pleistocene Epochs, ca. 1,600,000–3,500,000 years ago.

Pliocene Geological epoch dating 2,600,000–5,300,000 years ago.

Plunging (terminated) fracture Fracture that terminates recursively below and away from the plane of fracture propagation surface.

Pluvial Hypothetical periods of increased rainfall in Equatorial Africa thought to have coincided with northern hemisphere glaciations.

Polish Microscopic topographic flattening of stone surfaces.

Polished axe See celt, groundstone celt.

Pot-lid flake Flat hemispherical detached piece that forms when heated rocks cool quickly.

Prehistory The period before written historical records.

Pressure flaking Initiating a fracture by slowly increasing loading.

Primitive A morphology or behavior present in a common ancestor of descendant organisms.

Processual archaeology Archaeological research focusing on behavioral variability.

Processualizing Period (of prehistoric research in Eastern Africa) Since 1965.

Pulverizing tool Implement used to break seeds, pigments, or other materials into smaller particles through percussion and abrasion.

Quartz A rock crystal comprised mostly of silica.

Quern Catch-all term for various kinds of grinding slabs and other pulverizing tools.

Recycling Using a formerly discarded stone tool again, after substantial modification.

Reduction Removing a series of large flakes from a core.

Refitting Reconstructing sequences of toolmaking actions and geological processes by fitting flake scars from separate artifacts to one another.

Residues Particles of organic and inorganic media adhering to stone tool surfaces.

Retouch 1. The act of detaching a series of relatively small <20 mm flakes from the edge of a flake or a core, 2. Edge damage resulting from retouch.

Retouched piece Retouched flake fragment.

Reuse Using a formerly discarded stone tool without substantial modification.

Saddle quern Former term for a concave linear grinding slab.

Scaled piece See **Bipolar flake**.

Scraper Retouched piece with at least one relatively sharp orthogonally retouched edge.

Scraper retouch Orthogonal retouch that creates a relatively sharp edge.

Scrapers/notches/denticulates (SNDs) Orthogonally retouched pieces with relatively acute retouched edges.

Sedimentary rock Rock that formed as the result of pressure (e.g., chert, flint, jasper, chalcedony, shale, sandstone).

Shaping Retouch and reduction strategies intended to impose shape on a core (aka *façonnage*).

Shear fracture Fracture that forms in a single flat plane directly under the point of loading.

Side-struck flake A flake whose longest axis is perpendicular to the axis of fracture propagation, i.e., a flake that is wider than it is long.

Sidescraper Scraper with orthogonal retouch on lateral edge/edges.

Silicate General term for rocks comprised mainly of silica, regardless of their origin (e.g., quartz = crystal, obsidian = igneous, quartzite = metamorphic).

Sinew-frayer Former term for a truncated piece.

Site, archaeological See **Archaeological site**.

Site complex See **Archaeological site complex**.

SNDs Acronym for scrapers, notches, and denticulates.

Soft-hammer percussion Initiating a fracture by forcefully striking a rock with a piece of wood, bone, horn, or antler.

Spheroid Roughly spherical percussion-damaged piece.

Stack A series of adjacent step-terminated fracture scars.

Step (terminated) fracture A fracture that terminates at a right angle to the plane of fracture propagation and the fracture propagation surface.

Stone Age Archaeological periodization of earlier sub-Saharan African prehistory

Stone Tool Artifact made of rock, shaped by abrasion and/or fracture.

Stoneworker A human or earlier hominin who purposefully modifies stone.

Stoneworking Making and using stone tools.

Stoneworking Modes A–I Taxonomic framework for describing how primates modify stone. For detailed definitions, see Chapter 5.

Striation Linear concavities ("scratches") on rock surfaces that result from abrasion.

Striking platform The remnant part of the fracture initiation surface preserved at a flake's proximal end.

Subspheroid Subspherical to subangular percussion-damaged piece.

Subassemblage A group of artifacts from the same assemblage sharing similar properties (e.g., raw material, refitting, retouch pattern, stratigraphic or spatial association, etc.).

Surface collection Artifact samples collected from a site surface.

Systematics Discipline-specific terms used to describe scientific observations and inferences.

Technocomplex See **Technological complex**.

Technological complex Group of assemblages preserving evidence for similar toolmaking strategies.

Technology/Technological variables Artifact morphological or metric variables thought to be affected mainly by manufacturing techniques and strategies.

Teleolith A lithic artifact modified in the course of individuals learning how to make and use stone tools.

Thermal alteration Modifying rock fracture properties by exposing them to high temperatures.

Thinned piece Retouched piece from which deeply invasive, shallow flake scars have been detached.

Thumbnail scraper Small (<20–30 mm long) scraper with retouch on distal and both lateral edges.

Time-averaging Assuming that all artifacts enclosed in the same sedimentary deposit were actually contemporary with one another.

Torus Relatively large and symmetrical ring-shaped perforated groundstone artifact (aka bored stone, digging stick weight).

Typological variables See **Morphological variables**.

Typology 1. A list of recognized artifact-types. 2. Synonym for artifact morphological variation.

UHC Acronym for unifacial hierarchical core.

Victoria West Core Relatively large preferential bifacial hierarchical core.

Volcanic General term for various coarse-grained nonsilicate igneous rocks (e.g., basalt, rhyolite, phonolite).

Worked edge On cores, the intersection of fracture initiation and propagation surfaces from which flakes were detached. Also known as "working edge."

SUGGESTED READINGS

ABOUT AFRICAN ARCHAEOLOGY

Barham, Lawrence, and Peter Mitchell. 2008. *The First Africans: African Archaeology from the Earliest Toolmakers to Most Recent Foragers*. New York: Cambridge University Press.

Mitchell, Peter and Paul Lane, eds. 2013. *The Oxford Handbook of African Archaeology*. Oxford: Oxford University Press.

Phillipson, David W. 2005. *African Archaeology*. Third Edition. Cambridge: Cambridge University Press.

ABOUT STONE TOOLS

Andrefsky, William J. 2005. *Lithics: Macroscopic Approaches to Analysis*, Second Edition. New York: Cambridge University Press.

Inizan, Marie-Louise, M. Reduron-Ballinger, Hélène Roche, and Jacques Tixier. 1999. *Technology and Terminology of Knapped Stone (translated by J. Féblot-Augustins), Préhistoire de la Pierre Taillée, Tome 5*. Meudon, France: Cercle de Recherches et d'Etudes Préhistoriques (CNRS).

Odell, George H. 2004. *Lithic Analysis*. New York: Kluwer.

Schick, Kathy D. and Nicholas P. Toth. 1993. *Making Silent Stones Speak: Human Evolution and the Dawn of Technology*. New York: Simon and Schuster.

Shea, John J. 2017. *Stone Tools in Human Evolution: Behavioral Differences among Technological Primates*. New York: Cambridge University Press.

Whittaker, John C. 1994. *Flintknapping: Making and Understanding Stone Tools*. Austin: University of Texas Press.

BIBLIOGRAPHY

Adams, J. L. 2014. *Ground Stone Analysis: An Anthropological Approach*. Salt Lake City, UT: University of Utah Press.

Addington, L. 1986. *Lithic Illustration: Drawing Flaked Stone Artifacts for Publication*. Chicago, IL: University of Chicago Press.

Aiello, L. C. and P. Wheeler. 1995. The expensive-tissue hypothesis: The brain and digestive system in human and primate evolution. *Current Anthropology* 36:199–221.

Ambrose, S. H. 1983. "The Introduction of Pastoral Adaptation to the Highlands of East Africa," in *From Hunters to Farmers: The Causes and Consequences of Food Production in Africa*. Edited by J. D. Clark and S. A. Brandt, pp. 212–39. Berkeley, CA: University of California Press.

Ambrose, S. H. 1984. "*Holocene Environments and Human Adaptations in the Central Rift Valley, Kenya*." PhD Dissertation, University of California at Berkeley.

Ambrose, S. H. 1985. Excavations at Masai Gorge Rockshelter, Naivasha. *Azania: Archaeological Research in Africa* 20:29–67.

Ambrose, S. H. 1998. Chronology of the Later Stone Age and food production in East Africa. *Journal of Archaeological Science* 25:377–92.

Ambrose, S. H. 2001. "Middle and Later Stone Age Settlement Patterns in the Central Rift Valley, Kenya: Comparisons and Contrasts," in *Settlement Dynamics of the Middle Paleolithic and Middle Stone Age*. Edited by N. Conard, pp. 21–43. Tuebingen: Kerns Verlag.

Ambrose, S. H. 2002. "Small Things Remembered: Origins of Early Microlithic Industries in Sub-Saharan Africa," in *Thinking Small: Global Perspectives on Microlithization*. Edited by R. G. Elston and S. L. Kuhn, pp. 9–30. Washington, DC: American Anthropological Association (Archaeological Paper No. 12).

Ambrose, S. H., D. Collett, D. Collett, and F. Marshall. 1984. Excavations at Deloraine, Rongai, 1978. *Azania: Archaeological Research in Africa* 19:79–104.

Ambrose, S. H., and N. E. Sikes. 1991. Soil carbon isotope evidence for holocene habitat change in the Kenya Rift Valley. *Science* 253:1402–25.

American Psychiatric Association. 2013. *Diagnostic and Statistical Manual of Mental Disorders*, 5th Edition. Arlington, VA: American Psychiatric Association.

Andrefsky, W. J. 2005. *Lithics: Macroscopic Approaches to Analysis*, Second Edition. New York: Cambridge University Press.

Anthony, B. W. 1978. *The Prospect Industry: A Definition*. Doctoral Dissertation, Harvard University.

Aprahamian, G. D. 2001. "Le dessin du materiel lithique," in *Beyond Tools: Redefining the PPN Lithic Assemblages of the Levant*. Edited by I. Caneva, C. Lemorini, D. Zampetti, and P. Biagi, pp. 93–106. Berlin: ex oriente.

Asfaw, B., Y. Beyene, S. Semaw, G. Suwa, T. White, and G. WoldeGabriel. 1991. Fejej: A new paleoanthropological research area in Ethiopia. *Journal of Human Evolution* 21:137–43.

Ashley, C. Z. and K. M. Grillo. 2015. Archaeological ceramics from eastern Africa: Past approaches and future directions. *Azania: Archaeological Research in Africa* 50:460–80.

Barham, L. Editor. 2000. *The Middle Stone Age of Zambia, South Central Africa*. Bristol, U.K.: Western Academic & Specialist Press.

Barham, L. 2002. Systematic pigment use in the Middle Pleistocene of South-Central Africa. *Current Anthropology* 43:181–90.

Barham, L. and P. Mitchell. 2008. *The First Africans: African Archaeology from the Earliest Toolmakers to Most Recent Foragers*. New York: Cambridge University Press.

Barham, L., M. J. Simms, M. Gilmour, and N. Debenham. 2000. "Twin Rivers, Excavation and Behavioural Record," in *The Middle Stone Age of Zambia, South Central Africa*. Edited by L. Barham, pp. 165–216. Bristol, U.K.: Western Academic & Specialist Press.

Barnes, A. S. 1939. The difference between natural and human flaking in prehistoric flint implements. *American Anthropologist* 41:99–112.

Barsky, D., C. Chapon-Sao, J.-J. Bahain, Y. Beyene, D. Cauche, V. Celiberti, E. Desclaux, H. De Lumley, M.-A. De Lumley, F. Marchal, P.-E. Moullé, and D. Pleurdeau. 2011. The Early Oldowan Stone-Tool Assemblage from Fejej FJ-1a, Ethiopia. *Journal of African Archaeology* 9:207–24.

Barthelme, J. W. 1985. *Fisher-Hunters and Neolithic Pastoralists in East Turkana, Kenya*. Oxford: British Archaeological Reports International Series 254 (Cambridge Monographs in African Archaeology 13).

Bar-Yosef, O. and S. L. Kuhn. 1999. The big deal about blades: Laminar technologies and human evolution. *American Anthropologist* 101:322–38.

Beauchamp, E. K. and B. A. Purdy. 1986. Decrease in fracture toughness in chert by heat treatment. *Journal of Materials Science* 21:1963–6.

Beck, H. C. 1928. *Classification and Nomenclature of Beads and Pendants*. Oxford: John Johnson.

Belfer-Cohen, A. and L. Grosman. 2007. "Tools or Cores? And Why Does It Matter: Carinated Artifacts in Levantine Late Upper Paleolithic Assemblages," in *Tools versus Cores: Alternative Approaches to Stone Tool Analysis*. Edited by S. McPherron, pp. 143–63. Newcastle: Cambridge Scholars Publishing.

Beyene, Y., S. Katoh, G. WoldeGabriel, W. K. Hart, K. Uto, M. Sudo, M. Kondo, M. Hyodo, P. R. Renne, G. Suwa, and B. Asfaw. 2013. The characteristics and chronology of the earliest Acheulean at Konso, Ethiopia. *Proceedings of the National Academy of Sciences* 110:1584–91.

Beyin, A. 2010. *Prehistoric Settlements on the Red Sea Coast of Eritrea: Archaeological Investigations of the Buri Peninsula and the Gulf of Zula*. Saarbrücken, Germany: Lambert.

Biittner, K. M., E. A. Sawchuk, J. M. Miller, J. J. Werner, P. M. Bushozi, and P. R. Willoughby. 2017. Excavations at Mlambalasi Rockshelter: A terminal Pleistocene to recent Iron Age record in Southern Tanzania. *African Archaeological Review* 34:275–95.

Binford, L. R. 1979. Organization and formation processes: Looking at curated technologies. *Journal of Anthropological Research* 35:255–73.

Binford, L. R. 1981. *Bones: Ancient Men and Modern Myths*. New York: Academic Press.

Bishop, L. C., T. W. Plummer, J. V. Ferraro, D. Braun, P. W. Ditchfield, F. Hertel, J. D. Kingston, J. Hicks, and R. Potts. 2006. Recent research into Oldowan hominin activities at Kanjera South, western Kenya. *African Archaeological Review* 23:31.

Bishop, W. W. and J. D. Clark. Editors. 1967. *Background to Evolution in Africa*. Chicago, IL: University of Chicago Press.

Bisson, M. S. 2000. Nineteenth century tools for twenty-first century archaeology? Why the Middle Paleolithic typology of François Bordes must be replaced. *Journal of Archaeological Method and Theory* 7:1–48.

Bisson, M. S. 2001. Inteview with a Neanderthal: An experimental approach for reconstructing scraper production rules, and their implications for imposed form in Middle Palaeolithic tools. *Cambridge Archaeological Journal* 11:165–84.

Blegen, N. 2017. The earliest long-distance obsidian transport: Evidence from the ~200 ka Middle Stone Age Sibilo School Road Site, Baringo, Kenya. *Journal of Human Evolution* 103:1–19.

Blegen, N., J. T. Faith, A. Mant-Melville, D. J. Peppe, and C. A. Tryon. 2017. The Middle Stone Age after 50,000 years ago: New evidence from the Late Pleistocene sediments of the eastern Lake Victoria Basin, western Kenya. *PaleoAnthropology* 2017:139–69.

Blinkhorn, J. and M. Grove. 2018. The structure of the Middle Stone Age of eastern Africa. *Quaternary Science Reviews* 195:1–20.

Blumenschine, R. J. 1986. Carcass consumption sequences and the archaeological distinction of scavenging and hunting. *Journal of Human Evolution* 15:639–59.

Blumenschine, R. J., C. R. Peters, F. T. Masao, R. J. Clarke, A. L. Deino, R. L. Hay, C. C. Swisher, I. G. Stanistreet, G. M. Ashley, L. J. McHenry, N. E. Sikes, N. J. van der Merwe, J. C. Tactikos, A. E. Cushing, D. M. Deocampo, J. K. Njau, and J. I. Ebert. 2003. Late Pliocene *Homo* and hominid land use from western Olduvai Gorge, Tanzania. *Science* 299:1217–21.

Boëda, E. 1995. "Levallois: A Volumetric Construction, Methods, a Technique," in *The Definition and Interpretation of Levallois Technology.* Monographs in World Archaeology No. 23. Edited by H. L. Dibble and O. Bar-Yosef, pp. 41–68. Madison, WI: Prehistory Press.

Boëda, E. 2013. *Techno-logique & Technologie. Une Paléo-histoire des objets lithiques tranchants.* Paris: Archéo-éditions.

Boesch, C. and H. Boesch. 1984. Possible causes of sex differences in the use of natural hammers by wild chimpanzees. *Journal of Human Evolution* 13:415–40.

Bordes, F. 1961. *Typologie du Paléolithique ancien et moyen.* Bordeaux: Delmas.

Bower, J. 1991. The Pastoral Neolithic of East Africa. *Journal of World Prehistory* 5:49–82.

Bower, J. R. F. 1973. Seronera: Excavations at a stone bowl site in the Serengeti National Park, Tanzania. *Azania: Archaeological Research in Africa* 8:71–104.

Bower, J. R. F., C. M. Nelson, A. F. Waibel, and S. Wandibba. 1977. The University of Massachusetts' Later Stone Age/Pastoral 'Neolithic' comparative study in central Kenya: An overview. *Azania: Archaeological Research in Africa* 12:119–46.

Bowler, P. J. 1986. *Theories of Human Evolution: A Century of Debate, 1844-1944.* Baltimore, MD: Johns Hopkins University Press.

Brandt, S. 1982. "*A Late Quaternary Cultural and Environmental Sequence from Lake Besaka, Southern Afar, Ethiopia.*" PhD dissertation, University of California, Berkeley.

Brandt, S. A. and R. Fattovich. 1990. "Later Quaternary Archaeological Research in the Horn of Africa," in *A History of African Archaeology.* Edited by P. Robertshaw, pp. 95–108. Oxford: James Currey.

Brandt, S., E. Hildebrand, R. Vogelsang, J. Wolfhagen, and H. Wang. 2017. A new MIS 3 radiocarbon chronology for Mochena Borago Rockshelter, SW Ethiopia: Implications for the interpretation of Late Pleistocene chronostratigraphy and human behavior. *Journal of Archaeological Science: Reports* 11:352–69.

Brandt, S. A., A. Manzo, and C. Perlingieri. 2008. "Linking the Highlands and the Lowlands: Implications of a Test Excavation at Kokodan Rockshelter, Agordat, Eritrea," in *The Archaeology of Ancient Eritrea.* Edited by P. Schmidt, M. C. Curtis, and Z. Teka, pp. 33–49. Trenton, NJ: Red Sea Press.

Brandt, S. and K. J. Weedman. 1997. "The Ethnoarchaeology of Hide Working and Flaked Stone Tool Use in Southern Ethiopia.," in *Ethiopia in Broader Perspective: Papers of the 12th International Conference on Ethiopian Studies.* Edited by K. Fukui, F. Kuimoto, and M. Shigeta, pp. 351–61. Kyoto: Shokado Book Sellers.

Brézillon, M. 1977. *La dénomination des objets de Pierre Taillée (Second Edition). Gallia Préhistoire Fourth Supplement.* Paris: CNRS.

Brooks, A. S., and C. C. Smith. 1987. Ishango revisited: New age determinations and cultural interpretations. *The African Archaeological Review* 5:65–78.

Brooks, A. S., J. E. Yellen, R. Potts, A. K. Behrensmeyer, A. L. Deino, D. E. Leslie, S. H. Ambrose, J. R. Ferguson, F. d'Errico, A. M. Zipkin, S. Whittaker, J. Post, E. G. Veatch, K. Foecke, and J. B. Clark. 2018. Long-distance stone transport and pigment use in the earliest Middle Stone Age. *Science* 360:90.

Brown, J. 1966. The excavation of a group of burial mounds at Ilkek near Gilgil, Kenya. *Azania* 1:59–77.

Brown, K. S., C. W. Marean, A. I. R. Herries, Z. Jacobs, C. Tribolo, D. Braun, D. L. Roberts, M. C. Meyer, and J. Bernatchez. 2009. Fire as an engineering tool of early modern humans. *Science* 325:859–62.

Bruggemann, J. H., R. T. Buffler, M. M. M. Guillaume, R. C. Walter, R. von Cosel, B. N. Ghebretensae, and S. M. Berhe. 2004. Stratigraphy, palaeoenvironments and model for the deposition of the Abdur Reef limestone: Context for an important archaeological site from the last interglacial on the Red Sea coast of Eritrea. *Palaeogeography, Palaeoclimatology, Palaeoecology* 203:179–206.

Bunn, H. T. 1981. Archaeological evidence for meat-eating by Plio-Pleistocene hominids from Koobi Fora and Olduvai Gorge. *Nature* 291:574–77.

Cairncross, B. 2005. *Field Guide to Rocks & Minerals of Southern Africa.* Capetown: Penguin Random House South Africa.

Capra, D. 2017. Lithic manufacture at Medogwe, southwest of Aksum, Tigray, Ethiopia. *Azania: Archaeological Research in Africa* 52:407–27.

Carr, C. 1995. "A Unified Middle-Range Theory of Artifact Design," in *Style, Society, and Person: Archaeological and Ethnological Perspectives.* Edited by C. Carr and J. Neitzel, pp. 171–258. New York: Plenunm.

Chavaillon, J. and M. Piperno. Editors. 2004. *Studies on the Early Paleolithic Site of Melka Kunture, Ethiopia.* Florence: Istituto italiano di Preistoria e Protostoria.

Chazan, M. 1997. Redefining Levallois. *Journal of Human Evolution* 33:719–35.

Christel, M. 1994. Catarrhine primates grasping small objects: Techniques and hand preferences. *Current Primatology* 3:37–49.

Church, T. Editor. 1994. *Lithic Resource Studies: A Sourcebook for Archaeologists.* Tulsa, OK: Lithic Technology Special Publication #3.

Clark, G. 1969a. *World Prehistory: A New Outline.* Cambridge: Cambridge University Press.

Clark, G. 1970. *Aspects of Prehistory.* Berkeley, CA: University of California Press.

Clark, G. 1977. *World Prehistory in New Perspective*, Third edition. Cambridge: Cambridge University Press.

Clark, J. D. 1942. Further excavations (1939) at the Mumbwa Caves, Northern Rhodesia. *Transactions of the Royal Society of South Africa* 29:133–201.

Clark, J. D. 1954. *The Prehistoric Cultures of the Horn of Africa.* Cambridge: Cambridge University Press.

Clark, J. D. 1955. "The Stone Ball: Its Associations and Use by Prehistoric Man in Africa," in *Congrès Panafricain de Préhistoire: Actes de la IIe Session (Alger 1952).* Edited by L. Balout, pp. 403–17. Paris: Arts et Métiers Graphiques.

Clark, J. D. 1959. *The Prehistory of Southern Africa.* London: Penguin.

Clark, J. D. 1969. *Kalambo Falls Prehistoric Site, Vol. I: The Geology, Palaeoecology and Detailed Stratigraphy of the Excavations.* Cambridge: Cambridge University Press.

Clark, J. D. 1974. *The Kalambo Falls Prehistoric Site, Vol. II: The Later Prehistoric Cultures.* Cambridge: Cambridge University Press.

Clark, J. D. Editor. 1984. *The Cambridge History of Africa, Volume 1: From the Earliest Times to c. 500 BC.* Cambridge: Cambridge University Press.

Clark, J. D. 1988. The Middle Stone Age of East Africa and the beginnings of regional identity. *Journal of World Prehistory* 2:235–305.

Clark, J. D. Editor. 2001. *Kalambo Falls Prehistoric Site, Volume III, The Earlier Cultures: Middle and Earlier Stone Age.* Cambridge: Cambridge University Press.

Clark, J. D., Y. Beyene, G. WoldeGabriel, W. K. Hart, P. R. Renne, H. Gilbert, A. Defleur, G. Suwa, S. Katoh, K. R. Ludwig, J.-R. Boisserie, B. Asfaw, and T. D. White. 2003. Stratigraphic, chronological and behavioural contexts of Pleistocene *Homo sapiens* from Middle Awash, Ethiopia. *Nature* 423:747–52.

Clark, J. D. and S. A. Brandt. Editors. 1984. *From Hunters to Farmers: The Causes and Consequences of Food Production in Africa.* Berkeley, CA: University of California Press.

Clark, J. D., G. H. Cole, G. L. Isaac, and M. R. Kleindienst. 1966. Precision and definition in African archaeology. *The South African Archaeological Bulletin* 21:114–21.

Clark, J. D., and H. Kurashina. 1981. "A Study of the Work of a Modern Tanner in Ethiopia and Its Relevance for Archaeological Interpretation," in *Modern Material Culture: The Archaeology of Us.* Edited by R. A. Gould and M. B. Schiffer, pp. 303–20. New York: Academic Press.

Clark, J. D., K. W. Williamson, M. J. Michels, and C. A. Marean. 1984. A Middle Stone Age occurrence at Porc Epic Cave, Dire Dawa, Somalia. *African Archaeological Review* 2:37–71.

Clarke, D. L. 1978. *Analytical Archaeology*, Second Edition. New York: Columbia University Press.

Clarke, R. 1935. The flint-knapping industry at Brandon. *Antiquity* 9:38–56.

Clarkson, C. 2002. An index of invasiveness of the measurement of unifacial and bifacial retouch: A theoretical, experimental, and archaeological verification. *Journal of Archaeological Science* 29:65–75.

Cole, S. 1954. *The Prehistory of East Africa.* New York: Mentor.

Conard, N. J., M. Soressi, J. E. Parkington, S. Wurz, and R. Yates. 2004. A unified lithic taxonomy based on patterns of core reduction. *South African Archaeological Bulletin* 59:13–17.

Corbey, R., A. Jagich, M. Collard, and K. Vaesne. 2016. The Acheulean handaxe: More like bird song than a Beatles' tune? *Evolutionary Anthropology* 25:6–19.

Cornelissen, E. 1992. *Site GNJH-17 and Its Implications for the Archaeology of the Kapthurin Formation, Baringo, Kenya. Annals du Musée Royal de l'Afrique Centrale, Vol.133.* Tervuren, Belgium.

Cotterell, B., J. Kamminga, and F. P. Dickson. 1985. The essential mechanics of conchoidal flaking. *International Journal of Fracture* 29:205–21.

Cowling, S. A., P. M. Cox, C. D. Jones, M. A. Maslin, M. Peros, and S. A. Spall. 2008. Simulated glacial and interglacial vegetation across Africa: Implications for species phylogenies and trans-African migration of plants and animals. *Global Change Biology* 14:827–40.

Crabtree, D. 1972. *An Introduction to Flintworking,* Occasional Paper No. 28. Pocatello, ID: Idaho State Museum .

Crabtree, D. R. and R. Butler. 1964. Notes on experiments in flint knapping: Heat treatment of silica minerals. *Tebiwa* 7:1–6.

Crompton, R. H. and J. A. J. Gowlett. 1993. Multidimensional form in Acheulian bifaces from Kilombe, Kenya. *Journal of Human Evolution* 25:175–99.

Crowther, A., M. E. Prendergast, D. Q. Fuller, and N. Boivin. 2017. Subsistence mosaics, forager-farmer interactions, and the transition to food production in eastern Africa. *Quaternary International* 489:101–20

Cziesla, E. 1990. "On Refitting Stone Artefacts," in *The Big Puzzle: International Symposium on Refitting Stone Implements.* Edited by E. Cziesla, S. Eickhoff, N. Arts, and D. Winter, pp. 9–44. Bonn: Holos Press.

Daniel, G. E. and C. Renfrew. 1988. *The Idea of Prehistory.* Edinburgh: Edinburgh University Press.

Darwin, C. 1871. *Descent of Man, and Selection in Relation to Sex.* London: John Murray.

Davidson, I. and W. Noble. 1993. "Tools and Language in Human Evolution," in *Tools, Language and Cognition in Human Evolution.* Edited by K. R. Gibson and T. Ingold, pp. 363–88. Cambridge: Cambridge University Press.

de Heinzelin, J. 1962. Ishango. *Scientific American* 206:105–16.

de la Torre, I. 2004. Omo revisited: Evaluating the technological skills of Pliocene hominids. *Current Anthropology* 45:439–67.

de la Torre, I. 2011. The Early Stone Age lithic assemblages of Gadeb (Ethiopia) and the developed Oldowan/early Acheulean in East Africa. *Journal of Human Evolution* 60:768–812.

de la Torre, I., and R. Mora. 2005. *Technological Strategies in the Lower Pleistocene at Olduvai Beds I & II.* Liége: Université de Liége (ERAUL 112).

de la Torre, I., and R. Mora. 2009. "The Technology of the ST Site Complex," in *Peninj: A Research Project on Human Origins 1995-2005.* Edited by M. Domínguez-Rodrigo, L. Alcala, and L. Luque, pp. 145–89. Cambridge, MA: Oxbow Books (American School of Prehistoric Research).

de la Torre, I., R. Mora, A. Arroyo, and A. Benito-Calvo. 2014. Acheulean technological behaviour in the Middle Pleistocene landscape of Mieso (East-Central Ethiopia). *Journal of Human Evolution* 76:1–25.

De Maret, P. 2013. "Archaeologies of the Bantu Expansion," in *The Oxford Handbook of African Archaeology.* Edited by P. Mitchell and P. Lane, pp. 627–44. Oxford: Oxford University Press.

Debénath, A. and H. L. Dibble. 1994. *Handbook of Paleolithic Typology, Vol. 1: Lower and Middle Paleolithic of Europe.* Philadelphia: University of Pennsylvania Press.

Deino, A. L., A. K. Behrensmeyer, A. S. Brooks, J. E. Yellen, W. D. Sharp, and R. Potts. 2018. Chronology of the Acheulean to Middle Stone Age transition in eastern Africa. *Science* 360:95–8.

Delagnes, A., J.-R. Boisserie, Y. Beyene, K. Chuniaud, C. Guillemot, and M. Schuster. 2011. Archaeological investigations in the Lower Omo Valley (Shungura Formation, Ethiopia): New data and perspectives. *Journal of Human Evolution* 61:215–22.

Delagnes, A., A. Lenoble, S. Harmand, J.-P. Brugal, S. Prat, J.-J. Tiercelin, and H. Roche. 2006. Interpreting pachyderm single carcass sites in the African Lower and Early Middle Pleistocene record: A multidisciplinary approach to the site of Nadung'a 4 (Kenya). *Journal of Anthropological Archaeology* 25:448–65.

Delanges, A. and H. Roche. 2005. Late Pliocene hominid knapping skills: The case of Lokalalei 2C, West Turkana, Kenya. *Journal of Human Evolution* 48:435–72.

Dibble, H. L. 1987. The interpretation of Middle Paleolithic scraper morphology. *American Antiquity* 52:109–17.

Dibble, H. L. 1995. Middle Paleolithic scraper reduction: Background, clarification, and review of the evidence to date. *Journal of Archaeological Method and Theory* 2:299–368.

Dibble, H. L., and M. C. Bernard. 1980. A comparative study of edge angle measurement techniques. *American Antiquity* 45:857–65.

Dibble, H. L., S. J. Holdaway, S. C. Lin, D. R. Braun, M. J. Douglass, R. Iovita, S. P. McPherron, D. I. Olszewski, and D. Sandgathe. 2017. Major fallacies surrounding stone artifacts and assemblages. *Journal of Archaeological Method and Theory* 24:813–51.

Dibble, H. L., and Z. Rezek. 2009. Introducing a new experimental design for controlled studies of flake formation: Results for exterior platform angle, platform depth, angle of blow, velocity, and force. *Journal of Archaeological Science* 36:1945–54.

Dickson, F. P. 1982. *Australian Stone Hatchets: A Study in Design and Dynamics.* New York: Academic Press.

Dillian, C. 2016. "Current Questions and New Directions in Archaeological Obsidian Studies," in *Oxford Handbooks Online*, pp. 1–32. Oxford: Oxford University Press.

Domínguez-Rodrigo, M. 2002. Hunting and scavenging by early humans: The state of the debate. *Journal of World Prehistory* 16:1–54.

Domínguez-Rodrigo, M., L. Alcala, and L. Luque. Editors. 2009. *Peninj: A Research Project on Human Origins 1995-2005.* Cambridge, MA: Oxbow Books (American School of Prehistoric Research).

Domínguez-Rodrigo, M., R. Barba, and C. P. Egeland. Editors. 2007. *Deconstructing Olduvai: A Taphonomic Study of the Bed I Sites.* New York: Springer.

Domínguez-Rodrigo, M. and T. R. Pickering. 2003. Early hominid hunting and scavenging: A zooarchaeological review. *Evolutionary Anthropology* 12:275–82.

Douze, K. and A. Delagnes. 2016. The pattern of emergence of a Middle Stone Age tradition at Gademotta and Kulkuletti (Ethiopia) through convergent tool and point technologies. *Journal of Human Evolution* 91:93–121.

Dunbar, R. 2016. *Human Evolution: Our Brains and Our Behavior.* New York: Oxford University Press.

Dussubieux, L., C. M. Kusimba, V. Gogte, S. B. Kusimba, B. Gratuze, and R. Oka. 2008–2010. The trading of ancient glass beads: New analytical data from South Asian and East African soda–alumina glass beads. *Archaeometry* 50:797–821.

Elston, R. G. and P. J. Brantingham. 2002. "Microlithic Technology in Northern Asia: A Risk-Minimizing Strategy of the Late Paleolithic and Early Holocene," in *Thinking Small: Global Perspectives on Microlithization*, Archaeological Paper No. 12. Edited by R. G. Elston and S. L. Kuhn, pp. 103–16. Washington, DC: American Anthropological Association .

Elston, R. G., and S. L. Kuhn. Editors. 2002. *Thinking Small: Global Perspectives on Microlithization*, Archaeological Paper No. 12. Washington, DC: American Anthropological Association .

Eren, M. I., B. Buchanan, and M. J. O'Brien. 2015. Social learning and technological evolution during the Clovis colonization of the New World. *Journal of Human Evolution* 80:159–70.

Eren, M. I., M. Dominguez-Rodrigo, S. L. Kuhn, D. S. Adler, I. Le, and O. Bar-Yosef. 2005. Defining and measuring reduction in unifacial stone tools. *Journal of Archaeological Science* 32:1190–201.

Eren, M. I., A. J. Durant, M. Prendergast, and A. Z. P. Mabulla. 2014. Middle Stone Age archaeology at Olduvai Gorge, Tanzania. *Quaternary International* 322–23:292–313.

Eren, M. I., A. Greenspan, and C. G. Sampson. 2008. Are Upper Paleolithic blade cores more productive than Middle Paleolithic discoidal cores? A replication experiment. *Journal of Human Evolution* 55:952–61.

Eren, M. I., S. J. Lycett, R. J. Patten, B. Buchanan, J. Pargeter, and M. J. O'Brien. 2016. Test, model, and method validation: The role of experimental stone artifact replication in hypothesis-driven archaeology. *Ethnoarchaeology* 8:103–36.

Fagan, B. and F. van Noten. 1971. *The Hunter-Gatherers of Gwisho. Annals Series 8, Number 74.* Tervuren, Belgium: Koninklijk Museum voor Midden-Afrika.

Fattovich, R., H. Berhe, L. Phillipson, and L. Semicola. Editors. 2012. Archaeological Expedition at Aksum (Ethiopia) of the Università degli studi di Napoli, "L'Orientale" (2010 field season: Seglamen). *Newsletter di Archeologia del CISA, vol. 3.*

Finneran, N., S. Boardman, and C. Cain. 2000a. Excavations at the Late Stone Age site of

Baahti Nebait, Aksum, Northern Ethiopia, 1997. *Azania: Archaeological Research in Africa* 35:53–73.

Finneran, N., S. Boardman, and C. Cain. 2000b. A new perspective on the Late Stone Age of the northern Ethiopian highlands: Excavations at Anqqer Baahti, Aksum, Ethiopia 1996. *Azania: Archaeological Research in Africa* 35:21–51.

Flannery, K. V. Editor. 1976. *The Early Mesoamerican Village*. New York: Academic Press.

Fleagle, J. G. 2013. *Primate Adaptation and Evolution*, 3rd edition. Waltham, MA: Academic Press.

Fleagle, J. G. and F. E. Grine. 2014. "The Genus *Homo* in Africa," in *The Cambridge World Prehistory, Volume 1: Africa, South and Southeast Asia and the Pacific*. Edited by C. Renfrew and P. Bahn, pp. 85–105. New York: Cambridge University Press.

Foley, R. and M. M. Lahr. 2003. On stony ground: Lithic technology, human evolution, and the emergence of culture. *Evolutionary Anthropology* 12:109–22.

Frahm, E. and C. A. Tryon. 2018. Later Stone Age toolstone acquisition in the Central Rift Valley of Kenya: Portable XRF of Eburran obsidian artifacts from Leakey's excavations at Gamble's Cave II. *Journal of Archaeological Science: Reports* 18:475–86.

Frison, G. C. 1969. A functional analysis of certain chipped stone tools. *American Antiquity* 33:149–55.

Fuller, D. and E. Hildebrand. 2013. "Domesticating Plants in Africa," in *The Oxford Handbook of African Archaeology*. Edited by P. Mitchell and P. Lane, pp. 131–44. Oxford: Oxford University Press.

Gabel, C. 1965. *Stone Age Hunters of the Kafue: The Gwisho A Site*. Boston, Mass.: African Studies Center, Boston University.

Gabel, W. C. 1969. Six rockshelters on the Northern Kavirondo shore of Lake Victoria. *African Historical Studies* 2:205–54.

Gallagher, J. P. 1977. Contemporary stone tools in Ethiopia: Implications for archaeology. *Journal of Field Archaeology* 4:406–14.

Gamble, C. 2013. *Settling the Earth: The Archaeology of Deep Human History*. New York: Cambridge University Press.

Gamble, C. and R. Kruszynski. 2009. John Evans, Joseph Prestwich and the stone that shattered the time barrier. *Antiquity* 83:461–75.

Gasse, F., F. Chaliè, A. Vincens, M. A. J. Williams, and D. Williamson. 2008. Climatic patterns in equatorial and southern Africa from 30,000 to 10,000 years ago reconstructed from terrestrial and near-shore proxy data. *Quaternary Science Reviews* 27:2316–40.

Gero, J. M. 1991. "Genderlithics: Women's Roles in Stone Tool Production," in *Engendering Archaeology: Women in Prehistory*. Edited by J. M. Gero and M. W. Conkey, pp. 163–93. Oxford: Blackwell.

Giemsch, L., C. Hertler, M. Märker, G. Quénéhervé, C. Saanane, and F. Schrenk. 2018. Acheulean sites at Makuyuni (Lake Manyara, Tanzania): Results of archaeological fieldwork and classification of the lithic assemblages. *African Archaeological Review* 35:87–106.

Gilbert, W. H., V. B. Doronichev, L. V. Golovanova, L. E. Morgan, and L. Nunez, Renne, Paul. 2016. Archaeology and context of Hugub, an important new Late Acheulean locality in Ethiopia's Northern Rift. *PaleoAnthropology* 2016:58–99.

Gillespie, J. D., S. Tupakka, and C. Cluney. 2004. Distinguishing between naturally and culturally flaked cobbles: A test case from Alberta, Canada. *Geoarchaeology* 19:615–33.

Gliganic, L. A., Z. Jacobs, R. G. Roberts, M. Domînguez-Rodrigo, and A. Z. P. Mabulla. 2012. New ages for Middle and Later Stone Age deposits at Mumba rockshelter, Tanzania: Optically stimulated luminescence dating of quartz and feldspar grains. *Journal of Human Evolution* 62:533–47.

Goder-Goldberger, M., N. Gubenko, and E. Hovers. 2016. "Diffusion with modifications": Nubian assemblages in the central Negev highlands of Israel and their implications for Middle Paleolithic inter-regional interactions. *Quaternary International* 408:121–39.

Goldman-Neuman, T. and E. Hovers. 2012. Raw material selectivity in Late Pliocene Oldowan sites in the Makaamitalu Basin, Hadar, Ethiopia. *Journal of Human Evolution* 62:353–66.

Goldstein, S. 2018. The lithic assemblage from Sugenya, a pastoral Neolithic site of the Elmenteitan tradition in southwestern Kenya. *Azania: Archaeological Research in Africa*:1–29.

Goldstein, S., E. Hildebrand, M. Storozum, E. Sawchuk, J. Lewis, C. Ngugi, and L. H. Robbins. 2017. New archaeological investigations at the Lothagam harpoon site at Lake Turkana. *Antiquity* 91:e5.

Goodwin, R. J. and C. van Riet Lowe. 1929. The Stone Age cultures of South Africa. *Annals of the South African Museum* 27:1–289.

Gould, R. A., D. A. Koster, and A. Sontz. 1971. The lithic assemblage of the Western Desert Aborigines of Australia. *American Antiquity* 36:149–68.

Gould, S. J. 1981. *The Mismeasure of Man.* New York: W.W. Norton.

Gowlett, J. A. J. 1990. "Archaeological Studies of Human Origins & Early Prehistory in Africa," in *A History of African Archaeology*. Edited by P. Robertshaw, pp. 13–38. Oxford: James Currey.

Gowlett, J. 1993. Le site Acheuleen de Kilombe: stratigraphie, geochronology, habitat et industrie lithique. *L'anthropologie* 97:69–84.

Gowlett, J. A. J., J. W. K. Harris, E. Walton, and B. A. Wood. 1981. Early archaeological sites, hominid remains and traces of fire from Chesowanja, Kenya. *Nature* 294:125–9.

Gramly, R. M. 1976. Upper Pleistocene archaeological occurrences at Site GvJM/22, Lukenya Hill, Kenya. *Man* 11:319–44.

Graziosi, P. 1940. *L'Eta della Pietra in Somalia.* Fiernza, Italy: Universita degli Studi di Fiernza.

Gregory, J. W. 1921. *The Rift Valleys and Geology of East Africa.* London: Seeley, Service.

Gresham, T. 1984. "*An Investigation of an Upper Pleistocene Archaeological Site in Northern Somalia.*" Master's Thesis, University of Georgia.

Grillo, K. M., M. E. Prendergast, D. A. Contreras, T. Fitton, A. O. Gidna, S. T. Goldstein, M. C. Knisley, M. C. Langley, and A. Z. P. Mabulla. 2018. Pastoral Neolithic settlement at Luxmanda, Tanzania. *Journal of Field Archaeology* 43:102–20.

Guichard, J. and G. Guichard. 1968. "Contributions to the Study of the Early and Middle Paleolithic of Nubia," in *The Prehistory of Nubia*, vol. 1. Edited by F. Wendorf, pp. 57–116. Dallas, TX: Southern Methodist University Press.

Gutherz, X., A. Diaz, C. Ménard, F. Bon, K. Douze, V. Léa, J. Lesur, and D. Sordoillet. 2014. The Hargeisan revisited: Lithic industries from Shelter 7 of Laas Geel, Somaliland and the transition between the Middle and Late Stone Age in the Horn of Africa. *Quaternary International* 343:69–84.

Gutherz, X., J. Lesur, J. Cauliez, V. Charpentier, A. Diaz, M. O. Ismaël, J.-M. Pène, D.

Sordoillet, and A. Zazzo. 2015. New insights on the first Neolithic societies in the Horn of Africa: The site of Wakrita, Djibouti. *Journal of Field Archaeology* 40:55–68.

Hammond, G. and N. Hammond. 1981. Child's play: A distorting factor in archaeological distribution. *American Antiquity* 46:634–6.

Harmand, S. 2007. "Raw Materials and Techno-Economic at Oldowan and Acheulean Sites in the West Turkana Region, Kenya," in *Lithic materials and Palaeolithic societies*. Edited by A. B. and B. Blades, pp. 1–14. Oxford: Blackwell Publishers.

Harmand, S., J. E. Lewis, C. S. Feibel, C. J. Lepre, S. Prat, A. Lenoble, X. Boes, R. L. Quinn, M. Brenet, A. Arroyo, N. Taylor, S. Clement, G. Daver, J.-P. Brugal, L. Leakey, R. A. Mortlock, J. D. Wright, S. Lokorodi, C. Kirwa, D. V. Kent, and H. Roche. 2015. 3.3-million-year-old stone tools from Lomekwi 3, West Turkana, Kenya. *Nature* 521:310–15.

Harrower, M. J., J. McCorriston, and C. D'Andrea. 2010. General/specific, local/global: Comparing the beginnings of agriculture in the Horn of Africa (Ethiopia/Eritrea) and Southwest Arabia (Yemen). *American Antiquity* 75:452–72.

Haslam, M., A. Hernandez-Aguilar, V. Ling, S. Carvalho, I. de la Torre, A. DeStefano, A. Du, B. Hardy, J. Harris, L. Marchant, T. Matsuzawa, W. McGrew, J. Mercader, R. Mora, M. Petraglia, H. Roche, E. Visalberghi, and R. Warren. 2009. Primate archaeology. *Nature* 460:339–44.

Hayden, B. 1989. "From Chopper to Celt: The Evolution of Resharpening Techniques," in *Time, Energy and Stone Tools*. Edited by R. Torrence. Cambridge: Cambridge University Press.

Hayden, B. 1990. "The Right Rub: Hide Working in High RankingH," in *The Interpretive Possibilities of Microwear Analysis (AUN 14)*. Edited by B. Graslund, pp. 89–102. Uppsala: Societas Archaeologica Uppsaliensis.

Hayden, B., and M. W. Nelson. 1981. The use of chipped lithic material in the contemporary Maya Highlands. *American Antiquity* 46:885–98.

Hildebrand, E. A., K. M. Grillo, E. A. Sawchuk, S. K. Pfeiffer, L. B. Conyers, S. T. Goldstein, A. C. Hill, A. Janzen, C. E. Klehm, M. Helper, P. Kiura, E. Ndiema, C. Ngugi, J. J.

Shea, and H. Wang. 2018. A monumental cemetery built by eastern Africa's first herders near Lake Turkana, Kenya. *Proceedings of the National Academy of Sciences* 115:8942.

Hivernel, F. 1974. "*A Study of the Kenya Capsian of Gamble's Cave (Kenya).*" PhD Dissertation, University of London.

Holdaway, S., and M. Douglas. 2012. A twenty-first century archaeology of stone artifacts. *Journal of Archaeological Method and Theory* 19:101–31.

Holmes, W. W. 1919. *Handbook of American Aboriginal Antiquities, Part 1: Introductory and the Lithic Industries (Bureau of American Ethnology Bulletin 60).* Washington, DC: U.S. Government Printing Office.

Hovers, E. 2009. "Learning from Mistakes: Flaking Accidents and Knapping Skills in the Assemblage of A.L. 894 (Hadar, Ethiopia)," in *The Cutting Edge: New Approaches to the Archaeology of Human Origins.* Edited by K. Schick and N. Toth, pp. 151–70. Gosport, IN: Stone Age Institute Press.

Howell, F. C., G. H. Cole, M. R. Kleindienst, and E. Haldemann. 1962. *Isimila: An Acheulian Occupaton Site in the Iringa Highlands, Southern Highlands Province, Tanganyika*: Musée Royal de l'Afrique Centrale.

Howell, F. C., P. Haesaerts, and J. de Heinzelin. 1987. Depositional environments, archeological occurrences, and hominids from Members E and F of the Shungura Formation (Omo basin, Ethiopia). *Journal of Human Evolution* 16:665–700.

Hromnik, C. A. 1986. A weighed view of the weighted digging stick. *South African Archaeological Bulletin* 41:90–3.

Inizan, M.-L., M. Reduron-Ballinger, H. Roche, and J. Tixier. 1999. *Technology and Terminology of Knapped Stone (translated by J. Féblot-Augustins). Préhistoire de la Pierre Taillée, Tome 5.* Meudon, FR: Cercle de Recherches et d'Etudes Préhistoriques (CNRS).

Isaac, G. L. 1977. *Olorgesailie: Archaeological Studies of a Middle Pleistocene Lake Basin in Kenya.* Chicago: The University of Chicago Press.

Isaac, G. L. 1983. "Bones in Contention: Competing Explanations for the Juxtaposition of Early Pleistocene Artefacts and Faunal Remains," in *Animals and Archaeology: Hunters and Their Prey.* Edited by J. Clutton-Brock and G. Grigson, pp. 3–19. Oxford: British Archaeological Reports International Series 163.

Isaac, G. L., and B. Isaac. Editors. 1997. *Koobi Fora Research Project Series, Volume 5: Plio-Pleistocene Archaeology.* Oxford: Clarendon.

Jenkins, K. E., S. Nightingale, J. T. Faith, D. J. Peppe, L. A. Michel, S. G. Driese, K. P. McNulty, and C. A. Tryon. 2017. Evaluating the potential for tactical hunting in the Middle Stone Age: Insights from a bonebed of the extinct bovid, *Rusingoryx atopocranion. Journal of Human Evolution* 108:72–91.

Johnson, C. R. and S. McBrearty. 2010. 500,000 year old blades from the Kapthurin Formation, Kenya. *Journal of Human Evolution* 58:193–200.

Johnson, L. L. 1978. A history of flint-knapping experimentation, 1838-1976. *Current Anthropology* 19:337–72.

Jones, P. R. 1979. Effects of raw materials on biface manufacture. *Science* 204:835–6.

Jones, P. R. 1994. "Results of Experimental Work in Relation to the Stone Industries of Olduvai Gorge," in *Olduvai Gorge, Volume 5: Excavations in Beds III, IV and the Masek Beds, 1968-1971.* Edited by M. D. Leakey and D. A. Roe, pp. 254–98. Cambridge: Cambridge University Press.

Jones, S. C. and B. Stewart. Editors. 2016. *Africa from MIS 6-2: Population Dynamics and Paleoenvironments.* New York: Springer.

Keeley, L. H. 1980. *Experimental Determination of Stone Tool Uses: A Microwear Analysis.* Chicago: University of Chicago Press.

Keeley, L. H. 1982. Hafting and retooling: Effects on the archaeological record. *American Antiquity* 47:798–809.

Keeley, L. H., and N. P. Toth. 1981. Microwear polishes on early stone tools from Koobi Fora, Kenya. *Nature* 293:464–5.

Kelly, A. 1996. "*Intra-regional and Inter-regional Variability in the East Turkana (Kenya) and Kenyan Middle Stone Age.*" PhD Dissertation, Rutgers University.

Kelly, R. L. 1992. Mobility/sedentism: Concepts, archaeological measures, and effects. *Annual Review of Anthropology* 21:43–66.

Kessy, E. T. 2013. The transition from the Later Stone Age to Iron Age in Kondoa, Central Tanzania. *African Archaeological Review* 30:225–52.

Key, A., M. R. Fisch, and M. I. Eren. 2018. Early stage blunting causes rapid reductions in stone tool performance. *Journal of Archaeological Science* 91:1–11.

Key, A. J. M. and S. J. Lycett. 2014. Are bigger flakes always better? An experimental assessment of flake size variation on cutting efficiency and loading. *Journal of Archaeological Science* 41:140–6.

Key, A. J. M. and S. J. Lycett. 2017. Influence of handaxe size and shape on cutting efficiency: A large-scale experiment and morphometric analysis. *Journal of Archaeological Method and Theory* 24:514–41.

Kibunjia, M. 1994. Pliocene archaeological occurrences in the Lake Turkana basin. *Journal of Human Evolution* 27:159–71.

Kimbel, W. H., R. C. Walter, D. C. Johanson, K. E. Reed, J. L. Aronson, Z. Assefa, C. W. Marean, G. G. Eck, R. Bobe, R. Hovers, Y. Rak, C. Vondra, T. Yemane, D. York, Y. Chen, N. M. Evensen, and S. P.E. 1996. Late Pliocene Homo and Oldowan tools from the Hadar formation (Kada Hadar Member), Ethiopia. *Journal of Human Evolution* 31:549–61.

Kingdon, J. 1993. *Self-Made Man: Human Evolution from Eden to Extinction*. New York: John Wiley.

Kingston, J. D. and A. Hill. 2005. "When It Rains It Pours: Legends and Realities of the East African Pluvials," in *Interpreting the Past: Essays on Human, Primate, and Mammal Evolution in Honor of David Pilbeam*. Edited by D. E. Lieberman, R. J. Smith, and J. Kelly, pp. 189–206. Boston, MA: Brill.

Kleindienst, M. R. 1961. Variability within the Late Acheulian Assemblage in East Africa. *South African Archaeological Bulletin* 16:35–52.

Kleindienst, M. R. 1962. "Component of the East African Acheulian Assemblage: An Analytic Approach," in *Actes du IVe Congrès Panafricain de Préhistoire et de l'Étude du Quaternaire*. Edited by G. Mortelmans and J. Nenquin, pp. 81–105. Tervuren, Belgium: Musée Royale de l'Afrique Centrale.

Kleindienst, M. 1967. "Questions of Terminology in Regard to the Study of Stone Age Industries in Eastern Africa: 'Cultural Stratigraphic Units'," in *Background to Evolution in Africa*. Edited by W. W. Bishop and J. G. D. Clark, pp. 861–78. Chicago, IL: University of Chicago Press.

Kohn, M., and S. Mithen. 1999. Handaxes: Products of sexual selection? *Antiquity* 73:518–26.

Kraybill, N. 1977. "Pre-agricultural Tools for the Preparation of Foods in the Old World," in *Origins of Agriculture*. Edited by C. Reed, pp. 485–521. The Hague: Mouton.

Kuhn, S. L. 1990. A geometrical index of reduction for unifacial stone tools. *Journal of Archaeological Science* 17:583–93.

Kuhn, S. L. 1995. *Mousterian Lithic Technology: An Ecological Perspective*. Princeton, NJ: Princeton University Press.

Kuhn, T. S. 1962. *The Structure of Scientific Revolutions*. Chicago, IL: University of Chicago Press.

Kukucka, J., S. M. Kassin, P. Zapf, and I. Dror. 2017. Cognitive bias and blindness: A global survey of forensic science examiners. *Journal of Applied Research in Memory and Cognition* 6:452–9.

Kurashina, H. 1978. "*An Examination of Prehistoric Lithic Technology in East-Central Ethiopia*," PhD thesis, University of California at Berkeley.

Kusimba, C. M. and S. Barut Kusimba. Editors. 2003. *East African Archaeology: Foragers, Potters, Smiths and Traders*. Philadelphia, PA: University of Pennsylvania Museum of Archaeology and Anthropology.

Kusimba, C. M., D. J. Killick, and R. G. Cresswell. 1994. Indigenous and imported metals at Swahili sites on the coast of Kenya. *Society, Culture, and Technology in Africa* 11:63–77

Kusimba, S. B. 2001. The early Later Stone Age in East Africa: Excavations and lithic assemblages from Lukenya Hill. *African Archaeological Review* 18:77–123.

Kusimba, S. B. 2003. *African Foragers: Environments, Technology, Interactions*. Walnut Creek, CA: Altamira Press.

Lane, P. 2013. "The Archaeology of Pastoralism and Stock-Keeping in East Africa," in *The Oxford Handbook of African Archaeology*. Edited by P. Mitchell and P. Lane, pp. 585–602. Oxford: Oxford University Press.

Larson, M. L. 1986. "*A Reconsideration of Cultural Remains from the Site of Prolonged Drift, Kenya*." Undergraduate Honors Thesis, Harvard University.

Laughlin, J. P. and R. L. Kelly. 2010. Experimental analysis of the practical limits of lithic refitting. *Journal of Archaeological Science* 37:427–33.

Leakey, L. S. B. 1931. *The Stone Age Cultures of Kenya Colony*. Cambridge: Cambridge University Press.

Leakey, L. S. B. 1936. *Stone Age Africa*. London: Oxford University Press.

Leakey, L. S. B. 1937. *White African: An Early Autobiography.* New York: Schenkman.

Leakey, L. S. B. 1960. *Adam's Ancestors* (Fourth Edition). New York: Harper and Row.

Leakey, L. 1968. Bone smashing by late Miocene Hominidae. *Nature* 218:528–30.

Leakey, L. S. B. 1977. *The Southern Kikuyu before 1903.* London: Academic Press.

Leakey, L. S. B. and S. Cole. Editors. 1952. *Proceedings of the Pan-African Congress on Prehistory, 1947.* New York: Philosophical Society.

Leakey, M. D. 1966. A Review of the Oldowan culture from Olduvai Gorge, Tanzania. *Nature* 210:462–6.

Leakey, M. D. 1967. Excavation of a burial mound at Ngorongoro Crater. *Tanzania Notes and Records* 66:123–35.

Leakey, M. D. 1971. *Olduvai Gorge: Excavations in Beds I and II, 1960-1963.* Cambridge: Cambridge University Press.

Leakey, M. D., R. L. Hay, D. L. Thurber, R. Protsch, and R. Berger. 1972. Stratigraphy, archaeology, and age of the Ndutu and Naisiusiu Beds, Olduvai Gorge, Tanzania. *World Archaeology* 3:328–41.

Leakey, M. D., L. S. B. Leakey, P. M. Game, and A. J. H. Goodwin. 1943. Report on the Excavations at Hyrax Hill, Nakuru, Kenya Colony, 1937–1938. *Transactions of the Royal Society of South Africa* 30:271–409.

Leakey, M. D., and L. S. B. Leakey. 1950. *Excavations at the Njoro River Cave: Stone Age Burials in Kenya Colony.* Oxford: Clarendon Press.

Leakey, M. D., and D. A. Roe. Editors. 1994. *Olduvai Gorge, Volume 5: Excavations in Beds III, IV and the Masek Beds, 1968-1971.* Cambridge: Cambridge University Press.

Leakey, M., P. V. Tobias, J. E. Martyn, and R. E. F. Leakey. 1969. An Acheulean industry with prepared core technique and the discovery of a contemporary hominid mandible at Lake Baringo, Kenya. *Proceedings of the Prehistoric Society* 35:48–76.

Leakey, R., and V. Morell. 2001. *Wildlife Wars: My Fight to Save Africa's Natural Treasures.* New York: St. Martin's.

Lemmonier, P. 1992. *Elements for an Anthropology of Technology*, Paper No. 88. Ann Arbor, MI: University of Michigan Museum of Anthropology.

Leplongeon, A., D. Pleurdeau, and E. Hovers. 2017. Late Pleistocene and Holocene lithic variability at Goda Buticha (Southeastern Ethiopia): Implications for the understanding of the Middle and Late Stone Age of the Horn of Africa. *Journal of African Archaeology* 15:202–33.

Lepre, C. J., H. Roche, D. V. Kent, S. Harmand, R. L. Quinn, J.-P. Brugal, P.-J. Texier, A. Lenoble, and C. S. Feibel. 2011. An earlier origin for the Acheulian. *Nature* 477:82–5.

Leroi-Gourhan, A. 1964. *Le geste et la parole.* Paris: Éditions Albin Michel.

Levi-Sala, I. 1996. *A Study of Microscopic Polish on Flint Implements,* British Archaeological Reports International Series No. 629. Oxford: Archaeopress .

Liebenberg, L. 1990. *The Art of Tracking: The Origin of Science.* Cape Town, SA: David Phillip Publishers.

Lieberman, P. 2015. Language did not spring forth 100,000 years ago. *PLOS Biology* 13: e10002064.

Lieberman, P. and R. C. McCarthy. 2014. "The Evolution of Speech and Language," in *Handbook of Paleoanthropology.* Edited by W. Henke and I. Tattersall, pp. 1–33. Berlin: Springer.

Lin, S., Z. Rezek, D. Braun, and H. Dibble. 2013. On the utility and economization of unretouched flakes: The effects of exterior platform angle and platform depth. *American Antiquity* 78:724–45.

Loftus, E. 1996. *Eyewitness Testimony.* Cambridge, MA: Harvard University Press.

Luedtke, B. E. 1979. The identification of sources of Chert artifacts. *American Antiquity* 44:744–9.

Luedtke, B. E. 1992. *An Archaeologist's Guide to Flint and Chert.* Vol. 7. Archaeological Research Tools. Los Angeles: University of California at Los Angeles Press.

Marean, C. W. 2015. An evolutionary anthropological perspective on modern human origins. *Annual Review of Anthropology* 44:533–56.

Marks, A. and N. Conard. 2008. "Technology vs. Typology: The Case For and Against a Transition from the MSA to the LSA at Mumba Cave, Tanzania," in *Space and Time: Which Diachronies, Which Synchronies, Which Scales? Typology vs Technology.* Edited by T. Aubry, F. Almeida, A.C. Araújo, and M. Tiffagom, pp. 123–31. Oxford: Archaeopress.

Marshall, F. and E. Hildebrand. 2002. Cattle before crops: The beginnings of food production in africa. *Journal of World Prehistory* 16:99–143.

Marzke, M. W. 2013. Tool making, hand morphology and fossil hominins. *Philosophical Transactions of the Royal Society B: Biological Sciences* 368.

Marzke, M. W., and K. L. Wullstein. 1996. Chimpanzee and human grips: A new classification with a focus on evolutionary morphology. *International Journal of Primatology* 17:117–39.

Masao, F. 1979. *The Later Stone Age and the Rock Paintings of Central Tanzania Studien zur Kulturkunde.* Frankfurt, Germany: Steiner.

Maslin, M. 2017. *The Cradle of Humanity: How the Changing Landscape of Africa Made Us So Smart.* Oxford: Oxford University Press.

Mason, R. 1962. *The Prehistory of the Transvaal.* Johannesburg: University of Witwatersrand Press.

McBrearty, S. 1981a. The Sangoan-Lupemban sequence at the Muguruk Site, Western Kenya. *World Archaeology* 19:388–420.

McBrearty, S. 1981b. Songhor: a Middle Stone Age site in Western Kenya. *Quaternaria* 23:171–90.

McBrearty, S. 1992. Sangoan technology and habitat at Simbi, Kenya. *Nyame Akuma* 38:34–9.

McBrearty, S. 2005. "The Kapthurin Formation: What We Know Now that We Didn't Know Then," in *Interpreting the Past: Essays on Human, Primate, and Mammal Evolution in Honor of David Pilbeam.* Edited by D. E. Lieberman, R. J. Smith, and J. Kelly, pp. 263–74. Boston: Brill.

McBrearty, S., and A. S. Brooks. 2000. The revolution that wasn't: A new interpretation of the origin of modern human behavior. *Journal of Human Evolution* 39:453–563.

McBurney, C. B. M. 1960. *The Stone Age of Northern Africa.* London: Penguin.

McCall, G. 2012. Ethnoarchaeology and the organization of lithic technology. *Journal of Archaeological Research* 20:157–203.

McGrew, W. C. 1992. *Chimpanzee Material Culture: Implications for Human Evolution.* Cambridge: Cambridge University Press.

McKenna, A. Editor. 2011. *The History of Central and Eastern Africa (Britannica Guide to Africa).* New York: Rosen Education Service

McPherron, S. 2006. "What Typology Can Tell Us about Acheulian Handaxe Production," in *Axe Age: Acheulian Toolmaking from Quarry to Discard.* Edited by N. Goren-Inbar and G. Sharon, pp. 267–86. London: Equinox.

McPherron, S. Editor. 2007. *Tools versus Cores: Alternative Approaches to Stone Tool Analysis.* Newcastle: Cambridge Scholars Publishing.

McPherron, S., Z. Alemseged, C. W. Marean, J. G. Wynn, D. Reed, D. Geraads, R. Bobé, and H. Béarat. 2010. Evidence for stone tool-assisted consumption of animal tissues before 3.39 million years ago at Dikika, Ethiopia. *Nature* 466:857–60.

Mehlman, M. J. 1989. "Later Quaternary Archaeological Sequences in Northern Tanzania." PhD dissertation, University of Illinois.

Mellars, P. A. 1989. "Technological Changes at the Middle-Upper Palaeolithic Transition: Economic, Social, and Cognitive Perspectives," in *The Human Revolution: Behavioural and Biological Perspectives on the Origins of Modern Humans.* Edited by P. Mellars and C. Stringer, pp. 338–65. Edinburgh: Edinburgh University Press.

Ménard, C. 2015. "*Ruptures et continuités dans le Late Stone Age de la Corne de l'Afrique : apports des industries lithiques du Rift éthiopien.*" PhD dissertation, Université de Toulouse, France.

Ménard, C., F. Bon, A. Dessie, L. Bruxelles, K. Douze, F.-X. Fauvelle, L. Khalidi, J. Lesur, and R. Mensan. 2014. Late Stone Age variability in the Main Ethiopian Rift: New data from the Bulbula River, Ziway–Shala basin. *Quaternary International* 343:53–68.

Mercader, J., H. Barton, J. Gillespie, J. Harris, S. Kuhn, R. Tyler, and C. Boesch. 2007. 4,300-Year-old chimpanzee sites and the origins of percussive stone technology. *Proceedings of the National Academy of Sciences* 104:3043–8.

Mercader, J. and A. S. Brooks. 2001. Across forests and savannas: Later Stone Age assemblages from Ituri and Semliki, Democratic Republic of Congo. *Journal of Anthropological Research* 57:197–217.

Merrick, H. V. 1975. "*Change in Later Pleistocene Lithic Industries in Eastern Africa.*" PhD Dissertation, University of California at Berkeley.

Merrick, H. V., and F. Brown. 1984. Obsidian source and patterns fo source utilization in Kenya and northern Tanzania. *African Archaeological Review* 2:129–52.

Merrick, H. V. and J. P. S. Merrick. 1976. "Archaeological Occurrences of Earlier Pleistocene Age from the Shungura Formation," in *Earliest Man and Environments in the Lake Rudolf Basin: Stratigraphy, Paleoecology, and Evolution.* Edited by Y. Coppens, F. C. Howell, G. L. Isaac, and R. E. F. Leakey, pp. 574–84. Chicago, IL: University of Chicago Press.

Miller, S. E. F. 1969. "*The Nachikufan Industries of the Later Stone Age in Zambia.*" PhD Dissertation, University of California at Berkeley.

Mills, B. J. and S. Fowles. Editors. 2017. *The Oxford Handbook of Southwestern Archaeology.* New York: Oxford University Press.

Mitchell, P. 2002. *The Archaeology of Southern Africa.* Cambridge: Cambridge University Press.

Mitchell, P. and P. Lane. Editors. 2013. *The Oxford Handbook of African Archaeology.* Oxford,: Oxford University Press.

Monnier, G. F., J. L. Ladwig, and S. T. Porter. 2012. Swept under the rug: The problem of unacknowledged ambiguity in lithic residue identification. *Journal of Archaeological Science* 39:3284–300.

National Audobon Society 1979. *National Audubon Society Field Guide to Rocks and Minerals: North America.* New York: Knopf.

Ndiema, E., C. Dillian, and D. Braun. 2010. "Interaction and Exchange across the Transition to Pastoralism, Lake Turkana, Kenya," in *Trade and Exchange: Archaeological Studies from Prehistory and History.* Edited by C. Dillian and C. White, pp. 95–110. New York: Springer

Nelson, C. M. 1973. "*A Comparative Analysis of 29 Later Stone Age Occurrences from East Africa.*" PhD Dissertation, University of California at Berkeley.

Nelson, C. 1993. A standardized site enumeration system for the continent of Africa. *Nyame Akuma* 40:62–7.

Nelson, C. M. and M. Posnansky. 1970. The stone tools from the re-excavation of Nsongezi Rock Shelter, Uganda. *Azania: Archaeological Research in Africa* 5:119–72.

Newcomer, M. H. and F. Hivernell-Guerre. 1974. Nucleus sur éclat: Technologie et utilisation par différentes cultures préhistoriques. *Bulletin de la Société Préhistorique Française* 71:119–28.

Noten, V. 1982. *The Archaeology of Central Afridca* Graz: Akademische Druk – u Verlagsanstalt.

Nowell, A. 2010. Defining behavioral modernity in the context of Neandertal and anatomically modern human populations. *Annual Review of Anthropology* 39:437–52.

Nowell, A., C. Walker, C. E. Cordova, C. J. H. Ames, J. T. Pokines, D. Stueber, R. DeWitt, and A. S. A. al-Souliman. 2016. Middle Pleistocene subsistence in the Azraq Oasis, Jordan: Protein residue and other proxies. *Journal of Archaeological Science* 73:36–44.

O'Brien, T. P. 1939. *The Prehistory of the Uganda Protectorate.* Cambridge: Cambridge University Press.

Odell, G. H. 1981. The morphological express at function junction: Searching for meaning in lithic tool types. *Journal of Anthropological Research* 37:319–42.

Odell, G. H. 2004. *Lithic Analysis.* New York: Kluwer.

Odner, K. 1972. Excavations at Narosura, a stone bowl site in the southern Kenya highlands. *Azania* 7:24–92.

Odney-Obul, B. 1996. "Unstandardised Stone Tool Assemblages in the Context of Pastoral Neolithic Technological Variation in the Central Rift Valley, Kenya," in *Aspects of African Archaeology: Papers from the 10th Congress of the PanAfrican Association for Prehistory and Related Studies.* Edited by G. Pwiti and R. Soper, pp. 281–90. Harare, Zimbabwe: University of Zimbabwe.

Oliver, R. A. 1975. *Africa in the Iron Age, c. 500 B.C. to A.D. 1400.* New York: Cambridge University Press.

Omi, G. Editor. 1988. *An Interim Report of the East and Northeast African Prehistory Research Project −1986: Mtongwe and Mgonga.* Matsumoto, Japan: Shinshu University.

Orton, J. 2008. Later Stone Age ostrich eggshell bead manufacture in the Northern Cape, South Africa. *Journal of Archaeological Science* 35:1765–75.

Panger, M., A. S. Brooks, B. G. Richmond, and B. Wood. 2003. Older than the Oldowan? Rethinking the emergence of hominin tool use. *Evolutionary Anthropology* 11:226–34.

Pargeter, J. 2016. Lithic miniaturization in Late Pleistocene southern Africa. *Journal of Archaeological Science: Reports* 10:221–36.

Pargeter, J., and M. Eren. 2017. Quantifying and comparing bipolar versus freehand flake morphologies, production currencies, and reduction energetics during lithic miniaturization. *Lithic Technology.* https://doi.org/10.1080/01977261.2017.1345442

Pargeter, J. A. and J. J. Shea. 2019. Going big vs. going small: Lithic miniaturization in hominin lithic technology. *Evolutionary Anthropology* 28:1–14.

Patten, B. 2009. *Old Tools–New Eyes: A Primal Primer of Flintknapping*, Second Edition. Denver, CO: Stone Dagger Publications.

Patterson, L. W. 1983. Criteria for determining the attributes of man-made lithics. *Journal of Field Archaeology* 10:296–307.

Phillipson, D. W. 1976. *The Prehistory of Eastern Zambia*. Nairobi: British Institute in Eastern Africa.

Phillipson, D. W. 1977a. The excavation of Gobedra Rock-shelter, Axum: An early occurrence of cultivated finger millet in Northern Ethiopia. *Azania: Archaeological Research in Africa* 12:53–82.

Phillipson, D. W. 1977b. *The Later Prehistory of Eastern and Southern Africa*. London: Heinemann.

Phillipson, D. W. 1977c. Lowasera. *Azania* 7:1–32.l

Phillipson, D. W. 2005. *African Archaeology*, Third edition. Cambridge: Cambridge University Press.

Phillipson, D. and D. Gifford. 1981. Kulchurdo rock shelter and the Stone Age of Mount Marsabit. *Azania: Archaeological Research in Africa* 16:164–74.

Phillipson, D. W., J. S. Phillips, and A. Tarekegn. 2000. *Archaeology at Aksum, Ethiopia, 1993-7*. Nairobi, Kenya: British Institute in Eastern Africa.

Phillipson, L. 2009. *Using Stone Tools: The Evidence from Aksum, Ethiopia. Cambridge Monographs in African Archaeology 77.* Oxford: Archaeopress.

Phillipson, L. 2013. Lithic tools used in the manufacture of pre-Aksumite ceramics. *Azania: Archaeological Research in Africa* 48:380–402.

Phillipson, L. 2017. Lithic evidence for the peopling of northern Ethiopia. *African Archaeological Review* 34:177–91.

Phillipson, L., and F. Sulas. 2005. Cultural continuity in Aksumite lithic tool production: The evidence from Mai Agam. *Azania: Archaeological Research in Africa* 40:1–18.

Pickford, M. 1986. Did Kenyapithecus utilise stones? *Folia Primatologica* 47:1–7.

Pleurdeau, D. 2005. Human technical behavior in the African Middle Stone Age: The lithic assemblage of Porc-Epic Cave (Dire-Dawa, Ethiopia). *African Archaeological Review* 22:177–97.

Plummer, T., L. C. Bishop, P. Ditchfield, and J. Hicks. 1999. Research on Late Pliocene Oldowan sites at Kanjera South, Kenya. *Journal of Human Evolution* 36:151–70.

Potts, R. 1988. *Early Hominid Activities at Olduvai*. New York: Aldine de Gruyter.

Potts, R., A. K. Behrensmeyer, and P. Ditchfield. 1999. Paleolandscape variation and Early Pleistocene hominid activities: Members 1 and 7, Olorgesailie Formation, Kenya. *Journal of Human Evolution* 37:747–88.

Potts, R., A. K. Behrensmeyer, J. T. Faith, C. A. Tryon, A. S. Brooks, J. E. Yellen, A. L. Deino, R. Kinyanjui, J. B. Clark, C. M. Haradon, N. E. Levin, H. J. M. Meijer, E. G. Veatch, R. B. Owen, and R. W. Renaut. 2018. Environmental dynamics during the onset of the Middle Stone Age in eastern Africa. *Science* 360:86.

Prinz, M., G. E. Harlow, and J. Peters. Editors. 1978. *Simon and Schuster's Guide to Rocks and Minerals*. New York: Simon and Schuster.

Ranhorn, K. L., Justin A. Pargeter, Luke S. Premo, and PaST Collaborators. 2020. Investigating the evolution of human social learning through collaborative experimental archaeology. *Evolutionary Anthropology* 29.

Riede, F., N. N. Johannsen, A. Högberg, A. Nowell, and M. Lombard. 2018. The role of play objects and object play in human cognitive evolution and innovation. *Evolutionary Anthropology: Issues, News, and Reviews* 27:46–59.

Robbins, L. H. 1974. *The Lothagam Site: A Late Stone Age Fishing Settlement in the Lake Rudolf Basin, Kenya*. East Lansing, MI: Michigan State University Museum Anthropological Series.

Robbins, L. H. 1980. *Lopoy: A Late Stone Age Fishing and Pastoralist Settlement in the Lake Turkana Basin, Kenya*. East Lansing, MI: Michigan State University Museum Anthropological Series 3(1).

Robbins, L. H., S. A. McFarlin, J. L. Brower, and A. E. Hoffman. 1977. Rangi: A Late Stone Age site in Karamoja District, Uganda. *Azania: Archaeological Research in Africa* 12:209–33.

Robertshaw, P. 1990a. "The Development of Archaeology in Eastern Africa," in *A History of African Archaeology*. Edited by P. Robertshaw, pp. 78–94. Oxford: James Currey.

Robertshaw, P. 1990b. *Early Pastoralists of South-Western Kenya. Memoirs of the British Institute in*

Eastern Africa. Nairobi, Kenya: British Institute in Eastern Africa.

Robertshaw, P. 1991. Gogo Falls: Excavations at a complex archaeological site east of Lake Victoria. *Azania: Archaeological Research in Africa* 26:63–195.

Robertshaw, P. 1995. The last 200,000 years (or thereabouts) in Eastern Africa: Recent archaeological research. *Journal of Archaeological Research* 3:55–86.

Roche, H., J.-P. Brugal, D. Lefevre, S. Ploux, and P.-J. Texier. 1988. Isenya: état des recherches sur un nouveau site acheuléen d'Afrique orientale. *African Archaeological Review* 6:27–55.

Roche, H., J.-P. Brugal, A. Delagnes, C. Feibel, S. Harmand, M. Kibunjia, S. Prat, and P.-J. Texier. 2003. Les sites archeologiques plio-pleistocenes de la formation de Nachukui, Ouest-Turkana, Kenya: bilan synthetique 1997-2001. *Comptes Rendus Palevol* 2:663–73.

Roche, H., I. de la Torre, A. Arroyo, J.-P. Brugal, and S. Harmand. 2018. Naiyena Engol 2 (West Turkana, Kenya): A case study on variability in the Oldowan. *African Archaeological Review* 35:57–85.

Roe, D. A. 1994. "A Metrical Analysis of Selected Sets of Handaxes and Cleavers from Olduvai Gorge," in *Olduvai Gorge, Volume 5: Excavations in Beds III, IV and the Masek Beds, 1968-1971*. Edited by M. D. Leakey and D. A. Roe. Cambridge: Cambridge University Press.

Rolland, N. 1981. The interpretation of Middle Paleolithic variability. *Man* 16:15–42.

Rollefson, G. 1994. Protocols of the first workshop on PPN chiped lithics industries, Berlin, 29 March–2 April 1993. *Neo-Lithics* 1:1–5.

Rosen, S. A. 1996. "The Decline and Fall of Flint," in *Stone Tools: Theoretical Insights into Human Prehistory*. Edited by G. H. Odell, pp. 129–58. New York: Plenum.

Rosen, S. A. 1997. *Lithics after the Stone Age: a Handbook of Stone Tools from the Levant*. Walnut Creek, CA.: Altamira Press.

Rosenberg, D. 2010. Early maceheads in the Southern Levant: A "Chalcolithic" hallmark in Neolithic context. *Journal of Field Archaeology* 35:204–16.

Rots, V. 2003. Towards an understanding of hafting: The macro- and microscopic evidence. *Antiquity* 77:805–15.

Rots, V., B. L. Hardy, J. Serangeli, and N. J. Conard. 2015. Residue and microwear analyses of the stone artifacts from Schöningen. *Journal of Human Evolution* 89:298–308.

Sackett, J. 1982. Approaches to style in lithic archaeology. *Journal of Anthropological Archaeology* 1:59–112.

Sahle, Y., L. E. Morgan, D. R. Braun, B. Atnafu, and W. K. Hutchings. 2014. Chronological and behavioral contexts of the earliest Middle Stone Age in the Gademotta Formation, Main Ethiopian Rift. *Quaternary International* 331:6–19.

Sahle, Y., A. Nagash, and Braun. 2012. Variability in ethnographic hidescraper use among the Hadiya of Ethiopia: Implications for reduction analysis. *African Archaeological Review* 29:383–97.

Sahnouni, M., S. Semaw, and M. Rogers. 2013. "The African Acheulean: An Archaeological Summary," in *The Oxford Handbook of African Archaeology*. Edited by P. Mitchell and P. Lane, pp. 307–24. Oxford: Oxford University Press.

Sandgathe, D. M. 2004. Alternative interpretations of the Levallois reduction technique. *Lithic Technology* 29:147–59.

Sassoon, H. 1968. Excavation of a burial mound at Ngorongoro Crater. *Tanzania Notes and* 582_94

Scerri, E. M. L., M. G. Thomas, A. Manica, P. Gunz, J. T. Stock, C. Stringer, M. Grove, H. S. Groucutt, A. Timmermann, G. P. Rightmire, F. d'Errico, C. A. Tryon, N. A. Drake, A. S. Brooks, R. W. Dennell, R. Durbin, B. M. Henn, J. Lee-Thorp, P. deMenocal, M. D. Petraglia, J. C. Thompson, A. Scally, and L. Chikhi. 2018. Did our species evolve in subdivided populations across Africa, and why does it matter? *Trends in Ecology & Evolution* 33: 582–94.

Schick, K. D. 1986. *Stone Age Sites in the Making: Experiments in the Formation and Transformation of Archaeological Occurrences*. Oxford, UK: British Archaeological Reports International Series 314.

Schick, K. D., and N. P. Toth. 1993. *Making Silent Stones Speak: Human Evolution and the Dawn of Technology*. New York: Simon and Schuster.

Schick, K. D., and N. Toth. 1994. "Early Stone Age Technology in Africa: A Review and Case Study into the Nature and Function of Spheroids and Subspheroids," in *Integrative Paths to the Past: Paleoanthropological Advances in Honor of F. Clark Howell.* Edited by S. C. Robert and R. L. Ciochon, pp. 429–49. Englewood Cliffs, NJ: Prentice-Hall.

Schick, K., and N. Toth. 2017. Acheulean industries of the Early and Middle Pleistocene, Middle Awash, Ethiopia. *L'Anthropologie* 121:451–91.

Schiffer, M. B. and J. M. Skibo. 1997. The explanation of artifact variability. *American Antiquity* 62:51–85.

Schlüter, T. 1997. *Geology of East Africa.* Stuttgart, Germany: Schweizerbart Science Publishers.

Scholz, C. A., T. C. Johnson, A. S. Cohen, J. W. King, J. A. Peck, J. T. Overpeck, M. R. Talbot, E. T. Brown, L. Kalindekafe, P. Y. O. Amoako, R. P. Lyons, T. M. Shanahan, I. S. Castaneda, C. W. Heil, S. L. Forman, L. R. McHargue, K. R. Beuning, J. Gomez, and J. Pierson. 2007. East African megadroughts between 135 and 75 thousand years ago and bearing on early-modern human origins. *Proceedings of the National Academy of Sciences* 104:16416–21.

Seitsonen, O. 2010. Lithics use at Kansyore sites in East Africa: Technological organisation at four recently excavated sites in Nyanza Province, Kenya. *Azania: Archaeological Research in Africa* 45:49–82.

Sellet, F. 1993. *Châine opératoire*: The concept and its applications. *Lithic Technology* 18:106–12.

Semaw, S., M. J. Rogers, and D. Stout. 2009. "Insights into Late Pliocene Lithic Assemblage Variability: The East Gona and Ounda Gona South Oldowan Archaeology (2.6 Million years Ago) Afar, Ethiopia," in *The Cutting Edge: New Approaches to the Archaeology of Human Origins.* Edited by K. Schick and N. Toth, pp. 211–46. Gosport, IN: Stone Age Institute Press.

Semenov, S. A. 1964. *Prehistoric Technology.* London: Corey Adams Mackay.

Shackley, M. S. Editor. 2011. *X-Ray Fluorescence Spectrometry (XRF) in Geoarchaeology.* New York: Springer.

Sharon, G. 2010. Large Flake Acheulian. *Quaternary International* 223–4:226–33.

Sharon, G., and P. Beaumont. 2006. "Victoria West: A Highly Standardized Prepared Core Technology," in *Axe Age: Acheulian Tool-Making from Quarry to Discard.* Edited by N. Goren-Inbar and G. Sharon, pp. 181–99. London: Equinox.

Shea, J. J. 2006. Child's play: Reflections on the invisibility of children in the paleolithic record. *Evolutionary Anthropology* 15:212–16.

Shea, J. J. 2008. The Middle Stone Age archaeology of the Lower Omo Valley Kibish Formation: Excavations, lithic assemblages, and inferred patterns of early *Homo sapiens* behavior. *Journal of Human Evolution, Special Issue: Paleoanthropology of the Kibish Formation, Southern Ethiopia)* 55:448–85.

Shea, J. J. 2010. "Stone Age Visiting Cards Revisited: A Strategic Perspective on the Lithic Technology of Early Hominin Dispersal," in *Out of Africa 1: The First Hominin Colonization of Eurasia.* Edited by J. G. Fleagle, J. J. Shea, F. E. Grine, A. L. Baden, and R. Leakey, pp. 47–64. New York: Springer.

Shea, J. J. 2011a. *Homo sapiens* is as *Homo sapiens* was: Behavioral variability vs. "behavioral modernity" in Paleolithic archaeology. *Current Anthropology* 52:1–35.

Shea, J. J. 2011b. Stone tool analysis and human evolution: Some advice from Uncle Screwtape. *Evolutionary Anthropology* 20:48–53.

Shea, J. J. 2013a. Lithic Modes A-I: A new framework for describing global-scale variation in stone tool technology illustrated with evidence from the East Mediterranean Levant. *Journal of Archaeological Method and Theory* 20:151–86.

Shea, J. J. 2013b. *Stone Tools in the Paleolithic and Neolithic of the Near East: A Guide.* New York: Cambridge University Press.

Shea, J. J. 2015. Making and using stone tools: Advice for learners and teachers and insights for archaeologists. *Lithic Technology* 40:231–48.

Shea, J. J. 2017a. Occasional, obligatory, and habitual stone tool use in hominin evolution. *Evolutionary Anthropology* 26:200–17.

Shea, J. J. 2017b. *Stone Tools in Human Evolution: Behavioral Differences among Technological Primates.* New York: Cambridge University Press.

Shea, J. J., and J. D. Klenck. 1993. An experimental investigation of the effects of trampling on the results of lithic microwear analysis. *Journal of Archaeological Science* 20:175–94.

Shipman, P. 1983. "Early Hominid Lifestyle: Hunting and Gathering or Foraging, and Scavenging?," in *Animals and Archaeology. Volume 1. Hunters and Their Prey.* Edited by J. Clutton-Brock and C. Grigson, pp. 31–49. Oxford: BAR International Series 163.

Shipton, C. 2011. Taphonomy and behaviour at the Acheulean site of Kariandusi, Kenya. *African Archaeological Review* 28:141.

Shipton, C., A. Crowther, N. Kourampas, M. E. Prendergast, M. Horton, K. Douka, J.-L. Schwenninger, P. Faulkner, E. M. Quintana Morales, M. C. Langley, R. Tibesasa, L. Picornell-Gelabert, E. N. Wilmsen, C. Doherty, M.-A. Veall, A. K. Ali, M. D. Petraglia, and N. Boivin. 2016. Reinvestigation of Kuumbi Cave, Zanzibar, reveals Later Stone Age coastal habitation, early Holocene abandonment and Iron Age reoccupation. *Azania: Archaeological Research in Africa* 51:197–233.

Shipton, C., P. Roberts, W. Archer, S. J. Armitage, C. Bita, J. Blinkhorn, C. Courtney-Mustaphi, A. Crowther, R. Curtis, F. d' Errico, K. Douka, P. Faulkner, H. S. Groucutt, R. Helm, A. I. R Herries, S. Jembe, N. Kourampas, J. Lee-Thorp, R. Marchant, J. Mercader, A. Pitarch Marti, M. E. Prendergast, B. Rowson, A. Tengeza, R. Tibesasa, T. S. White, M. D. Petraglia, N. Boivin. 2018. 78,000-year-old record of Middle and Later stone age innovation in an East African tropical forest. *Nature Communications* 9. doi: 10.1038/s41467-018-04057-3.

Shoemaker, A. C., M. I. J. Davies, and H. L. Moore. 2017. Back to the grindstone? The archaeological potential of grinding-stone studies in Africa with reference to contemporary grinding practices in Marakwet, Northwest Kenya. *African Archaeological Review* 34:415–35.

Shott, M. J. 1996. An exegesis of the curation concept. *Journal of Anthropological Research* 52:259–80.

Shott, M. J. 2003. *Chaîne opératoire* and reduction sequence. *Lithic Technology* 28:95–105.

Siiriäinen, A. 1984. *Excavations in Laikipia: An Archaeological Study of the Recent Prehistory in the Eastern Highlands of Kenya Suomen Muinaismuistoyhdistyksen Aikakauskirja, 86.* Helsinki, Finland: Vammalan kirjapaino.

Sinclair, P. J. J., A. Juma, and F. Chami. 2006. "Excavations in Kuumbi Cave on Zanzibar in 2005," in *The African Archaeology Network: Research in Progress.* Edited by J. Kinahan and J. H. A. Kinahan, pp. 95–106. Dar es Salaam: Dar es Salaam University Press.

Sisk, M. L. and J. J. Shea. 2008. Intrasite spatial variation of the Omo Kibish Middle Stone Age assemblages: Artifact refitting and distribution patterns. *Journal of Human Evolution* 55:486–500.

Sisk, M. L. and J. J. Shea. 2009. Experimental use and quantitative performance analysis of triangular flakes (Levallois points) used as arrowheads. *Journal of Archaeological Science* 36:2039–47.

Skertchly, S. B. J. 1879. *On the Manufacture of Gun-Flints, the Methods of Excavating for Flint, the Age of Palaeolithic Man, and the Connection Between Neolithic Art and the Gun-Flint Trade. Memoirs of the Geological Survey.* London: Royal Stationery Office.

Soriano, S., P. Villa, and L. Wadley. 2007. Blade technology and tool forms in the Middle Stone Age of South Africa: the Howiesons Poort and post Howiesons Poort at Rose Cottage Cave. *Journal of Archaeological Science* 34:681–703.

Stahl, A. B. Editor. 2005. *African Archaeology: A Critical Introduction.* Oxford: Blackwell.

Sullivan, A. P., III and K. C. Rozen. 1985. Debitage analysis and archaeological interpretation. *American Antiquity* 50:755–79.

Sutton, J. E. G. 1973. *The Archaeology of the Western Highlands of Kenya. Memoirs of the British Institute in Eastern Africa.* Nairobi, Kenya: British Institute in Eastern Africa.

Sutton, J. 1998. Hyrax Hill and the later archaeology of the Central Rift Valley of Kenya. *Azania* 33:73–112.

Sutton, J. E. G. 2006. Denying history in colonial Kenya: The anthropology and archeology of G.W.B. Huntingford and L.S.B. Leakey. *History in Africa* 33: 287–320.

Taylor, N. 2016. "Across Woodlands and Rainforests: A Systematic Re-appraisal of the Lupemban Middle Stone Age in Central Africa," in *Africa from MIS 6-2: Population Dynamics and Paleoenvironments.* Edited by S. Jones and B. Stewart, pp. 273–99. Dordrecht: Springer.

Teka, Z. and D. Okubatsion. 2008. "Lithic Artifacts from Archaeological Sites in the Greater Asmara Area," in *The Archaeology of Ancient Eritrea.* Edited by P. Schmidt, M. C. Curtis, and Z. Teka, pp. 189–206. Trenton, NJ: Red Sea Press.

Tennie, C., L. S. Premo, D. R. Braun, and S. P. McPherron. 2017. Early stone tools and cultural transmission: Resetting the null hypothesis. *Current Anthropology* 58:652–72.

Texier, P. J. 1995. The Oldowan assemblage from NY 18 site at Nyabusosi (Toro-Uganda).

Comptes Rendus de l'Academie des Sciences Paris II 320:647–53.

Thomas, D. H. 1986. Points on points: A reply to Flenniken and Raymond. *American Antiquity* 51:619–27.

Tixier, J. 1963. *Typologie de l'epipaleolithique du Maghreb*. Paris: Arts et Metiers Graphiques.

Tostevin, G. B. 2012. *Seeing Lithics: A Middle-Range Theory for Testing for Cultural Transmission in the Pleistocene. American School of Prehistoric Research Publications, Peabody Museum, Harvard University.* Oakville, CT: Oxbow.

Toth, N., J. D. Clark, and G. Ligabue. 1992. The last stone axe makers. *Scientific American* 263:88–93.

Toth, N., K. D. Schick, E. S. Savage-Rumbaugh, R. Sevcik, and D. Rumbaugh. 1993. Pan the tool-maker: Investigations into the stone tool-making and tool-using abilities of a bonobo (*Pan paniscus*). *Journal of Archaeological Science* 20:81–91.

Trauth, M. H., M. A. Maslin, A. L. Deino, M. R. Strecker, A. G. N. Bergner, and M. Dünforth. 2007. High- and low-latitude forcing of Plio-Pleistocene East African climate and human evolution. *Journal of Human Evolution (Special Issue: African Paleoclimate and Human Evolution)* 53:475–86.

Trauth, M. H., M. A. Maslin, A. L. Deino, A. Junginger, M. Lesoloyia, E. O. Odada, D. O. Olago, L. A. Olaka, M. R. Strecker, and R. Tiedemann. 2010. Human evolution in a variable environment: The amplifier lakes of Eastern Africa. *Quaternary Science Reviews* 29:2981–8.

Trigger, B. G. 2006. *A History of Archaeological Thought*, Second Edition. Cambridge: Cambridge University Press.

Tryon, C. A. 2019. The Middle/Later Stone Age transition and cultural dynamics of late Pleistocene East Africa. *Evolutionary Anthropology* 28(5):267–282.

Tryon, C. A., I. Crevecoeur, J. T. Faith, R. Ekshtain, J. Nivens, D. Patterson, E. N. Mbua, and F. Spoor. 2015. Late Pleistocene age and archaeological context for the hominin calvaria from GvJm-22 (Lukenya Hill, Kenya). *Proceedings of the National Academy of Sciences*.

Tryon, C. A., and J. T. Faith. 2013. Variability in the Middle Stone Age of Eastern Africa. *Current Anthropology* 54:S234–S254.

Tryon, C. A., and J. T. Faith. 2016. A demographic perspective on the Middle to Later Stone Age transition from Nasera rockshelter, Tanzania. *Philosophical Transactions of the Royal Society B: Biological Sciences* 371. DOI:10.1098/rstb.2015.0238.

Tryon, C., J. Lewis, K. Ranhorn, A. Kwekason, B. Alex, M. Laird, C. Marean, E. Niespolo, J. Nivens, and A. Mabulla. 2018. Middle and Later Stone Age chronology of Kisese II Rockshelter (UNESCO World Heritage Kondoa Rock-Art Sites), Tanzania. *PLOS ONE* 13:e0192029.

Tryon, C. A., S. McBrearty, and P.-J. Texier. 2005. Levallois lithic technology from the Kapthurin Formation, Kenya: Acheulian origin and Middle Stone Age diversity. *African Archaeological Review* 22:199–229.

Usik, V. I., J. I. Rose, Y. H. Hilbert, P. Van Peer, and A. E. Marks. 2013. Nubian complex reduction strategies in Dhofar, southern Oman. *Quaternary International* 300:244–66.

Van Noten, F. 1977. Excavations at Matupi cave. *Antiquity* 51:35–40.

Van Peer, P. 1991. Interassemblage variability and Levallois styles: The case of the North African Middle Paleolithic. *Journal of Anthropological Archaeology* 10:107–51.

Van Perlo, B. 2009. *Birds of Eastern Africa (Collins Field Guide)*. London: HarperCollins.

Villa, P. 1983. *Terra Amata and the Middle Pleistocene Archaeological Record of Southern France*. Berkeley, CA: University of California Press.

Vrba, E. S. 1988. "Late Pliocene Climatic Events and Hominid Evolution," in *Evolutionary History of the "Robust" Australopithecines*. Edited by F. E. Grine, pp. 405–26. New York: Aldine de Gruyter.

Waldron, S. R. 1987. Weighted digging sticks in Ethiopia. *South African Archaeological Bulletin* 42:69–71.

Waweru, V. 2002. New excavations at the Middle Stone Age Cartwright's Site, Kenya. *Nyame Akuma* 58:26–33.

Waweru, V. 2007. "*Middle Stone Age Technology of the Cartwright's Site, Kenya.*" PhD Dissertation, University of Connecticut.

Wayland, E. 1924. Palaeolithic types of implements in relation to the Pleistocene deposits of Uganda. *Proceedings of the Prehistoric Society of East Anglia* 4:96–112.

Wayland, E. 1929. African pluvial periods. *Nature* 123:607.

Weedman, K. 2006. An ethnoarchaeological study of hafting and stone tool diversity among the Gamo of Ethiopia. *Journal of Archaeological Method and Theory* 13:188–237.

Weedman Arthur, K. 2010. Feminine knowledge and skill reconsidered: Women and flaked stone tools. *American Anthropologist* 112:228–43.

Weedman Arthur, K. 2018. *The Lives of Stone Tools: Crafting the Status, Skill, and Identity of Flintknappers*. Tucson, AZ: University of Arizona Press.

Wendorf, F. and R. Schild. 1974. *A Middle Stone Age Sequence from the Central Rift Valley, Ethiopia*. Warsaw: Polska Akademia Nauk.

Werdelin, L. and W. J. Sanders. Editors. 2010. *Cenozoic Mammals of Africa*. Berkeley, CA: University of California Press.

Werner, J. J. and P. R. Willoughby. 2017. Middle Stone Age technology and cultural evolution at Magubike Rockshelter, Southern Tanzania. *African Archaeological Review* 34:249–73.

White, T. D. 2000. A view on the science: Physical anthropology at the millennium. *American Journal of Physical Anthropology* 113:287–92.

Whittaker, J. C. 1994. *Flintknapping: Making and Understanding Stone Tools*. Austin, TX: University of Texas Press.

Whittaker, J. C. 2004. *American Flintknappers: Stone Age Art in the Age of Computers*. Austin: University of Texas Press.

Wilkins, J. and M. Chazan. 2012. Blade production~ 500 thousand years ago at Kathu Pan 1, South Africa: Support for a multiple origins hypothesis for early Middle Pleistocene blade technologies. *Journal of Archaeological Science* 39:1883–900.

Will, M., A. Mackay and N. Phillips. 2015. Implications of Nubian-like core reduction systems in southern Africa for the identification of early modern human dispersals. *PLoS ONE* 10:e0131824.

Will, M., C. Tryon, M. Shaw, E. M. Scerri, K. L. Ranhorn, J. Pargeter, J. McNeil, A. Mackay, A. Leplongeon, H. S. Groucutt, K. Douze, and A. S. Brooks. 2019. Comparative analysis of Middle Stone Age artifacts in Africa (CoMSAfrica). *Evolutionary Anthropology* doi.org/10.1002/evan.21772.

Willoughby, P. 1985. Spheroids and battered stones in the African Early Stone Age. *World Archaeology* 17:44–60.

Wilshaw, A. 2016. The current status of the Kenya Capsian. *African Archaeological Review* 33:13–27.

Wright, D. K. 2005. "*Environment, Chronology, and Resource Exploitation of the Pastoral Neolithic in Tsavo, Kenya.*" PhD dissertation, University of Ilinois at Chicago.

Wright, K. 1992. A classification system for ground stone tools from the prehistoric Levant. *Paléorient* 18:53–81.

Wynn, T. 1989. *The Evolution of Spatial Competence*. Chicago, IL: University of Illinois Press.

Wynn, T. and J. Gowlett. 2018. The handaxe reconsidered. *Evolutionary Anthropology: Issues, News, and Reviews* 27:21–9.

Yellen, J. E. 1998. Barbed bone points: Tradition and continuity in Saharan and Sub-Saharan Africa. *African Archaeological Review* 15:173–98.

Yellen, J., A. Brooks, D. Helgren, M. Tappen, S. Ambrose, R. Bonnefille, J. Feathers, G. Goodfriend, K. Ludwig, P. Renne, and K. Stewart. 2005. The archaeology of the Aduma Middle Stone Age sites in the Awash Valley, Ethiopia. *PaleoAnthropology* 10:25–100.

INDEX